Explaining Family Interactions

Explaining Family Interactions

Mary Anne Fitzpatrick
Anita L. Vangelisti
Editors

SAGE Publications
International Educational and Professional Publisher
Thousand Oaks   London   New Delhi

For information address:

SAGE Publications, Inc.
2455 Teller Road
Thousand Oaks, California 91320

SAGE Publications Ltd.
6 Bonhill Street
London EC2A 4PU
United Kingdom

SAGE Publications India Pvt. Ltd.
M-32 Market
Greater Kailash I
New Delhi 110 048 India

Printed in the United States of America

Library of Congress Cataloging-in-Publication Data

Main entry under title:

Explaining family interactions/edited by Mary Anne Fitzpatrick,
    Anita L. Vangelisti.
        p.   cm.
    Includes bibliographical references (p.   ) and index.
    ISBN 0-8039-5478-6 (cloth: acid-free paper).—ISBN
    0-8039-5479-4 (pbk.: acid-free paper)
        1. Communication in the family. 2. Family. I. Fitzpatrick, Mary
    Anne, 1949-   . II. Vangelisti, Anita L.
HQ518.E94   1995
306.87—dc20   95-7701

This book is printed on acid-free paper.

95 96 97 98 99 10 9 8 7 6 5 4 3 2 1

Sage Production Editor: Astrid Virding

Contents

Preface

Researchers and theorists who study the family generally agree that the values, social constraints, and behaviors that affect family structures have changed a great deal over the past two decades. The ability of families to survive in the face of such changes suggests that families are flexible—that "they absorb such external changes and . . . adapt accordingly" (Berardo, 1990). What is it about family members that allows for this type of flexibility? Increasingly, scholars have turned to family communication as a means of answering this question. Whether the change involves factors that are external to the family, such as employment opportunities (Barling, 1990), or events that occur within the family context, such as the birth of a child (MacDermid, Huston, & McHale, 1990), family communication influences how members adapt and function.

This volume, one of the first to synthesize the work of scholars who take a quantitative approach to the study of family interaction (but see Handel & Whitchurch, 1994, for an excellent collection of qualitative work), provides readers with at least four benefits. First, the book presents a detailed review of current research centering on an issue—family communication—that family scholars see as increasingly important. Although edited books on marital communication abound (e.g., Fincham & Bradbury, 1990; Gottman, 1979; Hahlweg & Jacobson, 1984; Noller & Fitzpatrick, 1988), volumes emphasizing the interaction patterns of family members are comparatively rare (but see Socha & Stamp, 1995, and Stafford & Bayer, 1993, for recent works focusing specifically on parent-child communication). Many of the books that do focus on family interaction are undergraduate textbooks (e.g., Arliss, 1993; Galvin & Brommel, 1986; Pearson, 1989; Yerby, Buerkel-Rothfuss, & Bochner, 1990). The current volume, therefore, fills a demand from scholars in family studies and communication studies for a more advanced, research-based work.

Second, because this book is based on a relatively new area of research, it exposes readers to unique, state-of-the-art ideas concerning both communication processes and family functioning. Those interested in the area of children's interpersonal communication will find new ideas about how children's social skills are influenced by parent-child relations in Chapter 2, by Brant Burleson, Jesse Delia, and James Applegate. Those who study adolescence will discover findings concerning the impact of various communication patterns on relationship outcomes in Chapter 3, by Patricia Noller. And those interested in the structure of the family will find in Chapter 7, by Susan Gano-Phillips and Frank Fincham, that communication represents an integral part of creating and maintaining family structures.

Third, this volume provides readers with an overarching set of questions that they can use to examine their own and others' research. In spite of the variety of topics covered here, all of the authors were asked to address a set of four general questions concerning family communication:

1. How do you define family communication?
2. Why is communication, per se, important to your specific area of research?
3. What implications do the findings of your study have for family members?
4. What implications do the findings of your study have for future theory and research on family communication?

Fourth, all of this volume's contributors are recognized scholars in marriage and the family. Because they are known nationally and internationally for their unique contributions to communication and family studies, their responses to the four questions vary. All of the authors approach these questions from different theoretical and/or methodological stances. Consequently, we believe we provide students, scholars, and practitioners with a broad base of theory and research with which to compare their own and others' perspectives.

The volume is organized around three sections. Part I begins with a focus on interaction in the family of origin between the primary caregiver and the neonate. It then moves to consideration of communication between parents and young children and then to that between parents and adolescents. The section ends with an examination of patterns of interaction during courtship among young adults. Part II comprises chapters that investigate interaction processes during times of crisis or change in relationships. It starts with a chapter that highlights the transition to parenthood, and then considers family interaction during problem solving and the association of this type of interaction to outcomes for young boys. This section concludes with two chapters on the various effects of family conflict and divorce on outcomes for both children and adults. Part III, the final section of the book, takes us beyond structural definitions of the family to examine many different types of family forms. Given the diversity of the modern family, the choices for this section were virtually unlimited. We had to focus on just a few of many relevant issues. The contributors to Part III not only adopt a transactional definition of the family, they problematize previously taken-for-granted assumptions about family interaction. Issues such as power, sexuality, inclusion, age, and cultural diversity are covered.

We are indebted to many people for their invaluable contributions to this volume. The authors who wrote for us put a great deal of time, effort, and thought into their work; this book came about only because of their excellent contributions. Our editor, Sophy Craze, and her assistant, Renee Piernot, have tirelessly nagged, encouraged, and prompted us. Without their persistence and patience, the idea we had to edit this book would likely still be hidden away in file folders. Also deserving of our gratitude are the families, couples, and individuals who participated in the research reported in these pages. We have learned a great deal because these people were willing to give of their time.

Finally, we would like to thank our own families—our husbands, Roman and John, and our children, Moira, Johnny, and Erin. They have taught us our most valuable lessons about family communication.

REFERENCES

Arliss, L. P. (1993). *Contemporary family communications: Messages and meanings*. New York: St. Martin's.

Barling, J. (1990). Employment and marital functioning. In F. D. Fincham & T. N. Bradbury (Eds.), *The psychology of marriage: Basic issues and applications* (pp. 201-225). New York: Guilford.

Berardo, F. M. (1990). Trends and directions in family research in the 1980s. *Journal of Marriage and the Family, 52,* 809-817.

Fincham, F. D., & Bradbury, T. N. (Eds.). (1990). *The psychology of marriage: Basic issues and applications*. New York: Guilford.

Galvin, K. M., & Brommel, B. J. (1986). *Family communication: Cohesion and change* (2nd ed.). Glenview, IL: Scott, Foresman.

Gottman, J. M. (1979). *Marital interaction*. New York: Academic Press.

Hahlweg, K., & Jacobson, N. S. (1984). *Marital interaction: Analysis and modification*. New York: Guilford.

Handel, G., & Whitchurch, G. G. (1994). *The psychosocial interior of the family* (4th ed.). New York: Aldine.

MacDermid, S. M., Huston, T. L., & McHale, S. M. (1990). Changes in marriage associated with the transition to parenthood: Individual differences as a function of sex-role attitudes and changes in the division of household labor. *Journal of Marriage and the Family, 52,* 431-440.

Noller, P., & Fitzpatrick, M. A. (Eds.). (1988). *Perspectives on marital interaction*. Clevedon, England: Multilingual Matters.

Pearson, J. C. (1989). *Communication in the family: Seeking satisfaction in changing times*. New York: Harper & Row.

Socha, T., & Stamp, G. (1995). *Parents, children, and communication: Frontiers of theory and research*. Hillsdale, NJ: Lawrence Erlbaum.

Stafford, L., & Bayer, C. L. (1993). *Interaction between parents and children*. Newbury Park, CA: Sage.

Yerby, J., Buerkel-Rothfuss, N., & Bochner, A. P. (1990). *Understanding family communication*. Scottsdale, AZ: Gorsuch Scarisbrick.

PART I

The Development of Family Communication Patterns

The chapters in this section provide an orientation to communication in the family by tracing the development of communication practices and skills and the connections between various communication behaviors and a variety of social, emotional, and cognitive outcomes for family members. Each chapter adapts a *transactional model* that posits a continual adaptation as parents and children, husbands and wives, and premarital dating partners mutually influence and respond to one another. The chapters also display sensitivity to the potential impact of cultural or class differences on the development of family communication patterns.

Appropriately enough, Chapter 1 takes up interaction between neonates and their parents. Marguerite Stevenson Barratt maintains that neonates are primed to engage in social interaction, as their parents are primed to respond. Although these universal propensities for mutual responsiveness guide early social interactions, they are modified on an ongoing basis by characteristics of the participants, their social settings, and their cultures. The author reviews a number of the factors that affect the mutual responsiveness of caregiver and infant.

For a number of years, Brant Burleson, Jesse Delia, and James Applegate have been centrally concerned with the question of how parents foster, even implicitly, the acquisition of communication skills in their young children. For these authors, communication is functional in that it can be used to achieve a variety of goals. The question is: How are different styles of functional communication *transmitted* from parents to their children? In Chapter 2, Burleson and his colleagues discuss their pursuit of this question using a variety of innovative methodological approaches. Of particular interest are their hierarchical communication coding schemes designed to tap differences in the ability to engage in person-centered persuasion, comforting, informative communication, identity management, and resistance to compliance. Like Barratt, Burleson and his colleagues demonstrate sensitivity to the interrelationship of culture and communication.

Similar to Burleson and his associates, Patricia Noller adopts a functional view of family communication. As she notes in Chapter 3, the important functions of communication in families with adolescents are (a) enabling the renegotiation of rules, roles, and relationships; (b) providing a climate for identity exploration; (c) enhancing adolescent self-esteem; (d) providing appropriate problem-solving models; and (e) allowing the adolescent to make important decisions that affect his or her life. For Noller, the quality of family communication serving these functions is crucial in determining the competence and confidence with which young people face the transition from childhood to adolescence. In helping adolescents cope with the transition to adulthood, families need to maintain a balance between closeness and control.

Most young adults marry, and Catherine Surra, Michelle Batchelder, and Debra Hughes are interested in understanding the dating and courtship process as it leads up to marriage. In Chapter 4 they summarize two major programs of research on accounts of courtship and then employ the findings of this research to debunk four myths about courtship. Courtship cannot be viewed as a period when partners manage their impressions with one another and delude themselves in order to win one another's love. Rather, as Surra and her associates demonstrate, courtship has more to do with navigating the complexities in the individual, interpersonal, and social interactions that influence partners' decisions to commit to marry. The interactions surrounding this commitment decision have surprising long-term implications for marriages.

1

Communication in Infancy

MARGUERITE STEVENSON BARRATT

Optimal family communication during infancy brings together a skilled infant and an adult tuned to respond. In the case of a typical infant in a typical family, this communication provides the context for a gradual unfolding of the child's potential (Scarr, 1992), and responsive communication from parents sets the course for optimizing cognitive, social, and language development. The transactional model (Sameroff & Chandler, 1975) posits a continual adaptation as parents and infants influence each other. Infant behaviors such as looking, vocalizing, smiling, and crying are potent signals that serve to elicit and maintain caregiving, and parents seem to be particularly inclined to respond to these signals (Bowlby, 1969; Newson, 1979; Stern, 1985).

Infants arrive primed for social interaction (Rosenblith, 1992). Vision focuses best at about the distance between faces when infants are held in parents' arms. Infants prefer looking at shapes with contrasts and contours, such as faces. Infants can identify their own mothers by using their sense of smell. Infants are particularly receptive to proprioceptive stimulation such as that provided when they are held and

AUTHOR'S NOTE: This work was supported in part by a research grant from the Graduate School Research Committee, University of Wisconsin—Madison. Special thanks to Dr. Mary A. Roach and Dr. Lewis Leavitt for their input into the thinking reflected in this chapter. Thanks also to the Waisman Center for Research on Human Development and Mental Retardation at the University of Wisconsin—Madison and to the Department of Psychology at Smith College for providing the settings for this work. Please address correspondence to M. S. Barratt at the Department of Child and Family Studies, University of Wisconsin, 1430 Linden Drive, Madison, WI 53706.

5

rocked. Infants prefer the high-pitched voices that parents tend to use with them, and infants can soon identify mother and father by voice. Even though infants' brains are a long way from maturity, infants arrive competent and skillful.

Parents support infant development by responding to signals from their skillful infants (Bornstein & Tamis-LeMonda, 1989; Gunnar, 1980; Martin, 1989; Skinner, 1986). For optimal communication, parents immediately and consistently follow infant behavior with behavior of their own that is appropriate and sensitive (Skinner, 1986). Theoretical support for the importance of parental behavior that is contingently tied to infant behavior comes from several sources (Lamb & Easterbrooks, 1981; Skinner, 1986): Psychoanalysts emphasize the role of early maternal sensitivity for later personality development (Brody & Axelrad, 1978); ethological-attachment theorists propose that adult responsiveness to infant signals is innate (e.g., Fleming, 1989), and that it is an essential component of the development of infants' attachment to their mothers (Ainsworth, Blehar, Waters, & Wall, 1978); organismic theorists (Brazelton, Koslowski, & Main, 1974) and ethological-attachment theorists (Bowlby, 1969) emphasize the role of infants' early signaling capacities in communicating with sensitive parents; social learning theorists suggest that the infant's competence and sense of efficacy are derived from parental behaviors that are contingent upon the infant's own behavior (Gewirtz, 1977; Watson, 1979).

Communication in parent-infant dyads is the result of ongoing adaptations by parents and infants. The process of adaptation is shaped by aspects of infants and aspects of parents (Belsky, 1984; Lamb & Easterbrooks, 1981). Parent-infant interactions are also influenced by the context of interaction (Belsky, 1984; Bronfenbrenner, 1979; Lamb & Easterbrooks, 1981). Not all interactions between parents and their infants are characterized by sensitivity, appropriateness, and responsiveness, and individual differences in parental responsiveness to signals from their infants may be seen as reflections of the influence of parental factors, infant factors, and the context within which the interactions take place. In this chapter, after presenting a general discussion of early communication, I will explore factors that influence individual differences in communications between parents and infants.

EARLY COMMUNICATION

As parents respond to early signals from their infants, they set up a pattern of turn taking that resembles conversation. For example, Kaye (1977) describes an early action dialogue wherein the mother fills pauses in the newborn's feeding by jiggling the nipple. Although the early pattern of vocal interaction includes considerable simultaneous vocalization (Ginsburg & Kilbourne, 1988; Stern, Jaffe, Beebe, & Bennett, 1975), by 4 months the pattern of vocal turn taking between mothers and infants begins to approximate the pattern of alternations seen in adult conversation (Ginsburg & Kilbourne, 1988; Stevenson, VerHoeve, Roach, & Leavitt, 1986). Thus when mothers and infants are attending to one another, a vocalization by either partner increases the likelihood of a subsequent vocalization by the other (Stevenson et al., 1986). After an infant vocalization, the initial increase in the likelihood of a vocalization is followed by a suppression of the likelihood of vocalization. This vocal suppression may result in the augmentation of maternal speech with frequent pauses designed to encourage infant participation (Jasnow & Feldstein, 1986). Although it has been suggested that the developmental decrease in simultaneous vocalization and the increase in alternating vocalization across the first few months is largely the result of mothers' management of the conversations (Collis, 1985; Elias & Broerse, 1989), infants also make significant contributions to the conversational patterns (Stevenson et al., 1986).

Linguistic analysis of the communication between parents and infants has included consideration of the content and structure of the parent's language. *Motherese,* or *baby talk,* refers to the set of modifications that are made in speaking to language-learning children. In particular, when speaking to infants, mothers vary the frequency contours of their speech more than they do when speaking to adults; they also use increased intensity and higher pitch in speaking to infants (Cooper & Aslin, 1989). Indeed, infants are particularly attracted to speech with such characteristics, and these features may help infants identify speech that is directed to them (Shute, 1987). Research with mothers who speak Mandarin Chinese, a tonal language, indicates that Mandarin motherese is similar to the motherese that has been recorded in other languages (Grieser & Kuhl, 1988); thus modifications that mothers make when speaking to infants may be universal.

Empirical Evidence for the Importance of Responsiveness

In the cognitive domain there is clear empirical evidence linking parental responsiveness in infancy to child competence (e.g., Clarke-Stewart, 1973; Coates & Lewis, 1984). Dunham and Dunham (1990) found that 3-month-old infants who experienced more vocal turn taking with their mothers performed better on a subsequent nonsocial contingency task than did infants who experienced less vocal turn taking with their mothers. Yarrow, Rubenstein, and Pedersen (1975) found that responsiveness in the social (and nonsocial) home environment was related to infant cognitive performance during the first year. When Goldberg, Lojkasek, Gartner, and Corter (1989) followed pre-term infants until they were 4 years old, significant relations were found between maternal responsiveness during infancy and intelligence at 4 years. One of the longest-term studies of the effects of maternal responsiveness during the first year on later cognitive competence found that contingent maternal vocalization at 8 months was linked to intelligence at age 12 (Beckwith & Cohen, 1989).

There is also empirical evidence linking parental responsiveness during infancy to social development, particularly infants' attachment to their mothers (Ainsworth, Bell, & Stayton, 1971; Ainsworth et al., 1978): Mothers who are particularly sensitive and responsive to their infants tend to have infants who are securely attached to them. Replications of this early research in the United States (Isabella & Belsky, 1991; Pederson et al., 1990; Smith & Pederson, 1988) and Japan (Kanaya & Miyake, 1985) have confirmed the relations between sensitive and responsive maternal behavior and securely attached infants. However, Lewis and Feiring (1989) suggest that there is a greater role for individual differences among infants than for differences in maternal behavior in explaining variation in infant attachments. Indeed, in a meta-analysis, Goldsmith and Alansky (1987) found the link between early maternal interaction and the security of the infant's attachment to the mother, as reflected in behavior during a series of separations and reunions in the laboratory, to be small. Rosen and Rothbaum's (1993) recent empirical research adds to the accumulating evidence that associations between parental behavior and infant attachment are less strong than previously presumed.

Assessments of social outcomes that go beyond the first year and beyond the assessment of attachment have revealed evidence of an association between parental responsiveness in infancy and social development. For example, Goldberg et al. (1989) found that preterm children whose mothers had been more responsive during the first year showed fewer behavior problems as 4-year-olds and performed better on an assessment of peer interaction strategies than did preterm children with less responsive mothers. In their longitudinal study of preterm infants, Beckwith and Cohen (1989) found positive links between maternal responsiveness during infancy and children's perceptions of their own social competence when they were 12 years old.

The reciprocity of early parent-infant dialogues may also serve to lay the foundation for infants' language acquisition (Bruner, 1977). Thus experience with protoconversation may be critical for the mastery of later communication skills. For example, lexical acquisition is more rapid where infants have experienced more verbally responsive early environments (Murphy, Menyuk, Liebergott, & Schultz, 1983). Other aspects of mothers' speech to their infants that are associated with facilitated language acquisition include maternal language focused on the objects of the infants' attention (Dunham & Dunham, 1992; Smith, Adamson, & Bakeman, 1988) and maternal language that is simplified for infants (Low & Moely, 1988; Murray, Johnson, & Peters, 1990).

Measurement Issues in the Assessment of Responsiveness

There is considerable theoretical and empirical support for the notion that parents' responsiveness to signals from their infants is a crucial aspect of communication within parent-infant dyads. There is, however, no consensus about the optimal approach to the assessment of individual differences in patterns of communication that appear during family interactions with young children (Maccoby & Martin,

1983). Global summary ratings of parental contingencies of responsiveness during parent-infant interaction have been used to capture individual differences in the likelihood of parents' responses to their infants (e.g., Ainsworth & Bell, 1974; Crnic, Ragozin, Greenberg, Robinson, & Basham, 1983; for a review, see Cairns, 1979). Other researchers have used a single summary rating to capture the synchrony of parents *and* infants (Bernieri, Reznick, & Rosenthal, 1988). Global ratings, in effect, are human summaries of patterns within the ongoing stream of behavior of parents and infants.

Although the reliability and validity of such global rating systems can be established, *microanalytic* approaches provide more direct access to the moment-by-moment behavior of parent and infant. For example, it becomes possible to examine parental response to each instance of infant vocalization throughout the stream of behaviors being emitted by both partners. The early research considered as responsive any behavior occurring within the same or subsequent 10-second interval (e.g., Clarke-Stewart, 1973). Alternatively, when Stern (1985) examined transitional probabilities among gaze states during mother-infant interaction, records were segmented into 0.6-second units. These approaches are limited, however, by the arbitrariness of the selected time unit (Messer & Vietze, 1988; Watson & Hayes, 1981). More recently, and more accurately, the continuous stream of mother and infant behavior has been examined for patterns of contingency using event lag sequential analyses (Barratt, Roach, & Leavitt, 1992; Messer & Vietze, 1988; Stevenson et al., 1986). There are at least three distinct approaches. One approach for event lag sequential analyses is the use of loglinear analyses to compare the observed contingencies with those that would be expected by chance (e.g., Barratt et al., 1992). A second approach uses information theoretical statistics (derived from communication engineering) to consider the behavior of mother and infant as influenced by the previous behavior of each partner and the combined synergic influence of both (Palthe, Hopkins, & Vos, 1990). And a third approach compares contingencies in the observed data with those in randomly shuffled data (Messer & Vietze, 1988). These approaches extend previous research by making comparisons with chance levels; as yet, none has emerged as the primary choice in the field.

The assessment of early communication is made more complex by the difficulty of disentangling the joint impact of behavior that is dependent on one's own behavior (Maccoby & Martin, 1983). Thus consideration of the autodependence of behavior is an essential component of understanding communication (Gottman, 1979). This becomes a particular concern in the conversations of infancy because self-dependent vocalizations seem predominant in some mother-infant dyads (Stevenson et al., 1986).

The immediate context of the interaction is also methodologically important when parent-infant communication during infancy is considered. Some researchers position infants in infant seats facing parents for brief recordings of interactions (e.g., Feldstein & Crown, 1986; Fogel, 1982; Lester, Hoffman, & Brazelton, 1985). Though this can allow excellent-quality audio and video recording of the interactions (including split-screen images), it may violate the assumption of the ecological validity of the observations. Indeed, Fogel, Dedo, and McEwen (1992) found that mother-infant interaction differed when 3- to 6-month-old infants were in sitting, reclining, and supine positions. Other researchers make longer naturalistic observations in the home or laboratory and abstract from the ongoing stream of behaviors those sections of interest where parent and infant are attending to one another and potentially engaged in interaction (e.g., Barratt et al., 1992; Stevenson et al., 1986). The interactional context also includes the parent's task during interaction: Mothers have been found to be more responsive when instructed to play with their 3-month-old infants or to imitate their infants than when instructed to hold the infants' attention (Symons & Moran, 1987). In comparisons of mothers' behavior during feeding, caretaking, and close interactions, variations across situations have, in fact, been found to be greater than variations caused by status variables such as social class and infant gender (Seifer, Sameroff, Anagnostopolou, & Elias, 1992).

PARENTAL FACTORS INFLUENCING COMMUNICATION

Some of the individual differences in parents' responsiveness to signals from their infants reflect characteristics of the parents themselves. In particular, parent gender effects suggest that there are differences in the ways that mothers and fathers interact with their infants (e.g., Lamb, 1981). Parental age is also an important factor, as there is some evidence that adolescent mothers communicate with their infants in ways that are different from the ways adult mothers communicate with their infants (e.g., Barratt, Roach, & Colbert, 1991). In addition, maternal mental health, particularly depression, may affect mothers' responsiveness during interactions with their infants (Belsky, 1984; Lamb & Easterbrooks, 1981). These influences on the communication between infants and their parents are reviewed below.

Mothers/Fathers

Increasingly, research on communication and interaction between infants and parents includes both fathers and mothers. The stereotype of the traditional father who is little involved with his infant is fading now that research from around the world is available on fathers' participation in the lives of their infants (Lamb, 1987; Nugent, 1991). Early research in the United States on father-infant interaction examined qualitative differences in the nature of the interaction: Interactions with fathers tend to focus on play, whereas interactions with mothers tend to focus on caregiving and teaching (Lamb, 1981). More recent research confirms this distinction (e.g., Stevenson, Leavitt, Thompson, & Roach, 1988), even for parents of preterm infants (Levy-Shiff, Sharir, & Mogilner, 1989). Examinations of the content of speech to infants also support this distinction: Game routines are more common in mothers' speech than in fathers' speech (Kruper & Uzgiris, 1987).

Although mothers and fathers both modify their speech during communication with infants, fathers adjust their speech less than mothers do (Kruper & Uzgiris, 1987; Rondal, 1980). Belsky, Gilstrap, and Rovine's (1984) hour-long observations in homes when infants were 1, 3, and 9 months old led them to conclude that the fathers in their sample were less engaging, responsive, stimulating, and positively affectionate than were the mothers. These researchers' discussion of their findings brings in support from Israel and Sweden for the idea that fathers' contributions to their infants during interaction may indeed be qualitatively different from mothers' contributions. For example, although both mothers and fathers respond to infant vocalizations, fathers respond vocally and mothers tactilely (Parke & Sawin, 1977).

Research has also explored factors that may influence individual differences among fathers in their communication and interaction with their infants. For example, Levy-Shiff, Hoffman, Mogilner, Levinger, and Mogilner (1990) found that fathers of preterm infants who visited their infants more frequently during the infants' hospital stays were more involved with the babies' caregiving and more affectionate toward them even when the infants were 18 months old. In contrast, Pannabecker, Emde, and Austin (1982) found that fathers who received an experimental intervention designed to increase their early contact with their infants did not interact with their infants any differently when the infants were 1 month old than did fathers who had not had the extra contact during the newborn period. On the other hand, Pedersen, Suwalsky, Cain, Zaslow, and Rabinovich (1987) report that fathers who had extra contact with their infants on an ongoing basis—taking care of their infants when the mothers were away from home—were more interactive with their infants in a greater variety of ways than were fathers who had less contact with their infants. Comparisons between fathers who are primary caregivers of their infants and secondary caregiving fathers indicate that the father-infant interactions of primary caregiving fathers are more similar to mother-infant interactions than are the father-infant interactions of secondary caregiving fathers (Field, 1978). This accumulating research suggests that fathers who have more contact with their infants begin to interact in ways that are similar to mother-infant interactions. Other factors that influence fathers' participation with their infants include mothers' employment status (Zaslow, Pedersen, Suwalsky, Rabinovich, & Cain, 1986) and fathers' stress (Noppe, Noppe, & Hughes, 1990), as well as fathers' personality, marriage, and work characteristics (Volling & Belsky, 1991).

Adolescent Parents

Approximately half a million adolescent women give birth each year in the United States (U.S. Bureau of the Census, 1992, Table 82,

p. 65), and some research suggests that adolescent mothers provide less stimulation for their infants than do adult mothers (Field, Widmayer, Stringer, & Ignatoff, 1980; García Coll, Hoffman, & Oh, 1987; Landy, Montgomery, Schubert, Cleland, & Clark, 1983). In particular, adolescent mothers vocalize to their infants less often than do adult mothers when the infants are newborns (Culp, Applebaum, Osofsky, & Levy, 1988), 1 to 3 months olds (Roosa, Fitzgerald, & Carlson, 1982), 4 months old (Barratt et al., 1992; García Coll et al., 1987), 6 months old (Culp, Culp, Osofsky, & Osofsky, 1991), and 8 months old (Field, 1980; Levine, García Coll, & Oh, 1985). Recent short-term longitudinal research indicates that the communicative limitation associated with adolescent parenthood during the early months is particularly a limitation in the frequencies of behaviors that are directed toward the infants. When their infants were 4 months old, adolescent mothers in one study—relative to adult mothers approximately matched on family background—were found to vocalize less, smile less, and offer or show toys to their infants less often (Barratt & Roach, 1995).

Because of the importance of parents' responsiveness to signals from their infants, research must go beyond tallying behavior frequencies to consider the relations over time between the behaviors of infants and parents. Detailed examination of the patterns of interaction between adolescent mothers and their infants suggests that adolescent mothers are less responsive to signals from their infants than are adult mothers (Field, 1980; Roosa, et al., 1982). The Barratt and Roach (1995) short-term longitudinal study cited above used microanalysis to compare the responsiveness of adolescent and adult single mothers who were approximately matched on family background. When the infants were 12 months old, the adolescent mothers were found to be less vocally responsive to their infants and, perhaps as a consequence, their 12-month-old infants were less vocally responsive than were 12-month-old infants with adult mothers.

Although the number of adolescent fathers is only about one-fourth the number of adolescent mothers, these young fathers are at an educational and financial disadvantage relative to older fathers (Hardy & Duggan, 1988), and this may be reason for concern. In general, little is known about adolescent fathers (Elster & Lamb, 1986), but their youth, plus their other disadvantaged circumstances, may influence their ability to respond to their infants. In comparing adolescent mothers' and adolescent fathers' interactive skills with their 4-month-old infants, McGovern (1990) found that the *type* of play was similar, but that adolescent mothers communicated more successfully with their infants than did adolescent fathers. The fathers missed cues and their responses were more often slow or inappropriate relative to mothers' responses. Thus the developmental immaturity of both adolescent mothers and adolescent fathers may lead to communicative interactions with infants that are less sensitive than the interactions that adult parents have with their infants.

Maternal Mental Health

Theoretical models addressing sources of influence on parenting suggest mental well-being as a concomitant of optimal parenting (Belsky, 1984; Lamb & Easterbrooks, 1981). For example, scores on three scales of the MMPI have been found to be related to observed maternal behavior with 3-month-old infants (Kaeller & Roe, 1990). Additional empirical evidence from research with single mothers and adolescent mothers supports the idea that there is a relation between mental health and parenting. Comparisons among single mothers of 4-month-old infants have found that mothers with fewer psychological symptoms are able to provide more appropriate social and physical environments for their infants (Barratt et al., 1991). For adolescent mothers, research suggests similar results: Emotional health has been found to be positively related to optimal mother-infant interactions (LeResche, Strobino, Parks, Fischer, & Smeriglio, 1983).

Maternal depression that interferes with daily functioning occurs in 10-15% of postpartum women (O'Hara, Neunaber, & Zekoski, 1984). Accumulating research suggests that depressed mothers are less able to engage in active and responsive interactions with their infants than are mothers who are not depressed (Cohn, Campbell, Matias, & Hopkins, 1990; Field, Healy, Goldstein, & Guthertz, 1990; Gelfand, Teti, & Fox, 1992; Wilfong, Saylor, & Elksnin, 1991). Even subclinical depression following childbirth seems to interfere with mother-infant interaction (Bettes, 1988). These findings of impaired communication between depressed mothers and their infants are of particular concern because mothers' interactive behavior may be the mechanism that contributes to observed deleterious effects of maternal depression on the infants themselves (Field, 1992; Murray, 1992; Whiffen & Gotlib, 1989).

INFANT CHARACTERISTICS
INFLUENCING COMMUNICATION

Bell and Harper (1977) assert that developmentalists must attend to the effects of children on their parents; more recently, Scarr (1992) has argued that children evoke responses from their parents that serve to structure the children's environments. Individual differences among infants have the clear potential to influence the ways in which their parents interact with them (Sameroff & Chandler, 1975). Thus parents who are presented with atypical infants adapt by modifying their parenting behavior (Field, 1987). In this section I review the literature to indicate some of the ways in which social interactions experienced by infants are influenced by infant characteristics, such as preterm birth and mental retardation.

Preterm Infants

The event of preterm birth imposes considerably on the interaction between mothers and infants (Goldberg, 1979; Kopp & Krakow, 1983). These effects are probably jointly influenced by parental expectations and anxieties and by characteristics of the infants themselves. Infants who are born prematurely are less attentive and more fussy during interaction with their mothers and, in addition, are less likely to smile and vocalize than are infants who are born at term (Barratt et al., 1992; Crawford, 1982; Crnic et al., 1983). Perhaps in response to infant inactivity, the mothers of young preterm infants do more holding and stimulating than do mothers of term infants (Beckwith & Cohen, 1978; Crawford, 1982; Crnic et al., 1983; Field, 1980). Mothers of preterm infants often seem to be making an extra effort, compared with mothers of term infants (Brown & Bakeman, 1980; Goldberg & Divitto, 1983).

When researchers have gone beyond counting the frequencies of behaviors to examine the patterns of interaction between mothers and their preterm infants, they have found mothers of preterm infants to be more responsive than mothers of term infants (Greene, Fox, & Lewis, 1983). In our own short-term longitudinal study of interactions between preterm infants and their mothers, my colleagues and I first made naturalistic observations at home when the infants were 4 months old (Barratt et al., 1992). Mothers of preterm infants, relative to mothers of term infants, were particularly responsive to their infants' signals within the attentional, vocal, and affective channels. During feeding at 8 months, preterm infants were more fussy than term infants, and their mothers were more attentive than were mothers of term infants (Stevenson, Roach, VerHoeve, & Leavitt, 1990). Mothers of preterm infants, who may be particularly concerned about infant weight gain, responded to different behavioral cues during the dialogue of feeding than did mothers of term infants: When preterm infants vocalized, mothers tended to offer food; when preterm infants took food, mothers marked the event with vocalization. During observations in the laboratory playroom at 12 months, however, there were no longer any differences between the mothers of preterm and term infants in their likelihood of responding to infant vocalizations (Barratt, Roach, & Leavitt, in press). Instead, at 12 months, mothers of preterm infants attempted more control of their infants by providing manual assistance and by intruding into their infants' play.

Thus it has been suggested that mothers of preterm infants may be running a natural compensatory program as they carry an extra burden of responsibility for the interaction with their relatively inactive and perhaps unresponsive infants (Beckwith & Cohen, 1978; Brown & Bakeman, 1980; Field, 1980; Greenberg & Crnic, 1988). Heightened maternal responsiveness during the first year may be a particularly appropriate adaptation to the needs of preterm infants; the appropriateness of the maternal adaptations is supported by findings that the effects of prematurity greatly diminish with age (Cohen, Parmelee, Beckwith, & Sigman, 1986; Field, Dempsey, & Shuman, 1981; Greenberg & Crnic, 1988; Holwerda-Kuipers, 1987; Lee & Barratt, 1993).

What about fathers of preterm infants? Comparisons of fathers' teaching interactions with preterm and term 3-month-old infants have indicated that fathers' interactions are more responsive and reciprocal with preterm infants that with term infants (Harrison, 1990). This finding suggests compensatory efforts on the part of fathers of preterm infants that parallel the compensatory efforts of mothers. In sum, having an infant who is born prematurely and with low birth weight seems to call forth extra effort from both mothers and fathers.

Developmentally Delayed Infants

Comparisons between mothers' interactions with their developmentally delayed young children and mothers' interactions with typically developing young children who have the same mental age indicate that mothers of developmentally delayed children use more maternal directives and more control (Marfo, 1984, 1990). One reason for the greater directiveness of mothers of developmentally delayed infants may be that signals from these infants are more difficult to read (Yoder, 1987); young children with mental retardation have been characterized as less active, less vocal, and less responsive than typically developing children (Marfo, 1984). Recent thinking suggests that maternal directiveness may be an adaptive way of structuring the interaction, rather than an aberration to be eradicated through intervention (Marfo, 1990).

In the case of developmentally delayed infants who also have cerebral palsy, mothers of handicapped infants have been found to use more verbal and physical directive behavior than do mothers of typically developing infants who are matched on mental age (Hanzlik, 1990). In considering the combined effects of physical handicaps and mental retardation on mother-infant interaction, maternal behavior has been found to vary with the amount of retardation (Wasserman, Shilansky, & Hahn, 1986). A greater degree of mental retardation has been associated with more maternal interaction and more maternal management of the interaction. This maternal sensitivity to infants' developmental level suggests that the mother's behavior is being shaped by input from the infant.

CONTEXTUAL CHARACTERISTICS
INFLUENCING COMMUNICATION

Children's development must be considered within its proximal and distal contexts (Bronfenbrenner, 1979), and a salient aspect of the proximal context of parenting is the social support that a mother receives (Belsky, 1984). At an intermediate level of examination, parenting reflects its social class and ethnic context. At a distal level of analysis, culture is a crucially important aspect of the developmental context (Bornstein, 1991; Rogoff & Morelli, 1989). Thus early parenting reflects its milieu, and parents strive to raise their children in ways that will facilitate the children's success in the environments that parents foresee (Belsky, 1984; Ogbu, 1981). I review below the following contextual influences on communication between parents and infants: social support, social class and ethnicity, and culture, particularly comparisons among Japan, France, and the United States.

Social Support

Support for the mother from people who are close to her may help her to parent her infant successfully (Belsky, 1984). For example, research suggests a positive association between mothers' reports of satisfaction with their marriages and their sensitive interactions with their infants (Belsky, 1981; Cox, Owen, Lewis, & Henderson, 1989; Goldberg & Easterbrooks, 1984). In a sample of disadvantaged mothers of preterm infants, supportive services from the infants' fathers were positively associated with the quality of the mothers' proximal interactions with their infants (Feiring, Fox, & Jaskir, 1987). In a cross-cultural study of Japan and the United States, mothers in both countries who perceived more support from their husbands provided better home environments for their infants (Durrett, Richards, Otaki, Pennebaker, & Nyquist, 1986). Thus satisfactory marital relationships and the support of spouses may enhance the experiences parents provide for their infants. There are also links between social support provided from outside the nuclear family and early parenting. For example, Feiring et al. (1987) found that mothers who received more material goods from friends and relatives had higher-quality interactions with their infants than did mothers who received less material assistance.

The multiple ties that reflect the breadth of the mother's social network may in fact include relationships that are supportive and relationships that are stressful (Zarling, Hirsch, & Landry, 1988). For full-term 6-month-old infants, close networks of friends and family who know each other have been found to be associated with higher maternal sensitivity. In contrast, for preterm infants close networks have been found to be associated with lower maternal sensitivity, perhaps because of concern and worry for infant well-being and ambiguity about expectations. Research on adolescent and adult mothers has shown that young mothers who live with their own mothers receive more support than those who live away from their families of origin; however, mothers living away from their families of origin provide more enriching environments for their infants (Barratt et al., 1991; Wasserman, Brunelli, & Rauh, 1990). Thus the ties between support and parenting cannot be viewed simplistically—more support is not always associated with better parenting. For example, there may be developmental changes in the need for support; Unger and Wandersman (1988) found that mothers who provided the best environments for their 8-month-old babies were found to be more satisfied than other mothers with support from their families prenatally and more satisfied than other mothers with support from their partners at 8 months.

Social Class and Ethnicity

Research on the effects of physical trauma associated with preterm birth indicates that the effects of preterm birth on long-term outcomes for children are small compared with the effects of social class differences (Drillien, 1964; Pfeiffer & Aylward, 1990). Social class effects are most likely transmitted to children through social class differences in parents' interactions with children (e.g., Gecas, 1979), and it has been suggested that social class accounts for about half of the variation in early home environments (MacPhee, Ramey, & Yeates, 1984). For example, higher socioeconomic status mothers have been found to be more verbal with their newborn infants than lower socioeconomic status mothers (Kilbride, Johnson, & Streissguth, 1977). When maternal responsiveness is considered, middle-class mothers have been found to respond to their infants' vocalizations with vocalizations of their own, whereas lower-class mothers are more likely to respond to infants' vocalizations with touch (Lewis & Wilson, 1972). Tulkin (1977) found more reciprocity in the interactions of middle-class mothers and their infants than in working-class mother-infant dyads. Social class differences in parent-infant interactions such as those described here may be part of the explanation for the findings of relations between socioeconomic status and later academic achievement (White, 1982).

In planning interventions for parents of preterm infants, Fajardo and Freedman (1981) realized that it would be important to consider the effects of ethnicity on the interactions between mothers and their full-term infants. The research that followed indicated that African American, Euro-American, and Navajo mothers all used the rhythm of interactions to engage their infants; however, techniques for sustaining interactions differed with ethnicity. In making detailed analyses of interactions between Euro-American, Hopi, and Navajo mothers and their infants, Callaghan (1981) found that Euro-American mothers were the most active across several behavior modes, the Hopi mothers less active, and the Navajo mothers least active. Field, Widmayer, Adler, and De Cubas (1990) compared African American and Cuban mothers in Miami and found that the Cuban mothers were more actively engaged with their infants vocally, tactilely, and affectively. Clearly, it is important not to interpret ethnic differences in early parenting from a deficit perspective; rather, we should consider the differences as reflecting different cultures and beliefs (García Coll, 1990; Laosa, 1981).

Culture

Whiting's (1963) classic study of childbearing in six cultures is an important landmark in the examination of the effects of culture on interactions between parents and children. Recent compilations of research compare interaction between parents and children around the world (Bornstein, 1991; LeVine, Miller, & West, 1988; Roopnarine & Carter, 1992). Comparisons between communication during infancy in the United States and in Japan provide an opportunity to compare parenting between cultures that are economically and educationally similar but have different cultural values and different beliefs about children (Azuma, 1986; Bornstein, 1989; Fogel, Stevenson, & Messinger, 1992). The Judeo-Christian heritage of the United States emphasizes the importance of shaping and molding infants; the Shinto heritage of Japan cherishes an inherent goodness in the infant (Fogel et al., 1992; Kojima, 1986).

The Japanese infant is cared for in the context of a close and fairly exclusive relationship with the mother; infants in the United States, in contrast, receive more care from fathers and other caregivers (Barratt, Negayama, & Minami, 1993). Perhaps because of this more exclusive relationship between mother and infant, and because of the valuing of interdependence, Japanese mothers have been found to be particularly vocally responsive to signals from their infants and to include more vocal and physical interactions with their infants than mothers in the United States. Perhaps because of their greater valuing of independence, mothers in the United States provide their infants with a greater variety of toys and experiences and use various infant equipment that places infants at a distance from mothers. Thus the interaction between Japanese infants and their mothers is an intensely interpersonal social interaction, with its focus on the dyad itself. In contrast, in the United States, interactions between infants and their mothers seem to be more didactic, as mothers provide greater structuring of the interaction and provide more varied experiences. Perhaps as they encourage independence, mothers in the United States focus interaction outside the dyad. Differences are also reflected in the content of mothers' speech in the two countries: Japanese mothers' speech is more affect oriented; the speech of mothers in the United States is more information oriented (Fernald & Morikawa, 1993; Toda, Fogel, & Kawai, 1990).

Comparisons between mother-infant interaction in the United States and France also suggest some particularly American ways of interacting with infants (Bornstein, Tamis-LeMonda, Pecheux, & Rahn, 1991). Mothers of 5-month-old infants in the United States have been found to be more likely than similar mothers in France to encourage their infants to attend to their mothers and other things in the environment. This indicates a more didactic style of interaction, as American mothers perhaps try to promote their infants' development. Yet comparisons between French mothers of 10- to 15-month-old infants and African mothers living in France indicate that French mothers are more didactic than African mothers, who structure more social interactions (Rabain-Jamin, 1989). In considering cross-cultural differences in early child rearing, it is clearly important to remember that a great deal of intracultural variability exists (van Ijzendoorn & Kroonenberg, 1988). Nevertheless, the cultural context in which parents make their moment-by-moment decisions during interactions with their infants accounts for some of the variation in communication between parents and their infants. Thus cultural values and expectations shape parents' goals for their children (LeVine, 1977; Richman, Miller, & LeVine, 1992), and these are expressed through communicative interactions.

CONCLUSION

In this review of the literature I have argued that infants arrive primed for social interaction and that parents are primed for response. Yet the details of the communication that emerge within any particular dyad are influenced by parent factors, infant factors, and the context of the interaction. In other words, the universal propensities that guide early social interactions are modified on an ongoing basis by characteristics of the participants and their social settings. Parents' interactive skills change with their own developmental maturity and with experience with their infants, and mothers' ongoing adaptations within the dyad may be limited by poor mental health. Parents who are presented with an infant who does not meet their expectations because of preterm birth or developmental delay seem to make extra efforts to elicit the best from their infants; this adaptation confirms that infants have a major role to play in the development of communication within the dyad. The context and setting in which the infant grows up seem to place limits on the adjustments that are possible by parents and their infants. Rearing infants within a circle of people who can provide support seems to make the process of mutual adaptation easier. The community expectations that accompany membership in an ethnic group, social class group, or cultural group also seem to constrain the adaptations that parents and infants make to one another.

Practitioners try to intervene in the parent-infant dyad to teach parents other ways to communicate with their infants or to provide support so that parents can try other ways. The success of some intervention programs at preventing the destructive communication patterns of abuse and neglect as well as promoting more optimal communication (e.g., Spiker, Ferguson, & Brooks-Gunn, 1993) indicates that infancy may be a particularly appropriate time for intervention. Though deleterious effects of insult to the organism during infancy can be somewhat remedied later (e.g., Clarke & Clarke, 1979), patterns of communication that are established during infancy tend to persist. Under the best of circumstances, the nascent social skills of infants will elicit appropriate responses from parents as infants teach parents to communicate. However, where circumstances are less than optimal because of, for example, poor mental health in the mother, interventionists attempt to support the emergence of appropriate and responsive communication between parents and infants. Thus the most successful interventions target both parents and infants (Shonkoff & Hauser-Cram, 1987).

REFERENCES

Ainsworth, M. D. S., & Bell, S. M. (1974). Mother-infant interaction and the development of competence. In K. S. Connolly & J. S. Bruner (Eds.), *The growth of competence* (pp. 97-118). New York: Academic Press.

Ainsworth, M. D. S., Bell, S. M., & Stayton, D. J. (1971). Individual differences in strange-situation behavior of one-year-olds. In H. R. Shaffer (Ed.), *The origins of human social relations* (pp. 17-52). New York: Academic Press.

Ainsworth, M. D. S., Blehar, M. C., Waters, E., & Wall, S. (1978). *Patterns of attachment: A psychological study of the strange situation.* Hillsdale, NJ: Lawrence Erlbaum.

Azuma, H. (1986). Why study child development in Japan? In H. Stevenson, H. Azuma, & K. Hakuta (Eds.), *Child development and education in Japan* (pp. 3-12). New York: W. H. Freeman.

Barratt, M. S., Negayama, K., & Minami, T. (1993). The social environments of early infancy in Japan and the United States. *Early Development and Parenting, 2,* 51-64.

Barratt, M. S., & Roach, M. A. (1995). Early interactive processes: Parenting by adolescent and adult single mothers. *Infant Behavior and Development, 18,* 97-109.

Barratt, M. S., Roach, M. A., & Colbert, K. K. (1991). Single mothers and their infants: Factors associated with optimal parenting. *Family Relations, 40,* 448-454.

Barratt, M. S., Roach, M. A., & Leavitt, L. A. (1992). Early channels of mother-infant communication: Preterm and term infants. *Journal of Child Psychology and Psychiatry, 33,* 1193-1204.

Barratt, M. S., Roach, M. A., & Leavitt, L. A. (in press). The impact of low-risk prematurity on maternal behavior and toddler outcomes. *Infant Behavior and Development.*

Beckwith, L., & Cohen, S. E. (1978). Preterm birth: Hazardous obstetrical and postnatal events as related to caregiver-infant behavior. *Infant Behavior and Development, 1,* 403-411.

Beckwith, L., & Cohen, S. E. (1989). Maternal responsiveness with preterm infants and later competency. In M. H. Bornstein (Ed.), *Maternal responsiveness: Characteristics and consequences* (pp. 75-87). San Francisco: Jossey-Bass.

Bell, R., & Harper, L. V. (1977). *Child effects on adults.* Hillsdale, NJ: Lawrence Erlbaum.

Belsky, J. (1981). Early human experience: A family perspective. *Developmental Psychology, 17,* 3-23.

Belsky, J. (1984). The determinants of parenting: A process model. *Child Development, 55,* 83-96.

Belsky, J., Gilstrap, B., & Rovine, M. (1984). The Pennsylvania infant and family development project: I. Stability and change in mother-infant and father-infant interaction in a family setting at one, three, and nine months. *Child Development, 55,* 692-705.

Bernieri, F. J., Reznick, J. S., & Rosenthal, R. (1988). Synchrony, pseudosynchrony, and dissynchrony: Measuring the entrainment process in mother-infant interactions. *Journal of Personality and Social Psychology, 54,* 243-253.

Bettes, B. A. (1988). Maternal depression and motherese: Temporal and intonational features. *Child Development, 59,* 1089-1096.

Bornstein, M. H. (1989). Cross-cultural developmental comparison: The case of Japanese-American infant and mother activities and interactions. What we know, what we need to know, and why we need to know. *Developmental Review, 9,* 171-204.

Bornstein, M. H. (Ed.). (1991). *Cultural approaches to parenting.* Hillsdale, NJ: Lawrence Erlbaum.

Bornstein, M. H., & Tamis-LeMonda, C. S. (1989). Maternal responsiveness and cognitive development in children. In M. H. Bornstein (Ed.), *Maternal responsiveness: Characteristics and consequences* (pp. 49-61). San Francisco: Jossey-Bass.

Bornstein, M. H., Tamis-LeMonda, C. S., Pecheux, M. G., & Rahn, C. W. (1991). Mother and infant activity and interaction in France and in the United States: A comparative study. *International Journal of Behavioral Development, 14,* 21-43.

Bowlby, J. (1969). *Attachment and loss: Vol. 1. Attachment.* New York: Basic Books.

Brazelton, T. B., Koslowski, B., & Main, M. (1974). The origins of reciprocity: The early mother-infant interaction. In M. Lewis & L. A. Rosenblum (Eds.), *The effects of the infant on its caregiver* (pp. 49-76). New York: John Wiley.

Brody, S., & Axelrad, S. (1978). *Mothers, fathers, and children.* New York: International Universities Press.

Bronfenbrenner, U. (1979). *The ecology of human development: Experiments by nature and by design.* Cambridge, MA: Harvard University Press.

Brown, J. V., & Bakeman, R. (1980). Relationships of human mothers with their infants during the first year of life: Effect of prematurity. In R. W. Bell & W. P. Smotherman (Eds.), *Maternal influences and early behavior* (pp. 353-373). New York: Spectrum.

Bruner, J. S. (1977). Early social interaction and language acquisition. In H. R. Schaffer (Ed.), *Studies in mother-infant interaction* (pp. 271-289). New York: Academic Press.

Cairns, R. B. (1979). *Analysis of social interaction: Methods, issues, and illustrations.* Hillsdale, NJ: Lawrence Erlbaum.

Callaghan, J. W. (1981). A comparison of Anglo, Hopi, and Navajo mothers and infants. In T. M. Field, A. M. Sostek, P. Vietze, & P. H. Leiderman (Eds.), *Culture and early interactions* (pp. 115-131). Hillsdale, NJ: Lawrence Erlbaum.

Clarke, A. M., & Clarke, A. D. B. (1979). *Early experience: Myth and evidence.* New York: Free Press.

Clarke-Stewart, K. A. (1973). Interactions between mothers and their young children: Characteristics and consequences. *Monographs of the Society for Research in Child Development, 38*(6-7, Serial No. 153).

Coates, D. L., & Lewis, M. (1984). Early mother-infant interaction and infant cognitive status as predictors of school performance and cognitive behavior in six-year-olds. *Child Development, 55,* 1219-1230.

Cohen, S. E., Parmelee, A. H., Beckwith, L., & Sigman, M. (1986). Cognitive development in preterm infants: Birth to 8 years. *Developmental and Behavioral Pediatrics, 7,* 102-110.

Cohn, J. F., Campbell, S. B., Matias, R., & Hopkins, J. (1990). Face-to-face interactions of postpartum depressed and nondepressed mother-infant pairs at 2 months. *Developmental Psychology, 26,* 15-23.

Collis, G. (1985). On the origins of turn-taking: Alternation and meaning. In M. Barrett (Ed.), *Children's single-word speech.* New York: John Wiley.

Cooper, R. P., & Aslin. R. N. (1989). The language environment of the young infant: Implications for early perceptual development. *Canadian Journal of Psychology, 43,* 247-265.

Cox, M. J., Owen, M. T., Lewis, J. M., & Henderson, V. K. (1989). Marriage, adult adjustment, and early parenting. *Child Development, 60,* 1015-1024.

Crawford, J. W. (1982). Mother-infant interaction in premature and full-term infants. *Child Development, 53,* 957-962.

Crnic, K. A., Ragozin, A. S., Greenberg, M. T., Robinson, N. M., & Basham, R. B. (1983). Social interaction and developmental competence of preterm and full-term infants during the first year of life. *Child Development, 54,* 1199-1210.

Culp, R. E., Applebaum, M. I., Osofsky, J. D., & Levy, J. A. (1988). Adolescent and older mothers: Comparison between prenatal maternal variables and newborn interaction measures. *Infant Behavior and Development, 11,* 353-362.

Culp, R. E., Culp, A. M., Osofsky, J. D., & Osofsky, H. J. (1991). Adolescent and older mothers' interaction patterns with their six-month-old infants. *Journal of Adolescence, 14,* 195-200.

Drillien, C. M. (1964). *The growth and development of the prematurely born infant.* Baltimore: Williams & Wilkins.

Dunham, P., & Dunham, F. (1990). Effects of mother-infant social interactions on infants' subsequent contingency task performance. *Child Development, 61,* 785-793.

Dunham, P., & Dunham, F. (1992). Lexical development during middle infancy: A mutually driven infant-caregiver process. *Developmental Psychology, 28,* 414-420.

Durrett, M. E., Richards, P., Otaki, M., Pennebaker, J. W., & Nyquist, L. (1986). Mother's involvement with infant and her perception of spousal support, Japan and America. *Journal of Marriage and the Family, 48,* 187-194.

Elias, G., & Broerse, J. (1989). Timing in mother-infant communications: A comment on Murray & Travarthen (1986). *Journal of Child Language, 16,* 703-706.

Elster A. B., & Lamb, M. E. (1986). Adolescent fathers: The understudied side of adolescent pregnancy. In J. B. Lancaster & B. A. Hamburg (Eds.), *School-age pregnancy and parenthood: Biosocial dimensions.* New York: Aldine de Gruyter.

Fajardo, B. F., & Freedman, D. G. (1981). Maternal rhythmicity in three American cultures. In T. M. Field, A. M. Sostek, P. Vietze, & P. H. Leiderman (Eds.), *Culture and early interactions* (pp. 133-147). Hillsdale, NJ: Lawrence Erlbaum.

Feiring, C., Fox, N. H., & Jaskir, J. (1987). The relation between social support, infant risk status and mother-infant interaction. *Developmental Psychology, 23,* 400-405.

Feldstein, S., & Crown, C. L. (1986, April). *The measurement of interpersonal influence in mother-infant interactions.* Paper presented at the International Conference on Infant Studies, Los Angeles.

Fernald, A., & Morikawa, H. (1993). Common themes and cultural variations in Japanese and American mothers' speech to infants. *Child Development, 64,* 637-656.

Field, T. M. (1978). Interaction behaviors of primary versus secondary caretaker fathers. *Developmental Psychology, 14,* 183-184.

Field, T. M. (1980). Interactions of preterm and term infants with their lower- and middle-class teenage and adult mothers. In T. M. Field, S. Goldberg, D. Stern, & A. M. Sostek (Eds.), *High-risk infants and children: Adult and peer interactions* (pp. 113-132). New York: Academic Press.

Field, T. M. (1987). Interaction and attachment in normal and atypical infants. *Journal of Consulting and Clinical Psychology, 55,* 853-859.

Field, T. M. (1992). Infants of depressed mothers. *Development and Psychopathology, 4,* 49-66.

Field, T. M., Dempsey, J., & Shuman, H. H. (1981). Five-year follow-up of preterm respiratory distress syndrome and post-term postmaturity syndrome infants. In T. M. Field & A. Sostek (Eds.), *Infants born at risk: Physiological, perceptual and cognitive process* (pp. 317-335). New York: Grune & Stratton.

Field, T. M., Healy, B., Goldstein, S., & Guthertz, M. (1990). Behavior state matching in mother-infant interactions of nondepressed versus depressed mother-infant dyads. *Developmental Psychology, 26,* 7-14.

Field, T. M., Widmayer, S. M., Adler, S., & De Cubas, M. (1990). Teenage parenting in different cultures, family constellations, and caregiving environments: Effects on infant development. *Infant Mental Health Journal, 11,* 158-174.

Field, T. M., Widmayer, S. M., Stringer, S., & Ignatoff, E. (1980). Teenage, lower class, black mothers and their preterm infants: An intervention and developmental follow up. *Child Development, 51,* 426-436.

Fleming, A. S. (1989). Maternal responsiveness in human and animal mothers. In M. H. Bornstein (Ed.), *Maternal responsiveness: Characteristics and consequences* (pp. 31-48). San Francisco: Jossey-Bass.

Fogel, A. (1982). Early adult-infant interaction: Expectable sequences of behavior. *Journal of Pediatric Psychology, 7,* 1-22.

Fogel, A., Dedo, J. Y., & McEwen, I. (1992). Effect of postural position and reaching on gaze during mother-infant face-to-face interaction. *Infant Behavior and Development, 15,* 231-244.

Fogel, A., Stevenson, M. B., & Messinger, D. (1992). A comparison of the parent-child relationship in Japan and the United States. In J. L. Roopnarine & D. B. Carter (Eds.), *Parent-child relations in diverse cultural settings* (pp. 35-51). Norwood, NJ: Ablex.

García Coll, C. T. (1990). Developmental outcome of minority infants: A process-oriented look into our beginnings. *Child Development, 61,* 270-289.

García Coll, C. T., Hoffman, J., & Oh, W. (1987). The social ecology and early parenting of Caucasian adolescent mothers. *Child Development, 58,* 955-963.

Gecas, V. (1979). The influence of social class on socialization. In W. R. Burr, R. Hill, F. I. Nye, & I. L. Reiss (Eds.), *Contemporary theories about the family* (Vol. 1, pp. 365-404). New York: Free Press.

Gelfand, D. M., Teti, D. M., & Fox, C. E. R. (1992). Sources of parenting stress for depressed and nondepressed mothers of infants. *Journal of Clinical Child Psychology, 21,* 262-272.

Gewirtz, J. L. (1977). Maternal responding and the conditioning of infant crying: Directions of influence within the attachment acquisition process. In B. C. Etzel, J. M. LeBlanc, & D. M. Baer (Eds.), *New developments in behavioral research: Theory, method, and application* (pp. 31-57). Hillsdale, NJ: Lawrence Erlbaum.

Ginsburg, G. P., & Kilbourne, B. K. (1988). Emergence of vocal alternation in mother-infant interchanges. *Journal of Child Language, 15,* 221-235.

Goldberg, S. (1979). Premature birth: Consequences for the parent-infant relationship. *American Scientist, 67,* 214-220.

Goldberg, S., & Divitto, B. A. (1983). *Born too soon: Preterm birth and early development.* San Francisco: W. H. Freeman.

Goldberg, S., Lojkasek, M., Gartner, G., & Corter, C. (1989). Maternal responsiveness and social development in preterm infants. In M. H. Bornstein (Ed.), *Maternal responsiveness: Characteristics and consequences* (pp. 89-104). San Francisco: Jossey-Bass.

Goldberg, W. A., & Easterbrooks, M. A. (1984). The role of marital quality in toddler development. *Developmental Psychology, 20,* 504-514.

Goldsmith, H. H., & Alansky, J. A. (1987). Maternal and infant temperamental predictors of attachment: A meta-analytic review. *Journal of Consulting and Clinical Psychology, 55,* 805-816.

Gottman. J. M. (1979). Detecting cyclicity in social interaction. *Psychological Bulletin, 86,* 338-348.

Greenberg, M. T., & Crnic, K. A. (1988). Longitudinal predictors of developmental status and social interaction in premature and full-term infants at age two. *Child Development, 59,* 554-570.

Greene, J. G., Fox, N. A., & Lewis, M. (1983). The relationship between neonatal characteristics and three-month mother-infant interaction in high-risk infants. *Child Development, 54,* 1286-1296.

Grieser, D. L., & Kuhl, P. K. (1988). Maternal speech to infants in a tonal language: Support for universal prosodic features in motherese. *Developmental Psychology, 24,* 14-20.

Gunnar, M. R. (1980). Contingent stimulation: A review of its role in early development. In E. Levine (Ed.), *Coping and health* (pp. 101-119). New York: Plenum.

Hanzlik, J. R. (1990). Nonverbal interaction patterns of mothers and their infants with cerebral palsy. *Educational Training and Mental Retardation, 25,* 333-343.

Hardy, J. B., & Duggan, A. K. (1988). Teenage fathers and the fathers of infants of urban, teenage mothers. *American Journal of Public Health, 78,* 919-922.

Harrison, M. J. (1990). A comparison of parental interactions with term and preterm infants. *Research in Nursing and Health, 13,* 173-179.

Holwerda-Kuipers, J. (1987). The cognitive development of low-birthweight children. *Journal of Child Psychology and Psychiatry, 28,* 321-328.

Isabella, R. A. (1993). Origins of attachment: Maternal interactive behavior across the first year. *Child Development, 64,* 605-621.

Isabella, R. A., & Belsky, J. (1991). Interactional synchrony and the origins of infant-mother attachment: A replication study. *Child Development, 62,* 373-384.

Jasnow, M., & Feldstein, S. (1986). Adult-like temporal characteristics of mother-infant vocal interaction. *Child Development, 57,* 754-761.

Kaeller, M. G., & Roe, K. V. (1990). Personality variables as assessed by the MMPI and their relationship to mother-infant interactional behaviors at age three months. *Psychological Reports, 66,* 899-904.

Kanaya, Y., & Miyake, K. (1985). *The relation between mother-infant interactional characteristics in early infancy and later attachment as assessed in the strange situation.* Unpublished manuscript, Kokugakuin Women's Junior College, Takikawa, Hokkaido, Japan.

Kaye, K. (1977). Toward the origin of dialogue. In H. R. Schaffer (Ed.), *Studies in mother-infant interaction* (pp. 89-117). New York: Academic Press.

Kilbride, H. W., Johnson, D. I., & Streissguth, A. P. (1977). Social class, birth order, and newborn experience. *Child Development, 48,* 1686-1688.

Kojima H. (1986). Japanese concepts of child development from the mid-17th to mid-19th century. *International Journal of Behavioral Development, 9,* 315-329.

Kopp, C. B., & Krakow, J. B. (1983). The developmentalist and the study of biological risk: A view of the past with an eye toward the future. *Child Development, 54,* 1086-1108.

Kruper, J. C., & Uzgiris, I. C. (1987). Fathers' and mothers' speech to young infants. *Journal of Psycholinguistic Research, 16,* 597-614.

Lamb, M. E. (1981). *The role of the father in child development.* New York: John Wiley.

Lamb, M. E. (1987). *The father's role: Cross-cultural perspectives.* Hillsdale, NJ: Lawrence Erlbaum.

Lamb, M. E., & Easterbrooks, M. A. (1981). Individual differences in parental sensitivity: Origins, components and consequences. In M. E. Lamb & L. R. Sherrod (Eds.), *Infant social cognition: Empirical and theoretical considerations* (pp. 127-153). Hillsdale, NJ: Lawrence Erlbaum.

Landy, S., Montgomery, J. S., Schubert, J., Cleland, J. F., & Clark, C. (1983). Mother-infant interaction of teenage mothers and the effect of experience in observational sessions on the development of their infants. *Early Child Development and Care, 10,* 165-186.

Laosa, L. M. (1981). Maternal behavior: Sociocultural diversity in modes of family interaction. In R. W. Henderson (Ed.), *Parent-child interaction: Theory, research, and prospects* (pp. 125-167). New York: Academic Press.

Lee, H., & Barratt, M. S. (1993). The cognitive development of preterm low birth weight children at 5 to 8 years. *Journal of Developmental and Behavioral Pediatrics, 14,* 242-249.

LeResche, L., Strobino, D., Parks, P., Fischer, P., & Smeriglio, V. (1983). The relationship of observed maternal behavior to questionnaire measures of parenting knowledge, attitudes, and emotional state in adolescent mothers. *Journal of Youth and Adolescence, 12,* 19-31.

Lester, B. M., Hoffman, J., & Brazelton, T. B. (1985). The rhythmic structure of mother-infant interaction in term and preterm infants. *Child Development, 56,* 15-27.

Levine, L., García Coll, C. T., & Oh, W. (1985). Determinants of mother-infant interaction in adolescent mothers. *Pediatrics, 75,* 23-29.

LeVine, R. (1977). Child rearing as cultural adaptation. In P. H. Leiderman, S. R. Rulkin, & A. Rosenfeld (Eds.), *Culture and infancy: Variations in the human experience* (pp. 15-27). New York: Academic Press.

LeVine, R., Miller, P., & West, M. (Eds.). (1988). *Parental behaviors in diverse societies.* San Francisco: Jossey-Bass.

Levy-Shiff, R., Hoffman, M. A., Mogilner, S., Levinger, S., & Mogilner, M. B. (1990). Fathers' hospital visits to their preterm infants as a predictor of father-infant relationship and infant development. *Pediatrics, 86,* 289-293.

Levy-Shiff, R., Sharir, H., & Mogilner, M. B. (1989). Mother- and father-preterm infant relationship in the hospital preterm nursery. *Child Development, 60,* 93-102.

Lewis, M., & Feiring, C. (1989). Infant, mother, and mother-infant interaction behavior and subsequent attachment. *Child Development, 60,* 831-837.

Lewis, M., & Wilson, C. D. (1972). Infant development in lower-class American families. *Human Development, 155,* 112-127.

Low, J. M., & Moely, B. E. (1988). Early word acquisition: Relationships to syntactic and semantic aspects of maternal speech. *Child Study Journal, 18,* 47-59.

Maccoby, E. E., & Martin, J. A. (1983). Socialization in the context of the family: Parent-child interaction. In P. H. Mussen (Ed.). *Handbook on child psychology: Vol. 4. Socialization, personality, and social development* (pp. 1-101). New York: John Wiley.

MacPhee, D., Ramey, C. T., & Yeates, K. O. (1984). Home environment and early cognitive development: Implications for intervention. In A. W. Gottfried (Ed.), *Home environment and early cognitive development* (pp. 343-377). New York: Academic Press.

Marfo, K. (1984). Interactions between mothers and their mentally retarded children: Integration of research findings. *Journal of Applied Developmental Psychology, 5,* 45-69.

Marfo, K. (1990). Maternal directiveness in interactions with mentally handicapped children: An analytical commentary. *Journal of Child Psychology and Psychiatry, 31,* 531-549.

Martin, J. A. (1989). Personal and interpersonal components of responsiveness. In M. H. Bornstein (Ed.), *Maternal responsiveness: Characteristics and consequences* (pp. 5-14). San Francisco: Jossey-Bass.

McGovern, M. A (1990). Sensitivity and reciprocity in the play of adolescent mothers and young fathers with their infants. *Family Relations, 39,* 427-431.

Messer, D. J., & Vietze, P. M. (1988). Does mutual influence occur during mother-infant social gaze? *Infant Behavior and Development, 11,* 97-110.

Murphy, R. L., Menyuk, P., Liebergott, J., & Schultz, M. C. (1983, April). *Predicting rate of lexical acquisition.* Paper presented at the biennial meeting of the Society for Research in Child Development, Detroit.

Murray, A. D., Johnson, J., & Peters, J. (1990). Fine-tuning of utterance length to preverbal infants: Effects on later language development. *Journal of Child Language, 17,* 511-525.

Murray, L. (1992). The impact of postnatal depression on infant development. *Journal of Child Psychology and Psychiatry, 33,* 543-561.

Newson, J. (1979). Intentional behavior in the young infant. In D. Shaffer & J. Dunn (Eds.), *The first year of life* (pp. 91-96). New York: John Wiley.

Noppe, I. C., Noppe, L. D., & Hughes, F. P. (1990). Stress as a predictor of the quality of parent-infant interactions. *Journal of Genetic Psychology, 152,* 17-28.

Nugent, J. K. (1991). Cultural and psychological influences on the father's role in infant development. *Journal of Marriage and the Family, 53,* 475-485.

Ogbu, J. U. (1981). Origins of human competence: A cultural-ecological perspective. *Child Development, 52,* 413-429.

O'Hara, M. W., Neunaber, D. J., & Zekoski, E. M. (1984). Prospective study of postpartum depression: Prevalence, course, predictive factors. *Journal of Abnormal Psychology, 93,* 158-171.

Palthe, T. V. W., Hopkins, B., & Vos, J. E. (1990). Quantitative description of early mother-infant interaction using information theoretical statistics. *Behaviour, 112,* 117-147.

Pannabecker, B. J., Emde, R. N., & Austin, B. C. (1982). The effect of early extended contact on father-newborn interaction. *Journal of Genetic Psychology, 141,* 7-17.

Parke, R. D., & Sawin, D. B. (1977, March). *The family in early infancy: Social interaction and attitudinal analyses.* Paper presented at the biennial meeting of the Society for Research in Child Development, New Orleans.

Pedersen, F. A., Suwalsky, J. T. D., Cain, R. L., Zaslow, M. J., & Rabinovich, B. A. (1987). Paternal care of infants during maternal separations: Associations with father-infant interaction at one year. *Psychiatry, 50,* 193-205.

Pederson, D. R., Moran, G., Sitko, C., Campbell, K., Ghesquire, K., & Acton, H. (1990). Maternal sensitivity and the security of infant-mother attachment: A Q-sort study. *Child Development, 61,* 1974-1983.

Pfeiffer, S. I., & Aylward, G. P. (1990). Outcome for preschoolers of very low birthweight: Sociocultural and environmental influences. *Perceptual and Motor Skills, 70,* 1367-1378.

Rabain-Jamin, J. (1989). Culture and early social interactions: The example of mother-infant object play in African and Native French families. *European Journal of Psychology of Education, 4,* 295-305.

Richman, A. L., Miller, P. M., & LeVine, R. A. (1992). Cultural and educational variations in maternal responsiveness. *Developmental Psychology, 28,* 614-621.

Rogoff, B., & Morelli, G. (1989). Perspectives on children's development from cultural psychology. *American Psychologist, 44,* 343-348.

Rondal, J. A. (1980). Fathers' and mothers' speech in early language development. *Journal of Child Language, 7,* 353-369.

Roopnarine, J. L., & Carter, D. B. (Eds.). (1992). *Parent-child relations in diverse cultural settings.* Norwood, NJ: Ablex.

Roosa, M. W., Fitzgerald, H. E., & Carlson, N. A. (1982). Teenage and older mothers and their infants: A descriptive comparison. *Adolescence, 17,* 1-17.

Rosen, K. S., & Rothbaum, F. (1993). Quality of parental caregiving and security of attachment. *Developmental Psychology, 29,* 358-367.

Rosenblith, J. F. (1992). *In the beginning: Development from conception to age two* (2nd ed.). Newbury Park, CA: Sage.

Sameroff, A., & Chandler, M. (1975). Reproductive risk and the continuum of caretaking casuality. In F. Horowitz, E. M. Hetherington, S. Scarr-Salapatek, et al. (Eds.), *Review of child development research* (Vol. 4, pp. 187-244). Chicago: University of Chicago Press.

Scarr, S. (1992). Developmental theories for the 1990s: Development and individual differences. *Child Development, 63,* 1-19.

Seifer, R., Sameroff, A. J., Anagnostopolou, R., & Elias, P. K. (1992). Mother-infant interaction during the first year: Effects of situation, maternal mental illness, and demographic factors. *Infant Behavior and Development, 15,* 405-426.

Shonkoff, J. P., & Hauser-Cram, P. (1987). Early intervention for disabled infants and their families: A quantitative analysis. *Pediatrics, 80,* 650-658.

Shute, H. B. (1987). Vocal pitch in motherese. *Educational Psychology, 7,* 187-205.

Skinner, E. A. (1986). The origins of young children's perceived control: Mother contingent and sensitive behavior. *International Journal of Behavioral Development, 9,* 359-382.

Smith, C. B., Adamson, L. B., & Bakeman, R. (1988). Interactional predictors of early language. *First Language, 8,* 143-156.

Smith, P. B., & Pederson, D. R. (1988). Maternal sensitivity and patterns of infant-mother attachment. *Child Development, 59,* 1097-1101.

Spiker, D., Ferguson, J., & Brooks-Gunn, J. (1993). Enhancing maternal interactive behavior and child social competence in low birth weight, premature infants. *Child Development, 64,* 754-768.

Stern, D. N. (1985). *The interpersonal world of the infant.* New York: Basic Books.

Stern, D. N., Jaffe, J., Beebe, B., & Bennett, S. L. (1975). Vocalizing in unison and in alternation: Two modes of communication within the mother-infant dyad. In D. Aaronson & R. Rieber (Eds.), *Developmental psycholinguistics and communication disorders.* New York: New York Academy of Sciences.

Stevenson, M. B., Leavitt, L. A., Thompson, R. H., & Roach, M. A. (1988). A social relations model analysis of parent and child play. *Developmental Psychology, 24,* 101-108.

Stevenson, M. B., Roach, M. A., VerHoeve, J., & Leavitt, L. A. (1990). Rhythms in the dialogue of infant feeding: Preterm and term infants. *Infant Behavior and Development, 13,* 51-70.

Stevenson, M. B., VerHoeve, J. N., Roach, M. A., & Leavitt, L. A. (1986). The beginning of conversation: Early patterns of mother-infant vocal responsiveness. *Infant Behavior and Development, 9,* 423-440.

Symons, D. K., & Moran, G. (1987). The behavioral dynamics of mutual responsiveness in early face-to-face mother-infant interactions. *Child Development, 58,* 1488-1495.

Toda, S., Fogel, A., & Kawai, M. (1990). Maternal speech to three-month-old infants in the United States and Japan. *Journal of Child Language, 17,* 279-294.

Tulkin, S. R. (1977). Social class differences in maternal and infant behavior. In P. H. Leiderman, S. R. Tulkin, & A. Rosenfeld (Eds.), *Culture and infancy: Variations in the human experience* (pp. 495-538). New York: Academic Press.

Unger, D. G., & Wandersman, L. P. (1988). The relation of family and partner support to the adjustment of adolescent mothers. *Child Development, 59,* 1056-1060.

U.S. Bureau of the Census. (1992). *Statistical abstracts of the United States.* Washington, DC: Government Printing Office.

van Ijzendoorn, M. H., & Kroonenberg, P. M. (1988). Cross-cultural patterns of attachment: A meta-analysis of the strange situation. *Child Development, 59,* 147-156.

Volling, B. L., & Belsky, J. (1991). Multiple determinants of father involvement during infancy in dual-earner and single-earner families. *Journal of Marriage and the Family, 53,* 461-474.

Wasserman, G. A., Brunelli, S. A., & Rauh, V. A. (1990). Social supports and living arrangements of adolescent and adult mothers. *Journal of Adolescent Research, 5,* 54-66.

Wasserman, G. A., Shilansky, M., & Hahn, H. (1986). A matter of degree: Maternal interaction with infants of varying levels of retardation. *Child Study Journal, 16,* 241-253.

Watson, J. S. (1979). Perception of contingency as a determinant of social responsiveness. In E. Thoman (Ed.), *The origins of the infant's social responsiveness.* Hillsdale, NJ: Lawrence Erlbaum.

Watson, J. S., & Hayes, L. A. (1981, April). *A new method of infant-environment interaction analysis.* Paper presented at the biennial meeting of the Society for Research in Child Development, Boston.

Whiffen, V. E., & Gotlib, I. H. (1989). Infants of postpartum depressed mothers: Temperament and cognitive status. *Journal of Abnormal Psychology, 98,* 274-279.

White, K. R. (1982). The relation between socioeconomic status and academic achievement. *Psychological Bulletin, 91,* 461-481.

Whiting, B. B. (Ed.). (1963). *Six cultures: Studies of childrearing.* New York: John Wiley.

Wilfong, E. W., Saylor, C., & Elksnin, N. (1991). Influences on responsiveness: Interactions between mothers and their premature infants. *Infant Mental Health Journal, 12,* 31-40.

Yarrow, L. J., Rubenstein, J. L., & Pedersen, F. A. (1975). *Infant and environment: Early cognitive and motivational development.* New York: John Wiley.

Yoder, P. J. (1987). Relationship between degree of infant handicap and clarity of infant cues. *American Journal of Mental Deficiency, 91,* 639-641.

Zarling, C. L., Hirsch, B. J., & Landry, S. (1988). Maternal social networks and mother-infant interactions in full-term and very low birthweight, preterm infants. *Child Development, 59,* 178-185.

Zaslow, M., Pedersen, F., Suwalsky, J., Rabinovich, B., & Cain, R. (1986). Fathering during the infancy period: Implications of the mother's employment role. *Infant Mental Health Journal, 7,* 225-234.

2

The Socialization of Person-Centered Communication

Parents' Contributions to Their Children's Social-Cognitive and Communication Skills

BRANT R. BURLESON
JESSE G. DELIA
JAMES L. APPLEGATE

The socialization process has become an increasingly important focus of work in a broad range of social sciences in recent years, including diverse areas in communication research. Simultaneously, the sub-field of family communication has taken shape as an increasingly well defined domain of interdisciplinary research concerned, in part, with issues of socialization as an interpretive and communicative process. The work on parents' and children's communication with which we have been associated (e.g., Applegate, Burke, Burleson, Delia, & Kline, 1985; Applegate, Burleson, & Delia, 1992; Applegate & Delia, 1980; Burleson, 1983; Burleson, Delia, & Applegate, 1992; O'Keefe & Delia, 1985) fits comfortably within this broad turn toward socialization and interpretive processes in everyday family communication practices. One of our major objectives has been to extend our general cognitive and social constructivist framework (see Applegate, 1990; Burleson, 1987, 1989; Delia, O'Keefe, & O'Keefe, 1982; O'Keefe & Delia, 1982) to conceptualize and assess several important aspects of parental communication, their determinants, and their consequences for children's social-cognitive and communication skills and peer relationships.

This chapter summarizes and extends our work on parental communication and children's social-cognitive and communicative development, and in so doing seeks to clarify some key issues in the analysis of intergenerational cultural and behavioral processes. More broadly, the chapter presents our formulation of the complex interconnections among culture, cognition, and communication. We begin by delineating the major theoretical issues addressed in our empirical work on socialization processes and effects. Next, we describe some conceptual and methodological tools frequently used in our work. The major portion of the chapter presents our model of the socialization of functional communication skills in childhood and reviews research testing aspects of this model.

THE SOCIALIZATION OF FUNCTIONAL COMMUNICATION SKILLS

An axiom widely shared by both philosophers and social theorists maintains that the social world is both produced and reproduced through the communicative activities of its members. But how, exactly, does this happen? How do humans, through their ordinary communicative activities, construct and reproduce social reality? What aspects of the social world are reproduced? What aspects are not?

Questions such as these have traditionally been answered in terms of the socialization process. Socialization may be understood as "the comprehensive and consistent induction of an individual into the objective world of a society or a sector of it" (Berger & Luckmann, 1967, p. 130). At a minimum, socialization involves the social and communicative processes through which cultural knowledge, resources, and practices are made available to and internalized by an individual. Hence any useful approach to the study of socialization should facilitate an appreciation of the integration of culture, cognition, and communication.

Communication is the primary process through which culture is conveyed to and internalized by the individual, as well as the primary process through which the individual externalizes his or her internal states, making them accessible to others. Thus the communication system of a culture (language, conversation, sociolinguistic rules, functional strategies) both makes socialization possible and serves a key function in virtually all aspects of both primary and secondary socialization. Because of its crucial role, the communication system "constitutes both the most important content and the most important instrument of socialization" (Berger & Luckmann, 1967, p. 133).

Research examining the acquisition of the communication system within the context of primary socialization has focused on how the child learns to communicate at all, as well as on how the child comes to acquire communicative practices characteristic of his or her group. Most research examining communicative competence in children has explored the child's acquisition of the linguistic code (language acquisition studies) and social rules for the appropriate use of that code (developmental sociolinguistic studies). Although these are vital areas of study, Clark and Delia (1979) have noted that neither of these two areas adequately addresses the child's development of *functional communication competence* or the ability to use communicative resources strategically to accomplish personal and social goals—to persuade, inform, console, appease, compromise, or the like. Clark and Delia suggest that scholars from the academic discipline of communication, with their rich heritage in rhetorical studies, are best positioned to address the acquisition and development of functional competence.

The development of functional competence can be seen as the product of both nature and nurture: Its emergence is a function of both internal dynamics (ontogenetic physical, intellectual, and psychological changes that occur naturally in the developing child) and external dynamics (the socializing influences of parents, peers, schools, and other social institutions). Elsewhere, we have presented detailed analyses of ontogenetic changes in several aspects of functional communication competence during childhood and adolescence (e.g., Burleson, 1984; Delia, Kline, & Burleson, 1979). Here, however, we are concerned with the *socialization* of functional communication skills in childhood. That is, the primary question addressed here (and in the studies reviewed below) is how socializing agents, especially parents, foster (however implicitly) the acquisition of functional communication skills by their children.

Our focal concern is not simply how parents teach their children to communicate functionally; rather, we are interested in how different *styles* of functional communication are passed from parents to their children. We have found it useful to address this issue within an individual differences framework. The strategic pursuit of certain social goals through communication (e.g., disciplining others, persuading others, comforting others, informing others) requires skills— skills at which individuals differ. Several interrelated questions about these skills and their intergenerational transmission can be asked, including the following: Do some cultural formations promote more than others the development of certain functional communication skills? Are individual differences in functional skills transmitted from one generation to the next? If so, how does this happen? What are the mechanisms through which individual differences in functional communication skills are transmitted or socialized? And what are some of the social effects of individual differences in functional communication skills within the culture in which they are transmitted?

Our approach to such questions has involved the development of parallel, integrated analyses of the cultural, communicative, and cognitive processes of both children and adults. Our theoretical and empirical work has consistently made use of the notion of *complexity* as a construct for differentiating types of messages and cognitive systems and relating them to differences in cultural formations. Following Werner (1957), we define *complexity* as the degree of differentiation, articulation, and integration within a system. Systems composed of a greater number of finely articulated and highly integrated components are more complex than are systems with fewer, less specialized, and less organized elements. Thus, for example, a complex cognitive system is composed of a comparatively large number of abstract, hierarchically organized elements. Complex message structures are those reflecting the coherent, integrated pursuit of multiple instrumental and relationship objectives.

We have much more to say about complexity in messages and cognitive systems and their relationship to culture in the subsequent sections of this chapter. We begin by explicating our idea of message complexity (or behavioral complexity; see O'Keefe & Delia, 1982) in the context of what we have termed *person-centered communication*. We discuss communication first, because it is the crucial process linking culture and cognition as well as the central mechanism through which socialization occurs.

PERSON-CENTERED COMMUNICATION AS A FOCUS FOR SOCIALIZATION RESEARCH

The Concept of Person-Centered Parental Communication

Our perspective on parental communication is part of a broad range of approaches that have identified sharp divergences in everyday parenting practices within American families. Virtually all of these lines of work have focused on differences in parental styles in either disciplining or providing nurturance. The conceptual schemes used in characterizing parental discipline have employed such general distinctions as power-assertive versus inductive, authoritarian versus authoritative, position centered versus person centered, parent centered versus child centered, punishment oriented versus reason oriented, and harsh/restrictive versus positive/nonrestrictive (see the review by Rollins & Thomas, 1979). Parental nurturance is an even less differentiated concept, with analysis typically stopping at the articulation of global categorical distinctions: warm versus cold behaviors, positive versus negative acts, accepting versus rejecting styles (see Radke-Yarrow & Zahn-Waxler, 1986). Our analysis has sought to provide a conceptual framework for parental behavior that goes beyond simple categorical classifications and dichotomous contrasts, representing instead a wide range of behaviors in both discipline and nurturance.

Consistent with our interest in functional communication competence, we have focused on variations in behavior in response to concrete discipline- or nurturance-relevant situations at a functional level of analysis. Our concern has been less with discourse form or the negotiation of meaning than with how communication is used as a functional resource to shape the child's conduct and thought. Our functional analysis of parental communication is rooted in a systematic conceptualization of "reflection-enhancing" parental behavior (see Applegate et al., 1985, 1992). Reflection-enhancing parenting is itself tied to a more general analysis of person-centered forms of communication (see Applegate, 1990; Applegate & Delia, 1980; Burleson, 1989; O'Keefe & Delia, 1982).

The conceptualization of reflection-enhancing communication integrates and builds upon Hoffman's (1977) analysis of power-assertive versus inductive parenting and Bernstein's (1974) ideas contrasting position- and person-centered communication. (Similar ideas have been presented by Baumrind [e.g., 1989] in her contrasting of authoritarian and authoritative parenting.) Power-assertive/authoritarian/position-centered parenting involves the direct assertion of parental authority through physical punishment, control of material resources, or verbal means (imperatives, commands, threats, rule invocations). Inductive/authoritative/person-centered parenting, by contrast, involves offering reasons, particularly consequence-focused reasons, to guide the child's thought and conduct. Considerable research has shown that power-assertive parenting is associated with greater aggression in children's behavior, whereas inductive parenting is associated with the internalization of self-guiding principles and altruistic behavior (see the reviews by Brody & Shaffer, 1982; Maccoby & Martin, 1983).

Bernstein's (1974) framework ties the analysis of position- and person-centered communication to a general model of the relationships among and the reproduction of linguistic processes, cultural formations, and cognitive structures. Bernstein argues that the position- and person-centered modes of communication are organized by cognitive orientations to, respectively, similarity and difference in the psychological experiences underlying social relations. Each of these modes of communication is reflected in a sociolinguistic code. The *restricted* code fosters and expresses a focus on the identities of others and the meanings of their actions as given in conventionally defined social roles within particular contexts. In contrast, the *elaborated* code focuses on the motivations, feelings, and intentions of individuals who are presumed to have distinctive psychological perspectives within contexts.

These two codes are grounded within and reproduce both their sustaining cognitive orientations and correspondent forms of social life that reflect two differing social structures (a system of shared social roles versus a system of contextually negotiated identities and relationships). Thus the restricted code fosters a *position-centered ori-*

entation that discourages language usage focused on the perspectives of unique individuals while promoting communication grounded in culturally shared definitions of situations, roles, and behavioral norms (e.g., those defining the conventional authority relationship between parent and child). In contrast, the elaborated code fosters a *person-centered orientation* that promotes communication as a medium for adaptation and interaction essential for bridging the gap between individuals with highly differentiated identities and perspectives.

Bernstein's theory has the virtue of wedding the analysis of different parenting modes to models of families as systems that reproduce themselves through communication. Although building directly upon Bernstein's socialization theory, we have sought to transcend a number of limiting factors in his perspective (e.g., the tight tie to the analysis of social class in British society, the primary focus on lexical and syntactic levels in analyses of language practices, the omission of any detailed analysis of psychological processes; see Applegate & Delia, 1980; Applegate et al., 1985, 1992). For present purposes, it is most important to note that the analysis of communicative practices is shifted to a functional level. We have proposed a continuum for parental communication designed to capture the extent to which messages embody the pursuit of complex goal structures that encourage children to reflect upon their experience or behavior, the consequences of their actions, and how their conduct might affect others behaviorally and psychologically. Messages defined as more *reflection enhancing* pursue more differentiated and integrated sets of goals, are responsive to the complex exigencies in the situations addressed, and direct the child's attention to behavioral consequences and psychological processes.

The Semiotic and Historical Situation of Person-Centered Communication

As a sociolinguist, Bernstein places primary emphasis on the association of the elaborated and restricted codes with particular social classes and the extent to which these codes are revealed in particular patterns of class-based linguistic usage. Much recent work in sociolinguistics reflects "semiotic" and "practice" perspectives that stress how the world is precoded and predefined through linguistic and other historically embedded codes (see Wertsch, 1991). These studies typically feature semiotically coded social power relations. Bernstein's analysis (and our own) is more dynamic than many of these perspectives, though some semiotic perspectives have recently been elaborated in ways that emphasize their "contextuality" (hence historically embedded codes are seen as appropriated within particular contexts and as operating in complex combinations). However, the tradition of semiotic analysis gives little attention to how behavior gets organized for the sustained tasks of everyday life by individuals who position themselves as active, interacting agents (but see Miller, Potts, & Fung, 1990, for a situated, pragmatic analysis of language socialization processes within the Vygotskian "practice" tradition). A focus on communication as a functionally organized activity is at the heart of our own analysis.

Our position recognizes that the world is predefined and precoded with semiotic representations that interlace everyday interactions and serve to reproduce themselves. Much of what happens in socialization is that these forms of "precoding" are made manifest in the speech of parents (and others), and thereby become accessible to the child and shape his or her developing constructs and practices. Communication is the medium of semiotic reproduction, but "reproduction" is a localized interpretive process, not a brute force or automatic outcome. Children must recognize, orient to, and appropriate particular distinctions embedded in the speech, behavior, dress, and so on of the social actors they confront. Socialization is not simply (and certainly is not only) a matter of transmitting content through social learning; it is also a process of actively interpreting, representing, and appropriating deep structural distinctions that organize everyday life. Though historical content is seldom the focus of interaction, any contemporary interactional moment will always be laced with history.

The semiotic and behavioral structures of position- and person-centered communication are not socially organized in a purely contemporary sense. Rather, they have been patterned into families and other social institutions across long periods of history. Moreover, any given family or individual expresses this historical patterning not as a pure form, but as it has entered into concrete and local sites of social life. We need not pursue the point very far here, but it is important to underscore that position- and person-centered modes of communication are deeply historical semiotic and behavioral structures. They are bound up with broad modes of interpretation and social organization that have arisen within Western cultures over the centuries, and their various formations embody distinct strands in the webs of that history.

For example, in his classic studies of the development of civility in European society, Elias (1982) shows that our contemporary patterns of polite and civil behavior are deeply intertwined with the promotion of particular forms of thinking that emphasize forethought and social perspective taking. Elias maintains that these very forms of thought emerged reciprocally with the behavioral patterns they support. Mintz and Kellogg (1988), in their history of the evolving patterns of American family life, trace the development of what we have termed the person-centered or reflection-enhancing parenting orientation. This mode of parenting emerged gradually throughout the nineteenth century. Those who argued for this new approach to parenting saw it as especially suited to promoting the child's capacity for behavioral "self-government" (a view with some marked similarities to Hoffman's analysis of induction). This emerging shift from the dominance of power-assertive parenting to person-centered parenting was tied to revolutionary concepts within the American zeitgeist, such as liberty and equality (see Wood, 1992), and to broadscale changes in the organization of everyday economic life associated with the rise of industrialization, increased differentiation of work roles, and a greatly expanded middle class (see Sellers, 1991). It also was highly gender inflected in its promotion of women as the primary agents of reflection-enhancing parenting. In addition, this shift was intertwined with the emergence of social formations that were less patriarchal and formal, and more egalitarian and concerned with individual feelings and overt nurturance.

There are some striking similarities between contemporary descriptions of inductive, person-centered parenting behavior and descriptions of "democratic parenting" that appeared in the early nineteenth century. An appreciation of these similarities emphasizes that any analysis of socialization processes that fails to consider the ways social life is historically organized through semiotic and cultural practices will miss something fundamental. We have sought to elaborate our understanding of socialization in ways that give it a strong cultural and sociohistorical aspect. Our perspective retains a robust psychological focus, but it also increasingly explores how psychological structures and processes are connected through communication with the organization of culture and society.

In sum, person-centered forms of social cognition and communication have entered into contemporary culture not as a unified body that integrates the entire society, but as a fragmented, partially distributed set of understandings. There is no universal social consensus on the appropriateness and utility of reflection-enhancing parenting, for example. Our Wernerian comparative perspective, with its analytic concepts built around the core idea of complexity, thus provides one framework for examining parenting orientations across individuals, families, and sociocultural groups. We believe our comparative approach, with its focus on complexity in cognitive systems and message structures and their relationship to cultural formations, is particularly well suited to comparing how individuals, families, and sociocultural groups utilize person-centered forms of social cognition and communication.

METHODOLOGICAL COMMITMENTS

The conceptual framework outlined above directly informs our methodological practices in several ways. One strength of our conceptual framework is that it encourages the use of varied methods for collecting data (e.g., in-depth interviews, naturalistic observation of behavior, role-playing exercises, survey questionnaires, laboratory experimentation). Most of the methods we have employed, however, reflect our commitments to (a) a developmental logic informing human action (a "genetic epistemology"; Piaget, 1970); (b) the functional, goal-based organization of communication; (c) the integrated effect of psychological and communicative processes on social functioning; and (d) a commitment to the search for the deep structures of development in "thick data" (with apologies to Geertz, 1973) grounded in the language and social constructions of actors themselves.

Commitment to a Developmental Logic

First, and most centrally, our approach assesses the interpretive and communication practices of individual family members using tools forged within a comparative-organismic developmental framework (Werner, 1957; Werner & Kaplan, 1963). The coding systems we have developed are hierarchical in nature, indexing comparative differences in the complexity of the perceptions and messages of children and adults along particular developmental axes. Our work has focused on the particular axes of development suggested by Werner's (1957) orthogenetic principle: "Wherever development occurs, it proceeds from a state of relative globality and lack of differentiation to a state of increasing differentiation, articulation, and hierarchic integration" (p. 126). In unpacking this idea as a foundation for coding systems indexing differences in psychological and communicative functioning, we have examined variations in the complexity with which individuals represent and act toward other people in social situations. To what extent can people differentiate between and multidimensionally represent alternate perspectives (e.g., self, other, society) on social situations? How well can individuals adapt to others as autonomous reasoning agents, articulating the feelings, dispositions, and basic ideological assumptions informing their own and others' perspectives? How well can individuals create strategic responses to situations that address the multiple demands posed by the people, norms, and communicative goals informing the situation?

Our efforts to represent and evaluate behavior in terms of these questions have led us to develop several hierarchical coding systems that index increases in person-centered communication. Reflecting an integration of Bernstein (1974) and the developmental perspectives of Werner, we view communicative development as marked by a shift from the use of egocentric and rigid forms of speech to forms that are progressively more sensitive to psychological states of the other, individual differences, the desire for personal autonomy, and the negotiated character of social situations. As indicated previously, person-centeredness is a general quality of communication with a variety of separable aspects, including the extent to which a message is responsive to the aims and utterances of the interactional partner, is adapted or tailored to meet the specific characteristics and needs of a particular listener, topically addresses persons' psychological and affective qualities, encourages self and other to reflect on the nature and assumptions of their circumstance, and implicitly seeks to enhance personal relationships and interpersonal identities (adapted from Applegate et al., 1985, pp. 134-135). In developing coding systems that array hierarchically these qualities of messages within family communication, we have focused on mothers' strategies for regulating and nurturing children and children's strategies for influencing, informing, and comforting. For example, mothers' regulative strategies range from coercive efforts that assume authority (e.g., "You will go to bed now or you will be punished!") to those that reflect more complex perceptions of the child's feelings, beliefs, and dispositions and address the child as an autonomous, reasoning agent (e.g., "John, what do you have on tap for tomorrow? . . . Hmmmm. Sounds like a full day. I know you really like this TV show, but remember what happened the last time you tried to stay up late before a big day? Wasn't a good time was it? Okay, I want you to go to bed now so tomorrow can be a good day for you.") Within our methodological framework, such differences are not seen in terms of dichotomous categories or content-driven typologies. Rather, they are hierarchically ordered as representing progressively more differentiated, articulated, and integrated accommodations to the complex demands of communication in a family context, and are viewed as reflective of specific developments in perception and communication.

The commitment to hierarchy does not, in itself, limit analyses of communication or its effects to a particular axis of development. Indeed, we see development as driven by the demands of the social environment. Context and culture are both resources for, and constraints on, the development of communication competencies through the particular goals and definitions of social contexts they encourage. We expect that developmental research across cultural boundaries will continue to suggest multiple and varied axes of development.

Commitment to the Functional
Nature of Communication

Our development of methods for assessing the person-centered quality of communication grew directly from our conception of communication as a functional tool for addressing the challenges of social situations. Consistent with the analysis of Clark and Delia (1979), we view communication as pragmatic action informed by goals. We see messages as rationally designed to address those goals made salient by the sociohistorical context of interaction. Clark and Delia (1979) argue that situated rational goal structures recurrently encompass identity goals (e.g., self-presentation and altercasting), relational goals (e.g., negotiating intimacy and control), and instrumental goals (e.g., persuasion, comforting, instruction).

Rational here does not mean logical in any formal sense. Rather, behavior is rational that is organized around and directed at the accomplishment of goals addressing the ever-recurrent demands of social life. Of course, actors are not always consciously aware of the goals informing their communication. In fact, sociolinguistic research has documented the fruitfulness of explaining communication in terms of culturally induced goals for which there is usually little or no situated awareness. The degree to which actors are able to recognize and attend to the multiple goals present in any situation is itself one index of their social cognitive and communicative development.

Our coding systems for indexing the person-centered quality of verbal and nonverbal behavior are differentiated along pragmatic, goal-defined lines. As noted above, for example, we have developed hierarchical systems (Applegate et al., 1985, 1992) for indexing increases in the reflection-enhancing and person-centered quality of parental communication in situations where the dominant communicative goal is either to regulate or to nurture (see Table 2.1). Other coding systems have been designed to tap differences in the ability to engage in person-centered persuasion (e.g., Delia et al., 1979), comforting (Burleson, 1984), identity management (e.g., Applegate & Woods, 1991; Hale, 1986), informative communication (Hale, 1980), and compliance resistance (Kline & Hennen-Floyd, 1990). All of these coding systems tap individual differences in the ability to recognize and adapt to the individuality of the other person and the multiple, functional demands of the situation.

Research participants have been presented with hypothetical situations constructed to provide stringent tests of their person-centered communication skills. For example, a mother may be presented with a situation depicting her child as (a) having brought home a flower to show her affection, but the flower was picked without permission from a neighbor's yard, or (b) being sad about not getting invited to a classmate's birthday party. College students have been asked to generate messages aimed at changing the irresponsible behavior of a roommate whose friendship they value. Children have been asked to produce messages persuading mothers to host a slumber party. The messages elicited by these tasks are coded within the multilevel hierarchical systems for their level of person-centeredness. Considerable evidence supports the validity of this approach to data collection and analysis (see Applegate, 1990; Delia et al., 1982). In particular, the validity of these coding systems is supported by appropriate associations with both (a) psychological characteristics of the message producer and (b) instrumental and social outcomes resulting from the use of particular message forms (see Burleson, 1987, 1994).

The surface content of the messages gleaned by these methods is generally only of incidental interest. Instead, the deeper logic of the messages structuring the social situation is the focus of the interpretive coding. The same is true when coding is done of videotapes of role-played conflict interactions (Applegate, 1980; Waldron & Applegate, 1994) and naturalistic or field observations of situated behavior over extended periods (Applegate, 1980; Kline & Ceropski, 1984; Zimmerman & Applegate, 1992). A primary research goal in many studies has been to answer the question, What does more person-centered communication look like in various functional, relational, and institutional contexts (e.g., children comforting peers on the playground, parents disciplining children at home, police officers persuading fellow officers at work, health providers informing patients in a clinical setting, and so on)? What remains constant across variations in coding systems is the methodological commitment to using developmental

TABLE 2.1 Coding Systems Used in Scoring Mothers' Disciplinary and Comforting Messages

Regulative Strategies	*Comforting Strategies*
Mother's regulative strategies were scored for the extent to which they promoted the development of the child as a responsible and autonomous agent by encouraging the child to modify his or her behavior through reflecting on and reasoning through the nature and consequences of the sanctionable behavior for him- or herself and other parties.	Mother's comforting strategies were scored for the extent to which they granted legitimacy to the child to reflect upon and seek understanding of his or her feelings and the circumstances producing them.

Discouragement of Reflection

1. Explicit discouragement of the child's self-definition as a responsible and autonomous agent; relying on threats, simple commands, physical punishment, and other tactics; failing to provide any reason for modification of behavior other than avoidance of punitive sanctions.	1. Explicit discouragement of the child's understanding of his or her feelings by condemning or by asserting the inappropriateness of his or her feelings.
"I'd tell him to take it back to the store and ground him."	"Stop being such a baby about the party. She whines and I just put a stop to it when she does."
"Jackie, go to bed. If she didn't go I'd just take her by the hand and put her there."	"You're being disrespectful to your father. Now apologize to him. He has no right to treat his father that way."
2. Implicit discouragement of the child's self-definition as a responsible and autonomous agent by forwarding and demanding acceptance of rules assumed by the parent to be self-evident, necessary, and sufficient reasons for modification of behavior.	2. Implicit discouragement of the child's understanding of his or her feelings by asserting how the child should feel or act in the situation.

(continued)

TABLE 2.1 Continued

"Taking people's things without asking is wrong. Now go apologize for taking the flower."	"I'd just tell him we're all human and forget things. He should forgive and forget."
"All children must go to school and you are no exception."	"She can't expect to be invited to every party. She should just put it out of her mind. There'll be other parties."

Implicit Encouragement of Reflection

3. Implicit encouragement of the child's self-definition as a responsible and autonomous agent by providing an emergent opportunity for social reasoning through offering minimal, preemptive justifications for rules invoked to modify the child's behavior.

"As a child you have to go to school. It's your job like I have to do my job. Now get the clothes on or you'll be late."

"Stealing is wrong. It's against the law and you can end up in jail if you keep doing it."

4. Implicit encouragement of the child's self-definition as a responsible and autonomous agent by requiring the child to deal with parent-controlled concessions, contingent rewards, or sanctions as reasons for modification of behavior.

"They usually say they're sick and I'd tell him if he was sick he didn't have to go to school but he would stay in bed all day with no friends and no going outside so he could get better. Then I'd ask him if he still wanted to stay home."

3. Implicit encouragement of the child's understanding of his or her feelings by providing an emergent acknowledgment of those feelings through the use of diversionary tactics intended to ease the child's distress.

"Oh, I'd probably just take her out shopping or to a movie to get her off it. There's not much else you can do."

"I'd tell her Daddy or I would make it up to her with another surprise."

4. Implicit encouragement of the child's understanding of his or her feelings through an explicit acknowledgment of those feelings (may be coupled with the invocation of clichés intended to "explain away" the child's behavior).

"I know you're disappointed about the surprise, I would be too, but these things happen sometimes, though, and we have to understand."

(continued)

TABLE 2.1 Continued

"I know you want to stay up, but it's a school night. You go to bed and maybe you can stay up for a special show on the weekend."	"I'd tell her I know she was hurt. Sometimes I wasn't invited to things when I was little but the hurt goes away in a little while."

Explicit Encouragement of Reflection

5. Explicit encouragement of the child's self-definition as a responsible and autonomous agent by (a) encouraging the child to think about parent-articulated general causes or consequences of his or her behavior and (b) viewing these typical causes or consequences of his or her behavior as reasons for the modification of behavior.

5. Explicit encouragement of the child's understanding of his or her feelings by explaining and attempting to alleviate those feelings in terms of mitigating features of the situation or general principles cited by the parent.

"When people hurt us we want to call them names. It doesn't do any good, though. Next time why don't you tell them you're angry at what they did. Then maybe they won't do it again. If they do, then just don't play with them. Just calling someone a name doesn't make you feel better or your friend stop."

"I'd probably tell him that most people don't have houses big enough to invite everybody to parties. That his friend's mother probably told him he could only invite so many and he just invited his very closest friends. That when people don't invite you to one party there can be a lot of reasons and it doesn't mean they don't like you."

"When people work hard to have things [flowers] they usually want to keep them to appreciate. Mrs. Jones might have given you a flower if you'd asked, but taking things from people without asking upsets them a lot."

"When people are very busy they can forget things even when they don't mean to. Everyone forgets sometimes and when they do it doesn't mean they meant to make anyone feel bad, just that they got too busy."

(continued)

TABLE 2.1 Continued

6. Explicit encouragement of the child's self-definition as a responsible and autonomous agent by (a) encouraging the child to articulate in his or her own terms the causes and consequences of his or her behavior, (b) helping the child to articulate how these causes and consequences are relevant to a broader context involving past or future experiences of the child or affect the perspectives of other people salient to the child, and (c) teaching the child to view these factors as reasons for the modification of behavior.	6. Explicit encouragement of the child's understanding of his or her feelings by actively eliciting the child's definition of his or her feelings and the causes of them and encouraging the child to see the situation producing the distressful feelings in a broader context involving specific past or future experiences or the perspectives of other people salient to the child.
"First, I'd get him to tell me why he called his friend a name like that. You know, talk about why he felt that way. He's had names thrown at him, in fact not long ago. I'd ask him how he felt when it happened and tell him his friends felt the same way. If he wants to have his friend to play with at school he probably should apologize and tell his friend why he did it. Otherwise he might lose his friend. Is that what he wants?"	"Well, he can't invite everyone in the class to his parties. I'd remind him of his birthday party and ask him who he invited and why. Did that mean he didn't like the other people? He forgot one of his friends then too. I'd ask him if the boy was one he invited to his party. And I'd encourage him not to exclude this friend from his parties since he knows how it feels now. Let him figure this out for himself so he can deal with it when it happens again, like it will."
"If that [refusing to attend school] happened now, she's practicing for the Christmas play, so I'd say she'd miss seeing her friends [in the play] and exchanging Christmas cards. Jackie [a friend] won't get a card from you and she'll be sad. I think she'd react to that. Her friends are important to her."	"I'd ask him why he wasn't talking to his dad. Depending on what he said I'd probably remind him of the times he's forgotten to do things he promised to me. He forgets to make his bed a lot. I'd ask him if I treat him like he's doing. He knows his dad feels sorry about it and I'd just ask him to go talk about it with him so they'd both feel better."

logics to examine multifunctional forms of communication in an array of interactional, relational, institutional, and cultural contexts. Corresponding results have been obtained with behavioral role-play methods and field observations of behavior (e.g., Applegate, 1980).

Commitment to an Integrated Analysis of Psychological and Communicative Development

From the outset, constructivist analyses of communication generally, and family communication specifically, have integrated parallel codings of psychological (particularly social-cognitive) development and communicative development. Although communication between parents and their children is influenced by both family history and features of the interactional context, it also reflects relatively enduring individual differences in social-cognitive and communication development of the persons involved. Our coding systems are noteworthy for tying specific messages, interactions, and family histories to the stable interpretive and communicative capacities of individual family members.

Certain social-cognitive developments are viewed as necessary but insufficient causes for developments in person-centered communication. For example, perspective-taking skill may be necessary to produce messages adapted to the other's point of view. However, understanding the other's point of view does not guarantee that an individual will have mastered the linguistic and strategic skills required to develop a sophisticated persuasive message. Thus conceptual and empirical analyses must address *both* social-cognitive and communicative developments, as well as the relationships between them, as these unfold within the context of particular cultural forms.

Our approach conceptualizes the social-cognitive system as made up of interpersonal constructs and schemata (see Delia et al., 1982; Sypher & Applegate, 1984), which develop in accord with Wernerian principles. Interpersonal constructs are bipolar structures organized into systems that compare and contrast features of persons, thereby allowing perceivers to interpret, anticipate, and evaluate the thoughts and behaviors of others. Various social perception processes (e.g., attributional inference, perspective taking, impression integration, defining social situations) occur through the application of the system of constructs. Past research indicates that social perceptions vary with age and, even within age groups, in complexity, acuity, stability, and sensitivity to the psychological states of others (see Delia et al., 1982). These differences have been viewed as manifestations of underlying developmental changes in the number, quality, and organization of interpersonal constructs. Our developmental focus leads us to code differences in interpersonal construct systems along such axes as globality-differentiation, concreteness-abstractness, diffuseness-integration, and egocentrism-perspectivism.

Considerable research shows that individual differences in social-cognitive development are significantly associated with more complex perceptions of social situations and the use of more sophisticated message forms. Individuals with more differentiated, abstract, and integrated systems of interpersonal constructs typically represent communicative situations in more complex and multifunctional ways. They also tend to use message strategies that address complex communicative goals in highly person-centered ways (see the reviews by Applegate, 1990; Burleson, 1987, 1989; Delia et al., 1982).

A variety of coding systems have been developed to assess the developmental quality of interpersonal construct systems within and across age groups. The most commonly used instrument has been a version of Crockett's (1965) Role Category Questionnaire (RCQ) measure of interpersonal construct differentiation. This measure assesses differences in the number and quality of interpersonal constructs persons employ when forming impressions of liked and disliked others. The RCQ is a simple and straightforward measure; it possesses good reliability and validity, and it consistently predicts sophisticated perceptual and communicative functioning (see Burleson & Waltman, 1988; O'Keefe & Sypher, 1981).

This integrated, developmental approach to cognitive and communicative functioning makes possible the exploration of models tying the conceptual and social skills of mothers to parallel cognitive and communication developments within their children. Methods that allow investigation of parallel developments in social-cognitive and communication functioning within specific social contexts (e.g., discipline within the family), and that further tie such developments to more general analyses of individual differences, provide a rich base for understanding the dynamics of family communication.

Commitment to "Thick Data"

Geertz (1973) has written eloquently about the need for "thick descriptions" of social life if researchers are to comprehend the subtle complexities of human culture. Our approach to communication in families is grounded in a commitment to methods that provide "thick data." The dense, open texture of data generated by these methods permits researchers to provide more convincing descriptions of the forms taken by person-centered communication and social-cognitive development across cultural, institutional, and functional contexts. Reliance upon thick data also opens up the possibility of discovering new ways that people go about addressing communication problems.

Coding cognitions and communication in terms of certain developmental axes is the particular methodological "wedge" we find useful for inserting ourselves into the stream of family life. Certainly, there are other useful wedges, many of which are illustrated in other chapters of this book (e.g., discourse-analytic techniques focusing on conversational management processes within the family, interpretive analyses of discourse forms such as family narratives, and systems approaches that study the family in terms of interactional problematics, such as identity and power). The case for our particular developmental approach is best made through a demonstration of the insights into family communication this approach provides. We make that case in the next section of this chapter.

THE SOCIALIZATION OF FUNCTIONAL COMMUNICATION SKILLS IN THE CONTEXT OF CULTURE: THEORY AND A RESEARCH SUMMARY

A Model of Socialization Processes and Outcomes

The conceptual relations we have posited between cognition and behavior have led to the articulation of a loose model that relates (a) cultural factors to individual differences in parental thought and behavior, (b) parental communication practices to individual differences in the thought and behavior of their children, and (c) individual differences in the communication practices of both parents and children to children's acceptance by members of their peer group and performance in contexts such as school.

Specifically, we propose that cultural differences, indexed (however poorly) by variables such as socioeconomic status, will be predictive of patterns of social cognition and communication exhibited by parents. In particular, we have predicted that socioeconomic status is positively related to complex forms of social cognition and the use of behaviorally complex, person-centered forms of communicating when disciplining and nurturing children. Further, we have expected that parental use of complex, person-centered forms of communication would have significant impact on the growth of social-cognitive and communication skills in children. We hypothesize that the more person-centered parents are in communicating with their children, the more likely it is the children will develop complex social-cognitive structures and sophisticated, person-centered communication skills. Finally, in contemporary middle-class culture, person-centered communication skills appear to facilitate the development of rewarding peer relationships, especially during childhood. Thus we anticipate that children with comparatively developed communication skills will be better liked and more accepted by peers than will children with less developed communication skills. This general model is depicted in Figure 2.1. This loose model has been a source of hypotheses that we have examined empirically. It has also served as an integrative framework for interpreting findings reported by others. In this section we review evidence pertinent to this model and the predictions flowing from it.

Sociocultural Foundations of Individual Differences in Parental Communication

Our analysis of the sociocultural foundations of parenting practices suggests that the communication strategies parents use when disciplining and nurturing their children should vary as a function of the subculture within which they are embedded. In this, our approach is consistent with that of many other researchers (see the review by Gecas, 1979) who have predicted sociocultural, in particular social class, differences in parents' disciplinary and nurturant communica-

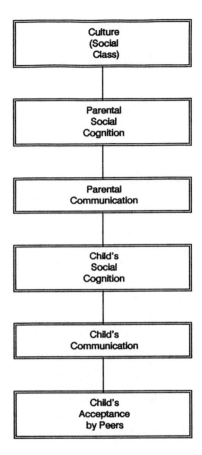

Figure 2.1. Primary Linkages Among Variables Involved in the Socialization of Social-Cognitive and Communication Skills

tion. Most generally, the prediction has been that power-assertive and position-centered forms of communication are more valued by and will tend to be used by working-class parents, whereas more inductive and person-centered forms of communication will be used by middle-class parents.

This general prediction has received considerable empirical support. For example, lower-class parents have been found more likely to use direct, position-centered forms of discipline, such as commands, imperatives, simple invocations of rules, and physical punishments. In contrast, middle-class parents tend to employ disciplinary measures that rely on more complex forms of behavior, including reasoning, induction, and personal appeals (e.g., Bernstein, 1974; Dekovic & Gerris, 1992; Hart, Ladd, & Burleson, 1990; see the reviews by Gecas, 1979; Maccoby & Martin, 1983). Also, middle-class parents have been found more likely to endorse values supporting the child's autonomy and independence (e.g., Kohn, 1976) and are more likely to exhibit behaviorally complex forms of nurturance conveying acceptance of, support for, sensitivity to, and involvement with the child (e.g., Holden, 1988; Rothbaum, 1988).

From our perspective, the linkage between culture and the communicative practices of parents can be understood in terms of the historical association of these more complex forms of conceptualizing social relations with the middle class. Navigating social relations in middle-class American society is made complex by its constitutive assumptions concerning personality differentiation, personal identity, the contingencies of value relevance, and the importance of negotiation and compromise in social relationships. The meanings "available" to members of more person-centered cultures are less public, less intersubjective, and less inferable from the situations and roles persons publicly occupy. This historically sustained, more complex meaning structure of the middle class in the sphere of interpersonal relations requires the development of constructs for conceptualizing other persons and social relationships in more differentiated and abstract (i.e., complex) ways, the articulation of more complex goals for social situations, and the use of more complex and integrated forms of communicative behavior in managing those situations and negotiating social relationships within them.

Thus our specific way of formulating the links among culture, cognition, and communication has been to see more complex cultural forms giving rise to and sustaining more complex modes of thought and action that organize them. Concretely, we have predicted significant, positive associations between social class and, on the one hand, assessments of cognitive variables such as interpersonal construct system differentiation and abstractness and, on the other hand, parents' use of person-centered message strategies when engaged in parenting tasks such as disciplining and nurturing. Moreover, within our framework, behavior is viewed as stemming most directly from the cognitions of social actors. Cultural factors are seen as influencing behavior through the mediation of the individual's cognitive system. Thus we have predicted that whereas indices of socioeconomic status will be positively associated with both the complexity of parental social cognition and the complexity (or person-centeredness) of parental behavior, cognition should mediate the effect of socioeconomic status on behavior.

These specific predictions were assessed in a study examining associations among social class (socioeconomic status), social-cognitive development, and ability to produce person-centered disciplinary and comforting messages (see Applegate et al., 1985). Utilizing tasks and methods described above, we obtained assessments of social class, interpersonal construct abstractness (psychological-centeredness), and the ability to produce person-centered messages when disciplining and comforting from participants (44 mothers of grade school children). As predicted, socioeconomic status was significantly associated with both the abstract quality of maternal social cognition ($r = .43$, $p < .01$) and the person-centeredness of mothers' disciplinary and comforting communication strategies ($r = .39$, $p < .01$). Further, the psychological-centeredness of maternal social-cognitive development was strongly associated with the use of person-centered disciplinary and comforting message strategies ($r = .54$, $p < .001$). It is important to note, however, that path-analytic procedures confirmed that maternal social cognition mediated the association between social class and communication: When the effect of maternal social cognition was partialed from the association between social class and maternal communication, only a small and nonsignificant path between social class and maternal communication remained. This pattern provides clear support for our model of the connections among culture, cognition, and communication. A very similar pattern of results was recently reported by Dekovic and Gerris (1992) in research with Dutch mothers and fathers and their children.

Our analysis of the sociocultural foundations of parental communication generates several other expectations. For example, if regularities in parental communication stem, to a significant extent, from underlying individual differences in social cognition, then there should be a fair degree of intraindividual consistency in the types of messages used across situations within a particular functional context (across, for example, different disciplinary situations), as well as across different functional contexts (across, for example, both disciplinary and comforting contexts).

There is some empirical support for each of these expectations. Applegate et al. (1985) found a high degree of internal consistency in the person-centeredness of mothers' responses to five disciplinary situations (alpha = .90) and two comforting situations (alpha = .80). Similar internal consistencies have been reported for multisituation assessments of the person-centeredness of the disciplinary strategies employed by both mothers (Dekovic & Gerris, 1992; Hart et al., 1990; Hart, DeWolf, Wozniak, & Burts, 1992) and fathers (Hart, DeWolf, Wozniak, & Burts, 1992). More important, perhaps, Kochanska, Kuczynski, and Radke-Yarrow (1989; also see Kochanska, 1990) found moderate to high levels of consistency in the types of messages parents produce in response to interviews about disciplinary communication and in the messages they actually use when disciplining their children. Applegate (1980) found similar parallels for the person-centeredness of the disciplinary and comforting messages day-care workers produced in response to interview questions and those they used when dealing with children in everyday situations. Additionally, Applegate et al. (1985) found that the level of person-centeredness exhibited in mothers' disciplinary messages was substantially associated ($r = .82$) with the level of person-centeredness displayed in their comforting messages. This finding suggests there is a considerable degree of coherence in the person-centered quality of communication across different functional contexts of parental communication. Similar results for children have been reported by Applegate et al. (1992), who found substantial associations among measures of children's comforting, persuasion, and listener-adapted communication skills. The substantial cross-situational consistencies in the person-centered quality of communicative behavior are just what would be expected if behavior stems, to a significant extent, from stable individual differences reflecting underlying sociocultural and social-cognitive orientations.

Our analysis further suggests that there should be a moderate level of intrafamilial consistency in the forms of communication parents use with their children. Specifically, if parental communication styles stem from underlying cultural orientations, and if most people marry within their particular subcultural groups (as much evidence suggests; see Duck, 1988), then there should be reasonable degrees of coherence in the person-centeredness of the messages used by mothers and fathers. Although only a few studies have obtained assessments of communication from both mothers and fathers, the available evidence is generally consistent with this prediction. For example, Hart, DeWolf, Wozniak, and Burts (1992) report that 65% of the mothers and fathers in their sample used disciplinary strategies reflecting nearly equivalent levels of person-centeredness. Weiss, Dodge, Bates, and Pettit (1992) found strong interparent correlations ($rs = .62$ to $.70$) for the harshness or power-assertiveness of parental discipline observed in their sample. The degree of interparent consistency found thus far, then, is consistent with the notion that parental communication styles reflect shared cultural orientations.

Taken together, the findings summarized here suggest that parenting styles are relatively stable individual differences with important cultural and cognitive groundings. Both parental communication and parental social cognition have consistently been found to be associated with socioeconomic status and other social class indicators. Culture manifests itself in how parents think and, through the mediation of thought, in how they communicate. We next examine how these culturally based patterns of cognition and communication are transmitted from one generation to the next.

The Socialization of Cognitive and Communicative Orientations in Children

One of the fundamental assumptions undergirding our analysis is that culture is produced—and reproduced—through the communicative practices of its members. Thus perhaps the most important consequence of parents' using a person-centered or position-centered mode of communicating with children is that these communicative forms are perpetuated through being re-created (albeit imperfectly) in children. Concretely, this analysis leads to the expectation that use by parents of a person-centered mode of communicating with their children will lead their offspring to think and communicate in a more person-centered fashion themselves.

Our work on the socialization of cognitive and communicative orientations in children is a part of a tradition in social and developmental psychology focusing on how the communicative practices of parents shape the conduct of children. Many theorists have suggested that the manner in which parents interact with their children is one of the most powerful determinants of children's social skills (e.g., Maccoby & Martin, 1983). Parental behavioral styles have been found to predict children's competencies related to prosocial and antisocial behavior (Zahn-Waxler, Radke-Yarrow, & King, 1979), moral reasoning and moral conduct (Brody & Shaffer, 1982), and general social-cognitive and inter-actional skills (Parke, MacDonald, Bertel, & Bhavnagri, 1988). Researchers such as Baumrind (1989), Hoffman (1977), and Sigel (1985) have examined particular features of parental communication for their effects on specific qualities of children's cognitive development. Other research has focused on parental communication in relation to the development of (a) specific role-taking and problem-solving abilities, (b) development of consequential thinking, and (c) general levels of social skill and peer acceptance (Hart, DeWolf, & Burts, 1992; Hart et al., 1990; Jones, Rickel, & Smith, 1980; Pettit, Dodge, & Brown, 1988; Putallaz, 1987).

Our analysis of how parental communication influences social-cognitive and communicative competencies in children has several distinctive aspects. In particular, our analysis differs from those advanced by others in its conception of (a) the key features of parental messages of interest, (b) the structures in the child affected by parental messages, and (c) the process through which parental communication affects children.

First, as discussed previously, we view variations in the person-centeredness of parental communication as reflecting different goal configurations. The analysis of these goal configurations involves considering not just context-defining instrumental goals (e.g., comforting, disciplining), but also how subsidiary goals involving identity, relational, or secondary instrumental concerns are addressed. The structural complexity of message behavior, as defined by underlying goal configurations, is central in our analysis of parental communication. Person-centered and reflection-enhancing messages are not simply more "inductive" or "authoritative"; they are structurally and functionally more complex forms of behavior (see O'Keefe & Delia, 1982).

As complex behavioral configurations, reflection-enhancing messages evince the desire not simply for the child to act a certain way (in disciplinary situations) or feel a certain way (in comforting situations), but rather to understand the situation in a broadened way and see that courses of action should follow from consideration of relevant situational features and enduring values. These complex forms of communicative behavior present greater accommodative challenges by calling upon the child to reason about situations and select behaviors based on considered needs, wants, and responsibilities.

What features of the child's developing psychobehavioral system are affected by parental communication varying in level of complexity? And what are the mechanisms through which parental communication exerts influence on the child's cognitive and behavioral structures?

We believe sustained exposure to more complex forms of parental behavior has a primary influence on the child's interpersonal cognitive structures rather than a direct effect on behavior (as might be predicted by a modeling or social learning analysis). Parental communication generally does not present the child with ready-made behavioral routines that can be executed in the social situations faced by the child. Rather, complex forms of parental communication point the child toward certain features of situations and suggest that it may be necessary for the child to pay attention to these features if he or she is to work out solutions to particular difficulties and conflicts. For example, many behaviorally complex messages make salient the desirability of maintaining a positive face for oneself and others across situations, the significance of identity and relationship management in complex social situations, and the importance of considering long-term as well as immediate consequences of actions. Thus, in being exposed to behaviorally complex messages, the child does not learn a specific set of beliefs or routines, but rather acquires a generalized interpretive orientation and set of constructs that guide his or her emergent assessment and management of situations.

Behaviorally complex parental communication should thus promote the development of more complex social-cognitive orientations in children (e.g., greater differentiation and psychologically centered construing). Enhanced social-cognitive development in the child is seen, in turn, as enabling the child to develop more person-centered communication abilities (e.g., the use of receiver-focused persuasive strategies and sophisticated comforting strategies). Contexts involving informing, persuading, and comforting make salient the child's ability to identify and adapt to relevant dispositional and motivational characteristics of others. Thus the development of a repertoire of strategies for responding to such situations in more skilled ways must build directly upon the child's social-cognitive abilities. Even if there are close parallels in the functional communicative domains assessed in the parent and the child, the path of influence should be from parental communication to the child's general social-cognitive abilities, and then to the child's specific communicative abilities.

We explain the effects of parental communication on the child's social-cognitive development in terms of the processes of semiotic mediation, social learning, and accommodation (the last of these concepts is understood from the perspective of cognitive-developmental theory). That is, we see socialization outcomes as realized through processes of social learning and cognitive development in a context that is semiotically mediated by the parents' communication. The messages of parents (and other socializing agents) code and direct attention to particular features of social contexts (e.g., the intrapsychic experiences of others) and, over time, the child is led to acquire cognitive schemes or constructs for representing, interpreting, and making inferences about those features of the social world (e.g., Dunn, Brown, & Beardsall, 1991). The behaviorally complex messages employed by person-centered parents code, and make more easily accessible, a wider range of interpersonal and intrapsychic features of contexts than do the structurally simpler messages used by position-centered parents. The presentation and elaboration of motivations, dispositions, feelings, social rules, and so on in behaviorally complex messages creates a more complicated social world for the child to construe. The recurrent presentation of such a world in parental discourse encourages the child to develop progressively more complex cognitive structures through which features of this social reality can be represented, interpreted, and acted upon. The growing complexity in the child's thought is further stimulated by the continual "re-presentation" of complexity in the parents' behavior and by the child's increasing capacity to represent that complexity through the schemes and constructs he or she has already acquired. In traditional cognitive-developmental terms, the child's development is channeled toward the elaboration of an interpersonal construct system sufficient in complexity to accommodate to and manage the complexity of the world the child is recurrently confronting. Over time, exposure to behaviorally complex, reflection-enhancing parenting and the person-centered interpretive premises it expresses should promote the child's development of more complex, psychologically centered social thinking.

Support for our specific analysis of the influence of parental communication on children's cognitive and communicative development comes from a two-year longitudinal study assessing associations among maternal communication, children's social cognition, and children's communication skills (Applegate et al., 1992). The participants in this study (51 first and third graders and their mothers) completed assessments of multiple cognitive and communicative skills: Mothers responded to tasks assessing their use of behaviorally complex disciplinary and comforting messages while children completed batteries of tasks assessing aspects of social cognition (construct system differentiation and abstractness, social perspective-taking ability, affective perspective-taking skill) and several communication skills (persuasion skill, comforting skill, listener-adaptation skill, referential skill). In both years of the study, maternal communication was a significant predictor of children's social-cognitive and communicative abilities, and remained so even when controlling statistically for the effect of variables such as social class, family size, and the sex, age, and birth order of the child. More important, a path analysis showed that, as predicted by our model, children's social-cognitive development mediated the effect of maternal communication on children's communication skills: Maternal communication primarily influenced development of the child's social-cognitive abilities, which in turn affected the child's communication skills.

Several other researchers have recently reported results consistent with those obtained by Applegate et al. (1992). For example, Weiss et al. (1992) found that parental "harsh discipline" (a construct conceptually similar to our notion of behaviorally simple, power-assertive messages) had the most direct impact on children's social information-processing skills, which in turn were linked most directly to displays of socially aggressive behavior. In three different studies, Hart and his colleagues (Hart, DeWolf, & Burts, 1992; Hart, DeWolf, Wozniak, & Burts, 1992; Hart et al., 1990) have found the person-centered quality of maternal disciplinary communication to predict features of children's social cognition and social behavior (see the summary in Hart, DeWolf, & Burts, 1993). In particular, Hart, DeWolf, and Burts (1992) found evidence that an aspect of children's social cognition (the ability to envision outcomes of various social strategies) mediated the influence of maternal discipline on some features of children's peer-related social behaviors. In sum, there is growing support for the notion that parental communication not only affects the child's behavior, but does so through influencing how the child thinks about the social world.

Parental Communication, Children's Skills,
and the Child's Peer Relationships and School Performance

Outside the family, perhaps no social relationships are as important to the child's development as those with peers. Friendships and other relationships with peers serve numerous constructive functions during childhood, including facilitating the development of cognitive and intellectual abilities, fostering emotional and moral maturation, and aiding the development of key social and communicative competencies (Burleson, 1986; Ginsberg, Gottman, & Parker, 1986). The importance of peer relationships has been demonstrated by numerous studies showing that children who lack peer relationships, particularly those actively rejected by their agemates, are at increased risk for a host of social, behavioral, and emotional problems, including poor performance in and dropout from school, delinquency, substance abuse, and emotional problems (see reviews by Kupersmidt, Coie, & Dodge, 1990; Ladd & Asher, 1985).

An expanding body of research indicates that children's social and communication skills are important determinants of their acceptance by peers (see reviews by Burleson, 1986; Coie, Dodge, & Kupersmidt,

1990; Hartup, 1983; Hymel & Rubin, 1985). In particular, several distinct lines of research have found that children with more person-centered communication skills—children who are more person cen-tered in their modes of comforting, persuading, informing, and managing conflicts with peers—tend to be better liked and more accepted by members of their peer group (e.g., Burleson et al., 1986; Renshaw & Asher, 1983). These findings suggest that, for the most part, peers prefer to be treated in person-centered ways that acknow-ledge their points of view, take their goals and motivations into account, and display concern for interpersonal relationships as well as instrumental goals. At least within the confines of middle-class American society, then, person-centered communication skills appear to be part of culturally preferred modes of acting and interacting.

Although considerable research links children's social skills to their acceptance by peers, only recently have researchers begun to examine how parental behavior might influence children's acceptance by their peer group (for reviews, see Cohn, Patterson, & Christopoulos, 1991; Putallaz & Heflin, 1990). Thus far, most research has focused on two theoretical mechanisms that might link parental behavior with chil-dren's peer acceptance: the independent-effects model and the medi-ated-effects model. The *independent-effects model* holds that parental communication has an impact on a child's peer acceptance apart from any effect it might have on the child's social-cognitive and communi-cation (i.e., social) skills. The *mediated-effects model* suggests that pa-rental behavior affects a child's peer acceptance primarily through its influence on the child's social skills. It is important to determine which of these models best fits the empirical associations among parental communication, child skills, and peer acceptance, because the two models imply different mechanisms through which parental behavior affects the child's social behaviors and social relationships and sug-gest different approaches to helping children who suffer from unsat-isfactory peer relationships.

Most research examining relations between parental behavior and child social status has implicitly assumed the mediated-effects model. Researchers have only recently begun to compare the independent- and mediated-effects models. For example, Pettit et al. (1988) report results providing weak support for the mediated-effects model: They found that the social problem-solving skills of preschoolers mediated relationships between some indices of parental practices and peer outcomes. In contrast, Hart et al. (1990) and Hart, DeWolf, and Burts (1992) found that the person-centered quality of maternal communication and children's social problem-solving skills each made independent contributions to children's peer acceptance. However, the results of four other recent studies consistently support the mediated-effects model, finding varied indices of child social competence mediating the relationship between assessments of parent discipline and children's peer acceptance (Dishion, 1990; Hart, DeWolf, Wozniak, & Burts, 1992; Pettit, Harrist, Bates, & Dodge, 1991; Weiss et al., 1992). It appears, then, that the preponderance of the (admittedly sparse) evidence supports the mediated-effects model.

Burleson et al. (1992) undertook a comparison of the independent- and mediated-effects models using the specific indices of maternal behavior (disciplinary and comforting communication) and child social competence (social-cognitive development and person-centered communication skills) obtained by Applegate et al. (1992). As noted above, Applegate et al. (1992) had found children's social-cognitive and communication skills to be strongly predicted by maternal person-centered communication. Burleson et al. (1992) found the assessments of children's social competence to be substantially associated with peer-acceptance indices, which included measures of popularity, peer acceptance, and mutual friendships. Burleson et al. further reasoned that maternal communication would primarily affect the quality of children's social relationships through the mediation of children's social skills (i.e., that the mediated-effects model would better fit the data in their study than would the independent-effects model). However, a path analysis indicated that the effect of maternal communication on children's peer acceptance was only slightly mediated by children's social skills. Thus, rather than fitting the hypothesized mediated-effects model, Burleson et al.'s (1992) data were more consistent with an independent-effects model, with maternal communication and children's skills each making distinct contributions to the child's peer acceptance.

It appears, then, that parental communication may have an effect on children's peer acceptance apart from any influence it has on children's social skills. Some theorists have suggested several alternative mechanisms by which parent discipline and nurturance might influence children's peer relationships (e.g., Putallaz & Heflin, 1990; Rubin & Sloman, 1984). For example, facilitative forms of discipline and nurturance can foster a sense of security and self-confidence in children. Secure and confident children may be more willing to explore the interpersonal environment, and thus may come into contact with a greater range of peers. In addition, the use of person-centered forms of discipline and nurturance may result in children's having more confirming and satisfying experiences with their parents, leading them to view interpersonal relationships in a generally more positive way. Such children may be more motivated to seek out and develop interpersonal associations, including those with peers, for the rewards they are perceived to bring. Other research indicates that some parents actively facilitate their children's relationships with peers by directly instructing the children in appropriate and relationship-enhancing forms of peer behavior (e.g., Ladd, Le Sieur, & Profilet, 1993; Pettit & Mize, 1993). Such parents may also be inclined to engage in more person-centered forms of discipline and nurturance with their children. Thus a full account of the influence of parental communication styles on children's acceptance by peers may require the development of complex models in which parental communication is seen to affect peer relations through its influence not only on children's social skills, but on a host of other variables as well.

As increasing empirical work has documented the effects of parental communication on children's relationships with peers, other research has examined how parental communication, especially forms of discipline and nurturance, influences somewhat different aspects of the child's social and intellectual development. One particularly important line of research has focused on how parental use of person-centered, reflection-enhancing forms of communication affect the child's performance in the social and academic arenas of the school environment.

Theorists have hypothesized that the reflection-enhancing quality of parental communication should promote children's thinking about the consequences of their behavior, means-ends relationships, the availability of multiple alternatives for varied situations, and so on (e.g., Baumrind, 1978; Shure, 1981). These enhanced cognitive capacities should enable the child to approach intellectual matters in a more reflective, open, considered, and sustained way, resulting in improved academic performance. The same cognitive capacities should also facilitate stronger conscience development, greater self-control, and more deeply internalized social norms, resulting in a less disruptive and problematic child in the classroom (see Maccoby & Martin, 1983). Consistent with these expectations, children exposed to more person-centered parenting have been found to perform more successfully than other children in the school environment, both academically (e.g., Lamborn, Mounts, Steinberg, & Dornbusch, 1991) and socially (e.g., Patterson & Stouthamer-Loeber, 1984). Thus parental communication, especially in relation to discipline and nurturance, appears to be an important vehicle for the transmission of a broad array of culturally valued cognitive and social competencies.

CONCLUSION

Although it is now a commonplace among social theorists that a culture reproduces itself through the communicative activities of it members, there are few detailed analyses available that document just how this reproductive process occurs. In this chapter, we have presented an account of how one feature of the social world, individual differences in the person-centered quality of functional communication, gets transmitted from one generation to the next. In concluding, we underscore some of the noteworthy features of our analysis, as well as draw attention to some of its limitations.

Our approach to the study of children's socialization in social-cognitive and communication skills strives to provide a coherent, integrative perspective on the interrelations of culture, cognition, and communication. The Wernerian notion of complexity has been useful in guiding the development of parallel concepts integrating cultural meaning systems, functional message structures, and social-cognitive systems. We think our focus on complexity captures something important about each of these domains and provides a way of depicting significant interconnections among them, and that its use to ground an analysis of the socialization of individual differences in social skills is a distinctive and noteworthy contribution to the study of family communication.

Our focus on complexity, however, also has significant limitations. Our analysis is narrow, we consider only a few aspects of social life, and we examine those aspects with a sharply focused lens. The development of an analysis of limited scope inevitably results in a constricted vision. There are a great many aspects of culture, cognition, and communication that remain untouched and unexamined by our analysis, and we have not provided anything approaching a general analysis of socialization.

The narrowness of our analysis does have the virtue, however, of permitting a very detailed examination of the phenomena encompassed within its frame. Many analyses of socialization are marred by overly global and diffuse conceptions of key structures and processes. For example, although many social theories assert that a culture is reproduced through the communicative activities of its members, few of these positions provide richly detailed, empirically testable accounts of just how this reproductive process supposedly occurs. In contrast, our analysis focuses on quite specific forms of thought (construct system features, social perspective-taking skills) and behavior (certain functional communication skills), and suggests quite specific connections among these forms of thought and action. The detailed explication of constructs and linkages among them means that our theory is very amenable to empirical specification and assessment, as demonstrated by the research reviewed in this chapter. Empirical tests are, of course, crucial for identifying where a particular theory is in need of further specification or is just wrong (as, for example, in our endorsement of the mediated-effects model of parental influence on children's acceptance by peers).

Although our theory focuses on only a small fraction of the modes of thinking and acting involved in social life and the transmission of culture, the particular set of skills we have examined appears to be quite consequential. The research we have reviewed clearly indicates that functional communication skills of parents play a critical role in the development of sophisticated, person-centered modes of thinking and acting in their children. Moreover, it is increasingly apparent that the functional communication skills of both parents and children have impacts on the child's acceptance by peers as well as on the child's performance and success in the school environment. There is mounting evidence, also, that the functional communication skills of parents not only influence the competencies of their children, but play a key role in the development of satisfying marriages (e.g., Burleson & Denton, 1992; Denton, Burleson, & Sprenkle, 1994), friendships (e.g., Burleson & Samter, 1994; Samter, 1992), and work relationships (Sypher & Zorn, 1986; Zorn, 1991). The few cognitive and communication variables on which we have focused our socialization research serve varied and important functions in multiple venues of social life. They deserve more extensive and systematic investigation.

REFERENCES

Applegate, J. L. (1980). Person- and position-centered communication in a day care center. In N. K. Denzin (Ed.), *Studies in symbolic interaction* (Vol. 3, pp. 59-96). Greenwich, CT: JAI.

Applegate, J. L. (1990). Constructs and communication: A pragmatic integration. In G. Neimeyer & R. Neimeyer (Eds.), *Advances in personal construct psychology* (Vol. 1, pp. 203-230). Greenwich, CT: JAI.

Applegate, J. L., Burke, J. A., Burleson, B. R., Delia, J. G., & Kline, S. L. (1985). Reflection-enhancing parental communication. In I. E. Sigel (Ed.), *Parental belief systems: The psychological consequences for children* (pp. 107-142). Hillsdale, NJ: Lawrence Erlbaum.

Applegate, J. L., Burleson, B. R., & Delia, J.G. (1992). Reflection-enhancing parenting as an antecedent to children's social-cognitive and communicative development. In I. E. Sigel, A. V. McGillicuddy-Delisi, & J. J. Goodnow (Eds.), *Parental belief systems: The psychological consequences for children* (Vol. 2, pp. 3-39). Hillsdale, NJ: Lawrence Erlbaum.

Applegate, J. L., & Delia, J. G. (1980). Person-centered speech, psychological development, and the contexts of language usage. In R. St. Clair & H. Giles (Eds.), *The social and psychological contexts of language* (pp. 245-282). Hillsdale, NJ: Lawrence Erlbaum.

Applegate, J. L., & Woods, E. (1991). Construct system development and attention to face wants in persuasive contexts. *Southern Communication Journal, 56*, 194-204.

Baumrind, D. (1978). Parental disciplinary patterns and social competence in children. *Youth & Society, 9*, 239-276.

Baumrind, D. (1989). Rearing competent children. In W. Damon (Ed.), *Child development today and tomorrow* (pp. 349-378). San Francisco: Jossey-Bass.

Berger, P. L., & Luckmann, T. (1967). *The social construction of reality: A treatise in the sociology of knowledge*. Garden City, NY: Anchor/Doubleday.

Bernstein, B. (1974). *Class, codes, and control: Theoretical studies toward a sociology of language* (rev. ed.). New York: Schocken.

Brody, G. H., & Shaffer, D. R. (1982). Contributions of parents and peers to children's moral socialization. *Developmental Review, 2,* 31-75.

Burleson, B. R. (1983). Interactional antecedents of social reasoning development: Interpreting the effects of parent discipline on children. In D. Zarefsky, M. O. Sillars, & J. R. Rhodes (Eds.), *Argument in transition: Proceedings of the Third Summer Conference on Argumentation* (pp. 597-610). Annandale, VA: Speech Communication Association.

Burleson, B. R. (1984). Age, social-cognitive development, and the use of comforting strategies. *Communication Monographs, 51,* 140-153.

Burleson, B. R. (1986). Communication skills and childhood peer relationships: An overview. In M. L. McLaughlin (Ed.), *Communication yearbook 9* (pp. 143-180). Beverly Hills, CA: Sage.

Burleson, B. R. (1987). Cognitive complexity. In J. C. McCroskey & J. A. Daly (Eds.), *Personality and interpersonal communication* (pp. 305-349). Newbury Park, CA: Sage.

Burleson, B. R. (1989). The constructivist approach to person-centered communication: Analysis of a research exemplar. In B. A. Dervin (Ed.), *Rethinking communication: Vol. 2. Paradigm exemplars* (pp. 29-46). Newbury Park, CA: Sage.

Burleson, B. R. (1994). Comforting messages: Features, functions, and outcomes. In J. A. Daly & J. M. Wiemann (Eds.), *Strategic interpersonal communication* (pp. 135-161). Hillsdale, NJ: Lawrence Erlbaum.

Burleson, B. R., Applegate, J. L., Burke, J. A., Clark, R. A., Delia, J. G., & Kline, S. L. (1986). Communicative correlates of peer acceptance in childhood. *Communication Education, 35,* 349-361.

Burleson, B. R., Delia, J. G., & Applegate, J. L. (1992). Effects of maternal communication and children's social-cognitive and communication skills on children's acceptance by the peer group. *Family Relations, 41,* 264-272.

Burleson, B. R., & Denton, W. H. (1992). A new look at similarity and attraction in marriage: Similarities in social-cognitive and communication skills as predictors of attraction and satisfaction. *Communication Monographs, 59,* 268-287.

Burleson, B. R., & Samter, W. (1994). A social skills approach to relationship maintenance: How individual differences in communication skills affect the achievement of relationship functions. In D. J. Canary & L. Stafford (Eds.), *Communication and relational maintenance* (pp. 61-90). San Diego, CA: Academic Press.

Burleson, B. R., & Waltman, M. S. (1988). Cognitive complexity: Using the Role Category Questionnaire measure. In C. H. Tardy (Ed.), *A handbook for the study of human communication: Methods and instruments for observing, measuring, and assessing communication processes* (pp. 1-35). Norwood, NJ: Ablex.

Clark, R. A., & Delia, J. G. (1979). Topoi and rhetorical competence. *Quarterly Journal of Speech, 65,* 187-206.

Cohn, D. A., Patterson, C. J., & Christopoulos, C. (1991). The family and children's peer relations. *Journal of Social and Personal Relationships, 8,* 315-346.

Coie, J. D., Dodge, K. A., & Kupersmidt, J.B. (1990). Peer group behavior and social status. In S. R. Asher & J. D. Coie (Eds.), *Peer rejection in childhood: Origins, consequences, and intervention* (pp. 17-59). New York: Cambridge University Press.

Crockett, W. H. (1965). Cognitive complexity and impression formation. In B. A. Maher (Ed.), *Progress in experimental personality research* (Vol. 2, pp. 47-90). New York: Academic Press.

Dekovic, M., & Gerris, J. R. M. (1992). Parental reasoning complexity, social class, and child-rearing behaviors. *Journal of Marriage and the Family, 54*, 675-685.

Delia, J. G., Kline, S. L., & Burleson, B. R. (1979). The development of persuasive communication strategies in kindergartners through twelfth-graders. *Communication Monographs, 46*, 241-256.

Delia, J. G., O'Keefe, B. J., & O'Keefe, D. J. (1982). The constructivist approach to communication. In F. E. X. Dance (Ed.), *Human communication theory: Comparative essays* (pp. 147-191). New York: Harper & Row.

Denton, W. H., Burleson, B. R., & Sprenkle, D. H. (1994). Motivation in marital communication: Comparison of distressed and nondistressed husbands and wives. *American Journal of Family Therapy, 22*, 17-26.

Dishion, T. J. (1990). The family ecology of boys' peer relations in middle childhood. *Child Development, 61*, 874-892.

Duck, S. (1988). *Relating to others*. Homewood, IL: Dorsey.

Dunn, J., Brown, J., & Beardsall, L. (1991). Family talk about feeling states and children's later understanding of others' emotions. *Developmental Psychology, 27*, 448-455.

Elias, N. (1982). *The history of manners* (E. Jephcott, Trans.). New York: Pantheon.

Gecas, V. (1979). The influence of social class on socialization. In W. R. Burr, R. Hill, F. I. Nye, & I. L. Reiss (Eds.), *Contemporary theories about the family* (Vol. 1, pp. 365-404). New York: Free Press.

Geertz, C. (1973). *The interpretation of cultures: Selected essays*. New York: Basic Books.

Ginsberg, D., Gottman, J. M., & Parker, J. G. (1986). The importance of friendship. In J. M. Gottman & J. G. Parker (Eds.), *Conversations of friends: Speculations on affective development* (pp. 3-50). Cambridge: Cambridge University Press.

Hale, C. L. (1980). Cognitive complexity-simplicity as a determinant of communication effectiveness. *Communication Monographs, 47*, 304-311.

Hale, C. L. (1986). Impact of cognitive complexity on message structure in a face-threatening context. *Journal of Language and Social Psychology, 5*, 135-143.

Hart, C. H., DeWolf, D. M., & Burts, D. C. (1992). Linkages among preschoolers' playground behavior, outcome expectations, and parental disciplinary strategies. *Early Education and Development, 3*, 265-283.

Hart, C. H., DeWolf, D. M., & Burts, D. C. (1993). Parental disciplinary strategies and preschoolers' play behavior in playground settings. In C. H. Hart (Ed.), *Children on playgrounds: Research perspectives and applications* (pp. 271-313). Albany: State University of New York Press.

Hart, C. H., DeWolf, D. M., Wozniak, P., & Burts, D. C. (1992). Maternal and paternal disciplinary styles: Relations with preschoolers' playground behavioral orientations and peer status. *Child Development, 63*, 879-892.

Hart, C. H., Ladd, G. W., & Burleson, B. R. (1990). Children's expectations of the outcomes of social strategies: Relationships with sociometric status and maternal disciplinary styles. *Child Development, 61*, 127-137.

Hartup, W. W. (1983). Peer relations. In E. M. Hetherington (Ed.), *Handbook of child psychology: Vol. 4. Socialization, personality, and social development* (pp. 103-196). New York: John Wiley.

Hoffman, M. L. (1977). Moral internalization: Current theory and research. In L. Berkowitz (Ed.), *Advances in experimental social psychology* (pp. 85-133). New York: Academic Press.

Holden, G. W. (1988). Adults' thinking about a child-rearing problem: Effects of experience, parental status, and gender. *Child Development, 59*, 1623-1632.

Hymel, S., & Rubin, K. H. (1985). Children with peer relationship and social skill problems: Conceptual, methodological, and developmental issues. In G. J. Whitehurst (Ed.), *Annals of child development* (Vol. 2, pp. 251-297). Greenwich, CT: JAI.

Jones, C. C., Rickel, A. U., & Smith, R. L. (1980). Maternal child-rearing practices and social problem-solving strategies among preschoolers. *Developmental Psychology, 16*, 241-242.

Kline, S. L., & Ceropski, J. M. (1984). Person-centered communication in medical practice. In J. T. Wood & G. M. Phillips (Eds.), *Human decision-making* (pp. 120-141). Carbondale: Southern Illinois University Press.

Kline, S. L., & Hennen-Floyd, C. (1990). On the art of saying no: The influence of social-cognitive development on messages of refusal. *Western Journal of Speech Communication, 54*, 454-472.

Kochanska, G. (1990). Maternal beliefs as long-term predictors of mother-child interaction and report. *Child Development, 61*, 1934-1943.

Kochanska, G., Kuczynski, L., & Radke-Yarrow, M. (1989). Correspondence between mothers' self-reported and observed child rearing practices. *Child Development, 60*, 56-63.

Kohn, M. L. (1976). Social class and parental values: Another confirmation of the relationship. *American Sociological Review, 41*, 538-545.

Kupersmidt, J., Coie, J. D., & Dodge, K. A. (1990). The role of poor peer relations in the development of disorder. In S. R. Asher & J. D. Coie (Eds.), *Peer rejection in childhood: Origins, consequences, and intervention* (pp. 274-305). New York: Cambridge University Press.

Ladd, G. W., & Asher, S. R. (1985). Social skill training and children's peer relations. In L. L'Abate & M. Milan (Eds.), *Handbook of social skills training* (pp. 219-244). New York: John Wiley.

Ladd, G. W., Le Sieur, K. D., & Profilet, S. M. (1993). Direct parental influences on young children's peer relations. In S. Duck (Ed.), *Learning about relationships* (pp. 152-183). Newbury Park, CA: Sage.

Lamborn, D. D., Mounts, N. S., Steinberg, L., & Dornbusch, S. M. (1991). Patterns of competence and adjustment among adolescents from authoritative, authoritarian, indulgent, and neglectful families. *Child Development, 62*, 1049-1065.

Maccoby, E. E., & Martin, J. A. (1983). Socialization in the context of the family: Parent-child interaction. In E. M. Hetherington (Ed.), *Handbook of child psychology: Vol. 4. Socialization, personality, and social development* (pp. 1-101). New York: John Wiley.

Miller, P. J., Potts, R., & Fung, H. (1990). Narrative practices and the social construction of self in childhood. *American Ethnologist, 17*, 292-311.

Mintz, S., & Kellogg, S. (1988). *Domestic revolutions: A social history of American family life.* New York: Free Press.

O'Keefe, B. J., & Delia, J. G. (1982). Impression formation and message production. In M. E. Roloff & C. R. Berger (Eds.), *Social cognition and communication* (pp. 33-72). Beverly Hills, CA: Sage.

O'Keefe, B. J., & Delia, J. G. (1985). Psychological and interactional dimensions of communicative development. In H. Giles & R. St. Clair (Eds.), *Recent advances in language, communication, and social psychology* (pp. 41-85). London: Lawrence Erlbaum.

O'Keefe, D. J., & Sypher, H. E. (1981). Cognitive complexity measures and the relationship of cognitive complexity to communication. *Human Communication Research, 8,* 72-92.

Parke, R. D. MacDonald, D. B., Bertel, A., & Bhavnagri, N. (1988). The role of the family in the development of peer relationships. In R. Peters & R. J. McMahon (Eds.), *Marriage and families: Behavioral treatments and processes* (pp. 17-44). New York: Brunner/Mazel.

Patterson, G., & Stouthamer-Loeber, M. (1984). The correlation of family management practices and delinquency. *Child Development, 55,* 1299-1307.

Pettit, G. S., Dodge, K. A., & Brown, M. M. (1988). Early family experience, social problem solving patterns, and children's social competence. *Child Development, 59,* 107-120.

Pettit, G. S., Harrist, A. W., Bates, J. E., & Dodge, K. A. (1991). Family interaction, social cognition, and children's subsequent relations with peers at kindergarten. *Journal of Social and Personal Relationships, 8,* 383-402.

Pettit, G. S., & Mize, J. (1993). Substance and style: Understanding the ways in which parents teach children about social relationships. In S. Duck (Ed.), *Learning about relationships* (pp. 118-151). Newbury Park, CA: Sage.

Piaget, J. (1970). *Genetic epistemology* (E. Duckworth, Trans.). New York: Columbia University Press.

Putallaz, M. (1987). Maternal behavior and children's sociometric status. *Child Development, 58,* 324-340.

Putallaz, M., & Heflin, A. H. (1990). Parent-child interaction. In S. R. Asher & J. D. Coie (Eds.), *Peer rejection in childhood: Origins, consequences, and intervention* (pp. 274-305). New York: Cambridge University Press.

Radke-Yarrow, M., & Zahn-Waxler, C. (1986). The role of familial factors in the development of prosocial behavior: Research findings and questions. In D. Olweus, J. Block, & M. Radke-Yarrow (Eds.), *Development of antisocial and prosocial behavior* (pp. 189-216). San Diego, CA: Academic Press.

Renshaw, P. D., & Asher, S. R. (1983). Children's goals and strategies for social interaction. *Merrill-Palmer Quarterly, 29,* 353-374.

Rollins, B. C., & Thomas, D. L. (1979). Parental support, power, and control techniques in the socialization of children. In W. R. Burr, R. Hill, F. I. Nye, & I. L. Reiss (Eds.), *Contemporary theories about the family* (Vol. 1, pp. 317-364). New York: Free Press.

Rothbaum, F. (1988). Maternal acceptance and child functioning. *Merrill-Palmer Quarterly, 34,* 162-184.

Rubin, K. H., & Sloman, J. (1984). How parents influence their children's friendships. In M. Lewis (Ed.), *Beyond the dyad* (pp. 223-250). New York: Plenum.

Samter, W. (1992). Communicative characteristics of the lonely person's friendship circle. *Communication Research, 19,* 212-239.

Sellers, C. G. (1991). *The market revolution: Jacksonian America, 1815-1846.* New York: Oxford University Press.

Shure, M. B. (1981). Social competence as problem solving. In J. D. Wine & M. D. Smye (Eds.), *Social competence* (pp. 158-185). New York: Guilford.

Sigel, I. E. (1985). A conceptual analysis of beliefs. In I. E. Sigel (Ed.), *Parental belief systems: The psychological consequences for children* (pp. 345-371). Hillsdale, NJ: Lawrence Erlbaum.

Sypher, H. E., & Applegate, J. L. (1984). Organizing communication behavior: The role of schemas and constructs. In R. N. Bostrom (Ed.), *Communication yearbook 8* (pp. 310-329). Beverly Hills, CA: Sage.

Sypher, B. D., & Zorn, T. E. (1986). Communication-related abilities and upward mobility: A longitudinal investigation. *Human Communication Research, 12,* 420-431.

Waldron, V. R., & Applegate, J. L. (1994). Interpersonal construct differentiation and conversational planning: An examination of two cognitive accounts for the production of competent verbal disagreement tactics. *Human Communication Research, 21,* 3-35.

Weiss, B., Dodge, K. A., Bates, J. E., & Pettit, G. S. (1992). Some consequences of early harsh discipline: Child aggression and a maladaptive social information processing style. *Child Development, 63,* 1321-1335.

Werner, H. (1957). The concept of development from a comparative and organismic point of view. In D. B. Harris (Ed.), *The concept of development* (pp. 125-146). Minneapolis: University of Minnesota Press.

Werner, H., & Kaplan, B. (1963). *Symbol formation.* New York: John Wiley.

Wertsch, J. V. (1991). *Voices of the mind: A sociocultural approach to mediated action.* Cambridge, MA: Harvard University Press.

Wood, G. S. (1992). *The radicalism of the American revolution.* New York: Alfred A. Knopf.

Zahn-Waxler, C., Radke-Yarrow, M., & King, R. A. (1979). Child rearing and children's prosocial initiations toward victims of distress. *Child Development, 50,* 319-330.

Zimmermann, S., & Applegate, J. L. (1992). Person-centered comforting in the hospice interdisciplinary team. *Communication Research, 19,* 240-263.

Zorn, T. E. (1991). Construct system development, transformational leadership, and leadership messages. *Southern Communication Journal, 56,* 178-193.

3

Parent-Adolescent Relationships

PATRICIA NOLLER

The quality of family relationships is a crucial determinant of the competence and confidence with which young people face the major transition from childhood to adulthood that we call adolescence. The quality of family relationships affects the success with which young people negotiate the major tasks of adolescence, the extent to which they become involved in the problem behaviors generally associated with this stage of life, and their ability to establish meaningful close relationships that are likely to last. The aspects of the family that seem to be particularly important are the amount of encouragement adolescents receive concerning autonomy and independence, the degree of control desired by parents, the amount of conflict among family members, the closeness of family bonds, and the amount of love and support available to the adolescents. In fact, the balance between closeness and control may be the most important aspect of the family environment during adolescence (Cooper, Grotevant, & Condon, 1984). Families that provide close, supportive environments for adolescents, while at the same time encouraging autonomy and independence, seem to produce adolescents who can cope best with the transition to adulthood.

In this chapter I focus on what I see as the important functions of communication in families with adolescents. I discuss five such functions: (a) enabling the renegotiation of roles, rules, and relationships; (b) providing an appropriate climate for identity exploration; (c) enhancing rather than diminishing self-esteem; (d) providing appropriate modeling and teaching of problem solving; and (e) enabling adolescents to make the important decisions that affect their lives.

There has been quite a deal of controversy over the problems of adolescence, with early writers assuming that most adolescents went through a time of storm and stress, or *Sturm und Drang* (Blos, 1979). Although there is currently less concern about the stress experienced by adolescents, there is certainly evidence that adolescence is a stressful time for the family, and particularly for parents. Olson and his colleagues (1983) found that families with adolescents reported higher levels of family stress and lower levels of family pride and cohesion than did families at other stages of the family life cycle. In addition, adolescent issues were seen as the most stressful issues experienced by families across the life cycle.

RENEGOTIATION OF ROLES AND RULES

Whereas phrases such as *breaking away* and *breaking free* used to be commonly employed in discussions of the need of adolescents to become independent of their parents, it is now more common to talk about adolescents as *renegotiating* their relationships with their parents and moving gradually toward having more autonomy and independence (Grotevant & Cooper, 1986). It seems clear that the quality of the parent-adolescent relationship depends on the extent to which the parent-child relationship can be renegotiated, so that parents show increasing respect for their adolescents' opinions and allow them greater control over their own lives, rather than treating them as children (Grotevant & Cooper, 1986). Through this process of renegotiation, adolescents aim to gain both higher status and more control (Hunter, 1985; Hunter & Youniss, 1982).

One of the problems that arises when parents and adolescents seek to renegotiate roles and rules in the family is that adolescents and their parents do not see their families in the same way; adolescents tend to see their families more negatively than do their parents. Barnes and Olson (1985), for example, found that the adolescents in their sample tended to report less openness and more problems in their families than did their parents. In my own previous work, I have found that adolescents are likely to see their families as less cohesive and less adaptable than do their parents (see, e.g., Noller & Callan, 1986). In a study that involved both clinic-referred and nonclinic adolescents, both groups of adolescents were equally negative about their families, but only the nonclinic adolescents were more negative about their families than their mothers were (Noller, Seth-Smith, Bouma, & Schweitzer, 1992). These adolescents saw their families as more conflicted, less intimate, and less democratic than did their mothers.

These differences in perception of the family by parents and adolescents are usually discussed in terms of the generational stake hypothesis posited by Bengtson and his colleagues (Bengtson & Kuypers, 1971; Bengtson & Troll, 1978). These researchers propose that each generation's view of family life is affected by that generation's own bias or stake. Parents are seen as emphasizing the positive aspects of family life because of their high levels of investment in the family, whereas adolescents are seen as emphasizing the negative aspects of family life because they are in the process of separating themselves from their families and establishing their own identities. According to Niemi (1968, 1974), parents are likely to be the most biased informants because of their need to see the results of their labors in a positive light. The findings of the Noller et al. (1992) study, however, suggest otherwise. If parents in nonclinic and clinic-referred families rate their families quite differently, whereas adolescents are equally negative irrespective of which type of family they belong to, it seems likely that the parents may be the least biased informants. It is hard to believe that there are no differences in the functioning of these two types of families, hence the similarity in ratings by the clinic and nonclinic adolescents suggests that the negativity of the nonclinic adolescents is unrelated to the reality of their family situations.

Not only do adolescents and parents disagree about the actual functioning of their families, they have difficulty agreeing about how they would like their families to be. In the Noller and Callan (1986) study mentioned above, we asked adolescents and parents to describe their ideal families as well as their actual families. Adolescents wanted their families to be highly cohesive, but not as cohesive as did their parents, and they wanted their families to be more cohesive than they currently were (or as they currently perceived them to be). Adolescents also wanted their families to be highly adaptable, and they were generally less satisfied than their parents with the current levels of adaptability in those families. It is interesting to note that the level of adaptability generally desired by these adolescents was in the chaotic range. In other words, they wanted to be free to do whatever they desired without having to negotiate with parents or other family members. At the same time, they wanted their parents to support them in their activities, and in their goals and plans.

How much conflict is engendered by an adolescent's moves toward autonomy will depend on the extent to which his or her parents accept and encourage these moves, or resist the inevitable changes and put their energies into trying to maintain control. Where parents are highly resistant of their adolescents' strivings for independence, conflict and rebellion are likely to ensue. Of course, no matter how much goodwill there is on the part of the parents, some conflict is inevitable. Adolescents are likely to want more change, and at a faster rate, than their parents can comfortably handle. As Stone and Church (1968) comment, one of the difficulties for parents and adolescents is that "readiness for adulthood comes about two years later than the adolescent claims and about two years before the parent will admit" (p. 447).

Steinberg and Silverberg (1986) suggest that, for adolescents, becoming autonomous involves learning to deal with both their emotional attachment to their parents and pressure from their peers. In developing emotional autonomy from parents and a more mature relationship with them, the adolescent needs to let go of the childish view that his or her parents are infallible or perfect and reduce dependence on them. As might be expected, when adolescents begin to realize that parents can make mistakes, there is likely to be increased conflict between adolescents and parents. Such adolescents are likely to challenge their parents and their parents' authority. Although many such adolescents may eventually accept their parents' advice, some may continue to argue with their parents and may become defiant toward them. Research has generally supported this view, showing that the transition from primary to secondary school is associated with increasing levels of conflict and more and more arguments with parents (Petersen & Taylor, 1980), although relationships tend to improve between middle and late adolescence.

Conflict between parents and adolescents may be further exacer-bated by the fact that adolescents tend to be disillusioned with the values of their parents. Today's adolescents are more concerned than previous generations have been about the environment, the conser-vation of resources and heritage, the uses of nuclear power, personal freedom, and the ideals of social and racial equality. They tend to believe that they have every reason to be very critical of their parents' generation and the way that generation has cared for the world. Although high levels of continued conflict are generally associated with negative outcomes, conflict with parents in early adolescence may be a necessary step in helping the adolescent to achieve necessary changes in roles and relationships. Parents and adolescents are then likely to settle reasonably happily into the new situation under the new rules. Jurkovic and Ulrici (1985) put it very nicely:

> Closer inspection of the self-report and observational findings sug-gests that maturational changes in normal adolescents are coincident with increased familial conflict and rigidity. Difficulties in adapta-tion, however, are followed by an increasingly pleasant mode of adolescent-parent relating, marked in part by a greater balance of power. (p. 239)

Where adolescents fail to negotiate more equal relationships with their parents, and these parents are highly critical and rejecting, the adolescents are likely to adopt negative identities (Harris & Howard, 1984). They may act out or behave badly to try to get their parents' attention or to punish their parents. Sadly, beneath the defiance may be depression caused by the adolescents' internalizing the rejection of their parents. (I discuss the issue of parental criticism further below, in the section on self-esteem.)

The adolescent's achievement of autonomy is likely to put him or her into very different relationships with peers as well as parents. The truly autonomous adolescent is able to make decisions independent of his or her parents, but is also able to resist pressure from peers to engage in undesirable behaviors. Unfortunately, as Steinberg and Silverberg (1986) show, these two aspects of autonomy are likely to be negatively correlated, particularly in younger adolescents. In other words, becoming autonomous from parents too early may increase a young person's susceptibility to peer pressure to engage in such behaviors as smoking, use of drugs and alcohol, and sexual activity. These findings underscore the need for parents of adolescents to establish a balance between allowing too much autonomy and being too controlling (Burt, Cohen, & Bjorck, 1988).

In summary, parents and adolescents need to renegotiate their relationships so that the adolescents can take increasing control over their own lives and start to see themselves as separate, autonomous individuals who are able to make their own decisions and stand on their own feet. These goals are best achieved in a family climate where the parents encourage the adolescent's moves toward autonomy and willingly relinquish control, compared with one where the parents resist moves toward autonomy and become even more controlling. On the other hand, it is also important that adolescents not be given complete control too early, as they may then be less able to deal effectively with the pressures of the peer group. Where parents and adolescents are able to work together to redefine the parent-child relationship so that it become more mutual and equal, the adolescent does not necessarily have to leave the relationship or break away from it. Thus a balance between closeness in the family and the encouragement of individuality and autonomy is crucial (Campbell, Adams, & Dobson, 1984; Cooper et al., 1984).

PROVIDING A CLIMATE FOR IDENTITY EXPLORATION AND FORMATION

As part of his stage theory of personality, Erikson (1963, 1968) argues that the establishment of a clear sense of ego identity is crucial for the adolescent, with a progressive strengthening of this sense of identity throughout adolescence. A clear sense of identity is also seen as necessary for the successful resolution of the following stage of initiating intimacy and the formation of stable intimate relationships. As Newman and Murray (1983) note, identity is "like a blueprint for future commitments and life choices. It is a set of beliefs and goals about one's relationship with family members, lovers and friends, one's roles as worker, citizen and religious believer and one's aspirations for achievement" (p. 294).

Two distinct but related processes are involved in identity formation: personal exploration and psychological differentiation (Campbell et al., 1984). *Personal exploration* involves working through alternative attitudes, values, and opinions and committing oneself to particular values and positions. *Psychological differentiation* refers to the gradually increasing awareness of one's nature and personality and an understanding of one's uniqueness and separateness from others.

There are also a number of different aspects of identity, including personal, sexual, religious, and political elements. Identity development includes an increased understanding of how one relates to others and of one's own preferences for particular types of work and activities, for being alone or with others, and for playing it safe or taking risks. One adolescent's self-description, for example, might include the following aspects of identity:

> I am a warm and friendly person who likes to be with other people, I like having fun and I don't really like working hard. I like to work with my hands rather than having to think a lot, and I prefer to be able to set my own pace. I don't really like study much but prefer outdoor activities, and enjoy taking risks in sporting activities. I enjoy being with the opposite sex and look forward to getting married and having a family someday, but not too soon. I would like to have plenty of fun first and maybe even do some traveling.

Another young person of similar age may have a quite different identity:

> I am quiet and shy and I hate being in a big group. Going to parties is not my scene at all, and I prefer going to a concert or a movie with just one or two friends. I need to spend a fair amount of time on my own, and feel hassled if I don't get that kind of time. I really enjoy reading and watching television. Study is very important to me and I hope to get to the top of my chosen career of law. I hate team sports and rough games and prefer swimming and jogging. My approach to life is generally pretty serious and it is important to me to be able to serve others. I am fairly religious and go to church each Sunday

and belong to a study group at the church. I hope to get married someday, but I would prefer to finish my studies and get established in a practice before committing myself to someone for life.

Basic to these differences in identity are the family experiences of adolescents, including the extent to which families provide a climate where adolescents are free to explore alternative ways of looking at the world and to discuss their hopes and aspirations and their doubts and fears. This issue of being free to explore alternatives is central to a theory of identity status developed by Marcia (1966, 1976). Marcia's four different identity statuses are defined in terms of two factors: (a) whether the individual has experienced some form of identity crisis and (b) whether the individual has committed him- or herself to a specific identity. Crisis involves giving serious consideration to alternative possibilities, such as different ideologies or life goals. Whether the individual has committed him- or herself to an alternative ideology is not the crucial issue; rather, more important is whether he or she has explored other alternatives and made a choice on the basis of some understanding of the alternatives and has internalized the values to which he or she has committed him- or herself.

Marcia labels the four identity statuses *identity achievement, foreclosure, moratorium,* and *identity diffusion.* Individuals in the identity achievement group have been through a period of questioning and exploration (or a crisis in this model) and have developed relatively firm commitments. Individuals in the foreclosure group have not been through a period of questioning and exploration, although they have committed themselves to particular goals and values that tend to reflect the wishes of the authority figures in their lives, usually their parents. Individuals in the moratorium group are currently in a state of questioning and exploration (they have experienced a crisis) and are seeking to make identity-related choices. Individuals in the identity diffusion group have no firm commitments, nor are they actively exploring or trying to form such commitments.

One reason for emphasizing the importance of identity status is the evidence of a clear relationship between adolescents' identity status and their overall psychological adjustment (Bernard, 1981; Donovan, 1975). Identity achievers are the healthiest of the four status groups in their general adjustment and also in their relationships with both peers and authority figures. Thus families that encourage identity exploration and achievement are also likely to produce adolescents with healthy psychological adjustment. These families are likely to be open in their communication, to tolerate differences, and to be democratic in terms of control. In such families, adolescents are encouraged to make their own decisions, although with the help and support of their parents. Identity achievers also tend to have better personal relationships than do other adolescents and young adults. They tend to be nurturant with their peers and to be high in internal control and self-esteem and low in anxiety, particularly if they are males. Identity achievers also seem to be more capable of forming close, stable relationships than are other adolescents (Kahn, Zimmerman, Csikszentmihalyi, & Getzels, 1985; Orlofsky, Marcia, & Lesser, 1973). Somewhat paradoxically, those in the identity achievement status, who are generally more confident and sure of themselves than are those in other status groups, tend to be cooperative in their relationships with authority figures.

As already noted, those in the foreclosure group tend to commit themselves to identities without doing the personal exploration of alternatives that is typical of identity achievers. Another concern about foreclosures is that they may not be very successful in the separation-individuation process (Kroger, 1989). In other words, these adolescents may adopt the values and goals of their parents because they do not really see themselves as separate from their parents. According to Parker (1983, 1991), who categorizes parental bonding behaviors in terms of the two dimensions of *care* and *overprotection*, foreclosures are likely to come from families that are high on both these dimensions. Parents are likely to be very nurturant and affectionate, but also highly controlling, and the adolescents are likely to be dependent, concerned about pleasing their parents, and somewhat in awe of them. Such adolescents are likely to have difficulty in exploring identity issues (Kroger, 1989). There is also evidence that the dependency associated with the foreclosure status may be more clearly part of the female than the male identity (Kahn et al., 1985). As would be expected, given that these young people have adopted the values and attitudes of their authority figures with little questioning, foreclosures tend to be in awe of authority figures. They also tend to be distant from their peers and to be manipulative and controlling in their attempts to get their own way.

Families influence the identity exploration of their adolescents by emphasizing either the importance of autonomy and independence for individuals or family togetherness, closeness, and loyalty. In families where there is an emphasis on independence, there is a greater possibility of identity exploration, especially for females (see Grotevant & Cooper, 1985). On the other hand, daughters engage in *less* identity exploration when they respect their mothers' views and are open and responsive to those views, and thus would be more likely to settle into the foreclosure status. Sons, however, are *more* likely to explore their identities when they are open and responsive to their fathers' views and know that their fathers respect their opinions and attitudes (see also Campbell et al., 1984).

Adolescents in different identity status groups have different relationships with their parents (Adams & Jones, 1983; Campbell et al., 1984). In particular, foreclosures have the closest relationships with parents, whereas those in the identity diffusion status tend to be distant from their parents and other family members. These young people see their parents as indifferent to them, as not understanding them, and/or as rejecting them. Thus diffusions and foreclosures are different in terms of their closeness to their families, and this dimension seems an important one in terms of identity exploration and development. Identity achievers and foreclosures are likely to be close to their parents, whereas those in the moratorium and diffusion statuses are likely to be distant. In contrast, both foreclosures and diffusions are likely to have controlling parents, whereas identity achievers and moratoriums are more likely to have parents low in control.

Newman and Murray (1983) see the extent to which parents use coercive power in the family as a crucial determinant of the willingness of adolescents to be involved in identity exploration. They argue that adolescents whose parents have authoritarian and coercive relationships with them are less likely to engage in identity exploration, more likely to adopt external moral standards, more likely to have lower self-confidence and self-esteem, and tend to have greater problems in using their own judgment as a guide to behavior. Because of their less developed sense of their own identity, these adolescents are likely to be less autonomous, less confident about their competence, and more susceptible to peer pressure.

Adolescents whose parents adopt an inductive, democratic style, on the other hand, are able to make their own decisions and formulate appropriate plans. Paradoxically, these adolescents also make decisions and plans that are more satisfactory to their parents and are more likely to seek the help and guidance of their parents. Such democratic families tend to produce adolescents who strongly identify with their parents and, in turn, internalize their parents' values and ideals. In these families, adolescents are likely to be encouraged to be assertive and to adopt their own points of view, and will, as a consequence, tend to have higher levels of ego development (Hauser et al., 1984). As these adolescents negotiate with parents to bring about changes in the family environment, the parents are also likely to show greater respect for the opinions of their growing adolescents. Certainly, older adolescents seem to be able to negotiate changes in their relationships with their parents and to develop styles of interaction that involve less conflict and more control (Jacob, 1974; Steinberg & Hill, 1978). Families that best promote adolescent identity exploration and adjustment do not emphasize individuality to the exclusion of connectedness or closeness, nor do they focus on family closeness and connectedness to the exclusion of autonomy and individuality. Rather, they tend to acknowledge the importance of both individuality and connectedness.

There is also evidence that security of attachment is related to identity exploration. Lapsley, Rice, and Fitzgerald (1990) explored the relations between security of attachment to parents and level of identity development in late adolescents leaving home to go to college. They found that communication with parents was significantly related to both personal (conception of self and feelings of uniqueness) and social (involvement in social roles and relationships) aspects of identity. Kroger (1985) found that identity-achieved adolescents were the most securely attached group, but results for insecure adolescents were mixed. For example, some foreclosures were anxiously attached, whereas others were emotionally detached. In a longitudinal study, Kroger and Haslett (1988) found no support for the hypothesis that earlier attachment would predict later identity status. Much more research is needed to clarify this issue.

Although identity in adolescence is often discussed as though it is a unitary construct, with a strong emphasis on personal identity, the development of identity actually needs to occur across a range of areas, including sexual identity, occupational identity, and religious or ideological identity. Coming to terms with one's sexual feelings and establishing a positive sexual identity are crucial aspects of identity development. The sexual development of adolescents involves anxiety for both parents and teenagers. Parents worry about whether their children are mature enough to make responsible decisions about their sexual activity, and to cope with the emotional demands of sexual relationships. Parents are also confused about their role in preparing their children for sexual activity and about the possible consequences of such activity, including pregnancy and contraction of sexually transmitted diseases.

The situation is further complicated by the need to consider sexual orientation. Whereas most adolescents develop heterosexual identities, a small percentage develop homosexual identities. Another important aspect of sexual identity includes an individual's concept of what it means to be male or female. Changing attitudes toward sex roles make it likely that females can consider an increasingly wide range of careers as appropriate, whereas young males can be expected to be able care for themselves and participate in household chores, whether single or married.

Adolescence is also a time for making choices about educational and career goals; choices such as whether or not to finish school, whether to participate in higher education, and what courses to take are all important. Some adolescents may also need help in sorting out their own interests from the expectations of their parents. (I address this issue below in the section on adolescents' decision making.)

Although there is little doubt that parents play an important role in influencing the attitudes of adolescents about religious beliefs (Hoge, Petrillo, & Smith, 1982), the effect their influence has depends mainly on the quality of the parent-adolescent relationship (Hauser, 1981). Where the parent-adolescent relationship is primarily positive and cooperative, the adolescent is more likely to follow the beliefs of the parents. It is important, however, to consider whether the adolescent accepts the parents' views without taking them for his or her own (that is, forecloses) or is able to achieve a religious identity of his or her own. In this respect, the important issue is likely to be the extent to which the adolescent is encouraged to deal openly and honestly with doubts and questions.

A recent study found evidence of relations among attachment to parents, attachment style with peers, and religious belief and commitment (Noller & Strahan, 1993). For males, maternal care was associated with religious belief and commitment, with the relation between the two variables being mediated by comfort with closeness. That is, males who came from families where maternal care was high were more likely to be comfortable with closeness and more likely to be strong in their religious commitment. For females, there were similar but weaker relations among maternal care, comfort with closeness, and religious belief and commitment. In addition, paternal overprotection was directly and negatively related to religious belief and commitment. It is important to keep in mind that the vast majority of the students in this study came from religious families.

In summary, family factors affect adolescents' willingness to explore identity issues. Families, however, differ in the extent to which they provide environments that encourage such exploration. Families high in care and moderate to low in control are likely to provide the kinds of environments that encourage identity exploration and facilitate adolescents' coming to terms with who they are and who they would like to be. Security of attachment also seems to be related to identity achievement.

ENHANCING RATHER THAN DIMINISHING SELF-ESTEEM

What type of communication between parents and adolescents promotes the development of high self-esteem in adolescents? Clearly, parental support and nurturance are very important. A number of studies have shown a positive relationship between parental support or nurturance and self-esteem (Buri, Kirchner, & Walsh, 1987; Gecas

& Schwalbe, 1986; Hoelter & Harper, 1987). Self-esteem is positively related to parents' use of support and induction techniques and negatively related to their use of coercion. The Noller et al. (1992) study cited above, which used a sample that included both clinic-referred and nonclinic adolescents, shows that adolescent self-esteem is higher in families where intimacy is high, conflict is low, and control is democratic. In another study involving American students, personal and family self-esteem were correlated similarly with family functioning (Noller, 1994).

Burt et al. (1988) examined the relationship between measures of the family environment and adolescents' anxiety, self-esteem, and depression. Where the family was perceived as cohesive, organized, and allowing members to express their feelings openly, adolescent family members tended to have higher self-esteem and to be less depressed and anxious than other adolescents. These researchers also found that perceptions of the family as conflictual and controlling were related to lower levels of self-esteem and higher levels of depression in adolescents. Burt et al. also reassessed the families in their sample after six months to see whether they could establish clearly that particular parenting styles were the cause of low self-esteem and depression. They found little evidence that perceptions of conflict and control at the earlier time were related to anxiety, depression, and self-esteem at the later time. As I have noted in previous work, however, the time frame of the Burt et al. study was rather short for these findings to be considered conclusive (Noller & Callan, 1991). A much longer period of observation would be needed to answer such an important question.

When parents coerce their children, the effects on the children's self-esteem are likely to be negative (Rollins & Thomas, 1979). Parents' use of coercive techniques tends to imply that their adolescent children are incompetent, untrustworthy, and poorly motivated. Overwhelmingly, the message is that the adolescent cannot cope without the parent. Less clearly coercive messages, such as those of overprotection and overnurturance (e.g., "Let me do that for you" or "Don't worry your pretty little head about that"), can have similar effects. In contrast, parents' use of supportive and inductive techniques tends to imply that adolescents are competent and can be trusted to make good decisions and to behave appropriately. It is not surprising, then, that these different styles of parenting have very different effects on adolescent self-esteem.

According to a study by Openshaw, Thomas, and Rollins (1984), adolescents' self-esteem is more clearly related to the extent to which their parents' behavior toward them confirms them as worthwhile and lovable individuals than it is to the self-esteem of the parents. In other words, adolescent self-esteem is a response to the treatment received from parents, rather than the result of adolescents' modeling their parents' self-esteem-related behavior. This finding is supported by the work of Gecas and Schwalbe (1986), who have shown that adolescent self-esteem is more closely related to the actual support adolescents receive from their parents (as coded by outsiders) than to the adolescents' perceptions of that support. Openshaw and his colleagues interpret their finding as supporting a symbolic interactionist theoretical perspective, rather than a social learning perspective.

The sex of the parent providing the support also has an effect on adolescent self-esteem, with perceptions of fathers' support and nurturance being more strongly related to self-esteem in adolescents than perceptions of mothers' nurturance, particularly for boys. There are at least two possible explanations for this finding, as I have suggested elsewhere (Noller & Callan, 1991). First, perhaps the adolescent still views the father as the most powerful figure in the family, and thus gives the father's views greater weight than the mother's. An alternative explanation is that mothers are generally supportive and nurturant of their children, with little discrimination between mothers on these characteristics. It is likely, then, that differences among fathers in levels of support and nurturance would be more salient.

Another important determinant of adolescents' self-esteem is the extent to which adolescents are criticized by their parents. In a study of this issue, Harris and Howard (1984) categorized adolescents according to whether they saw their parents as very accepting or not very accepting, and whether they saw themselves as being frequently or rarely criticized. Adolescents whose parents were accepting and not very critical had the most positive self-images, whereas adolescents whose parents were highly critical and not very accepting had the most negative self-images. Where parent-adolescent communication consists mainly of criticism, the adolescent develops a negative self-image, which leads to more negative behaviors and more criticism and rejection from the parents. Similarly, high levels of punishment and perceived control by parents seem to lower self-esteem and generate hostility in adolescents (Amoroso & Ware, 1986). Close supervision, for example, seems to provoke very negative attitudes and behavior in adolescents, probably because of the implication that the adolescent is incompetent or untrustworthy and therefore in need of such close monitoring. The hostility expressed by the adolescent in this context is likely to lead to the parent's trusting him or her less and increasing the monitoring. A vicious cycle is likely to be set up that will be hard to break.

Harris and Howard (1984) also found evidence that both sex of parent and sex of adolescent affect which behaviors are seen as acceptable and which are unacceptable. In this study, mothers tended to reject sons who were messy, not appreciative, and not sociable, whereas fathers were more likely to reject daughters who were not loving and affectionate. Fathers had little tolerance for foolish or silly behavior, whether it was their sons or daughters whom they perceived to be behaving foolishly.

A currently popular theoretical perspective that is relevant to the issue of self-esteem in adolescents is attachment theory (Ainsworth, Blehar, Waters, & Wall, 1978; Bowlby, 1969, 1973, 1980; Hazan & Shaver, 1987). Attachment theory posits that during the first year of life a child develops fairly stable attitudes about him- or herself and the world on the basis of the responsiveness of the child's primary caregiver. Where the caregiver is responsive, the child is likely to develop positive attitudes, both toward others (e.g., willingness to trust) and toward him- or herself (e.g., as a person who is worthy of being cared for). Different styles of attachment develop depending on whether the individual has positive or negative attitudes toward him- or herself and others (Ainsworth et al., 1978; Bartholomew & Horowitz, 1991; Hazan & Shaver, 1987). In other words, self-esteem is central to the definition of attachment style, especially in Bartholomew and Horowitz's (1991) four-category model. Those in the categories they label *preoccupied* and *fearful avoidant* are likely to be low in self-esteem, whereas those in the *secure* and *dismissing* categories are likely to be high in self-esteem. In our own work using Hazan and Shaver's (1987) three-category model, my colleagues and I have found that those in the category labeled *secure* are higher in self-esteem than those in either of the insecure groups (Feeney & Noller, 1990; Noller, 1994).

Greenberg and his colleagues found that positive affect and attachment to parents was correlated with measures of self-esteem and life satisfaction for both high school and university students in their sample. In addition, for the university students, parental attachment was related to adaptive emotional functioning, being negatively correlated with depression/anxiety, resentment/alienation, irritability/anger, and guilt (Armsden & Greenberg, 1987; Greenberg, Siegel, & Leitch, 1983). Richman and Flaherty (1987) used a sample of medical students and found relations between maternal and paternal care, as measured by the Parental Bonding Instrument (Parker, Tupling, & Brown, 1979), and self-esteem and interpersonal dependency over time. In addition, parental care at Time 1 was associated with depression at Time 2. Ryan and Lynch (1989) found that emotional detachment from parents was negatively associated with self-esteem, although only with the aspect of self-esteem labeled *lovability* and not with global self-esteem or competence. In other words, the emotional component of self-esteem seemed more clearly related to detachment from parents than was a sense of competence.

Rice (1990) carried out a meta-analysis of studies that related attachment to adjustment. He found that the relations were clearer for healthy adjustment than for unhealthy adjustment and that measures of self-esteem or self-concept were more clearly related to attachment than were other aspects of adjustment. Further, the relations between self-esteem and adjustment were stronger for females than for males. These studies suggest that for female adolescents, self-esteem may be particularly sensitive to attachment problems in their relations with their parents.

There is other evidence that the effects of parenting behaviors on self-esteem in adolescents are moderated by the sex of the adolescent (Gecas & Schwalbe, 1986; Openshaw et al., 1984). The clearest effect on the self-esteem of males seems to be the balance between parental control and the extent to which the adolescent is encouraged to be autonomous and independent. Boys who are encouraged to be independent and whose parents do not exert a lot of control tend to be high in self-esteem, whereas those who are strongly controlled by their parents and are not encouraged to be independent tend to be low in self-esteem. In contrast, the self-esteem of girls is most strongly affected by the level of support and nurturance they receive from their parents and is hardly affected at all by level of control versus autonomy. Adolescent girls whose parents are supportive tend to be high in self-esteem, whereas those whose parents are rejecting and unsupportive tend to be low in self-esteem.

High levels of pressure to succeed from parents have negative effects on adolescents' self-esteem, whereas feeling able to meet the goals set by parents contributes positively to self-esteem (see, e.g., Eskilson, Wiley, Muehlbauer, & Dodder, 1986). Thus it seems important that pressure from parents be related to realistic goals that are clearly attainable by the adolescent. Another possible consequence of parents' pressuring adolescents to achieve is that the adolescents are then more likely to become involved in deviant behaviors such as alcohol abuse, drug taking, and vandalism.

Other variables that have negative effects on the self-esteem of adolescents include physical abuse of the adolescent and conflict between parents. Being physically abused tends to be part of a downward spiral resulting in low self-esteem, poor social relationships, lack of empathy, and involvement in problem behaviors such as drug and alcohol abuse, delinquency, and suicide (Garbarino & Gillam, 1980). Part of the reason for the downward spiral may be that abused adolescents are likely to leave home very early and may even end up on the streets. These adolescents will consequently lack both the level of support and the level of control needed for healthy development.

Conflict between parents can also lead to low self-esteem, poor school performance, and emotional problems in children from families high in conflict (Amato, 1987; Emery & O'Leary, 1984; Ochiltree & Amato, 1983; Porter & O'Leary, 1980). Amato (1987) suggests two reasons conflict between parents may have negative effects on their children. First, the arguments between the parents are likely to create a stressful family environment. Perhaps the adolescent will feel responsible for the conflict or may experience divided loyalties. A second possibility is that the unhappy marriage "spills over" into the parent-adolescent relationship, producing deterioration in that relationship as well. I am currently involved in research that is looking at the links between the ways spouses communicate with one another in trying to resolve conflicts and how they report behaving when communicating with their adolescents.

In summary, the self-esteem of adolescents is affected by a number of parent-related variables, including support and nurturance received from the parents; the cohesiveness, openness, and organization in the family environment; the amount of conflict, coercion, and control in the family; the extent to which the adolescents are criticized by their parents; the pressure to succeed that adolescents receive from the parents; and physical and emotional abuse. In families where support is high, conflict is low, and control is relatively democratic, adolescents are more likely to develop positive concepts of themselves that will better enable them to face the world and deal with its challenges and problems.

PROVIDING APPROPRIATE MODELING
AND TEACHING OF PROBLEM SOLVING

Communication in the family should ideally provide an environment where adolescents can learn appropriate social skills that will enable them to deal effectively with interpersonal situations and to find constructive solutions to their problems. Some theorists argue that the stresses related to adolescence result from the fact that adolescents tend to lack the interpersonal skills they need to cope with moves toward greater independence and autonomy (Hartup, 1979; Montemayor, 1983). In supportive families, however, they are likely to develop better social and coping skills and more positive identities (Cooper, Grotevant, Moore, & Condon, 1982). Particularly in families where parents consistently demonstrate good coping and problem-solving skills, adolescents are likely to cope much better and be more confident about their ability to deal with the problems that arise. In addition, rather than developing a negative cycle of rebellion or depression, these adolescents are more likely to develop a positive cycle involving growing confidence and increasing competence.

Families with better parent-adolescent communication tend to be more close and loving, more flexible in their approaches to solving family problems, and more satisfied with their family life than those families where parent-adolescent communication is less effective (Barnes & Olson, 1985). It is interesting to note, however, that in democratic families where parents and children communicate and negotiate, adolescents tend to develop both a strong sense of independence and increasingly positive bonds of affection and closeness with their parents. In other words, families where there is positive communication between parents and children are most likely to produce adolescents who can stand on their own feet and function very effectively as independent adults.

Relationships with siblings are also an important part of the family environment and provide adolescents with experience in dealing with closely related peers of either the same or the opposite sex (or both). Unfortunately, at least some of the evidence on siblings suggests that these relationships are likely to be coercive and violent. In a national survey conducted by Straus, Gelles, and Steinmetz (1980), 62% of senior high school students admitted that they had hit a sibling in the past year. Given that sibling aggression seems to be related to aggression outside the family (Gully, Dengerink, Pepping, & Bergstrom, 1981) and that those who are violent with their siblings are more likely to be violent outside the family as well, this finding is particularly disturbing.

According to Patterson (1982), it is siblings who play the central role in triggering the violent behavior of highly aggressive boys, with younger siblings generally being dealt with more aggressively than older ones. Siblings are more likely than peers to reciprocate aggressive behaviors such as hitting, with each violent behavior likely to be followed by even more violent and aggressive behavior, until parents intervene or someone is hurt. The most likely outcome is that a coercive cycle will be set up involving continuing escalation of violence. Given the enforced closeness in which siblings generally operate and the competition among them for limited family resources, it seems unlikely that these relationships, particularly those between males, foster good negotiation and problem-solving skills.

When Montemayor and Hanson (1985) compared adolescents' reports of conflicts with parents and siblings, they found that more than half of all the reported conflicts occurred with siblings. Arguments were most likely to occur between adolescents and their mothers or between adolescents and their same-sex siblings. In our own recent work using a self-report questionnaire, my colleagues and I found that the nature of conflict interactions between siblings depended on the sex of the person doing the reporting and the sex of the sibling with whom they were interacting (Noller, Sheehan, Feeney, & Peterson, 1995). Females reported higher levels of mutuality in their interactions with siblings than did males. In addition, those reporting on interactions with sisters reported less coercion, more mutuality, and more postconflict distress than did those reporting on interactions with brothers. As we shall see later in this section, these findings, to some extent, reflect those based on the reports of the parents.

This idea that male and female children and adolescents are being socialized into different ways of approaching interpersonal conflicts is further supported by Dino, Barnett, and Howard's (1984) finding that there are sex differences in children's expectations of how mothers and fathers would respond to interpersonal problems raised by their sons and daughters. The children in Dino et al.'s sample, who were in grades 4 to 8, expected fathers to respond to sons with instrumental responses, suggesting ways of resolving problems without really listening to their sons and trying to understand the sons' perspectives. Mothers were expected to respond to daughters with expressive responses and to try to understand their daughters' feelings and perspectives rather than suggest ways of solving the problems. Given that these expectations based on sex role stereotypes are clearly evident even among these primary school children, it is highly likely that they themselves will react according to the stereotypes when they are problem solving in other close relationships, such as their own marriages later in life. Males who model their fathers are less likely to understand their wives' needs to talk about relationship problems and to work through such issues (for discussion of differences in the approaches of husbands and wives to solving problems in marriages, see Noller & Fitzpatrick, 1988).

In several studies on parent-adolescent communication, my colleagues and I have found clear differences related to gender of both parent and adolescent (Noller & Bagi, 1985; Noller & Callan, 1990; Noller et al., 1995). In one study, we found that late adolescents reported communicating more frequently and disclosing more deeply to mothers than to fathers across a range of topics (Noller & Bagi, 1985). There was only one topic on which they reported communicating more with fathers than with mothers, and that was politics. In addition, female adolescents reported more self-disclosure to mothers than did male adolescents across such areas as interests, sex roles, relationships, sexual information, and sexual problems, and they reported more self-disclosure to fathers in the areas of future plans, rules of society, and general problems. It seems that mothers and fathers are modeling different levels of disclosure, and daughters and sons are responding with similar levels of disclosure as those modeled by their same-sex parents.

In a follow-up study, we found that the tendency for female adolescents to talk more with their parents, particularly mothers, was evident across all the age groups from 13 to 17 years (Noller & Callan, 1990). Adolescent females also reported talking more to mothers than to fathers and disclosing more to mothers than fathers. Mothers were also seen as initiating more interactions across a number of areas and as recognizing and accepting the adolescents' opinions more than fathers. These findings again support the view that parents are providing models of communication that fit with sex role stereotypes and that adolescents are following these models in their own interactions, at least with their parents.

In a quite different study mentioned earlier, in which we were focusing primarily on interaction patterns during conflict, rather than on self-disclosure, we found similar evidence of gender differences in parent-child interactions that were also reflected in sibling interactions (Noller et al., 1995). Fathers tended to report more coercion and less mutuality in their interactions with their offspring than did mothers. In addition, the adolescents reported both more mutuality and more conflict distress in their interactions with mothers than with fathers. It seems that interactions with female family members tend to involve more mutuality (mutual discussion, expression, and nego-tiation, and less avoidance and withdrawal), but also more distress following the conflict, whereas interactions with male family mem-bers tend to involve less mutuality and distress, but more coercion. These findings again suggest that both sons and daughters are being effectively socialized into gender roles in their interactions with both their parents and their siblings.

An important issue relevant to the model of communication pro-vided by parents is the extent to which adolescent-peer interactions reflect adolescent-parent interactions. Hunter (1984, 1985) examined the types of interactions that occur between adolescents and their parents versus their peers, with particular emphasis on the relation-ship between the way adolescents interact with parents and the way they interact with peers. He found that both mothers and fathers were more directive and didactic with adolescents than were friends. In fact, parents spent more time explaining their own positions than listening to their adolescents and trying to understand their perspec-tives on the particular issues under discussion. Adolescents' interac-tions with friends were generally more mutual than those with their parents, with friends spending more time doing what the parents failed to do, listening and trying to understand. Adolescents' interac-tions with their parents seemed to have little impact on their interac-tions with friends, especially for females. Those adolescents whose parents were very directive were as likely as those with nondirective parents to have mutual interactions with their friends. In other words, even those adolescents with highly directive parents were able to be nondirective in their interactions with their peers.

Effective communication in the family also provides the adolescent with models of social competence, as well as training in skills such as self-disclosure and problem solving. There are several indications, for example, of a relationship between loneliness and an individual's social competence (Perlman & Peplau, 1981). Lonely people tend to avoid social situations and have difficulty taking the initiative in conversations, making friends, introducing themselves to others, and making phone calls to arrange social activities. Those whose parents have not provided them with good models in these areas, and have not helped them to overcome any reticence to initiate social contacts, are more likely to be lonely and to have problems doing anything about that loneliness.

Learning appropriate patterns of self-disclosure in the family is also likely to decrease the chances of adolescents' being lonely. Teenagers who learn to self-disclose appropriately in the family are more likely to self-disclose to their peers and, as a consequence, are less likely to feel lonely (Franzoi & Davis, 1985). It is important to remember that adolescents are more likely to model the social skills of parents with whom they have positive relationships. High school students report being more likely to self-disclose to parents who are warm and loving. Those who disclose to parents are also more likely to disclose to peers and thus to be less lonely. There is also evidence that mothers' social competence directly affects the social competence of their children. Filsinger and Lamke (1983), for example, show that mothers who are anxious and socially withdrawing tend to have adolescents who behave similarly. These adolescents are also likely to be low in social self-esteem and to have problems with intimate relationships. These are the adolescents who are most likely to be lonely and unhappy.

In summary, it seems important that parents provide an environment in which their children and adolescents are able to learn appropriate negotiation and problem-solving skills. Where there is positive, constructive communication between parents and adolescents, adolescents are more likely to develop a strong sense of independence and positive bonds of affection and closeness with parents. Relationships with siblings provide adolescents with experiences of resolving conflict with peers, but these relationships are likely to be coercive and violent, especially with male siblings. There is also evidence that male and female adolescents are being socialized into different ways of approaching conflict, in line with sex role stereotypes. A comparison of adolescents' interactions with peers with their interactions with parents reveals that parents are more directive than peers and generally fail to listen to what their adolescents are saying and to try to understand their points of view. Interestingly, even adolescents with highly directive parents are able to listen to their peers. Finally, adolescents whose parents model appropriate social skills for them are less likely to be lonely.

FACILITATING ADOLESCENTS' DECISION MAKING

One of the overarching conflicts of adolescence concerns the different perspectives of parents and their offspring about who should control the various aspects of the adolescents' lives. Adolescents tend to regard more and more areas of their lives as appropriately controlled by them. For example, adolescents have become less accepting of parents' attempts to influence them with regard to social events, dress styles, and choice of friends.

Smetana (1988) compared parents' and adolescents' ideas about which areas (moral issues, conventional issues, personal issues) should come under parental control and which should be controlled by the adolescent. Families with preadolescents were more likely to see issues as subject to parental authority than were families with adolescents, suggesting some changes as the children get older. On the other hand, as would be expected, parents tend to see issues as more under their authority than do children. Moral and conventional issues were seen to be legitimate areas of parental control by both parents and adolescents, but parents tended to want to retain control in personal areas as well. Smetana's data indicate that shifts in perceptions about parents' authority during adolescence occur primarily with personal issues, not moral or conventional ones. It is no wonder, then, that so much of the conflict between parents and adolescents is about these personal issues. An added problem is that some issues that parents see as moral (e.g., sexual behavior) are seen by the adolescents as personal, and therefore as issues about which they themselves should decide.

Thus decision making is a problem in adolescence for two related reasons. First, adolescents want to have more control over their lives than they have had in the past, often more control than their parents believe is appropriate. In fact, adolescents tend to want to make most of the decisions that directly affect them. At the same time, the decisions that adolescents make can have far-reaching consequences for both themselves and their families. These major decisions include whether to continue education, what kind of career to pursue, which peer group to spend most time with, whom to date, whether to be involved in sexual activity and with whom, whether to continue to live at home or to move out, and whom to marry and when. Understandably, parents can be very concerned about young persons' abilities to make decisions such as these, and, for this reason, they may try to have more influence than adolescents see as reasonable. Parents may also have more realistic ideas about the likely consequences of such decisions than do their adolescents. Ironically, however, parents who try to make decisions for their adolescents or who try to have too strong an influence may lose what influence they have, and may even alienate their offspring. The parents' anxieties are often further exacerbated by adolescents' lack of communication about their activities and hence their own lack of information about what is happening. The problem is that parents' expressions of anxiety may serve only to increase the chances that adolescents will make the decisions that parents fear most.

Poole and Gelder (1985) explored the perceptions of family decision making of 15-year-olds in an Australian sample. These adolescents generally saw themselves as making most of the decisions affecting their lives. Although the influences of the family were still evident, how much impact the family had on the adolescents depended on their sex, their social class, and their ethnic background. Female adolescents considered their mothers' opinions more important than did adolescent boys, whereas boys tended to be more influenced by their fathers' opinions than were girls. Females made more decisions for themselves than did boys, despite the evidence that girls tend to be dominated by boys in mixed-sex decision-making tasks with peers. Perhaps parents trust girls more, especially given that girls are more likely to have values similar to those of their parents.

Poole and Gelder also found class differences in attitudes toward the decision making of adolescents. High socioeconomic status families were more likely to emphasize the importance of adolescents' forming their own opinions while taking note of the opinions of other family members than were low socioeconomic status families. Families from ethnic backgrounds (such as Greek, Italian, Chinese) tended to be more cohesive than Australian families and less willing to encourage autonomy in their adolescents. These families also put less store in the opinions of outsiders. An important difference between the native-born Australian adolescents and those from immigrant groups was that the Australian adolescents, especially the boys, claimed larger networks of friends. Having larger networks probably gives these adolescents access to wider ranges of opinion about various issues. This exposure may add to their level of cognitive development and increase their confidence in forming and expressing opinions different from those of their parents.

Whether it is parents or peers who are seen as the most important influence on decision making for an adolescent depends on three important factors: (a) the relationship the adolescent has with his or her parents, (b) the relationship he or she has with peers, and (c) the particular type of decision being made. Overall, the findings tend to show that peers are important for decisions about current lifestyle, whereas parents are more important in decisions that have long-term impact. In fact, teenagers frequently use the standards of one group or the other depending on the decisions they are making (Glynn, 1981). For example, peers may be the reference group for music and dress, whereas parents are the reference group for long-term decisions about education and careers.

Wilks (1986) found that university students considered their parents to be the most important influences in their lives, and that parents' influence tended to be most important in future-oriented decisions such as educational and vocational choices (see also Sebald & White, 1980). Thus, despite the fact that the peer group assumes new importance in adolescence, the family is still seen as central to the well-being of the young person. In fact, Sheppard, Wright, and Goodstadt (1985) maintain that "the peer group, contrary to what is commonly believed, has little or no influence as long as the family remains strong. Peers take over only when parents abdicate" (p. 951). Although this view may be considered extreme, it certainly seems clear from all the research reviewed above that most adolescents want to maintain close, positive relationships with their parents and to be able to rely on their parents' support and help. Parents who have positive relationships with their children can remain more influential than the peer group throughout adolescence.

Both parents and peers tend to agree that parents' opinions are more important than those of peers in the consideration of educational and vocational choices, as well as decisions about money. Of course, parents' involvement may be important in these areas because parents are also likely to be important sources of financial support.

Peers tend to be more important than parents for advice about current decisions, such as social activities, hobbies, and reading material. In these areas, friends are clearly preferred as the reference group, and parents generally support the use of the peer group for guidance in most of these decisions. Fathers, however, tend to think that they should be consulted about issues related to dress, and both parents think that they should be used as guides about alcohol use, dating, and sex. As far as adolescents are concerned, however, their friends are more important sources of advice in these areas. In fact, even when problems arise, adolescents are more likely to turn to their closest friends than to their parents.

Johnson (1986) examined the relative influence of parents and peers on adolescents' use and abuse of alcohol and showed that the more involved adolescents were in their peer group, the more likely they were to drink alcohol. These findings suggest how important it is for parents to stand by their adolescents and support them, rather than throw them out of the home or withdraw love and support in some other way. If parents fail to support their adolescents, the young people can become more involved with their peers and even more committed to peer group values. Adolescents who rely on the peer group rather than the family for their main support are particularly vulnerable to peer pressure to engage not just in alcohol use and abuse but in other problem behaviors, such as smoking cigarettes and using illegal drugs (Sheppard et al., 1985).

Although adolescents tend to react negatively to parents who try to control them too much, some parental supervision seems to be important to their well-being, and particularly minimizes the chances of their deciding to become involved in problem behaviors. Those who spend a lot of time unsupervised are more likely to engage in a range of such behaviors. For example, females are less likely to smoke if they are subjected to more parental supervision and if they associate less with female friends who smoke.

Deciding to become involved in the use of illegal drugs is also related to amount of supervision, and is particularly high among young adults who are often on their own or who are living away from

home with friends (Thorne & DeBlassie, 1985). Of course, an important question concerns whether these young people use drugs more
because they are away from home or leave home in order to be free to
use drugs. It is clear, however, that being at home and being under
some supervision reduces involvement in drug use.

Adolescents' drug taking is also affected by the quality of their
relationships with parents. In fact, these relationships can even predict
changing patterns of drug use over a two-year period, as shown by
Norem-Hebeisen, Johnson, Anderson, and Johnson (1984). These researchers found that increasing use of drugs between grades 9 and 11
was associated with adolescents' perceptions that their parents did
not approve of them, did not care about them, or were openly angry
and rejecting of them. The adolescents who did not use drugs reported
more positive relationships with their parents between grades 9 and
11, with more affirmation from both mothers and fathers and less
hostility between themselves and their fathers.

A big decision that adolescents have to make is when to leave home
and separate from their families. For some the decision is dictated by
external circumstances, such as being accepted at a particular college
or obtaining employment in another city, but others must make a
specific decision that the time is right. Whereas adolescents whose
parents have healthy relationships tend to develop strong positive
identities and separate fairly smoothly from their parents, those whose
parents are in conflict may have more separation problems. Martin
(1987) suggests that separation from parents may be particularly
difficult if one of the parents is too involved with the adolescent, or if
one or both parents are maladjusted. Conflicted parent-child relationships can also make separation difficult, rather than easy, for the
adolescent because of the guilt, anxiety, resentment, and anger the
adolescent feels toward the parent.

In summary, making decisions is an important part of adolescence.
Adolescents expect that over time they will come to make more of the
decisions that affect their lives, particularly in personal areas. There
is often conflict between parents and adolescents about such decisions
because parents become anxious about the ability of adolescents to
make decisions and about the consequences of those decisions. Adolescents tend to rely on their parents when making future-oriented

decisions, such as educational and vocational choices, and to rely more on their peers in making decisions about current activities, such as those regarding clothes, music, hobbies, use of alcohol and drugs, and sexual behavior. Adolescents who have poor relationships with their parents tend to look more to the peer group and are more likely to become involved in problem behaviors.

In this chapter I have looked at the need for parents of adolescents to provide the type of family environment in which adolescents are most likely to be healthy and well-adjusted. I have discussed five characteristics of that environment and have argued that the ideal environment for adolescents is one in which (a) they are able to renegotiate roles, rules, and relationships with their parents in the direction of more adult-to-adult relationships characterized by a greater balance of power; (b) there is an appropriate climate for exploring alternative identities and achieving identities with which they are comfortable; (c) their self-esteem is enhanced through their caring relationships with their parents and they are able to establish realistic self-concepts that are not distorted through continual criticism, conflict, abuse, or overprotection; (d) parents provide appropriate models of competent communication skills that enable adolescents to learn constructive ways of dealing with the problems and challenges that face them; and (e) parents encourage and enable adolescents to take over responsibility for their lives and for making decisions about both current lifestyle and future educational and vocational goals. As we have seen, the quality of the communication between parents and adolescents is a critical feature of all these tasks.

REFERENCES

Adams, G. R., & Jones, R. M. (1983). Female adolescents' identity development: Age comparisons and perceived child-rearing experience. *Developmental Psychology, 19,* 249-256.

Ainsworth, M. D. S., Blehar, M. C., Waters, E., & Wall, S. (1978). *Patterns of attachment: A psychological study of the strange situation.* Hillsdale, NJ: Lawrence Erlbaum.

Amato, P. (1987). Children's reactions to parental separation and divorce: The views of children and custodial mothers. *Australian Journal of Social Issues, 22,* 610-623.

Amoroso, D. M., & Ware, E. E. (1986). Adolescents' perceptions of aspects of the home environment and their attitudes towards parents, self and external authority. *Adolescence, 21,* 191-204.

Armsden, G. C., & Greenberg, M. T. (1987). The inventory of parent and peer attachment: Individual differences and their relationship to psychological well-being in adolescence. *Journal of Youth and Adolescence, 16,* 427-453.

Barnes, H. L., & Olson, D. H. (1985). Parent-adolescent communication and the circumplex model. *Child Development, 56,* 437-447.

Bartholomew, K., & Horowitz, L. M. (1991). Attachment styles among young adults: A test of a four-category model. *Journal of Personality and Social Psychology, 61,* 226-244.

Bengtson, V. L., & Kuypers, J. A. (1971). Generational differences and the developmental stake. *Aging and Human Development, 2,* 240-260.

Bengtson, V. L., & Troll, L. (1978). Youth and their parents: Feedback and intergenerational influence in socialization. In R. M. Lerner & G. B. Spanier (Eds.), *Children's influences on marital and family interaction: A life-span perspective* (pp. 106-130). New York: Academic Press.

Bernard, H. S. (1981). Identity formation during late adolescence: A review of some empirical findings. *Adolescence, 16,* 349-358.

Blos, P. (1979). *The adolescent passage.* New York: International Universities Press.

Bowlby, J. (1969). *Attachment and loss: Vol. 1. Attachment.* New York: Basic Books.

Bowlby, J. (1973). *Attachment and loss: Vol. 2. Separation: Anxiety and anger.* New York: Basic Books.

Bowlby, J. (1980). *Attachment and loss: Vol. 3. Loss.* New York: Basic Books.

Buri, J. R., Kirchner, P. A., & Walsh, J. M. (1987). Familial correlates of self-esteem in young American adults. *Journal of Social Psychology, 127,* 583-588.

Burt, C. E., Cohen, L. H., & Bjorck, J. P. (1988). Perceived family environment as a moderator of young adolescents' life stress adjustment. *American Journal of Community Psychology, 16,* 101-122.

Campbell, E., Adams, G. R., & Dobson, W. R. (1984). Family correlates of identity formation in late adolescents: A study of the predictive utility of connectedness and individuality in family relations. *Journal of Youth and Adolescence, 13,* 509-525.

Cooper, C. R., Grotevant, H. D., & Condon, S. M. (1984). Family support and conflict: Both foster adolescent identity and role-taking skills. In H. D. Grotevant & C. R. Cooper (Eds.), *Adolescent development in the family: New directions for child development.* San Francisco: Jossey-Bass.

Cooper, C. R., Grotevant, H. D., Moore, M. S., & Condon, S. M. (1982). *Family support and conflict: Both foster adolescent identity and role-taking.* Paper presented at the annual meeting of the American Psychological Association, Washington, DC.

Dino, G. A., Barnett, M. A., & Howard, J. A. (1984). Children's expectations of sex differences in parents' responses to sons and daughters encountering interpersonal problems. *Sex Roles, 11,* 709-717.

Donovan, J. M. (1975). Identity status and interpersonal style. *Journal of Youth and Adolescence, 4,* 37-55.

Emery, R. E., & O'Leary, D. (1984). Marital discord and child behavior problems in a nonclinical sample. *Journal of Abnormal Child Psychology, 12,* 411-420.

Erikson, E. (1963). *Youth: Challenge and change.* New York: Basic Books.

Erikson, E. (1968). *Identity: Youth and crisis.* New York: W. W. Norton.

Eskilson, A., Wiley, M. G., Muehlbauer, G., & Dodder, L. (1986). Parental pressure, self-esteem and adolescent reported deviance: Bending the twig too far. *Adolescence, 21,* 501-515.

Feeney, J. A., & Noller, P. (1990). Attachment style as a predictor of adult romantic relationships. *Journal of Personality and Social Psychology, 58,* 281-291.

Filsinger, E. E., & Lamke, L. K. (1983). The lineage transmission of interpersonal competence. *Journal of Marriage and the Family, 45,* 75-80.

Franzoi, S. L., & Davis, M. H. (1985). Adolescent self-disclosure and loneliness: Private self-consciousness and parental influences. *Journal of Personality and Social Psychology, 48,* 768-780.

Garbarino, J., & Gilliam, G. (1980). *Understanding abusive families.* Lexington, MA: Lexington.

Gecas, V., & Schwalbe, M. L. (1986). Parental behavior and adolescent self-esteem. *Journal of Marriage and the Family, 48,* 37-46.

Glynn, T. (1981). *Drugs and the family* (U.S. DHHS, Research Issues 29). Washington, DC: Government Printing Office.

Greenberg, M., Siegel, J., & Leitch, C. (1983). The nature and importance of attachment relationships to parents and peers during adolescence. *Journal of Youth and Adolescence, 12,* 373-386.

Grotevant, H. D., & Cooper, C. R. (1985). Patterns of interaction in family relationships and the development of identity exploration in adolescents. *Child Development, 56,* 415-428.

Grotevant, H. D., & Cooper, C. R. (1986). Individuation in family relationships: A perspective on individual differences in the development of identity and role-taking skill in adolescence. *Human Development, 29,* 82-100.

Gully, K. J., Dengerink, H. A., Pepping, M., & Bergstrom, D. (1981). Research note: Sibling contribution to violent behavior. *Journal of Marriage and the Family, 43,* 333-337.

Harris, I. D., & Howard, K. I. (1984). Parental criticism and the adolescent experience. *Journal of Youth and Adolescence, 13,* 113-121.

Hartup, W. W. (1979). The social worlds of childhood. *American Psychologist, 34,* 944-950.

Hauser, J. (1981). Adolescents and religion. *Adolescence, 16,* 309-320.

Hauser, S. T., Powers, S. I., Noam, G. G., Jacobson, A. M., Wiess, B., & Follansbee, D. J. (1984). Familial contexts of adolescent ego development. *Child Development, 55,* 195-213.

Hazan, C., & Shaver, P. R. (1987). Romantic love conceptualized as an attachment process. *Journal of Personality and Social Psychology, 52,* 511-524.

Hoelter, J., & Harper, L. (1987). Structural and interpersonal family influences on adolescent self-conception. *Journal of Marriage and the Family, 49,* 129-139.

Hoge, D. R., Petrillo, G. H., & Smith, E. L. (1982). Transmission of religious and social values from parent to teenage children. *Journal of Marriage and the Family, 44,* 569-580.

Hunter, F. T. (1984). Socializing procedures in parent-child and friendship relations during adolescence. *Developmental Psychology, 20,* 1092-1099.

Hunter, F. T. (1985). Individual adolescents' perceptions of interactions with parents and friends. *Journal of Early Adolescence, 5,* 295-305.

Hunter, F. T., & Youniss, J. (1982). Changes in functions of three relations during adolescence. *Developmental Psychology, 18,* 806-811.

Jacob, T. (1974). Patterns of family conflict and dominance as a function of child age and social class. *Developmental Psychology, 10,* 1-12.

Johnson, K. A. (1986). Informal control networks and adolescent orientations toward alcohol use. *Adolescence, 21,* 767-784.

Jurkovic, G. J., & Ulrici, D. (1985). Empirical perspectives on adolescents and their families. In L. L'Abate (Ed.), *Handbook of family psychology and therapy* (pp. 215-257). Homewood, IL: Dorsey.

Kahn, S., Zimmerman, G., Csikszentmihalyi, M., & Getzels, J. W. (1985). Relations between identity in young adulthood and intimacy at midlife. *Journal of Personality and Social Psychology, 49,* 1316-1322.

Kroger, J. (1985). Separation-individuation and ego identity status in New Zealand university students. *Journal of Youth and Adolescence, 14,* 133-147.

Kroger, J. (1989). *Identity in adolescence.* London: Routledge.

Kroger, J., & Haslett, S. J. (1988). Separation-individuation and ego identity status in late adolescence: A two-year longitudinal study. *Journal of Youth and Adolescence, 17,* 59-79.

Lapsley, D. K., Rice, K. G., & Fitzgerald, D. P. (1990). Adolescent attachment, identity and adjustment to college: Implications for the continuity of adaptation hypothesis. *Journal of Counseling and Development, 68,* 561-565.

Marcia, J. E. (1966). Development and validation of ego identity status. *Journal of Personality and Social Psychology, 3,* 551-558.

Marcia, J. E. (1976). Identity six years after: A follow-up study. *Journal of Youth and Adolescence, 5,* 145-160.

Martin, B. (1987). Development perspectives on family theory and psychopathology. In T. Jacob (Ed.), *Family interaction and psychopathology: Theories, methods, and findings* (pp. 163-202). New York: Plenum.

Montemayor, R. (1983). Parents and adolescents in conflict: All families some of the time and some families most of the time. *Journal of Early Adolescence, 3,* 83-103.

Montemayor, R., & Hanson, E. (1985). A naturalistic view of conflict between adolescents and their parents and siblings. *Journal of Early Adolescence, 5,* 23-30.

Newman, B. A., & Murray, C. I. (1983). Identity and family relations in early adolescence. *Journal of Early Adolescence, 3,* 293-303.

Niemi, R. G. (1968). *A methodological study of political socialization in the family.* Ann Arbor, MI: University Microfilms.

Niemi, R. G. (1974). *How family members perceive each other: Political and social attitudes in two generations.* New Haven, CT: Yale University Press.

Noller, P. (1994). Relationships with parents in adolescence: Process and outcome. In R. Montemayor, G. R. Adams, & T. P. Gulotta (Eds.), *Personal relationships during adolescence* (pp. 37-77). Thousand Oaks, CA: Sage.

Noller, P., & Bagi, S. (1985). Parent-adolescent communication. *Journal of Adolescence, 8,* 125-144.

Noller, P., & Callan, V. J. (1986). Adolescent and parent perceptions of family cohesion and adaptability. *Journal of Adolescence, 9,* 97-106.

Noller, P., & Callan, V. J. (1990). Adolescents' perceptions of the nature of their communication with parents. *Journal of Youth and Adolescence, 19*, 349-362.

Noller, P., & Callan, V. J. (1991). *The adolescent in the family.* London: Routledge.

Noller, P., & Fitzpatrick, M. A. (Eds.). (1988). *Perspectives on marital interaction.* Clevedon, UK: Multilingual Matters.

Noller, P., Seth-Smith, M., Bouma, R., & Schweitzer, R. (1992). Parent and adolescent perceptions of family functioning: A comparison of clinic and nonclinic families. *Journal of Adolescence, 15,* 101-114.

Noller, P., Sheehan, G., Feeney, J. A., & Peterson, C. (1995). *Links between couple interaction, sibling interaction and parents' interactions with sons and daughters.* Manuscript in preparation.

Noller, P., & Strahan, B. J. (1993, November). *Attachment predictors of religious experience.* Paper presented at the meeting of the National Council on Family Relations, Baltimore.

Norem-Hebeisen, A., Johnson, D. W., Anderson, D., & Johnson, R. (1984). Predictors and concomitants of changes in drug use patterns among teenagers. *Journal of Social Psychology, 124,* 43-50.

Ochiltree, G., & Amato, P. R. (1983, November). *Family conflict and child competence.* Paper presented at the Australian Family Research Conference, Canberra.

Olson, D. H., McCubbin, H. I., Barnes, H. L., Larsen, A. S., Muxen, M. J., & Wilson, M. A. (1983). *Families: What makes them work?* Beverly Hills, CA: Sage.

Openshaw, D. K., Thomas, D. L., & Rollins, B. C. (1984). Parental influences on adolescent self-esteem. *Journal of Early Adolescence, 4,* 259-274.

Orlofsky, J. L., Marcia, C. E., & Lesser, I. (1973). Ego identity status and the intimacy versus isolation crisis of young adulthood. *Journal of Personality and Social Psychology, 27,* 211-219.

Parker, G. (1983). *Parental overprotection: A risk factor in psychosocial adjustment.* Sydney: Grune & Stratton.

Parker, G. (1991). Response to Quadrio & Levy's "Separation crises in over-attached families." *Australian and New Zealand Journal of Family Therapy, 10,* 27-33.

Parker, G., Tupling, H., & Brown, L. B. (1979). A parental bonding instrument. *British Journal of Medical Psychology, 52,* 1-10.

Patterson, G. R. (1982). *Coercive family processes.* Eugene, OR: Castalia.

Perlman, D., & Peplau, L. A. (1981). Toward a social psychology of loneliness. In S. Duck & R. Gilmour (Eds.), *Personal relationships 3: Personal relationships in disorder* (pp. 31-56). London: Academic Press.

Petersen, A. C., & Taylor, B. (1980). The biological approach to adolescence: Biological change and psychological adaption. In J. Adelson (Ed.), *Handbook of adolescent psychology* (pp. 117-155). New York: John Wiley.

Poole, M. E., & Gelder, A. J. (1985). Family cohesiveness and adolescent autonomy in decision making. *Australian Journal of Sex, Marriage and Family, 5,* 65-75.

Porter, B., & O'Leary, K. D. (1980). Marital discord and child behavior problems. *Journal of Abnormal Child Psychology, 8,* 287-295.

Rice, K. G. (1990). Attachment in adolescence: A narrative and meta-analytic review. *Journal of Youth and Adolescence, 19,* 511-538.

Richman, J. A., & Flaherty, J. A. (1987). Adult psychosocial assets and depressive mood over time: Effects of internalized childhood attachments. *Journal of Nervous and Mental Diseases, 175,* 703-712.

Rollins, B. C., & Thomas, D. L. (1979). Parental support, power and control techniques in the socialization of children. In W. R. Burr, R. Hill, F. I. Nye, & I. L. Reiss (Eds.), *Contemporary theories about the family* (Vol. 1, pp. 317-364). New York: Free Press.

Ryan, R. M., & Lynch, J. H. (1989). Emotional autonomy versus detachment: Revising the vicissitudes of adolescence and young adulthood. *Child Development, 60,* 340-356.

Sebald, H., & White, B. (1980). Teenagers' divided reference groups: Uneven alignment with parents and peers. *Adolescence, 15,* 979-984.

Sheppard, M. A., Wright, D., & Goodstadt, M. S. (1985). Peer pressure and drug use: Exploding the myth. *Adolescence, 20,* 949-958.

Smetana, J. G. (1988). Adolescents' and parents' conceptions of parental authority. *Child Development, 59,* 321-335.

Steinberg, L. D., & Hill, J. P. (1978). Patterns of family interaction as a function of age, the onset of puberty and formal thinking. *Developmental Psychology, 14,* 683-684.

Steinberg, L. D., & Silverberg, S. B. (1986). The vicissitudes of autonomy in early adolescence. *Child Development, 57,* 841-851.

Stone, L. J., & Church, J. (1968). *Childhood and adolescence: A psychology of the growing person* (2nd ed.). New York: Random House.

Straus, M. A., Gelles, R. J., & Steinmetz, S. K. (1980). *Behind closed doors: Violence in the American family.* Garden City, NY: Anchor/Doubleday.

Thorne, C. R., & DeBlassie, R. R. (1985). Adolescent substance abuse. *Adolescence, 22,* 335-347.

Wilks, J. (1986). The relative importance of parents and friends in adolescent decision making. *Journal of Youth and Adolescence, 15,* 323-335.

Accounts and the
Demystification of Courtship

CATHERINE A. SURRA
MICHELLE L. BATCHELDER
DEBRA K. HUGHES

Courtship is a period when two individuals, usually a man and a woman, try to win one another's affections and, ultimately, one another's commitment to a lasting marriage. The verb *to court* is defined in at least one popular American dictionary as follows: "to endeavor to gain the favor of or win over by attention" and "to flatter in order to get something" (*Webster's New Twentieth Century Dictionary*, 1979, p. 420). When applied to close relationships, the verb takes on specific meanings regarding what it is that is being pursued; namely, another's love, loyalty, and commitment to wed.

This definition of courtship emphasizes two central features of the experience. First, people court with intentionality, with goals in mind about what they would like the outcome of their relationship to be. This feature sets courting relationships apart from other close relationships. Even though partners in close relationships generally are concerned about the future status of their relationships and what form they want the future to take, this is much more true of people who are courting. Unlike individuals who are in more voluntaristic, temporary close relationships, courting individuals must consciously consider whether they want their future relationships to take the form of the social, legal, and economic union of marriage. Some people who end up considering marriage may not have had much awareness early on that their relationships were headed that way; at some point, however, most individuals who eventually wed decide with forethought and intentionality to press on with their commitment.

Second, the dictionary definition of courtship highlights the fact that it involves having to *entice* another to share one's goal of commitment to wed. We typically assume that the need to entice is so great that courtship by its very nature requires that the partners deceive one another about their true characters or, at the very least, manage very carefully the impressions they convey. The process of *character management* goes far deeper than what we usually think of as the management of first or early impressions. During courtship, coupled partners are assumed to present themselves positively over diverse social and private situations, for relatively long periods, and during frequent interactions with one another. What a job it is to make oneself so consistently attractive and desirable in another's eyes! Thankfully, the process of character management is facilitated, according to some scholars, by a tendency on the part of partners to idealize one another (see Huston, 1994; Waller, 1938). Idealization, which is prompted by the romanticism of courtship and the goal of marital commitment, means that partners will delude themselves about the other's true character and will overlook or misinterpret signs of the other's negative side. The result is believed to be an image of the other rooted in positive illusion, rather than an accurate and complete image of the other's character (see Murray & Holmes, 1993).

As we shall show below, this view of courtship as a period of character management and idealization does not jibe well with data derived from partners' own accounts of why they became committed to wed and other data. According to research on accounts, the processes by which individuals decide to wed are actually quite variable and multifaceted. The extent to which partners must manage their self-presentation or convince the other to wed varies across relationships. In some cases, the partners fall so agreeably into a comfortable relationship and into a common understanding of marriage as the desired goal that the need for either to woo the other is irrelevant. In still other cases, as we will demonstrate, some people are aware of the negative sides of both their partners and their relationships, perhaps because the partners are not very good at character management, do not recognize the value of character management, or believe it is undesirable to hide their true character from their partners. Some partners, the data suggest, may decide to commit in spite of the information they have about negativity in their relationships.

Other definitions of courtship underscore the fact that it is a social, as well as interpersonal, endeavor (Surra & Huston, 1987). Courtship is a social transition, which means that it entails changes in social roles not only for the individuals involved, but also for their family members and friends. Thus a partner's family members and friends have a vested interest in that individual's choice of a spouse. They are concerned with the solidarity of the group and with how easily and well the chosen one can be integrated into their established networks (Surra & Milardo, 1991). Because an individual's family members and friends have a stake in his or her marital choice, they themselves may become very active in "courting" or in "rejecting" the one who is chosen—much to the chagrin of partners, who mistakenly assume that courtship is just between them.

In this chapter, we examine the individual, interpersonal, and social features of courtship as they are subjectively experienced by partners themselves. In order to do so, we rely on data from accounts and narratives of how particular courtships developed. We first define accounts as one type of relational knowledge structure, and discuss how accounts differ from memories, scripts, social constructions, and attributions. We then review the results of two programs of research on accounts of courtship, our own and the work of Joseph Veroff and his colleagues at the University of Michigan. The review summarizes results in a way that dispels the following four myths about courtship, which are held to some degree by social scientists and laypersons alike: (a) courtships follow fixed scripts and similar pathways to marriage, (b) courting partners idealize and romanticize one another and their relationship, (c) people are naive about commitment and about why they get committed, and (d) relationships begin anew at marriage and have equal chances of becoming successful marriages.

ACCOUNTS AS CAUSAL KNOWLEDGE
STRUCTURES ABOUT RELATIONSHIPS

Our research on accounts takes the view that accounts are products of cognitive and social processes whereby partners seek to explain to themselves and to others why relationship events transpired as they did. In particular, our research is concerned with how heterosexual partners explain developmental changes, both increases and decreases, in their commitment to marrying one another. In this section, we clarify the definition of causal accounts, justify our ascribing to them the status of a relational knowledge structure, and discuss how our definition is similar to and different from other uses of the terms *attributions* and *accounts* in the literature. In addition, we describe the way in which accounts draw on other knowledge structures about relationships, which makes them an especially good source of data about relationships.

What Are Causal Accounts of Relationship Events?

Causal accounts of relationship events are organized, stored representations of how and why these events occurred that persist long after the events actually happened (Surra & Bohman, 1991). Accounts are packages of attributions (Harvey, Orbuch, & Weber, 1992) that draw on a variety of individual, interpersonal, social, and circumstantial explanations. The explanations are interwoven into a cohesive, storylike narrative that enables individuals to make sense of their relationship experiences for themselves and others.

A key controversy in the literature on accounts concerns the extent to which they reflect actual private explanations for events versus the degree to which they are socially constructed for the audience that is privy to them. Another debate centers on how much accounts are altered with the passage of time and how much they can be trusted to reflect the real objective and subjective occurrences that took place when the event that is being explained actually happened. The issue of the accuracy of accounts is especially relevant to many of the data reported in this chapter (Veroff's and our own) because, in the case of newlyweds, they are reconstructions of past events. In our view, the explanations are rooted in real relationship experiences, including representations of interactions that actually took place between partners and between them and third parties, in the partners' interpretations of interactions, in their beliefs about the qualities of their relationships, and in other individual and environmental occurrences. We believe that, although causal accounts for past relationship events are altered by more recent happenings and are colored by the present state of the relationship, they also serve as a good characterization of the history of the relationship. The question is: To what extent do accounts change over time, and what factors explain those changes?

From our perspective, account making is a type of social cognitive processing that comes into play whenever people have the processing goal of explaining why. (Other goals, such as the goal of gathering information about a partner, would call up other processing mechanisms; see Wyer & Srull, 1986.) Research on accounts suggests that inferential goals are triggered whenever incoming information is inconsistent with prior relational knowledge, including schemata for what relationships typically are like or should be like and schemata specific to the relationship and the partner in question (Planalp & Rivers, in press; Planalp & Surra, 1992). Account making also will be instigated whenever individuals are asked by third parties, including social others or researchers, why they behaved as they did. Finally, partners' attempts to make sense of their own experience and their motivation to understand, predict, and control their experiences will require inferential processing and the construction of private accounts.

This definition of accounts closely parallels the view taken by Harvey and his colleagues (1992), which emphasizes that people will construct accounts whenever they need to explain to themselves or others why they behave as they do, why their partners behave as they do, or why other social and external events happen to them or for them. Our definition is also very similar to the conception of narratives, and seems functionally the same as the usage of the term *narratives* in the literature (e.g., Gergen & Gergen, 1987; Harvey et al., 1992; Veroff, Sutherland, Chadiha, & Ortega, 1993a, 1993b). This view departs from the definition of accounts as justifying, face-saving devices that individuals offer as explanations for untoward behaviors (see, for example, McLaughlin, Cody, & Read, 1992). Following the work of Scott and Lyman (1968), the latter definition emphasizes the ways in which individuals account *for* negative behaviors *to* social others, and the processes of preserving self-esteem, making excuses, and rationalizing by which they do so. In contrast to this approach, our definition encompasses a broader range of occurrences and assumes that people need to account not only for negative relational events, but for positive ones (e.g., "Why did my partner buy me a special gift on an ordinary Wednesday?"). In addition, account making will result when partners are trying to make sense themselves of such relational behaviors as decisions to become more or less involved. Thus accounts of "why I am becoming more or less committed to marrying my partner" and "how I ended up married to my partner" are especially relevant to premarital relationships and to courtship.

Certainly, our definition of accounts has social elements and assumes that accounts are influenced by social processes, but we, along with Harvey et al. (1992), believe that accounts are not merely social constructions that are offered to others to save face or to present the self positively. Rather, accounts also arise out of personal needs and motivations to feel a greater sense of control over the environment, to enable individuals to cope with highly charged emotional occurrences, to give people a sense of completeness in their understanding, to help individuals find better ways of coping with the future (Harvey et al., 1992), or to understand or to give order to even mundane or accidental happenings in the day-to-day life of a relationship.

Causal accounts have private motivations, are privately constructed, and are deeply rooted in behavioral and environmental events that actually happened. This definition of accounts does not mean, for example, that the characterization of events apparent in accounts will be the same for different people involved in the events. Nor do we assume that the social or public account given to an outsider, even a researcher, will map exactly onto the private account (see Antaki, 1987). It does mean, however, that accounts contain representations of objective and subjective occurrences, and, if researchers are careful about how they ask for accounts, they can obtain valid, detailed reports of partners' private accounts for relationship events (e.g., by using nonleading, open-ended probes).

The emphasis on accounts as the products of explanation means that attributions and attribution theory have played a large part in attempts to understand account making. Attribution theory seems especially relevant in close relationships for understanding the sorts of happenings that trigger causal searches, the various sources of information that people draw upon in order to explain events, and the location of causes (e.g., internal versus external) to which events are attributed (Planalp & Rivers, in press). Attribution theory is also useful for understanding the powerful motives that drive sense making in everyday experience. Attributions, however, are not the same as causal accounts. The term *attributions* frequently is used to refer to the singular, momentary inferences people make during ongoing interaction with others (e.g., Fletcher & Fincham, 1991). The kinds of explanations utilized during interaction will be influenced by the causal knowledge structures, or accounts, already in place, but the content of accounts differs from "on-line" attributions. Whenever inferences take on the status of organized stores of explanatory information that can be reproduced when called upon or modified as new or inconsistent information becomes available, we refer to them as *causal accounts*.

The term *attributions* also is applied to the ascriptions individuals make to the personalities or characters of others (see Fletcher & Fincham, 1991). Although causal accounts contain such attributions, they are only a part of the richly networked set of attributions apparent in accounts. Because of the multiple uses of the term *attribution* in the literature, we refer to the separate explanations contained in accounts as individuals' *reasons* for behaving as they do. We turn now to a fuller examination of the types of relational knowledge contained in accounts.

Causal Accounts and Their
Connections to Relational Knowledge

In their model of cognition and close relationships, Surra and Bohman (1991) describe several different knowledge structures that operate in the development of relationships. Out of all of the knowledge structures that affect relationships, causal accounts may be the most interesting and the single most informative source of relational knowledge. This is because accounts contain elements of all other sources of relational knowledge. In their attempts to explain events, partners draw upon the relational knowledge structures that are already in place, integrating them into coherent explanations for events.

In attempting to account for relationship events, partners will utilize information from three knowledge structures that exist prior to the formation of the target relationship. *Generalized schemata for classes of relationships* contain information about what a relationship typically is like, normative beliefs about what makes a relationship good or bad, and rules and scripts for appropriate behavior. These schemata show up in accounts as explanations for both positive and negative events in which expectations for what should have occurred or what typically occurs are unmet (Planalp & Rivers, in press; Planalp & Surra, 1992), and they provide standards against which occurrences in the target relationship are evaluated and judged. Thus they provide sources of information about the target relationship (Surra & Milardo, 1991). As the target relationship progresses, it will affect and alter the preexisting knowledge structures (for a more detailed explanation of this process, see Surra & Bohman, 1991).

Relationship-specific schemata for other close relationships and *self-schemata* are two other preexisting knowledge structures that have a similar function in accounts: They are a means of finding out about and understanding a new partner or a close partner who is behaving in novel ways. When accounting for events, for example, individuals will compare the partner to the self as a means of understanding the other's behavior (e.g., "Just now, Doug doesn't know what he wants to do after college, whereas I have a more definite idea of what I want"; see Surra, 1994). Similarly, relationship-specific schemata for others who are or have been close partners provide information that serves as a comparison point for acquiring knowledge about the partner (e.g., "I had a better relationship with Sheila than anyone I had ever dated before"; Surra & Milardo, 1991).

Accounts also are valuable sources of information about *relationship-specific schemata*, or knowledge stores about the target relationship (see Planalp, 1985; Surra & Bohman, 1991). The following account obtained from a college-age woman, describing why commitment changed early in her relationship, illustrates some of the ways in which accounts are valuable sources of relationship-specific knowledge:

We got along real well and we had real similar goals and stuff. And so then it wasn't just like we were dating and having fun. . . . We could see something serious coming out of this, and we were only dating each other. He was 23. Maybe he was more ready to get married. . . . I was 19 when we first started dating. . . . He thought about it more at first than I did.

In order to explain why her relationship became more committed, the woman made assessments of prototypical relationship constructs, in this case how compatible she and her partner were. Partners frequently call upon prototypical knowledge (see Fehr, 1988) in order to weigh the value of and degree to which the characteristic is present in the relationship in question (e.g., how in love they are, how much they can trust their partners, or how committed they are). Accounts also contain references to beliefs about the partner and the relationship that are contained in relationship-specific schemata. In this instance, the woman referred to her beliefs that the relationship would lead to something serious and that both partners were exclusively dating. In still other cases, accounts draw on relationship-specific schemata to represent typical relationship behaviors and action sequences (e.g., "Every time we were together, we fought"). In addition, the woman's account illustrates the impact of generalized schemata for classes of relationships on accounts; she relies on her preconceived knowledge about appropriate age norms for marriage, then considers her partner's age, her own age, and what that meant for each partner's readiness to wed.

In the following sections, we review the results of recent research on accounts of the development of courtship. Our goal here is to elucidate how patterns of findings from two independent programs of research have converged to debunk myths about courtship.

RESEARCH ON ACCOUNTS OF COURTSHIP
DEVELOPMENT: DEBUNKING THE MYTHS

Research on accounts of courtship has made fruitful contributions to our knowledge about how partners decide to marry particular others and the advisability of those decisions. One of the outgrowths of this research is that we now know much more than we once did about the subjective processes by which people go about committing to wed. In this section, we draw primarily from the results of two research programs, our own and that of Joseph Veroff and his colleagues, to debunk four myths about courtship. The myths are rooted in beliefs about courtship apparent in the scholarly literature as well as laypersons' assumptions. Before addressing the myths, we summarize the methods used in each program of research and discuss how the methods might have affected the results that were obtained.

Methods for Studying Accounts
of Courtship Development

In the longitudinal study carried out by Veroff and his colleagues, newlywed couples constructed the stories or narratives of their courtships in joint interviews (Holmberg & Veroff, in press; Orbuch, Veroff, & Holmberg, 1993; Veroff et al., 1993a, 1993b). The researchers asked 373 African American and white same-race spouses to tell the stories of their relationships from their beginnings up to the future. A storyboard that "describes most people's storyline" was used to guide the interviews (Veroff et al., 1993a, p. 445). The storyboard represented progressive steps of developing relationships along a pathway from courtship to married life. It included the following steps, each of which was contained in a circle. The circles were arranged in a series that progressed upward: "how we met," "getting interested in each other," "becoming a couple," "planning to get married," "the wedding," "right after the wedding," "how things are now," and "the future" (Veroff et al., 1993a, p. 445). If partners did not move to different sections of the story line, the interviewer prompted them to ensure that all topics on the storyboard were covered.

The work of Surra and her colleagues centers on partners' accounts of why commitment to marrying particular partners changed over the course of relationships (Surra, 1987; Surra, Arizzi, & Asmussen, 1988; Surra & Hughes, 1994). Coupled partners, who were either newly married (in two samples) or dating (in one sample), separately graphed commitment to marriage, which was operationalized as the chance of marriage from 0% to 100%. In the case of newlyweds, the graph was drawn from the time the relationship began to the day of the wedding and 100% chance of marriage. In the case of daters, it was drawn to the present. Interviewers set the stage by emphasizing that we were not interested in how the respondent's relationship was similar to others, but in what his or her relationship was really like and how it was different or unique. The graph was constructed as a series of upturns or downturns, or turning points, in commitment. Each time a respondent said that he or she was aware of a change in the chance of marriage, the interviewer asked the respondent to tell what the percentage was and then to describe the shape of the line connecting the new point to the previous point. After drawing the line, the interviewer said, "Tell me in as specific terms as possible, what happened from [date] to [date] that made the chance of marriage go [up/down] __%." The respondent then gave his or her account for the turning point. The interviewer then asked, "Is there anything else that happened that made the chance of marriage go [up/down] __% from [date] to [date]?" This question was repeated until the respondent said that nothing else had happened. This series of questions was repeated for each turning point.

Although people's accounts of courtships constitute the data for both of these research projects, differences in the methods of the two projects may produce different results. In Veroff et al.'s studies, partners were interviewed together, so that they jointly constructed their stories. Surra et al., in contrast, interviewed partners separately. Joint interviews probably yield accounts about which both partners agree, and may make apparent places where they do not. Surra et al.'s interviews, on the other hand, yielded information about individuals' perceptions of their relationships, including events that sometimes only one partner knew about, and, in some cases, had concealed from the other. The questions asked also differentiate the two studies. Even though the storyboard may have evoked couples' unique sets of knowledge about their courtships, the standardized plotline of the storyboard may influence them to tailor their own stories to fit the suggested script. Veroff and colleagues (1993a) acknowledge the possible pitfalls associated with standardizing the plot. Surra et al.'s open-ended procedure, in contrast, granted respondents more leeway to determine the content of their accounts. In addition, contrary to the positively progressing circles in the storyboard, the graphing procedure allowed for regressions, as well as progressions, in the developmental path. With respect to coding the accounts, Veroff and colleagues concentrated on global coding of the whole narrative for the presence or absence of certain themes. Surra et al. divided every account into its separate reasons and then aggregated the reasons across turning points on the entire graph.

The two studies thus may yield somewhat different kinds of knowledge about relationships. What is surprising perhaps, is that, despite the methodological differences, the results of the two research programs converge to offer compelling insights about courtship.

Myth 1: Courtships Follow Fixed Scripts and Similar Pathways to Marriage

Researchers and laypersons frequently expect courtships to follow a set plot and believe that narratives about courtship coalesce on the same cultural script. Drawing on the work of Ross (1989), Holmberg and Veroff (in press), for example, argue that memories of courtship development are derived to a large extent from individuals' scripted theories about what courtships are like and should be like. Memories—and, by implication, accounts—are thought to be highly changeable because people are assumed to forget and/or misrepresent what actually occurred in their relationships. Gaps in their knowledge will be filled in with scriptlike information about what courtships typically and ideally are like.

Based on a review of research and on their own narratives, Holmberg and Veroff (in press) propose the following courtship script:

> The male initiates the relationship. The couple then grows steadily closer, forming an intrapersonal commitment which comes from within, rather than being spurred on by outside forces. The relationship is harmonious, with little conflict and few serious reversals. The male then proposes, and the couple is wed in a ceremony which is an important social occasion, bringing together not only the couple themselves, but also their friends and families. (p. 25)

The script emphasizes that courting relationships are motivated not by external forces, but by intrapersonal, internal forces. The partners' individual social networks are brought together at the wedding; they are not a factor in the developing commitment. The script assumes that relationships are nearly conflict free and proceed in a mostly positive direction. It also emphasizes traditional gender roles such that the male initiates the relationship and later proposes marriage.

Even though courtship is frequently assumed to follow a set script and accounts of courtship are believed to be shaped by that script, the results of both Veroff et al.'s research and Surra et al.'s research suggest otherwise. Instead, accounts are characterized by a rich variety of themes (Orbuch et al., 1993; Surra, 1987; Surra et al., 1988). The variety apparent in accounts is so great as to suggest that either different people are drawing upon a number of different scripts or that accounts just are not very scripted. Variety is apparent in two ways. First, there is great diversity with respect to the thematic content of accounts offered by different partners. Second, in Veroff et al.'s data, themes vary according to respondents' subcultural backgrounds; African Americans and whites report different courtship themes (Orbuch et al., 1993).

Regarding the first type of variation, no one courtship story predominated among Veroff et al.'s narratives. Instead, each couple presented one or more of 37 identifiable themes (Orbuch et al., 1993). For some partners, positive themes filled with romance—such as love at first sight, one partner's hot pursuit of the other, the relationship's fulfilling spiritual destiny, or the couple's beginning as childhood sweethearts—precipitated their love affair. Other partners described the progression of their relationships in more neutral and less romantic terms, as in the case where a marital relationship evolved from a friendship. In other narratives, partners became committed for pragmatic reasons; for example, because of children, a pregnancy, a partner's capacity as a parent, or simply because the partners were always together. Still other couples described courtship in terms of overcoming obstacles, such as illness, unemployment, physical distance, parental opposition, and conflict between the partners.

When Veroff et al.'s respondents recounted which partner initiated the relationship and the marriage proposal, their responses frequently departed from the script (Orbuch et al., 1993). Although almost half the couples did follow a traditional script, in which the husband was portrayed as the initiator of the courtship, the remaining respondents said that both partners, the wife, or a third party initiated it. Regarding who proposed marriage, one-third of the couples reported following the traditional script of husband proposing to the wife whereas one-fifth reported role reversal, with the wife proposing to the husband. For the remaining couples, marriage proposals reportedly resulted from the efforts of both partners.

Similar to the diversity of these global themes, Surra and her colleagues have found that many different subcategories are needed to capture the variety of separate reasons that constitute accounts. Accounts obtained from daters (Surra, 1994; Surra & Hughes, 1994) and from newlyweds (Surra et al., 1988) contained a similar diversity of reasons, ranging from 22 to 30 different coding categories, depending upon the particular coding scheme utilized in each study. The different reasons, which fall into four major themes, depart from the courtship script in several ways. Contrary to the courtship script, two of the major themes capture references to the impact of external forces, whereas only one theme is intrapersonal. *Social network* reasons make reference to interaction with or attributions about third parties who are external to the relationship, such as family members, friends, coworkers, or alternative partners. In contrast to the content of scripts, social network reasons are reported throughout the reconstruction of the courtship, and are not concentrated around the wedding. One man, for example, reported the following for the first three months of the relationship, when the chance of marriage increased from 5% to 15%: "I helped her mom move. . . . And her ma talked about her [the dating partner] when she was a kid. We sat and talked and stuff and that's when I started getting an inclination [toward marriage]." Social network reasons constituted nearly 20% of all reasons in a study of daters (Surra & Hughes, 1994) and 25% in a study of newlyweds (Surra at al., 1988). A second theme that contains references to external forces, events, and institutions comprises *circumstantial* reasons (e.g., "all of a sudden being thrown into a small efficiency apartment"). These reasons constituted about 7% of all reasons reported by daters (Surra & Hughes, 1994) and about 5% by newlyweds (Surra et al., 1988).

Courtship scripts do play a part in one type of internal theme we labeled *intrapersonal-normative* reasons, which made up about 1% of all reasons for daters (total number of reasons reported = 2,395; Surra & Hughes, 1994) and 4% for newlyweds. Here, partners make explicit their readiness to wed or evaluate whether their relationship measures up by evaluating it against preexisting norms and standards for relationships (e.g., "I knew she would make a good wife. She was very domestic").

Accounts deviate from courtship scripts in another way as well. They contain many references to lack of harmony between partners and to reversals in the progression of the relationship toward marriage. In Surra et al.'s coding scheme, such negative references to the relationship are captured by subcategories of *dyadic* reasons, which constituted about 70% of all reasons reported by daters (Surra & Hughes, 1994) and 66% by newlyweds (Surra et al., 1988). Dyadic reasons involve interaction between the partners or attributions about the partner or the relationship (e.g., "We just saw each other constantly"; "We just started fighting"; "We had similar goals and stuff"). Contrary to what the courtship script suggests, however, about 3% of all dyadic reasons are statements about conflict, suggesting that some individuals are aware of tensions and arguments exchanged between them. Other data from the graphs and the accounts that accompany them further indicate that regressions in involvement characterize courtship. The proportion of downturns in the graphs of daters averaged 19% of all turning points, with a range from 0% to 67%. As we shall demonstrate below, the average percentage of downturns is even higher in some types of commitments. In addition, reasons from the dyadic subcategory of agreements on stage of involvement, which constitute about 3% of all reasons reported, are references to both progressions and regressions in stage of involvement.

According to the results of research by Orbuch et al. (1993), variation in accounts also is apparent in the courtship narratives reported by people of different races. These researchers found that although African American couples and white couples were equally likely to voice nonromantic or pragmatic themes of courtship, significantly more African American couples than white couples recounted romantic courtships that positively progressed toward marriage. Relief about overcoming obstacles also was expressed more often by African Americans than by whites. The emotional tone of romantic themes or relief about overcoming hardships may reflect subcultural beliefs about the affective quality of courtship and marriage that are more common among African Americans than among whites.

Descriptions of couples' weddings also diverged by race. When African American couples discussed the wedding per se, they focused on the couple and described more drama and tension between partners than did white couples (Veroff et al., 1993a). Among African Americans, the meaning of the wedding ceremony appears to be couple oriented whereas among whites the wedding may serve as an announcement of the couple's social contract with and obligations to the community (Veroff et al., 1993a).

Thus results from two different programs of research on accounts of courtship that employed somewhat different methods point to the same conclusions. Accounts, whether coded globally or divided into separate reasons, are characterized by a great variety of content. The variety itself indicates that accounts of courtship are not very scripted, although scripts may affect some of their content (e.g., Surra et al.'s intrapersonal-normative reasons). Accounts depart from scripts with references to the impact of external forces and the social context on the relationship. Although themes that center on the partners' relationship often are romantic, they are just as often nonromantic, containing references to practical considerations and to overcoming obstacles. In addition, according to accounts, courtships do not always advance smoothly toward the social event of the wedding; rather, their movement frequently is characterized by fits and starts resulting from episodes of conflict, negativity, and ambivalence. Accounts also vary according to the subcultures of the people who report them.

Myth 2: Courting Partners Idealize and Romanticize One Other and Their Relationship

The research on accounts dispels another myth about courtship apparent in American popular culture and in social theory: that courting partners idealize one another and believe that romance and emotional bliss typify their courtship experiences. More than 50 years ago, Waller (1938) characterized courtship as a period when lovers abandon realistic perceptions and idealize each other. At the same time, partners engage in character management; they put their "best foot forward" and carefully control the impressions they convey. Like Waller's depiction of courtship, scripts about courtship advance the idea that courting is harmonious and minimize conflict and tension between partners (Holmberg & Veroff, in press). As we shall see below, courting partners are not so naive; tension and negative beliefs about their relationships are part of the knowledge that many people have about their own relationships during courtship.

In research based upon Veroff et al.'s data, most people discussed some tension in their descriptions of courtship (Orbuch et al., 1993). Tension and negativity can reside in different locations—for example, within one or both of the partners, between the two of them, or with people outside of the relationship (e.g., parents, friends, or coworkers). In only 14% of Veroff et al.'s courtship narratives were no tensions mentioned (Orbuch et al., 1993). In Surra, Jacquet, and Batchelder's (1994) study of daters, conflict accounted for about 3% of all reasons. In addition, references to negative attributions about the relationship made up 11% of all reasons, and negative attributions involving the social network made up 3%.

The following quotation, which is taken from one man's account of his dating history with his partner, Rachel, illustrates the ways in which negative beliefs and internal and external tensions can enter a relationship that previously had evolved with ease:

> The freshman class in [my college] was sporting a healthy crop of young women, and I wasn't sure, I was confused at what I wanted, whether I wanted to be committed to somebody at that point. I went out with a [technician] a couple of times. Rachel . . . kept telling me she wasn't sure whether we should see each other anymore because we weren't getting along. We were just having lots of arguments about trivial things which is fine now and then, but enough's enough.

As this excerpt illustrates, partners are aware of tensions that reside within them, as in the man's own doubts about commitment or his beliefs about his partner's concerns about their not getting along. He also mentioned arguments between them. Threats also came from extrarelationship sources, as in the case where an entering freshman class made available to the man new, attractive alternatives to Rachel. Thus partners understand that their relationships can slip into periods of conflict and negative interaction, even though these periods may be preceded by closeness and enjoyment. Courtships do not always progress positively toward marriage, but may fluctuate between good and bad times or between breaking up and getting back together (see Surra, 1990).

Contrary to prevailing views, the difficulties of courtship are often precipitated by third parties. Research on accounts demonstrates that people understand that social networks play a role in their relationships and that network members may have vested interests in relationships' success or failure. Parents of the partners sometimes oppose a relationship and become an obstacle to surmount (Orbuch et al., 1993; Surra et al., 1988). Partners may consider outside friendships a threat to the relationship; as one woman said, "We started fighting, and at first he paid all his attention to me and then to his friends and forgot about me." Her partner, on the other hand, believed the relationship was threatening his friendships: "Uh, I wanted to be with my friends more 'cause I was with her constantly, and she didn't want me to so we started getting into fights, and it was I just got a feeling of hemmed in already." The accounts of these coupled partners illustrate how negotiating a place for the partner and the relationship in one's existing network may have detrimental consequences for one or both partners.

Although myths about courtship assume that partners romanticize their experience, this was true in only roughly half of the accounts of courtship obtained from the studies examined here. In about an equal number of cases, courtships were accounted for in nonromantic, even mundane, terms. In the research by Orbuch et al. (1993), about 38% of the courtship narratives showed evidence of romantic positive augmentation themes. These themes are characterized by a steadily progressing, positive progression without disruptions in which courtship is described as a quest for love. For 54% of the narratives, however, there was evidence of positive and nonromantic themes; for 56%, pragmatic themes were found.

Likewise, in their study of daters, Surra and Hughes (1994) identified two types of commitment processes: *relationship driven* and *event driven.* Of the entire sample of 108 coupled partners, 43% had relation-ship-driven commitments. These partners had graphs that developed relatively smoothly, positively, and evenly. Only 6% of the turning points in their graphs, on average, were downturns, and the amount of change in each turning point averaged about 10% per month, regardless of whether the turning points were positive or negative. Event-driven commitments, in contrast, developed in more passion-ate and dramatic ways, with many reversals that were subsequently overcome. About 57% of the respondents' accounts fell into this type of commitment process. Partners who had event-driven commit-ments reported graphs that were comparatively rocky, with dramatic changes and many retreats from commitment. On average, about 30% of the turning points in their graphs were downturns, and the absolute amount of change per month across all turning points averaged nearly 20%.

With respect to their accounts, partners in relationship-driven com-mitments referred relatively more often to spending time together and engaging in specific activities together. Women in relationship-driven commitments reported more positive beliefs about their partners and their relationships than did those in event-driven commitments. Com-pared with men in event-driven commitments, men in relationship-driven commitments referred more to the couple's interaction with the network and less to each partner's separate interaction with the network; they also made more positive attributions about friends, family, and other network members. Women in relationship-driven commitments, compared with those in event-driven commitments, also were more similar to their partners on preferences for recreational activities done in their free time, and they reportedly had less conflict over activities and in general.

The accounts of commitment obtained from partners in relation-ship-driven commitments often sounded boring or dull. Indeed, dur-ing interviews with these partners they sometimes referred to their accounts that way (e.g., "I know this sounds boring, but . . . "). One man in a relationship-driven commitment described his turning points this way: "We just got to know each other more, much better. Did a lot of the same things together." Later, he said, "Oh, again, we got to know each other better. We opened up more to each other." Still later: "We spent a lot more time together. We saw a lot more of each other . . . and we still got along quite well." Consistent with the findings just reported, this man's account focused on activities and time together and positive attributions about the relationship.

Analysis of the accounts showed that event-driven partners made more frequent attributions to singular or episodic events and to negative events to explain changes in commitment than did relationship-driven partners. Relative to partners with relationship-driven commitments, men and women with event-driven commitments made more references to conflict episodes and more often made negative attributions about their relationships. In addition, women in event-driven commitments more often mentioned disclosure episodes and made negative comments about the social network. On other measures, event-driven women also were more ambivalent about their relationships than were relationship-driven women. One man in the event-driven group, for instance, explained a decrease in commitment this way: "Well, we had several arguments about our morals and what's right and what's wrong. . . . Just a lot of arguing." Later, however, he said the chance of marriage increased to an even higher point because "my sister got engaged . . . and all my grandparents and her grandparents kept describing her and I as her future husband and future wife. And I like the sound of that."

In contrast to the notion that romantic, passionate courtships foster relationships that thrive, the evidence from the research by Orbuch et al. (1993) and by Surra and Hughes (1994) suggests that more mundane, nonromantic courtships may have more optimistic futures. Results from the study of daters demonstrated that both men and women in relationship-driven commitments were more satisfied with their relationships at the first time of measurement. Women in relationship-driven commitments also had greater increases in relationship satisfaction over a one-year period than did women in event-driven commitments (Surra & Hughes, 1994). Similarly, respondents who had courtship accounts with nonromantic positive themes had higher levels of marital well-being after three years of marriage, compared with those whose accounts did not have such themes (Orbuch et al., 1993).

Myth 3: People Are Naive About Commitment and About Why They Get Committed

Psychologists who study individual and social behavior sometimes assume that people do not understand very well why they do what they do because people do not have cognitive access to the variety of motives and other factors that affect their behavior (e.g., Nisbett & Wilson, 1977). When applied to the study of relationships, this assumption becomes even more entrenched in the minds of laypersons and social scientists alike. The workings of relationships and the attractions between two people are thought to be mysterious and hard for anyone to grasp. With regard to commitment, in particular, it is often believed that individuals make commitment decisions in a haphazard, coincidental, or unaware manner. This myth about commitment sometimes is interpreted further to mean that, because people are naive about commitment, they cannot be taught prior to marriage anything about how to form healthy relationships. Even mental health professionals who work in premarital counseling sometimes scoff at the idea that they can help anyone make good commitment decisions.

The results of research on accounts of commitment suggest, however, that such beliefs are, at best, an overstatement and, at worst, misconceptions. When making commitment decisions, individuals do, in fact, consider many of the same factors that researchers and others who study relationships say they should. Their accounts of the factors they consider suggest that they frequently do so in a deliberate, thoughtful, and conscious manner. The more seriously they are considering marital commitment, the more deliberate their analyses of their commitment seems to become. Even though some individuals arrive at the commitment to wed for simplistic reasons, those reasons fit well with what theorists say are the constructs that are supposed to affect commitment. Thus, for example, people who say, in a cursory manner, "He asked me out so I went," are referring to what theorists would call behavioral interdependence. The woman who said, "My grandmother liked him so I decided to marry him," is referring to social reactions, a key construct in theories of commitment. As we shall see below, however, people do not always act on the information they possess about commitment in the way that theories predict they would.

Although the correspondence between people's subjective analyses of commitment and theories of commitment is far from perfect, there is considerable overlap (for more on this correspondence, see Surra et al., 1994). Reasons for commitment, for example, include references to positive and negative qualities of the relationship, which map onto theoretical constructs that concern attitudes toward the relationship and the satisfactions and rewards derived from it. Similarly, references to behavioral interdependence in accounts have parallels in the structure of outcome interdependence between partners, including spending time together, conflict, enjoyment derived from time together, and beliefs about correspondence of preferences. With respect to social network reasons, attributions about the separateness and jointness of the couple's network, alternative involvements, and positive and negative network attributions resemble the theoretical constructs of network overlap, comparison level for alternatives, and social reactions, respectively. Other reasons evident in accounts have no direct parallels in theories of commitment; these include references to agreements about stages of involvement, met and unmet normative expectations for relationships, and specific interactive episodes involving conflict or disclosures. Apparently, some reasons that are subjectively important to individuals who are deciding about commitment are not addressed by formal theories (see Surra et al., 1994).

Many of the findings regarding accounts and developmental changes in commitment fit well with the results obtained when other, more structured, methods are used by researchers. Using self-reports of scaled items, Rusbult (1980, 1983) found that commitment increases with satisfaction with the relationship; satisfaction, in turn, increases as the rewards derived from the relationship increase. These findings correspond well with findings from accounts showing that positive beliefs about the partnership are associated with increases and progressions in commitment, whereas negative beliefs about the partnership are associated with declines and delays in the development of commitment (Surra et al., 1988; Surra & Hughes, 1991). Rusbult also found that commitment decreases as the perceived quality of alternatives increases. This result jibes with findings from accounts showing that reasons that concern alternative partner involvements are associated with declines in commitment and with commitments that develop more slowly (Surra et al., 1988; Surra & Hughes, 1991).

Data from accounts also indicate that references to partners' joint interaction with the network are connected to increases and accelerations in commitment, but that separate network interaction is associated with decreases and slowdowns in commitment (Surra et al., 1988; Surra & Hughes, 1991). Similar results have been obtained in studies that have employed interaction records; dating partners who became more involved over time have been shown to withdraw from their separate networks (Milardo, Johnson, & Huston, 1983) and form joint couple networks (Milardo, 1982). Structured measures of support for the relationship and interference with it on the part of network members have frequently been found to predict involvement between partners in the same way data from accounts do. (For a review of research on support and interference, see Surra, 1990; for findings on accounts, see Surra et al., 1988; Surra & Hughes, 1991.)

The comparability between findings obtained from accounts and other techniques should dispel the myth that people are not very savvy thinkers about their relationships. The results from studies of accounts, contrary to the myth, indicate that some people explain changes in commitment in much the same way professional researchers do. Furthermore, the correspondence between findings from accounts and other methods lends support to the argument that accounts do, in fact, accurately represent perceptions of actual interactions, occurrences, and beliefs that have occurred over the history of the relationship.

Findings obtained from accounts, however, depart from those derived from studies that have employed more objective methods in one important respect: Data from accounts suggest that people do not always use the evidence available to them in the ways theorists say they do. Many of the data regarding the reasons associated with decreases in and slow development of commitment have been obtained from daters who stayed together over a one-year period (Surra & Hughes, 1994) and newlyweds who did, in fact, eventually wed (Surra et al., 1988). Apparently, some people who continued to date or who wed did so *in spite of the negative evidence that was evident to them.*

This negative evidence included references to unmet normative expectations, to conflict, to negative beliefs about the partnership, to the maintenance of separate networks, and to negative social reactions. The negative evidence, therefore, came from many different sources—intrapersonal, dyadic, and social. Although such factors are associated with changeable commitments that take a long time to develop, some people seem to stay together regardless of their subjective knowledge of negativity. Thus research on accounts points to a crucial question: Why do people who see the bad sides of their relationships continue their involvement in those relationships?

Myth 4: Relationships Begin Anew at Marriage and Have Equal Chances of Becoming Successful Marriages

Social scientists and laypersons alike often assume that the wedding day is a new beginning in the relationship between two individuals and that relationships that go bad do so after the wedding. The fact that all relationships that result in marriage have histories—some very lengthy histories—frequently is ignored. Moreover, the wedding itself is assumed to have a cleansing effect, in which problems that occurred before marriage are erased. The wedding is also assumed to have a homogenizing effect. Because the wedding transforms people and relationships, all couples are able to begin their lives together with equal chances of long-term happiness and relationship survival. Contrary to this view, studies of accounts of how courtships develop suggest that a more continuous view of relationships would be more accurate.

Explanations contained in accounts of courtship obtained from newlyweds do predict the future courses of marital relationships. When newlywed couples described their courtships as positive progressions toward marriage, black husbands and wives reported high levels of marital satisfaction three years later (Veroff et al., 1993b). In a more detailed analysis, narratives of positive relationship development were coded as either romantic or nonromantic stories. Similar to the findings for relationship-driven commitments described above (Surra & Hughes, 1994), nonromantic courtships that progressed positively toward marriage predicted greater satisfaction three years after marriage for African American husbands and wives and for white wives, but not for white husbands (Orbuch et al., 1993). Some reasons for changes in commitment to marriage reported by newlyweds also were related to marital satisfaction after four years of marriage (Surra et al., 1988). Higher marital satisfaction was associated with earlier references to spending time together and to disclosures whereas lower marital satisfaction was related to references to separate and joint network interaction, to alternative partner involvements, and to partners' agreeing on changes in their stage of involvement. Thus romantic, dramatic explanations of courtships are negatively related to the future success of marriages.

Accounts of hardships and external influences on courtship also foretell the quality of marital relationships, although the findings vary by race. The absence of themes about overcoming obstacles predicted marital satisfaction for white couples, but not for African American couples (Orbuch et al., 1993). Even though African Americans more often than whites described their courtships in terms of overcoming obstacles (Orbuch et al., 1993), only talking about finances and children were negatively related to later marital satisfaction, and only for African American males (Veroff et al., 1993b). Partners' feeling little control over their own lives and at the mercy of external forces likewise was associated with lower marital satisfaction several years later (Buehlman, Gottman, & Katz, 1992). Although courtships characterized by hardships and obstacles may bode ill for later relationship satisfaction, partners who are proud that they successfully conquered difficult times have more positive relationship outcomes several years later (Buehlman et al., 1992). Perhaps couples' beliefs that they are able to conquer difficulties temper the effects of courtships filled with barriers and hardships.

Thus findings from research on accounts of courtship suggest that, although the wedding is the beginning of the marriage, it is not the beginning of the relationship. Newlyweds' explanations for why their courtships evolved are connected to their marital outcomes years later. No one has yet studied the linkages between accounts obtained from people *while they were dating* and their subsequent marital success. These kinds of studies are needed to confirm the idea that there is continuity between why people wed and their later marital quality.

The data that are available so far, however, do seriously call into question the belief that relationships get fresh starts when people wed.

CONCLUSIONS

In this chapter, we have defined accounts as relational knowledge structures that are more or less permanent representations of explanations for why events happened as they did. We have argued that accounts are not merely social constructions or scripts, but that they reflect to a large extent people's own understandings of events. We have also argued that the content and structure of accounts changes as new events occur, but that accounts also reflect with some accuracy individuals' perceptions of interactions, feelings, attitudes, and circumstances that affected the events. Explanations contained in accounts capture something of the history of a relationship. Accounts, therefore, are good sources of information about other knowledge structures, including generalized schemata for classes of relationships, self-schemata, and relationship-specific schemata for the target relationship and for the individual's other close relationships. The extent to which accounts are accurate representations, the degree to which they change over time, and the factors that affect these changes are matters in need of much more research.

We then turned our attention to setting straight four myths that frequently underlie scholarly, as well as casual, observations about courtship. The first myth is that courtships follow a fixed script and the same pathways to marriage: boy meets girl, they fall in love, their relationship is harmonious, they get progressively closer, boy proposes to girl, and they and their families are drawn together at the wedding celebration. Contrary to this scripted view, people's accounts contain references to unique, personal events and experiences that vary across people, relationships, and subcultures. In addition, research on accounts indicates that a diversity of circumstances and social forces interact with intra- and interpersonal forces to shape the development of commitment.

The second myth is that courting partners idealize and romanticize one another and their relationships. Counter to this assumption, when daters and newlyweds were asked to describe why their commitments to marrying changed over time, they did not usually tell romantic tales of mutual adoration and unencumbered love. Instead, references to tension and conflict within the partners, between the partners, and between partners and third parties were common, as were references to external hardships to be overcome. Reversals in involvement and regressions in commitment are common. In addition, some commitments develop out of mundane and even practical analyses of the relationship and of the partners' life circumstances. These types of commitments actually seem to fare better with respect to relationship outcomes than do more romantic, dramatic analyses of commitment.

Third, it frequently is assumed that people are naive about relationships generally and that it is impossible to understand the magical and mysterious processes that underlie the development of commitment. Findings from the research on accounts contradict this view. The data suggest that people are frequently quite astute in their analyses of their commitments. Although the overlap between laypersons' attributions and scientific theories about the causes of commitment is incomplete, there is considerable correspondence between the two. The correspondence suggests that individuals who are making commitment decisions think about many of the same causes that theorists say are influential. One place where theories depart from laypersons' thinking about commitment is that individuals do not always act on their analyses in the ways theories would predict. Even though negative beliefs about the relationship, negative social reactions, and other reasons for commitment are associated with slowdowns and reversals in commitment, some individuals who have such information still opt to continue their relationships.

The last myth is that relationships begin anew at marriage and have equal chances of becoming successful marriages. Connected to this myth are beliefs that marital relationships sometimes go sour after the wedding, but that people would not enter marriage knowing that their relationship has serious problems or difficulties. The act of marrying itself is believed to make better any problems that were observed prior to marriage. Contrary to this view, the research on accounts indicates that there is some continuity between explanations for why people wed and marital outcomes. Nonromantic, positively developing commitments, in particular, seem to make for satisfying marriages in the long run (Orbuch et al., 1993). This finding fits well with findings from daters suggesting that smoothly developing commitments that focus on time spent together and positive beliefs about the relationship also are more satisfying over the long term (Surra & Hughes, 1994).

Most important, research on accounts suggests that it is time to discard the view of courtship as a period when partners manage their characters and delude themselves in order to win one another's loyalty and love. Contemporary courtship experiences have more to do with navigating the complexities of individual, interpersonal, social, and circumstantial forces that influence commitment decisions.

REFERENCES

Antaki, C. (1987). Performed and unperformable: A guide to accounts of relationships. In R. Burnett, P. McGhee, & D. Clarke (Eds.), *Accounting for relationships: Explanation, representation, and knowledge* (pp. 97-113). London: Methuen.

Buehlman, K. T., Gottman, J. M., & Katz, L. F. (1992). How a couple views their past predicts their future: Predicting divorce from an oral history interview. *Journal of Family Psychology, 5,* 295-318.

Fehr, B. (1988). Prototypical analysis of the concepts of love and commitment. *Journal of Personality and Social Psychology, 55,* 557-579.

Fletcher, G. J. O., & Fincham, F. D. (1991). Attribution processes in close relationships. In G. J. O. Fletcher & F. D. Fincham (Eds.), *Cognition and close relationships* (pp. 7-35). Hillsdale, NJ: Lawrence Erlbaum.

Gergen, K. J., & Gergen, M. (1987). Narratives as relationships. In R. Burnett, P. McGhee, & D. Clarke (Eds.), *Accounting for relationships: Explanation, representation, and knowledge* (pp. 269-288). London: Methuen.

Harvey, J. H., Orbuch, T. L., & Weber, A. L. (1992). Introduction: Convergence of the attribution and accounts concepts in the study of close relationships. In J. H. Harvey, T. L. Orbuch, & A. L. Weber (Eds.), *Attributions, accounts, and close relationships* (pp. 1-18). New York: Springer-Verlag.

Holmberg, D., & Veroff, J. (in press). Rewriting relationship memories: The effects of courtship and wedding scripts. In G. J. O. Fletcher & J. Fitness (Eds.), *Knowledge structures and interaction in close relationships.* Hillsdale, NJ: Lawrence Erlbaum.

Huston, T. L. (1994). Courtship antecedents of marital satisfaction and love. In R. Erber & R. Gilmour (Eds.), *Theoretical perspectives on personal relationships* (pp. 43-65). Hillsdale, NJ: Lawrence Erlbaum.

McLaughlin, M. L., Cody, M. J., & Read, S. J. (Eds.). (1992). *Explaining one's self to others: Reason-giving in a social context.* Hillsdale, NJ: Lawrence Erlbaum.

Milardo, R. M. (1982). Friendship networks in developing relationships: Converging and diverging social environments. *Social Psychological Quarterly, 45,* 162-172.

Milardo, R. M., Johnson, M. P., & Huston, T. L. (1983). Developing close relationships: Changing patterns of interaction between pair members and social networks. *Journal of Personality and Social Psychology, 44,* 964-976.

Murray, S. L., & Holmes, J. G. (1993). Seeing virtues in faults: Negativity and the transformation of interpersonal narratives in close relationships. *Journal of Personality and Social Psychology, 65,* 707-722.

Nisbett, R. E., & Wilson, T. D. (1977). Telling more than we can know: Verbal reports on mental processes. *Psychological Review, 84,* 231-259.

Orbuch, T. L., Veroff, J., & Holmberg, D. (1993). Becoming a married couple: The emergence of meaning in the first years of marriage. *Journal of Marriage and the Family, 55,* 815-826.

Planalp, S. (1985). Relational schemata: A test of alternative forms of relational knowledge as guides to communication. *Human Communication Research, 12,* 3-29.

Planalp, S., & Rivers, M. (in press). Changes in knowledge of personal relationships. In G. J. O. Fletcher & J. Fitness (Eds.), *Knowledge structures and interaction in close relationships.* Hillsdale, NJ: Lawrence Erlbaum.

Planalp, S., & Surra, C. A. (1992). The role of account-making in the growth and deterioration of close relationships. In J. H. Harvey, T. L. Orbuch, & A. L. Weber (Eds.), *Attributions, accounts, and close relationships* (pp. 71-92). New York: Springer-Verlag.

Ross, M. A. (1989). The relation of implicit theories to the construction of personal histories. *Psychological Review, 96,* 341-357.

Rusbult, C. E. (1980). Commitment and satisfaction in romantic associations: A test of the investment model. *Journal of Experimental Social Psychology, 16,* 172-186.

Rusbult, C. E. (1983). A longitudinal test of the investment model: The development (and deterioration) of satisfaction and commitment in heterosexual involvements. *Journal of Personality and Social Psychology, 45,* 101-117.

Scott, M. B., & Lyman, S. M. (1968). Accounts. *American Sociological Review, 33,* 46-62.

Surra, C. A. (1987). Reasons for changes in commitment: Variations by courtship type. *Journal of Social and Personal Relationships, 4,* 17-33.

Surra, C. A. (1990). Research and theory on mate selection and premarital relationships in the 1980's. *Journal of Marriage and the Family, 52,* 844-865.

Surra, C. A. (1994). *Turning point coding manual IV: Coding rules and definitions.* Unpublished manuscript, The University of Texas at Austin.

Surra, C. A., Arizzi, P., & Asmussen, L. A. (1988). The association between reasons for commitment and the development and outcome of marital relationships. *Journal of Social and Personal Relationships, 5,* 47-63.

Surra, C. A., & Bohman, T. (1991). The development of close relationships: A cognitive perspective. In G. J. O. Fletcher & F. D. Fincham (Eds.), *Cognition in close relationships* (pp. 281-305). Hillsdale, NJ: Lawrence Erlbaum.

Surra, C. A., & Hughes, D. (1991, November). *Reasons for commitment and commitment processes.* Paper presented at the meeting of the National Council on Family Relations, Denver.

Surra, C. A., & Hughes, D. (1994). *Commitment processes in the development of premarital relationships.* Manuscript submitted for publication.

Surra, C. A., & Huston, T. L. (1987). Mate selection as a social transition. In D. Perlman & S. Duck (Eds.), *Intimate relations: Development, dynamics, and deterioration* (pp. 88-120). Newbury Park, CA: Sage.

Surra, C. A., Jacquet, S. E., & Batchelder, M. L. (1994). *Commitment to marriage: A phenomenological approach.* Unpublished manuscript.

Surra, C. A., & Milardo, R. M. (1991). The social psychological context of developing relationships: Interactive and psychological networks. In W. H. Jones & D. Perlman (Eds.), *Advances in personal relationships* (Vol. 3, pp. 1-36). London: Kingsley.

Veroff, J., Sutherland, L., Chadiha, L., & Ortega, R. M. (1993a). Newlyweds tell their stories: A narrative method for assessing marital experiences. *Journal of Social and Personal Relationships, 10,* 437-457.

Veroff, J., Sutherland, L., Chadiha, L., & Ortega, R. M. (1993b). Predicting marital quality with narrative assessments of marital experience. *Journal of Marriage and the Family, 55,* 326-337.

Waller, W. (1938). *The family.* New York: Cordon.

Webster's new twentieth century dictionary of the English language (2nd ed.). (1979). New York: Simon & Schuster.

Wyer, R. S., & Srull, T. K. (1986). Human cognition in its social context. *Psychological Review, 3,* 322-359.

Family Relationships in Process

When we think of family relationships in process, we view the events and relationships among family members as dynamic, ongoing, ever-changing, yet continuous. A conceptual commitment to examining family relationships in process entails a certain methodological commitment. The chapters in this section employ two of the most insightful methods developed in the social sciences for examining family relationships in process. The first focuses on examining families at major transition points. In Chapter 5, Ted Huston and Anita Vangelisti examine the transition to parenthood and its impact on marital processes. In Chapter 8, Sandra Metts and William Cupach examine another common family transition—that involving a renegotiation of the relationship between former married partners.

The second method useful for examining family relationships in process involves an emphasis on interaction, or the give-and-take of focused responsive behavior among family members. Using this method, researchers explore family relationships by examining family members' intertwined verbal and nonverbal behaviors. In Chapter 6, Samuel Vuchinich and Joseph Angelelli focus on family interaction during problem solving, whereas Susan Gano-Phillips and Frank Fincham, in Chapter 7, explore the effects of family conflict on children's adjustment to divorce.

As we did for Part I, we have organized the chapters in Part II within a loose developmental framework. The section moves from an examination of the effects of parenthood on marital outcomes to problem-solving discussions in families with 10-year-olds. Subsequently, the section takes up the issues of the effects of family conflict and divorce on outcomes for children and how partners relate to one another after divorce.

For a number of years, the extant social science literature held a monolithic, negative view of parenthood. Parenthood was believed to create marital distress and to represent a crisis in the relationship between marital partners. In Chapter 5, Huston and Vangelisti summarize the results of a longitudinal investigation into the transition to parenthood. They argue that a paradigm shift is currently taking place, and that parenthood is being reconceptualized as creating a mix of consequences that produce a variety of adjustments and adaptations for couples, only some of which are negative. Huston and Vangelisti also identify the salient conceptual, design, and measurement issues that need to be addressed if we want to determine how parenthood affects marital well-being.

Parenthood may not be a crisis, but with the birth of a child the family clearly undergoes profound transformations. When the marital dyad (husband-wife) becomes a family triad (mother-father-child), the number of potential family relationships increases about 300%. To that one dyad of husband and wife, the family now adds the mother-child, father-child, and mother-father-child constellations. The family therapy literature generally emphasizes the importance of maintaining the mother-father coalition during family problem solving to maintain balance in the system. In Chapter 6, Vuchinich and Angelelli argue, however, that the optimal mother-father coalition is neither too strong nor too weak. These authors demonstrate how to measure various family coalitions reliably and how to link various coalitions to family problem-solving effectiveness.

Although a large body of research now exists linking divorce to a variety of childhood problems, Gano-Phillips and Fincham argue in Chapter 7 that these effects may not be caused by divorce per se, but by factors associated with divorce. Of particular concern is family conflict. After offering an overview of different types of family conflict (i.e., interparental, parent-child, and sibling), these authors outline four major issues that need to be addressed if we are to advance our understanding of the effects of family conflict on outcomes for children. Each of these four factors may help to clarify the relationship between family conflict and child outcomes.

Metts and Cupach are interested in what happens to relationships between former married partners after divorce. In Chapter 8, these authors argue that there is no culturally shared frame for postdivorce relationships. They then characterize the nature and quality of postdivorce relationships and identify the factors that contribute to the formation of these associations.

How Parenthood Affects Marriage

TED L. HUSTON
ANITA L. VANGELISTI

This chapter summarizes the results of a longitudinal study of the transition to parenthood and challenges the paradigm that presumes that parenthood generally causes a decline in marital satisfaction. Most of the writing on the transition to parenthood has emphasized its problematic and crisis elements. Researchers have assumed that the "big changes" that accompany parenthood and the stresses that attend to incorporating a child into a marriage erode marital well-being. The declines in marital satisfaction that sometimes occur from before to after childbirth have been readily interpreted as prima facie evidence that parenthood makes it more difficult for couples to maintain mutually satisfying marriages. There can be no doubt that marital lifestyles change with parenthood. However, as scholars have begun to examine correlates of the direction and extent of change in satisfaction following the birth of a child, they have increasingly recognized that parenthood may enhance some marriages, undermine others, and have little effect on still others (Belsky & Kelly, 1994; Cowan & Cowan, 1992).

The literature on the transition to parenthood, in short, is slowly undergoing a paradigm shift. Beginning with Hill's (1949) suggestion

AUTHORS' NOTE: Work on this chapter was supported by grants from the National Science Foundation (SBR-9311846) and the National Institute of Mental Health (MH 33938), Ted L. Huston, principal investigator.

that parenthood sets the stage for crisis and LeMasters's (1957) early study supporting Hill's prognostication, the premise that parenthood creates marital distress became the battle cry of researchers over the next 25 years (although occasionally a researcher, e.g., Russell, 1974, would come forward to propose that parenthood brings forth compensating gratifications). Longitudinal studies initiated in the early 1980s, however, began to create cracks in this monolithic negative view of parenthood. The research area is now primed to reconceptualize parenthood as creating a mix of consequences that produce a variety of adjustments and adaptations, only some of which lead to distress (e.g., Belsky, 1985; Cowan & Cowan, 1989; Fitzpatrick, Vangelisti, & Firman, 1994; McHale & Huston, 1985; White & Booth, 1985). In this chapter, we identify some of the larger conceptual, design, and measurement issues that researchers need to address if they are to delineate the conditions under which, and the ways in which, parenthood affects marital well-being. We then present an overview of our own longitudinal study of couples and place our work within the larger body of research on the effects of parenthood on marriage.

THEORETICAL AND METHODOLOGICAL ISSUES IN ANALYZING THE IMPACT OF PARENTHOOD ON MARRIAGE

Establishing Parenthood as a Causal Agent

The literature on the transition to parenthood has implemented successively more sophisticated strategies for establishing the role parenthood plays in marital life. Cook and Campbell (1979) identify three hallmarks of causal explanation that can be used to characterize the evolution of work on the transition to parenthood. Establishing that the presumed cause (parenthood) covaries with its effect (marital quality) is the first criterion for establishing causality. Studies comparing parents and nonparents at a single point in time meet this criterion (e.g., Figley, 1973; Miller, 1976). Cross-sectional studies that find parents less happily married than nonparents, however, are marked by three problems. First, couples who become parents may differ in satisfaction independent of their parental status. Parenthood often occurs early in marriage and without careful planning, and thus the lesser satisfaction of couples who become parents may have been present prior to parenthood. It is also possible, even if parenthood creates a greater propensity for the development of distress, that this tendency is limited to couples who become parents without already having built a strong foundation for their relationship. Second, because "the presence of a child or children deters many unhappily married persons from divorcing" (Glenn & McLanahan, 1982, p. 69; see also, Waite, Haggstrom, & Kanouse, 1985), any group of parents is likely to include a relatively large number of unhappy couples reluctant to subject their children to divorce (White, Booth, & Edwards, 1986). Third, couples who become parents may differ from nonparents in other ways that are reflected in their satisfaction (Menaghan, 1982). A cross-sectional comparison of married couples who are parents with those who are nonparents, for example, would include sets of couples who were married at different ages and who have been married different lengths of time. The parent group is apt to be younger and married for a shorter length of time than the nonparent group, and these factors, rather than parenthood status, may account for group differences in marital satisfaction or marital stability (Moore & Waite, 1981).

Cook and Campbell (1979) identify the temporal precedence of the putative cause as the second criterion for establishing its causal significance. With data gathered from couples before and after parenthood, longitudinal designs establish the temporal precedence of the putative cause. In the most common longitudinal design, a single group of couples in which the wives are pregnant is followed from before to after the births of the children. These studies typically (Belsky, Lang, & Rovine, 1985; Belsky, Spanier, & Rovine, 1983; Cowan et al., 1985; Feldman & Nash, 1984; Ruble, Fleming, Hackel, & Stangor, 1988; Tomlinson, 1987), although not invariably (Meyerowitz & Feldman, 1966; Miller & Sollie, 1980; Waldron & Routh, 1981; Wallace & Gotlib, 1990), report linear declines in marital well-being from before to after childbirth (but see Box 5.1). Although the designs used in most longitudinal investigations provide information that was unavailable in earlier cross-sectional studies, they have at least three limitations

All but a few (Belsky, Lang, & Rovine, 1985; Feldman & Nash, 1984; Miller & Sollie, 1980; Ruble, Fleming, Hackel, & Stangor, 1988) of the studies that report declines in marital satisfaction used scales that confound behavioral changes in marriage with global assessments of satisfaction. Standard measures of marital adjustment (e.g., Locke & Wallace, 1959; Spanier, 1976) define adjustment, in part, by reference to spouses' assessments of the extent to which they agree on various matters, how often they experience conflict, and how affectionate they are with each other. As a consequence, it is difficult to discern whether changes in adjustment, as assessed by these measures, reflect changes in the spouses' feelings toward each other or changes in their behavior (e.g., amount of companionship, conflict, and frequency of sexual activity). Because the terms *adjustment* and *satisfaction* are often used interchangeably, so-called declines in satisfaction may actually represent changes in marital behavior patterns (for commentaries on this issue, see Belsky et al., 1985; Fincham & Bradbury, 1987; Huston, McHale, & Crouter, 1986; MacDermid, Huston, & McHale, 1990; McHale & Huston, 1985).

Box 5.1. Confounding Marital Satisfaction and Behavior in Measures of Marital Adjustment

(Cook & Campbell, 1979). First, couples about to become parents may be, as a consequence of their pregnancies, temporarily happier with their marriages; thus changes in marital satisfaction may reflect regression toward the mean (regression effects). Second, as couples settle into marriage, their satisfaction may decline over time regardless of whether they become parents (maturation effects). This is important because a sizable proportion of couples become parents during the first few years of marriage, a period over which declines in satisfaction are normative. Third, the before/after design used in the studies that investigate the impact of parenthood on marriage, coupled with the participants' awareness of the general purposes of the investigation, may affect the data (testing effects).

The third criterion for establishing causality is the exclusion of alternative explanations for the putative cause-effect relationship (Cook & Campbell, 1979). The use of a comparison group of couples who do not make the transition to parenthood provides one way of eliminating alternative explanations such as maturation effects. The few studies that have included comparison groups of couples who have not made the transition over the same period provide little support for the idea that parenthood produces a decline in marital satisfaction. Couples become less satisfied with their marriages over time, regardless of whether they become parents (Cowan & Cowan, 1989; MacDermid, Huston, & McHale, 1990; McHale & Huston, 1985; White & Booth, 1985). Ryder (1973), the first researcher to use a comparison group, found that wives (but not husbands) who became parents declined in adjustment; however, he used the Locke-Wallace (1959) scale (see Box 5.1). White and Booth (1985) assessed marital satisfaction using a purely evaluative index in their three-year longitudinal study. They found that people who became parents did not differ from those who remained childless, either before or after the former group made the transition to parenthood. Both groups experienced declines in satisfaction, however, over the three years. Cowan and Cowan (1989) followed couples over two years and reported declines in satisfaction among couples who became parents, using the Spanier (1976) Dyadic Adjustment Scale. These researchers, however, did not compare the parenthood group directly with those who remained childless.

Temporal Aspects of the Impact of Parenthood on Marriage

Practical considerations have led most researchers to gather data on one or two occasions within a year after childbirth from couples who have become parents. Because the processes through which parenthood affects marital well-being are poorly understood, social scientists have given little attention to the timing of marital assessments. Kelly and McGrath (1988) argue that researchers need to incorporate temporal parameters into their conceptualization of causal agents and to articulate the hypothesized temporal path created by the putative cause. They describe a variety of ways an event, X (e.g., the birth of a child) might affect an outcome, Y (e.g., marital satisfaction).

Figures 5.1a and 5.1b portray parenthood as creating an immediate effect that persists over time in the first case and fades in the second.

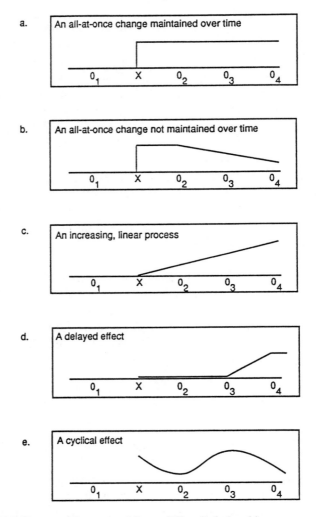

Figure 5.1. Temporal Patterns of Cause-Effect Relationships
SOURCE: Adapted from Kelly and McGrath (1988).

Research that uses data gathered from parents soon after childbirth assumes parenthood has an almost immediate impact. Much of this research, even that of a longitudinal nature, reports data gathered from new parents on only one or two occasions relatively soon after the birth of the first child. As a consequence, the studies may pick up short-term fluctuations in satisfaction, but may fail to detect more slowly emerging effects of parenthood. Thus, although this literature tends to characterize parenthood as a "crisis," it is unclear whether the crisis and its effects dissipate over time (Figure 5.1b) or whether the marital patterns stimulated by the crisis become ongoing and create long-lasting change in marital well-being (Figure 5.1a). Figure 5.1c suggests another possible pattern. Here, the effect of parenthood on marital satisfaction increases gradually over time. For example, if parenthood increases stress and conflict in marriage (Hill, 1949; Le-Masters, 1957), the impact of the conflictual and negative patterns may cumulate with time and erode satisfaction. On the other hand, parenthood may bring with it a sense of elation that might be reflected in a short-lived upswing in satisfaction, followed by a decline (see Miller & Sollie, 1980; Wallace & Gotlib, 1990). Figure 5.1d, in contrast, shows parenthood having a delayed impact on marriage. The influence of parenthood on marital satisfaction may surface years later, for example, as a consequence of spouses' having very different religious values or ideas about child rearing. Finally, Figure 5.1e shows a cyclical pattern reflecting modulations in spouses' marital satisfaction over time. Marital satisfaction contains both a relatively stable, traitlike component and a statelike element that resonates to the vicissitudes of day-to-day life (Robins, 1990; Wiggins, 1979). If the cyclical pattern of spouses' satisfaction is similar across couples, different conclusions might be reached about the impact of parenthood, depending on the timing of measurement. If the pattern is not timed similarly across couples, however, the effects of parenthood are likely to be masked. Parenthood could create highs and lows in the lives of couples, but the timing of these highs and lows may be largely idiosyncratic.

Links Among Parenthood, Marital Patterns, and Satisfaction

Although the birth of a couple's first child provides a discrete event that marks the onset of parenthood, the transition to parenthood is a process that takes place over a more extended period of time. A couple can anticipate their child's birth date and, accordingly, begin to make adjustments in their lifestyle long before the baby is born. Pregnancy may encourage spouses to be gentle and affectionate with each other, creating a temporary elevation in the expression of positive feelings. Parenthood also may bring about changes in marital role patterns, the extent to which spouses participate in enjoyable leisure activities together, and the involvement of the spouses with friends and kin.

These considerations suggest that parenthood "as a cause" can be viewed in a number of different ways. Following Cook and Campbell (1979), parenthood can be taken as a "macro" event that sets in motion a number of other adjustments of a macro nature (e.g., changes in spouses' labor force participation or economic well-being) that may affect marital satisfaction. According to Cook and Campbell, macro events may also set in motion other, more specific, events—referred to as "micromediational" events—that affect the satisfactoriness of the marriage. Thus, for example, parenthood may be the root cause of alterations in the division of household labor, sleep deficits, increases in the amount of stress spouses experience, or decreases in the opportunity for spouses to pursue enjoyable leisure activities—any of which may undermine partners' sense of satisfaction with their marriage. It is critical to identify how parenthood affects the day-to-day lives of marital couples and to pinpoint which of these changes make differences in how spouses come to feel about each other and their marriage. Parenthood may be a "big change" for many couples, as Cowan and Cowan (1992) suggest, but whether, on balance it is an unwelcome change for marriage is another matter.

THE PAIR PROJECT AND
THE TRANSITION TO PARENTHOOD

The PAIR (Processes of Adaptation in Intimate Relationships) project, a two-year longitudinal study of newlyweds, followed couples from shortly after they were married at yearly intervals until the beginning of their third year of marriage. Data were gathered initially approximately 2 months after couples were wed; the second and third

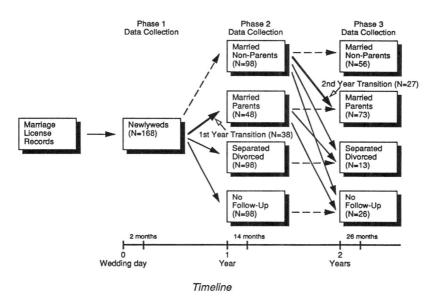

Figure 5.2. PAIR Project: Tracking Marital Transitions Over Time

phases took place 14 months and 26 months into marriage. The initial sample, drawn from marriage license records in four counties in central Pennsylvania, consisted of 168 first-time married couples, 129 of whom stayed married and were followed across all three phases of the study. Because many of the couples became parents while the study was being carried out, what was originally a study of adaptation in the early years of marriage serendipitously also became a study of the transition to parenthood. Figure 5.2 shows the progression of couples across time in terms of marital and parental status. Of the couples who were followed throughout the course of the study, 73 (57%) became parents by the beginning of their third year of marriage. Ten couples had children before we interviewed them the first time as newlyweds (before Phase 1), 38 became parents between Phase 1 and Phase 2, and another 27 became parents between Phases 2 and 3.

The study has several design strengths that are unusual for research on the transition to parenthood. First, we are able to compare couples about to become parents to childless couples, making it possible to see whether parents-to-be differ from nonparents before parenthood with regard to features of their marriages. Second, the comparisons over time of couples who become parents with those who do not become parents make it possible to determine whether it is parenthood, rather than the mere passage of time, that accounts for changes in the quality of marriage. Third, it is possible to examine the influence of the timing of parenthood on marriage. Fourth, participants were not sensitized to the nature of the investigation. The issue of parenthood was never identified to the participants as a focal point of the research, nor was the timing of births used to determine data collection periods. It is important, however, to recognize that this study, like most other longitudinal studies, examines a relatively short temporal interval.

The approach to collecting data used in the PAIR project was developed to overcome problems associated with global self-reports of marital patterns—such as who does what around the house or how much time spouses spend together in leisure activities—because it was assumed that such reports would be informed as much by beliefs about cultural norms and about desirable patterns as by the actual behavior patterns. Thus, for example, when asked to provide estimates of how much each partner does around the house, people subscribing to egalitarian gender role attitudes may minimize inequities, particularly if they are in love with their spouses. To make these kinds of overall estimates with any accuracy, individuals must (a) identify the activities and behaviors relevant to the category, (b) keep track of both their own and their spouses' participation in the activities over time, and (c) make judgments regarding how the patterns relate to the options presented to them by the researcher. Furthermore, different respondents must use the same criteria in identifying and weighing activities, be equally attuned to keeping track of both their own and their spouses' activities, use the same logic in converting their estimates to the metric used by the investigator, and be able to overcome any motivations to distort the report (Huston & Robins, 1982; Robins, 1990; Schwarz, 1990).

To minimize these problems, insofar as possible, we developed a telephone interview technique that required husbands and wives to provide information about specific activities they performed and interaction events that took place during the 24-hour period ending shortly before the call (see Huston, Robins, Atkinson, & McHale, 1987). Calls were made to each spousal pair on nine evenings during each phase of data collection, and the responses were aggregated to create profiles of various aspects of their marriage.

Husbands and wives both provided data about their participation in regard to a comprehensive list of 26 household activities, 14 child-care tasks, and more than 50 leisure activities. The questions were organized into groups based on their similarity, such that, for example, activities relating to "food preparation/cleanup" were clustered together, as were those associated with "playing sports and games." Spouses were asked to examine, in turn, each cluster of activities and to indicate for any activity they participated in whether or not they did the activity with their partners. In the case of leisure activities, each spouse was also asked to indicate whether anyone other than his or her partner participated in the activity and, if so, the nature of the respondent's relationship with that person. These data enable us to examine changes in instrumental and leisure patterns in marriage over time and thereby distinguish changes associated with parenthood from changes that take place independent of parenthood.

We also sought to capture the affective tone of the marital relationship by having spouses provide reports concerning the occurrence of each of 16 specific socioemotional events, such as their spouses saying, "I love you," or registering criticisms or complaints. These interpersonal events were subsequently grouped, based on a series of factor analyses, into three types of events: (a) the expression of affection, (b) negativity, and (c) sexual interest (Huston & Vangelisti, 1991).

The telephone interview procedures, by aggregating data about a variety of aspects of marriage across a representative sample of days, make it possible to examine a wide range of ways married life might change when couples become parents. Thus we were in a position to identify more specifically than heretofore possible what changes take place with parenthood and to examine how these changes mediate connections between parenthood and marital satisfaction and love.

The measures of marital satisfaction and love used in the study focus entirely on spouses' global assessments of their relationship so as to avoid confounding assessments of changes in behavioral patterns with spouses' evaluations of their marriage (see Box 5.1). The measures, as a consequence, allow us to determine empirically the behavioral features of marriage that both change with parenthood and covary with husbands' and wives' subjective assessments of their marriage.

MARITAL BEHAVIOR PATTERNS ASSOCIATED WITH THE TRANSITION TO PARENTHOOD

The marital behavioral patterns that we examine in connection with parenthood are broken down into three domains: division of labor, leisure and companionship, and socioemotional behavior (see Huston, McHale, & Crouter, 1986). This categorization centers attention, first, on whether parenthood traditionalizes marital roles; then, on whether parenthood undermines companionship; and finally, on whether it alters the affective tone of spouses' day-to-day lives together. The behavioral changes to be noted in each of these domains parallel changes found by previous research in spouses' psychological conceptions of their roles—both as parents and as romantic partners (Belsky et al., 1983; Cowan et al., 1985).

Division of Labor

The way couples organize their life together changes considerably upon the birth of a child. When wives become mothers, they typically reconfigure their commitments, often leaving the world of paid work and centering their day-to-day lives on the family. In contrast, husbands' participation in the work world changes minimally when they become fathers. The dramatic reconfiguration of their wives' commitments, however, changes the context within which new fathers live their daily lives at home.

The transition to parenthood, as shown in Figure 5.3, brings with it a striking expansion in the extent to which spouses, particularly wives, are involved in instrumental activities around the house. The relative size of the pie charts reflects the increase in the amount of household tasks couples carry out subsequent to parenthood. The birth of a child adds a significant new dimension to the marital

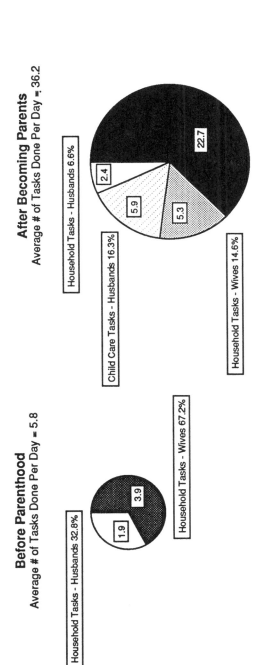

Before Parenthood
Average # of Tasks Done Per Day = 5.8

Household Tasks - Husbands 32.8%

1.9

3.9

Household Tasks - Wives 67.2%

After Becoming Parents
Average # of Tasks Done Per Day = 36.2

Household Tasks - Husbands 6.6%

Child Care Tasks - Husbands 16.3%

2.4

5.9

5.3

22.7

Household Tasks - Wives 14.6%

Child Care Tasks - Wives 62.5%

Figure 5.3. Division of Household Labor and Child Care

159

lifestyle. Inasmuch as parents feed, clothe, bathe, and nurture their new baby, the division of labor, both inside and outside the home, must be modified. Inside the home, new parents obviously have to deal with the demands of caring for their baby. Outside the home, these same demands may impinge upon one or both spouses' paid work activities. Typically, most of the burden of child care falls upon wives (Cowan et al., 1985; Ruble et al., 1988). As a group, wives who became parents in our sample reduced their involvement in work for pay outside the home and increased their involvement in household work (MacDermid et al., 1990). Mothers perform about 80% of all child-care duties.

In the vast majority of couples, husbands maintain their role in the paid labor force and, in cases where the wife leaves the labor force, become the sole breadwinner, at least temporarily. The number of hours husbands spend engaged in paid work and participating in household tasks does not change with the transition to parenthood. Their overall involvement in work activities at home, however, increases slightly when they become fathers, because they perform about 20% of the child-care tasks.

Leisure and Companionship

Although the total amount of time that parents and nonparents engaged in leisure activities does not differ, the addition of a child to the marriage often shapes the type of leisure activities that spouses are able to enjoy. As Figure 5.4 shows, the amount of time spouses spend together as a couple engaged in leisure activities (without their child) decreases drastically once they become parents. Most of the leisure time they have together is spent with their new baby. Compared with parents, spouses who do not have children tend to have a great deal of flexibility with regard to the way they structure their leisure time. They can engage in leisure activities together or separately, and they can select activities that are preferred by one, the other, or both partners. More important, they can freely participate in activities that would be difficult, if not impossible, to do with children. Parents, in contrast, are often limited to leisure pursuits that allow them simultaneously to attend to the needs of their child (MacDermid

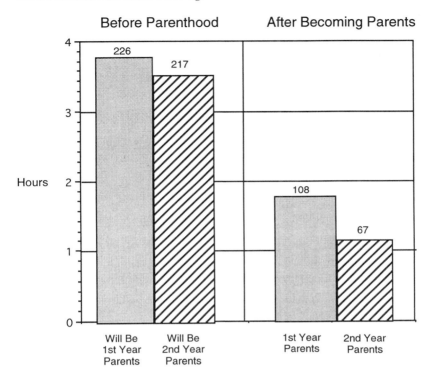

Figure 5.4. Marital Companionship: Joint Leisure Without Child
(minutes per day)

et al., 1990; McHale & Huston, 1985). If a parent participates in leisure
activities apart from his or her spouse, he or she must do something
that can be done with the child, persuade the partner to "watch the
baby," or ask a third party to do the child care. Often, even when
parents engage in leisure together, one or both of them must keep a
constant eye on the child.

On the surface, the fact that wives do the vast majority of child care
suggests that their leisure might be more restricted by the birth of a
child than that of their husbands. After all, much of wives' time is
occupied doing instrumental activities in the home. New fathers,
however, also have limited opportunities to engage in preferred leisure activities. An interesting pattern of results emerges when leisure

is examined in terms of (a) whether it is performed jointly or separately, and (b) the extent to which spouses do activities enjoyed by the father, the mother, or both partners (Crawford & Huston, 1993). New fathers spend less time in leisure activities apart from their spouses than do new mothers or nonparents. Mothers, in contrast, spend more time away from their husbands engaged in their own preferred leisure activities. Fatherhood reduces the opportunity for husbands to enjoy independent leisure activities. It is also associated with a decrease in the amount of time fathers spend in leisure pursuits that both they and their wives enjoy. For mothers, parenthood affords greater opportunities to engage in activities they like, but their husbands dislike.

Wives' ability to pursue preferred leisure activities may be due, in part, to the level of enjoyment new mothers experience when they spend leisure time with kin. It may be that new mothers like to do things with their own mothers and kin, and that these activities can be comfortably done with children, regardless of whether the new fathers are involved. As a consequence, the transition to parenthood may allow new mothers to engage in leisure activities apart from their husbands (but with their kin) while simultaneously taking care of the baby. Indeed, the amount of leisure time wives spend with kin is more stable for parents than it is for nonparents (McHale & Huston, 1985). In contrast, husbands' preferred leisure may focus more on their friendships and less on their kin relationships. Assuming that the activities husbands engage in with their friends are less baby centered than are wives' activities with kin, the birth of a baby is likely to restrict the amount of time husbands are able to spend doing preferred leisure activities. Furthermore, when wives spend much of their day apart from their spouses caring for their children, they may be displeased if their husbands choose to engage in leisure activities with friends. In most cases, such choices not only separate husbands from their wives and children, they allow husbands to relax and engage in leisure while their wives continue to perform child-care duties. Although a husband may feel he deserves this type of leisure after spending much of his day engaged in paid labor, his wife, who has spent much of her day working at home, is likely to see the situation as inequitable.

Socioemotional Behavior

Spouses' increased child-care responsibilities not only place limitations on the types of leisure activities in which they engage, they also restrict the amount of time spouses have to interact with each other as a couple. Indeed, parents spend less time conversing with each other than do nonparents (McHale & Huston, 1985). Given the centrality of communication to spouses' marital satisfaction (for a review, see Noller & Fitzpatrick, 1990), this reported decrease in partners' interaction time does not bode well for the quality of their marriage. For instance, we might expect parents to report that their partners engage in fewer positive behaviors than do nonparents. We may reason that the lack of interaction time experienced by parents, combined with their added child-care responsibilities, discourages them from taking the time and effort to engage in positive behaviors toward one another (Belsky et al., 1983). Data from the PAIR project, however, suggest that parents and nonparents do not differ in terms of the amount of affection they express in their marriages (MacDermid et al., 1990). New parents seem to make the most of their limited time together. Furthermore, the data show that in some cases the amount of affection that husbands express toward their wives actually increases during the transition to parenthood (McHale & Huston, 1985). Husbands who are married to wives who are pregnant either prior to or shortly after marriage are particularly affectionate toward their wives during pregnancy. Although these husbands decrease their affection subsequent to childbirth, they do not become less affectionate than husbands of wives who do not give birth during the first year of marriage.

Similarly, the frequency of negative behaviors in marriage does not differ for parents and nonparents—either before or after the parent group experiences the birth of their child (MacDermid et al., 1990). Because negativity is a particularly sensitive barometer of spouses' marital satisfaction (e.g., Broderick & O'Leary, 1986; Jacobson, Waldron, & Moore, 1980; Wills, Weiss, & Patterson, 1974), this finding lends further credence to the conceptualization of parenthood as a "change" rather than a "crisis" in marriage. Most parents do not seem to react to their more restricted schedules by increasing their negativity toward each other. Instead, they adjust by shifting their lifestyle toward a working partnership (Belsky et al., 1983): Wives' work becomes more focused on the child, husbands appear to sacrifice some of their preferred leisure activities, and both parents maintain levels of socioemotional behavior similar to those maintained by nonparent couples.

DOES PARENTHOOD NEGATIVELY INFLUENCE SPOUSES' EVALUATIONS OF MARITAL QUALITY?

Because the changes that accompany parenthood are multifaceted and occur in different domains of marriage, parents' evaluations of their relationship may differ from one domain to another. If changes in particular aspects of the relationship over time are unrelated to the transition to parenthood, then parenthood should not affect spouses' evaluations of those domains. It is also important to note that the evaluation of a given domain may or may not be associated with spouses' more global assessments of their relationship. It is possible, for instance, that parents who are relatively dissatisfied with the amount of leisure time they have together (an evaluation of a specific domain) may still be very satisfied or very much in love with each other (global evaluations of the relationship). If spouses' satisfaction with leisure has little bearing on their feelings of love, changes in satisfaction with the former will have little impact on the latter.

Division of Labor

Although satisfaction with the way household tasks are divided does not change over time for couples who remain childless, it changes a great deal for many of those who become parents (Vangelisti & Huston, 1994). Wives who give birth prior to their first wedding anniversaries show a sharp decline in satisfaction with the division of household tasks after a year of marriage, and this decline continues between their first and second wedding anniversaries. Because these wives become mothers so soon after they marry, they have little time to adjust to the changes that most of them experience in the division of household labor when they become parents. This limited period of adjustment, combined with the decreased time they have to interact with their husbands, may restrict their ability to modify their husbands' role expectations (see, e.g., Stamp, 1994). When childbirth is postponed until later, between the first and second wedding anniversaries, wives do not report a significant decline in their satisfaction with the division of household tasks.

It is important to note that for wives, decreases in satisfaction with the division of household labor are not associated with declines in martial satisfaction or their love for their husbands (see Ruble et al., 1988). Wives apparently separate their evaluation of the instrumental realm of their marriage from their overall assessment of the marital relationship. The same cannot be said of husbands. Regardless of whether they become fathers during the first or second year of marriage, husbands become less satisfied with how work is divided around the house after the transition to parenthood. Moreover, for husbands, dissatisfaction with the division of labor tasks is associated with declines in their love for their wives. Husbands' evaluation of this instrumental domain is not associated with the amount of household work done by their wives, but rather with the amount that the husbands themselves do. Those who do more household work are less satisfied with the way the tasks are distributed. This finding suggests that drawing husbands into household work creates dissatisfaction with the division of labor for husbands, which in turn is reflected in a reduction in their overall satisfaction with marriage.

Leisure and Companionship

The extent to which husbands are satisfied with the opportunities they have to pursue independent leisure activities and with the amount of time they have available to spend in leisure with their wives declines with time, regardless of whether the couple makes the transition to parenthood (Vangelisti & Huston, 1994). The decline in satisfaction with companionship is greater, however, for husbands who become fathers. Similarly, wives who become mothers experience more of a decline in satisfaction with the amount of time they have to pursue independent leisure than do those who do not become mothers.

Although these findings suggest that the restrictions attendant to parenthood bring with them feelings of disenchantment, we found no evidence supporting the idea that these feelings spill over to create declines in overall satisfaction or love. The lack of association between unhappiness about reduced companionship and more general feelings about the relationship may be explained, in part, by spouses' recognition that the decrease in companionship is an inevitable concomitant of parenthood. If spouses were to attribute the reduced companionship to decreased desire on the part of their partners to do things together, their disenchantment with their levels of companionship might be more reflective of their general evaluations of the relationship.

Socioemotional Behavior

Because the socioemotional aspects of marriage (the positivity and negativity spouses express toward each other) do not differ for parents and nonparents, it is reasonable to anticipate that the transition to parenthood will have little impact on the way spouses evaluate the quality of this domain of marriage. Indeed, data from the PAIR project largely support this supposition. Spouses who become parents are no more or less satisfied with their marital communication than are those who remain childless.

The similarity between parents and nonparents in regard to the frequency with which they enact positive socioemotional behaviors, as well as their more subjective evaluations of the quality of their communication, provides an important context for interpreting spouses' global assessments of their relationship. A substantial body of research suggests that spouses who express more negativity toward each other tend to become less satisfied with their relationship over time than do those who express less negativity (e.g., Gottman & Krokoff, 1989; Huston & Vangelisti, 1991; Levenson & Gottman, 1985; Markman, 1981). Furthermore, spouses' ratings of how satisfied they are with the quality of their communication consistently covary with their overall marital satisfaction (Vangelisti & Huston, 1994). Taken together, these findings suggest that because parents and nonparents do not differ in their socioemotional behavior, they should not differ in marital satisfaction. Not surprisingly, parents and nonparents report similar levels of marital satisfaction and love for each other (MacDermid et al., 1990). For both groups, marital satisfaction and love significantly decrease over the first two years of marriage (see White & Booth, 1985). Both parents and nonparents experience decreases in satisfaction with the quality of their communication, with the amount of influence they have in their marriages, and with their sexual relationships (Vangelisti & Huston, 1994).

STRAIN AND ADAPTATION IN
THE TRANSITION TO PARENTHOOD

What's Easy for Some Is Difficult for Others

Although the transition to parenthood represents a "big change" (Cowan & Cowan, 1992) in the way most couples organize their time, the transformations that accompany parenthood are more palatable for some couples than for others. Spouses with relatively traditional gender role attitudes move toward parenthood with comparative ease. These couples tend to become parents earlier in marriage than do those with less traditional attitudes. Indeed, by the time more traditional couples reach their second wedding anniversaries, they are quite likely to have established a pattern in which the husband is the primary breadwinner and the wife the primary caregiver (Huston & Geis, 1993). Furthermore, the beliefs these spouses hold concerning husbands' and wives' role behaviors fit well with many of the changes parenthood brings. Wives who have relatively traditional gender role attitudes prefer less involvement from their husbands with regard to child-care activities; these wives see child care as their domain. They tend to be more involved with their children than are wives with egalitarian gender-role attitudes, and they tend to engage in more child-care activities (McHale & Huston, 1984). In fact, mothers with more traditional gender-role attitudes who are in marriages with relatively equal division of labor report that they are less in love with their husbands and tend to be more negative. Likewise, fathers with more traditional gender-role attitudes who are highly involved with child-care and household tasks report being less in love with their wives and being more negative (MacDermid et al., 1990). These findings fit well within a larger literature that shows that women who are comfortable in "expressive" roles are relatively unaffected by the child-care demands that typically accompany motherhood (e.g., Belsky, Lang, & Huston, 1986; Hackel & Ruble, 1992).

In contrast, spouses with less traditional gender-role attitudes often organize their behavior in different ways. Their more egalitarian beliefs about husbands' and wives' roles in marriage do not coincide with the way most new parents divide household tasks and child care (Cowan et al., 1985; Lamb, 1978). Wives who have more egalitarian gender-role attitudes and role preferences tend to have husbands who are more involved in child-care tasks. Similarly, fathers who have nontraditional ideas about parenting roles are more involved in child-oriented activities and tend to do more caregiving, relative to play and leisure activities with their children (McHale & Huston, 1984).

The tendency of spouses—whether traditional or egalitarian—to engage in more child-care activity in part depends on their perceived skills (McHale & Huston, 1984). Fathers who feel skilled with regard to parenting are more involved in child-oriented activities than are those who feel unskilled. In addition, these fathers tend to do more caregiving, relative to play and leisure activities with their children. Fathers' perceived skill also tends to bring their families together. Those fathers who feel competent about performing child care are more involved in child-oriented activities with their wives.

For fathers, perceived skill in child care is a relatively stable trait. It does not significantly change or evolve when they become parents (McHale & Huston, 1984)—husbands who feel skilled at child care before becoming fathers also tend to feel skilled afterward. In contrast, wives' feelings of competence with regard to their child-care skills are more likely to change over the transition to parenthood. Mothers who are highly involved in child-oriented activities after their babies are born increase their perceptions of their own child-care skills as well as their preferences for doing child care. Although husbands' and wives' role preferences are not related to each other before they become parents, afterward, mothers' expressivity and their perceived skill are inversely related to fathers' preferences for being involved in child care. The more expressive mothers are, and the more skilled they perceive themselves to be in terms of child care, the less their husbands prefer to engage in child-care activities.

It appears that the changing role preferences of wives may influence husbands' involvement with their children. The associations between wives' role-related characteristics and their husbands' activities are stronger than the associations between husbands' characteristics and their own activities. Although husbands who are more expressive tend to believe that they are more skilled in terms of child care, husbands' expressivity does not by itself predict their tendency to engage in child-oriented activities. Wives' role preferences (measured after they become mothers), however, predict husbands' involvement with their children. Wives who prefer their husbands to be involved in child care after they become parents tend to have husbands who engage in more child-oriented activities. As we will see below, however, husbands' greater involvement in child care does not always bode well for the marriage.

Dual-Earner Marriage: Another Challenge

With the number of women who work for pay outside the home now in the majority, and the real earnings of both women and men on the decline, the tendency of spouses to choose a lifestyle in which one parent stays at home to care for the children is increasingly rare. Regardless of their role preferences, many new parents juggle the demands of both dual-earner marriages and their new babies. The limited time these parents have available to spend with their children clearly has an impact on the ways they organize their lives together.

The more new mothers work for pay outside the home, the less involved they are with their children, in terms of both child care and leisure activities (McHale & Huston, 1984). Part of this decreased involvement is a result of the restrictions that paid work places on these mothers' schedules. But data from the PAIR project also demonstrate that children are less central to the activities of these mothers when the mothers are at home. Similarly, the more hours mothers work for pay, the less central their children are to their leisure activities outside the home. One result of all this is that mothers who work more outside the home tend to spend less time alone with their children. They do not appear to choose leisure activities and home-oriented activities that center on their children as often as do other mothers. The amount of time these mothers spend with their children in larger social settings (e.g., with friends or family), however, is not affected by the number of hours mothers work for pay. Children's and mothers' activities together with others do not decrease when mothers spend more time at work.

Although mothers in dual-earner marriages adjust their activities so that they spend slightly less time alone with their children, fathers in these relationships spend more time alone with their children. In fact, fathers in dual-earner marriages report doing more than twice as many child-care activities on their own as do fathers in single-earner marriages (Crouter, Perry-Jenkins, Huston, & McHale, 1987). The more restricted schedules of dual-earner couples seem to create a context in which spouses choose efficiency (e.g., one parent caring for the child while the other engages in another activity) over companionship (e.g., both parents spending time with the child together). Indeed, fathers in dual-earner and single-earner marriages do not differ in the amount of child-care activities they do with their spouses.

Although new fathers in dual-earner marriages engage in more child care alone than do those in single-earner marriages, there is no connection between the dual-earner fathers' sense of skill with regard to child-care activities and their involvement (Crouter et al., 1987). Fathers in dual-earner marriages tend to be more involved in child care alone regardless of whether they feel confident about their child-care skills. Very likely because of the more restricted schedules of dual-earner couples, these fathers are drawn into doing child-care tasks even if they do not feel very competent about doing them. In contrast, fathers in single-earner marriages tend to stay relatively uninvolved in child-care duties when they do not feel skilled about performing such tasks. Those who perceive they are more skilled tend to participate more in child care with their spouses than do those who feel unskilled. Single-earner fathers seem to have the luxury of being able to modify the extent of their involvement based on their feelings of skill, whereas dual-earner fathers do not.

The finding that dual-earner fathers are drawn into child-care activities regardless of their perceived skill suggests that these fathers are performing child-care tasks more out of necessity than by choice. If this is the case, greater involvement on the part of dual-earner fathers may take a toll on their marriages. Dual-earner fathers who feel they are forced into child care by their wives' out-of-home work activities may begin to feel more negative about their marriages. When we examine spouses' marital interaction and the feelings these fathers report toward their wives, we find substantial support for this proposition (Crouter et al., 1987). The more involved fathers in dual-earner couples are with child care, either alone or with their wives, the more negativity there is in the marriage. Furthermore, fathers in dual-earner marriages who report more negative interaction tend to be less satisfied with the division of child-care tasks and also tend to be less in love with their wives. Conversely, fathers in dual-earner marriages who are less involved with their children (with regard to both child care and leisure activities) are more in love with their wives. And when these fathers are more in love with their wives, they also tend to be more satisfied with the division of child-care tasks. It is interesting to note that the same associations do not hold for wives. The link between negativity and husbands' level of participation in child care no doubt suppresses the impact of negativity on wives' love.

The connections among fathers' involvement in child care, their feelings toward their wives, and the quality of their marital interaction are unique to dual-earner couples. Indeed, the pattern of associations is quite different for single-earner couples. There is no link between the extent to which single-earner fathers are involved in child care and the negativity they report in their marriages. Further, single-earner fathers who are more in love with their wives tend to be more (rather than less) involved in child care and in leisure activities alone with their children.

CONCLUSIONS

The birth of a baby clearly has an impact on marital behavior patterns. Spouses change the way they organize their instrumental tasks and leisure time. Wives' day-to-day activities become more home and family centered. Husbands engage in fewer of the leisure activities they enjoy. The responsibilities that accompany child care limit the amount of time spouses have to spend together as a couple. Accordingly, parents report spending less time in conversation together than do nonparents. Although new parents change many of their behavioral patterns, the socioemotional aspects of their interaction do not differ from those of nonparents. Because socioemotional behavior is an important predictor of spouses' relational satisfaction, the lack of difference in this domain of marriage for parents and nonparents suggests that parenthood, per se, should not encourage decreases in spouses' marital satisfaction and love. Data from the PAIR project support this claim.

Having noted that parents do not differ from nonparents in terms of the way they evaluate the quality of their marriages, we feel it is important to acknowledge that the changes that accompany parenthood are more easily managed by some than by others. In particular, those with traditional gender role attitudes tend to hold beliefs about marriage that are congruent with many of the transformations spouses experience when they become parents. Those with more egalitarian gender role attitudes, in contrast, hold beliefs that clash with some of the changes that typically accompany parenthood. In addition, spouses' occupational status constrains the way they organize their time together. Dual-earner husbands, for instance, are slightly more involved in child care than are their single-earner counterparts. However, although drawing these husbands into child care may reduce marital tension by decreasing wives' workloads, it can have negative influences on the ways dual-earner husbands evaluate their marriages.

Our efforts to trace the multiple ways parenthood affects marriage and to identify the conditions under which parenthood affects satisfaction fit into a new, emerging paradigm that seeks to create a richer, more balanced portrait of the transition to parenthood. Researchers are poised, we believe, to recognize that parenthood creates opportunities as well as problems, and that the overall effect of parenthood on marriage reflects the operation of a number of causal dynamics. It is important to recognize, moreover, that our more optimistic portrait of couples undergoing the transition to parenthood may reflect our having drawn our sample from a rural, largely working-class area and that our couples underwent the transition to parenthood relatively early in marriage; most researchers have studied relatively well educated middle-class couples, large subsamples of whom were married for longer periods prior to becoming parents. In addition to studying the potential differences between working-class and middle-class couples, researchers need to expand work on the transition to parenthood to include unwed mothers and fathers, because first-time parenthood increasingly takes place outside marriage. Scholars are beginning to examine how the relational world of unmarried parents changes, in both the short run and the long run (Furstenberg, 1976; Furstenberg, Brooks-Gunn, & Morgan, 1987). Finally, as the longitudinal studies initiated in the 1980s continue into the 1990s, we will be in a position to examine the way parenthood affects marriage over longer stretches of time and to determine whether the number of children have influences on spouses' marital well-being.

REFERENCES

Belsky, J. (1985). Exploring individual differences in marital change across the transition to parenthood: The role of violated expectations. *Journal of Marriage and the Family, 47*, 1037-1044.

Belsky, J., & Kelly, J. (1994). *The transition to parenthood: How a first child changes a marriage.* London: Vermilion.

Belsky, J., Lang, M., & Huston, T. L. (1986). Sex typing and division of labor as determinants of marital change across the transition to parenthood. *Journal of Personality and Social Psychology, 50*, 517-522.

Belsky, J., Lang, M., & Rovine, M. (1985). Stability and change in marriage across the transition to parenthood: A second study. *Journal of Marriage and the Family, 47*, 855-865.

Belsky, J., Spanier, G., & Rovine, M. (1983). Stability and change across the transition to parenthood. *Journal of Marriage and the Family, 45*, 567-577.

Broderick, J. E., & O'Leary, K. D. (1986). Contributions of affect, attitudes, and behavior to marital satisfaction. *Journal of Consulting and Clinical Psychology, 54*, 514-517.

Cook, T., & Campbell, D. T. (1979). *Quasi-experimentation: Design and analysis issues for field settings.* Chicago: Rand McNally.

Cowan, C. P., & Cowan, P. A. (1992). *When partners become parents: The big life change for couples.* New York: Basic Books.

Cowan, C. P., Cowan, P. A., Heming, G., Heming, G., Garrett, E., Coysh, W. S., Curtis-Boles, H., & Boles, A. J. (1985). Transitions to parenthood: His, hers, and theirs. *Journal of Family Issues, 6*, 451-481.

Cowan, P. A., & Cowan, C. P. (1989). Changes in marriage during the transition to parenthood: Must we blame the baby? In G. Michaels & W. Goldberg (Eds.), *The transition to parenthood: Current theory and research* (pp. 114-154). Cambridge: Cambridge University Press.

Crawford, D. W., & Huston, T. L. (1993). The impact of the transition to parenthood on marital leisure. *Personality and Social Psychology Bulletin, 19,* 39-46.

Crouter, A. C., Perry-Jenkins, M., Huston, T. L., & McHale, S. M. (1987). Processes underlying father involvement in dual-earner and single-earner families. *Developmental Psychology, 23,* 431-440.

Feldman, S. S., & Nash S. C. (1984). The transition from expectancy to parenthood: Impact of the firstborn child on men and women. *Sex Roles, 11,* 61-78.

Figley, C. R. (1973). Child density and the marital relationship. *Journal of Marriage and the Family, 35,* 272-282.

Fincham, F. D., & Bradbury, T. N. (1987). The assessment of marital quality: A reevaluation. *Journal of Marriage and the Family, 49,* 797-809.

Fitzpatrick, M. A., Vangelisti, A. L., & Firman, S. M. (1994). Perceptions of marital interaction and change during pregnancy: A typological approach. *Personal Relationships, 1,* 101-122.

Furstenberg, F. F. (1976). *Unplanned parenthood: The social consequences of teenage childbearing.* New York: Free Press.

Furstenberg, F. F., Brooks-Gunn, J., & Morgan, S. P. (1987). *Adolescent mothers in later life.* Cambridge: Cambridge University Press.

Glenn, N. D., & McLanahan, S. (1982). Children and marital happiness: A further specification of the relationship. *Journal of Marriage and the Family, 44,* 63-72.

Gottman, J. M., & Krokoff, L. J. (1989). Marital interaction and satisfaction: A longitudinal view. *Journal of Consulting and Clinical Psychology, 57,* 47-52.

Hackel, L. S., & Ruble, D. N. (1992). Changes in the marital relationship after the first baby is born: Predicting the impact of expectancy disconfirmation. *Journal of Personality and Social Psychology, 62,* 944-957.

Hill, R. (1949). *Families under stress.* New York: Harper.

Huston, T. L., & Geis, G. (1993). In what ways do gender-related attributes and beliefs affect marriage? *Journal of Social Issues, 49,* 87-106.

Huston, T. L., McHale, S. M., & Crouter, A. C. (1986). When the honeymoon's over: Changes in the marriage relationship over the first year. In R. Gilmour & S. Duck (Eds.), *The emerging field of personal relationships* (pp. 263-286). Hillsdale, NJ: Lawrence Erlbaum.

Huston, T. L., & Robins, E. (1982). Conceptual and methodological issues in studying close relationships. *Journal of Marriage and the Family, 44,* 901-925.

Huston, T. L., Robins, E., Atkinson, J., & McHale, S. M. (1987). Surveying the landscape of marital behavior: A behavioral self-report approach to studying marriage. In S. Oskamp (Ed.), *Family processes and problems: Social psychological aspects* (pp. 45-72). Newbury Park, CA: Sage.

Huston, T. L., & Vangelisti, A. L. (1991). Socioemotional behavior and satisfaction in marital relationships: A longitudinal study. *Journal of Personality and Social Psychology, 61,* 721-733.

Jacobson, N. S., Waldron, H., & Moore, D. (1980). Toward a behavioral profile of marital distress. *Journal of Consulting and Clinical Psychology, 48,* 696-703.

Kelly, J. R. & McGrath J. E. (1988). *On time and method.* Newbury Park, CA: Sage.

Lamb, M. E. (1978). The influence of the child on marital quality and family interaction during the prenatal, perinatal, and infancy periods. In R. M. Lerner & G. B. Spanier (Eds.), *Child influences on marital and family interaction* (pp. 137-163). New York: Academic Press.

LeMasters, E. E. (1957). Parenthood as crisis. *Marriage and Family Living, 19,* 352-355.

Levenson, R., & Gottman, J. (1985). Physiological and affective predictors of change in relationship satisfaction. *Journal of Personality and Social Psychology, 49,* 85-94.

Locke, H. J., & Wallace, K. M. (1959). Short marital-adjustment and prediction tests: Their reliability and validity. *Marriage and Family Living, 21,* 251-255.

MacDermid, S. M., Huston, T. L., & McHale, S. M. (1990). Changes in marriage associated with the transition to parenthood: Individual differences as a function of sex-role attitudes and changes in the division of household labor. *Journal of Marriage and the Family, 52,* 475-486.

Markman, H. J. (1981). Prediction of marital distress: A 5-year follow-up. *Journal of Consulting and Clinical Psychology, 49,* 760-762.

McHale, S. M., & Huston, T. L. (1984). Men and women as parents: Sex role orientations, employment, and parental roles with infants. *Child Development, 55,* 1349-1361.

McHale, S. M., & Huston, T. L. (1985). The effect of the transition to parenthood on the marriage relationship: A longitudinal study. *Journal of Family Issues, 6,* 409-433.

Menaghan, E. (1982). Assessing the impact of family transitions on marital experience. In H. I. McCubbin, A. E. Cauble, & J. M. Patterson (Eds.), *Family stress, coping, and social support* (pp. 90-108). Springfield, IL: Charles C Thomas.

Meyerowitz, J. H., & Feldman, H. (1966). Transition to parenthood. *Psychiatric Research Reports, 20,* 78-84.

Miller, B. (1976). A multivariate developmental model of marital satisfaction. *Journal of Marriage and the Family, 38,* 643-657.

Miller, B. C., & Sollie, D. L. (1980). Normal stresses during the transition to parenthood. *Family Relations, 29,* 459-465.

Moore, K. A., & Waite, L. J. (1981). Marital dissolution, early motherhood and early marriage. *Social Forces, 60,* 20-40.

Noller, P., & Fitzpatrick, M. A. (1990). Marital communication in the eighties. *Journal of Marriage and the Family, 52,* 832-843.

Robins, E. (1990). The study of interdependence in marriage. In F. D. Fincham & T. Bradbury (Eds.), *The psychology of marriage: Basic issues and applications* (pp. 59-86). New York: Guilford.

Ruble, D. N., Fleming, A. S., Hackel, L. S., & Stangor, C. (1988). Changes in the marital relationship during the transition to first time motherhood: Effects of violated expectations concerning the division of labor. *Journal of Personality and Social Psychology, 55,* 78-87.

Russell, C. S. (1974). Transition to parenthood: Problems and gratifications. *Journal of Marriage and the Family, 36,* 294-302.

Ryder, R. G. (1973). Longitudinal data relating marriage satisfaction and having a child. *Journal of Marriage and the Family, 35,* 604-606.

Schwarz, N. (1990). Assessing frequency reports of mundane behaviors: Contributions of cognitive psychology to questionnaire construction. In C. Hendrick &

M. S. Clark (Eds.), *Research methods in personality and social psychology* (pp. 98-119). Newbury Park, CA: Sage.

Spanier, G. B. (1976). Measuring dyadic adjustment: New scales for assessing the quality of marriage and similar dyads. *Journal of Marriage and the Family, 38,* 15-28.

Stamp, G. H. (1994). The appropriation of the parental role through communication during the transition to parenthood. *Communication Monographs, 61,* 89-112.

Tomlinson, P. S. (1987). Spousal differences in marital satisfaction during the transition to parenthood. *Nursing Research, 36,* 239-243.

Vangelisti, A. L., & Huston, T. L. (1994). Maintaining marital satisfaction and love. In D. J. Canary & L. Stafford (Eds.), *Communication and relational maintenance* (pp. 165-186). San Diego, CA: Academic Press.

Waite, L. J., Haggstrom, G. W., & Kanouse, D. E. (1985). The consequences of parenthood for the marital stability of young adults. *American Sociological Review, 50,* 850-857.

Waldron, H., & Routh, D. K. (1981). The effect of the first child on the marital relationship. *Journal of Marriage and the Family, 43,* 785-788.

Wallace, P. M., & Gotlib, I. H. (1990). Marital adjustment during the transition to parenthood: Stability and predictors of change. *Journal of Marriage and the Family, 52,* 21-29.

White, L. K., & Booth, A. (1985). The transition to parenthood and marital quality. *Journal of Family Issues, 6,* 435-449.

White, L. K., Booth, A., & Edwards, J. N. (1986). Children and marital happiness: Why the negative correlation? *Journal of Family Issues, 7,* 131-147.

Wiggins, J. (1979). Dynamic theories of social relationships and resulting research strategies. In R. L. Burgess & T. L. Huston (Eds.), *Social exchange in developing relationships* (pp. 381-407). New York: Academic Press.

Wills, T. A., Weiss, R. L., & Patterson, G. R. (1974). A behavioral analysis of the determinants of marital satisfaction. *Journal of Consulting and Clinical Psychology, 42,* 802-811.

6

Family Interaction
During Problem Solving

SAMUEL VUCHINICH
JOSEPH ANGELELLI

Humans use communication to create, maintain, and change their social order through relationships and more complex social forms. This requires an array of communication patterns and structures. The fundamental role of communication in group functioning is most clearly exemplified in human families. The intense interpersonal bonds that characterize parent-child, marital, sibling, and other kin group relationships entail a wide range of distinctive communication patterns that are used over long periods of time and that adapt to developmental changes in individuals and families.

The communication demands of family life are considerable, and some individuals, relationships, and structures are unable to meet the demands. Indeed, adjusting communication patterns is one of the primary tools of family therapy and marital counseling designed to repair, maintain, enrich, and promote the well-being of family groups. One key aspect of family communication involved in these efforts is the process of family problem solving.

Our research program is designed to provide information useful for the improvement of family-based psychosocial treatment programs for the prevention of antisocial behavior in adolescence and intervention programs to reduce that behavior after it has become a problem. The most widely used and most successful programs for these problems are based on social learning research and emphasize the training

177

of parents to use better discipline practices and more positive reinforcement (Kazdin, Siegel, & Bass, 1992; Reid, 1993). More recent
treatments have added cognitive components aimed at training children to think differently about themselves and the behavior of others
(Kazdin et al., 1992). Such programs seem to be effective for children
in middle childhood, but are less effective with older children (Reid,
1993). This loss in effectiveness is a result of developmental changes
in children and families. Transformations in parent-child relationships
that take place as children approach puberty, move through the preadolescent and adolescent transitions, and increase in peer group
contact create new social and psychological contexts for treatment
(e.g., Baumrind, 1991; Steinberg, 1990).

Whereas social learning and cognitive theories are only beginning
to understand this transition in terms of family life, the family therapy
field has a well-developed theory of family systems that is applied to
this transition (e.g., Haley, 1976). As a child moves through preadolescence, basic features of the parent-child relationship should change to
provide for optimal development. The child's increasing need for
autonomy, identity, and peer relationships requires complex parental
social and emotional adaptation. There are many pitfalls in this transition that can result in family conflict, withdrawal, resentment, confusion, and, in extreme cases, psychopathology. As these problems
emerge, one family therapy perspective emphasizes the importance
of coalitions that form within the family (Haley, 1976; Madanes, 1981;
Minuchin, Rosman, & Baker, 1978). Serious problems are associated with
a parent-child coalition becoming stronger than the mother-father
coalition. We address this issue empirically in this report.

Because the family therapy literature is based largely on clinical case
studies, it may be of limited use in preventing problems in at-risk
families and other nonclinical families. However, such work has
inspired initial efforts at more systematic research on family systems
(e.g., Christensen & Margolin, 1988; Gilbert, Christensen, & Margolin,
1984; Vuchinich, Emery, & Cassidy, 1988). Some elements of that
literature place family communication at the core of some forms of
major mental illness (e.g., Jacob, 1987; Madanes, 1981).

In this analysis we apply the behavioral approach of social learning
theory to an exploration of the linkages between coalitions in the

family and problem-solving effectiveness. We also compare the behavior profiles of families with sons who exhibit antisocial behavior with those of families with less antisocial sons. We analyze the positive and negative communication patterns of mothers and fathers with 10-year-old sons as these families attempt to resolve problems that have recently come up in their homes. Our analysis integrates three levels of family communication.

DEFINING FAMILY COMMUNICATION

We define family communication in terms of three interlocking levels of analysis. First, family communication entails the transmission of information from one family member to another. Several features distinguish family communication. One is the strong affective nature of much of the information that gets transmitted in families. Another is the amount of information family members have about each other as a result of long-term relationships and frequent contact. This allows shared communication forms that may be unique to specific family members or relationships. We call this the *behavior exchange level* of family communication.

The second level of family communication requires that it be organized to allow the creation, maintenance, and change of specialized interpersonal relationships within the family. One such relationship is that between parent and child, which requires both nurturance and controlling behavior by parents and the appropriate responses from children. Another is the relationship between husband and wife (or other adult partners), which requires supportive communication to promote intimate sharing and commitment for long-term stability. Sibling relationships supply a balance of support and conflict that prepares children for peer relations outside the family. The communications that occur in the context of these relationships function to promote the well-being of individuals in healthy families. We refer to this as the *relationship level* of family communication.

The third level of family communication involves the integration of parent-child, marital, sibling, and other kin relations into a larger social unit known as the family. Family communication at this level includes behaviors, rituals, and events that express the identity, value, and unity of the family group. Family meals, birthday parties, and gift exchanges at Christmas are examples of communication at this level. But the day-to-day functioning of family groups requires other, less ritualized, communications that serve to maintain and repair the integration of the various subsystems within the family. For example, the demands of the parent-child system may conflict with those of the marital system for a given period of time. At the mundane level, for example, parents may be forced to choose between taking a child to a science fair, which would benefit the child's academic progress, and going out to dinner by themselves for some much-needed and well-deserved time to maintain their marital relationship. The family discussions that deal with such decisions represent another form of the third level of family communication. Links between family subsystems may be less mundane, as when a father becomes too intimate with his adolescent daughter as a response to marital problems. We refer to this as the *family system level* of family communication.

It is possible to distinguish the three levels of family communication and consider the components separately, but understanding at any level of analysis requires consideration of all levels. Because family problem solving involves the integration of family subsystems, consideration of all three levels is needed in the analysis of this process. Especially relevant in this regard are coalitions within the family, because they involve two family members taking sides against a third. Information exchange, dyadic relationships, and multiple family subsystems are involved in these coalitions.

FAMILY PROBLEM SOLVING

Problem solving is a process that occurs in individuals, dyads, and families. Coalitions are common in family problem solving and can have a major impact on how family problems are solved. The importance of coalitions in group problem solving has long been recognized (e.g., Mishler & Waxler, 1968; Simmel, 1908/1950). Coalitions in group decision making have been a topic in the experimental social psychology of small groups for some time (e.g., Steinhauer, 1987). Although this research contributes to the general theory of group process, it is of limited value for the analysis of families because most of it does not involve family groups and thus does not involve the distinctive features of family communication. Those studies that include family groups usually involve very artificial tasks that have low ecological validity (Bronfenbrenner, 1979; Reiss, 1981; Steinhauer, 1987).

Clinical work on family therapy has addressed the importance of family problem solving and the role of intrafamily coalitions in the family problem-solving process (e.g., Haley, 1976). This literature describes such coalition phenomena as *scapegoating*, in which parents (or other family subsystems) inaccurately blame one family member for all the problems in the family (Gurman & Kniskern, 1981); *detouring*, which occurs when marital problems are acted out through a child (Minuchin et al., 1978); and *triangulation*, which occurs when both parents try to draw the child into marital conflict by having the child side with them against the other parent. All of these patterns create distorted cognitive and emotional states in family members and make effective family problem solving difficult.

The family therapy literature generally emphasizes the importance of the mother-father coalition in sustaining a healthy balance of affective relations and a hierarchy to maintain order within the family (Haley, 1976; Madanes, 1981; Minuchin et al., 1978). If this coalition is supplanted by a stronger parent-child (intergenerational) coalition (e.g., mother-child), various affective and control problems emerge. These provide the basis for many pathological symptoms (e.g., Beavers, 1982; Madanes, 1981; Mann, Borduin, Henggeler, & Blaske, 1990; Schuham, 1970), especially in children. It is also possible, however, that the mother-father coalition may become too strong, as is the case in scapegoating, when the marital subsystem is excessive to the detriment of the parent-child subsystem (Vuchinich, Vuchinich, & Wood, 1993). The optimal mother-father coalition is thus neither too strong nor too weak.

ANALYSIS PLAN

There is some empirical evidence for the deleterious implications of intergenerational coalitions (e.g., Gilbert et al., 1984; Preli & Protinsky,

1988) and scapegoating (Seelig, Goldman-Hall, & Jerrell, 1992), but a barrier to research on family coalitions is the difficulty of adequate measurement. Intrafamily coalitions have been assessed in a variety of ways by different researchers, with little concern for the convergent validity of the different approaches. Because this inhibits cumulative research on family coalitions and problem solving, we begin by testing the convergent and predictive validity of three different measures of intrafamily coalitions.

After assessing the viability of different measurement approaches, we examine the exchange of positive and negative behaviors during mother-father-son family problem-solving sessions. In this part of the analysis we compare family behavior profiles across four different family characteristics. First, we compare families with strong mother-father (MF) coalitions with those that have weaker MF coalitions. Next, we compare families with strong mother-son (MS) coalitions with those with weaker MS coalitions. Third, we compare families that are most effective in solving problems with those that are least effective. And finally, we compare families that have antisocial sons with those whose sons are less antisocial. The goal in this part of the analysis is to isolate which types of behavior by which family members are associated with the presence of coalitions, effective problem solving, and the presence of antisocial sons. Coalitions are also important in families with more than one child and in families with female children. The inclusion of family size and gender of the child, however, is beyond the scope of this analysis.

Although behavior rates provide useful summaries of intrafamily behavior patterns, the problem-solving process unfolds over time. Behavior rates cannot capture the interactional processes that generate them (e.g., Gottman, 1987; Gottman & Roy, 1990; Vuchinich, Hetherington, Vuchinich, & Clingempeel, 1991). Behavior sequences have long been recognized as an important feature of family interaction (e.g., Haley, 1964) and group decision making (Rausch, Barry, Hertel, & Swain, 1974). To complete our analysis of family problem solving, we present the results of a sequential analysis designed to control for effects of sequential patterns that may distort behavior differences characteristic of coalitions, effective problem solving, and families with antisocial sons.

METHODS

Subjects

The subjects were 40 family triads (mother, father, and son; a total of 120 individuals) with the male child in the fourth grade (mean age 9.7 years) at the first assessment. Families were recruited from schools in neighborhoods that had juvenile delinquency rates above the 66th percentile in a metropolitan area with a population of about 150,000 people. Parents of all male fourth graders were contacted through the school system, and 74% agreed to participate in a study of child development. The socioeconomic status of the families was generally lower-middle-class, with a mean Hollingshead Four-Factor Socioeconomic Status Index of 32.1 and a mean per capita income of $4,612. Mean number of children in the home was 2.8 in the intact families and 2.5 in the stepfamilies. All families were Caucasian. Mean age of the mothers in intact families was 37.6 years; in stepfamilies, 32.9 years. Of the target children in this study, 4.4% were in the clinical range on the externalizing scale of the Child Behavior Checklist (Achenbach & Edelbrock, 1983) at Time 1, and 5.2% were in this range at Time 2. Families were paid for their participation in problem-solving sessions as part of their involvement in a larger assessment battery (Patterson, Reid, & Dishion, 1992).

Procedure

Family problem-solving sessions were conducted at a community research and counseling center. Families were given no education or treatment in this research study. Each family was taken to a room with chairs and a coffee table and a video camera mounted on the wall in full view, and members were informed that they would be video-taped. The parents were asked to select a problem to discuss from a list of 49 parent-child issues that are often a problem at home (e.g., allowance, bedtime, chores, punishment); the child also selected a problem, independent of the parents' selection. Family members were instructed to select problems that had been of some concern to them at home in the past month. Prior to the problem-solving sessions, the family triads were asked to plan, for 5 minutes, a "fun family activity" that they might actually do in the next two weeks while being video-taped. This served to accustom them to being videotaped. Next, they were asked to try to solve one of the problems they had selected for a period of 10 minutes. The parent-selected problem was first in half the cases, and the child-selected problem was first in the other half. The experimenter left the room while the sessions were videotaped. After 10 minutes, the experimenter reentered the room, asked if there were any questions, and then asked the family members to try to solve the second problem selected for the next 10 minutes. The experimenter again left the room and the second 10-minute session was videotaped.

Measurement

This analysis used two types of observational coding. Sequential coding was used to examine each behavior in a 10-minute problem-solving session to determine if it was positive, negative, or other. The speaker and recipient of each behavior in the session were entered into the sequential data file. In the second, completely independent, coding procedure, which we call global coding, different coders watched the entire 10-minute session and then made overall ratings about the families as described below.

Sequential Coding

A video time generator was used to place elapsed time from the beginning of the session on the videotape. An observational coding system was used to record information about each turn at talk by each family member in sequence. A "turn at talk" represents what is said from the time a speaker begins talking until he or she stops or is interrupted (Bakeman & Gottman, 1986). The following information was collected for each successive turn: who the speaker was (e.g., mother, father), to whom the speaker's talk was addressed (a special code was used when the speaker spoke to more than one person), the beginning time and ending time for each turn, and the type of verbal behavior displayed by the speaker. Coders were trained to evaluate each turn at talk based on its own characteristics, independent of any prior turns (Bakeman & Dorval, 1989).

The verbal behavior code was made up of three specific behavior categories. In *positive behavior,* the speaker expressed positive support, regard, or affect toward the child ("You look good tonight."); this behavior included compliments, agreements, and expressions of solidarity. In *negative behavior,* the speaker opposed some aspect of another directly or opposed something the other had said or done ("You're wrong."); this behavior included disagreements, challenges, rebukes, insults, and threats. *Other behavior* encompassed any verbal behavior from one person to another that was not positive or negative (i.e., neutral behavior). In the infrequent cases where a single turn at talk included more than one of the three behavior specific types, one type was judged to be predominant in that turn and was used as the code for that turn.

Reliability of the coding system was assessed by having at least two coders independently code the same session. The five coders who were involved in the coding were trained for an average of 56 hours. Agreement on the coding of a given turn at talk was defined to occur only if (a) the start times for the turn for both coders were within two seconds of each other, (b) the ending times for the turn for both coders were within two seconds of each other, and (c) the coders agreed on the speaker, recipient, and behavior type of the turn. Thus intercoder agreement occurred only if coders agreed that the same behavior occurred at the same time by the same person, toward the same recipient. Reliability checks were made on 15% of the data. Pairwise percentage agreements for the behavior coding categories were as follows: positive behavior, 77%; negative behavior, 82%; other behavior, 83%. The mean pairwise kappa for the entire coding system was 0.72.

Global Ratings

Videotapes of the problem-solving sessions were coded by a team of five coders. One 10-minute session was coded at a time. Coders made their ratings once after viewing the 10-minute session. Coders were trained for about 100 hours to attain reliability. Intercoder reliability was tested on 20% of the data.

Ratings of the mother-father coalition assessed the extent to which the mother and father took sides against the son in discussing the family problem during each 10-minute session. The ratings were based on coders' judgment of "how much the mother and father were in a coalition against the son" on a 7-point scale from 1 (*not at all*) to 7 (*almost always*). Parallel ratings were made on 7-point scales for the mother-son coalition and father-son coalition.

The measure of the effectiveness of family problem solving was based on the multiple indicator instrument developed by Forgatch (1989). The external and ecological validity of the observational assessments have been acknowledged as being especially good (e.g., Brody, Stoneman, McCoy, & Forehand, 1992).

In this study, family problem-solving effectiveness was rated on three separate 7-point scales. The first measured the quality of the solutions proposed; the scale ranged from *no solutions proposed* (1) to *excellent solutions proposed* (7). The second measured the extent of resolution, from *no resolution-total disagreement* (1) to *problem resolved* (7). This score represents an overall assessment of how close the family came to a final solution to the problem, regardless of how much agreeing or disagreeing went on in the discussion. The third component of the problem-solving effectiveness score was an overall problem-solving score that assessed how well the family members took one another's perspectives during the sessions and promoted group participation, a *perspective-taking* score. This included taking into account others' views and feelings (Selman, Beardslee, Schultz, Krupa, & Podorefsky, 1986). The three components (i.e., quality of solutions, extent of resolution, and perspective taking) were combined to provide a more comprehensive assessment of different key elements of family problem solving than is possible with any single item.

Intercoder reliability for global codes was calculated using the Pearson correlation coefficient between independent ratings of the same session. Pearson reliability correlations for problem-solving effectiveness were as follows: 0.77 for quality of solutions proposed, 0.81 for extent of resolution, and 0.76 for perspective taking. The total problem-solving effectiveness score is the sum of the quality, extent, and perspective-taking scores. Cronbach's alpha for this total scale was 0.86. We evaluated test-retest reliability in two ways. First, we calculated the correlations between observational scores for the 10-

minute problem-solving session in which the child selected the problem and the 10-minute session in which the parents selected the problem for each wave of assessment. Because one of these sessions occurred immediately after the other, and involved the same task and participants, these correlations give an indication of short-term test-retest reliability of the ratings.

Measuring Coalitions

To assess the convergent validity of family coalition measures, we used three methods for measuring the strength of mother-father, mother-son, and father-son coalitions in this analysis. The simplest was the global method described above, which involved rating the strength of each of these coalitions on a 7-point scale. The second method followed previous research (Christensen & Margolin, 1988; Gilbert et al., 1984; Schuham, 1970) and used the sequential coding of positive and negative behavior to construct composite coalition scores. This method, which we call the *sociometric* method, was based on the turn-by-turn rating of every behavior in the session. The strength of a coalition was calculated from the rates of positive and negative behaviors directed toward the relevant family members. Consider the mother-father coalition against the child. First, as an indication of mutual support, the rate of positive behavior from mother to father was added to the rate of positive behavior from father to mother. Next, because conflict can counterbalance such support, the rates of negative behavior between mother and father were summed. This negative behavior sum was subtracted from the positive behavior sum to yield an indicator of mother-father supportiveness, adjusted for parental conflict. Strong coalitions involve opposition toward the third party in question, so the negative behaviors from father to son and from mother to son were summed. The result was then added to the mother-father supportiveness score to create our final mother-father coalition score. Parallel composite scores for the mother-son coalition against father and father-son coalition against mother were calculated for each family.

The third method of assessing coalitions was based on the idea that the best context for observing intrafamily coalitions is during conflict episodes. By carefully coding who took sides with whom during family conflicts, we could infer the strength of the coalitions. A method for locating conflict episodes and coding who takes sides with whom had been developed previously (Vuchinich et al., 1988) and was applied to the data in this study. We assessed the strength of the mother-father coalition by summing the number of times the mother took sides with the father and the number of times the father took sides with the mother during conflicts that emerged during the family problem-solving session. To control for variation in the frequency of conflict, we divided the side-taking counts by the number of opportunities each family member had to take sides (Vuchinich et al., 1988). We used the same approach to construct mother-son coalition scores and father-son coalition scores.

Measuring Child Antisocial Behavior

Assessments of the level of antisocial behavior of the sons in this study were obtained through a multiple-measure index based on reports from the parents, the sons' teachers, and the sons' peer groups, and self-reports by the sons (Capaldi & Patterson, 1989; Vuchinich, Bank, & Patterson, 1992). *Antisocial behavior* refers to aggressive, noncompliant, and rule-breaking behaviors that may be viewed as behavior against other people or property. This composite antisocial measure is correlated with the assessments of externalizing from the Achenbach Child Behavior Checklist (Achenbach & Edelbrock, 1983). Because of the multiple sources and contexts of the composite antisocial measure, we use it here, but include some reports on externalizing scores.

RESULTS

Analysis of Family Behavior Profiles

Table 6.1 presents the correlations among the sociometric global and side-taking measures of the mother-father, mother-son, and father-son coalitions. There was significant convergence among all three methods for the MF coalition. The global and sociometric methods converged

TABLE 6.1   Correlations Among Measures of Family Coalitions

	Coding Methods		
	Global	Sociometric	Side Taking
Mother-father coalition			
global	1.00		
sociometric	0.51*	1.00	
side taking	0.49*	0.48*	1.00
Mother-son coalition			
global	1.00		
sociometric	0.50*	1.00	
side taking	-0.10	0.16	1.00
Father-son coalition			
global	1.00		
sociometric	0.15	1.00	
side taking	-0.08	-0.26	1.00

* Significant at the 0.01 level.

for MS coalitions. There was no convergence for the FS coalitions; this may be a result of the low incidence of this coalition type.

Table 6.2 displays the predictive validity of the coalition measures, using correlations with family problem-solving effectiveness, child antisocial behavior, and child externalizing. These correlations show that stronger MF coalitions are associated with less effective family problem solving and having a more antisocial son. This pattern is consistent with the scapegoat pattern, in which the mother-father coalition is too strong (e.g., Gurman & Kniskern, 1981). Elevated MS coalitions are also associated with poor problem solving and child antisocial behavior, but only for the side-taking measure. This is evidence for family problem links to cross-generational coalitions (Madanes, 1981). When mother and son become closer to each other than the mother and father, problems often develop in the family. At one level, the father tends to become jealous of the son and more negative toward him. The mother, in turn, often will defend the son against the father, creating even more marital tension. At another level, the primary authority hierarchy in the family, which typically relies on the mother-father coalition, begins to break down and order gives way to chaos.

TABLE 6.2 Correlations Between Coalition Measures and Family Characteristics

	Problem Solving	Antisocial	Externalizing
MF coalition			
global	−0.56***	0.40**	0.30[+]
side taking	−0.23	0.35*	0.13
sociometric	−0.59***	0.41**	0.27[+]
MS coalition			
global	0.17	−0.13	−0.03
side taking	−0.34**	0.48**	0.48**
sociometric	0.02	0.06	−0.06
Coalition difference			
MF − MS	−0.64***	0.41**	0.32*
MF − FS	−0.61**	0.42**	0.35*

[+]Significant at the 0.10 level; *significant at the 0.05 level; **significant at the 0.01 level; ***significant at the 0.001 level.

Because more than one coalition may form during problem solving, we calculated the relative strength of the MF coalition compared with MS and FS coalitions by subtraction (e.g., MF − MS yields a coalition difference score). Correlations of these difference scores with problem solving, child antisocial behavior, and child externalizing are given in Table 6.2. These coalition difference scores exhibit the highest and most consistent correlations with the variables of interest, as has been previously found (Gilbert et al., 1984).

The correlations shown in Table 6.2 might be accounted for by the presence of more conflict in families with stronger coalitions rather than by the coalitions themselves. To test for this alternative hypothesis, we conducted multiple regression analyses, with conflict frequency and each coalition score that was found to be viable in the correlational analysis of Table 6.2 as independent variables and the effectiveness of family problem solving as the dependent variable. To control for other variables, we also included the child antisocial score and the mean of the mother and father Dyadic Adjustment Scale (Spanier, 1976) score as independent variables. The regression results are given in Table 6.3. Conflict frequency had no effect on problem solving. This is consistent with research showing that conflict may be

TABLE 6.3 Regression Coefficient for Testing Discriminant Validity of the Effect of Coalitions on Family Problem Solving

	Regression Models		
	Model 1	*Model 2*	*Model 3*
Coalition			
MF global	−0.50**	—	—
MF sociometric	—	0.56**	—
MS side taking	—	—	−0.12
Conflict frequency	−0.01	0.01	−0.24
Antisocial child	−0.24	0.26	−0.35*
Marital adjustment	−0.01	0.01	0.04
R^2	0.42	0.45	0.27

*Significant at the 0.05 level; **significant at the 0.01 level.

beneficial, depending on how it is managed (Grych & Fincham, 1990) and whether or not it is resolved (Cummings, Ballard, El-Sheikh, & Lake, 1991). We conclude that MF coalitions can be validly assessed in this context and are associated with problem-solving effectiveness and child antisocial behavior.

Tables 6.4 and 6.5 give the family behavior profiles for positive and negative behavior separately. These profiles are the mean frequencies per 10 minute-session of each type of behavior. To distinguish the dynamics of coalitions more clearly, we give in Table 6.4 profiles for the top and bottom quartiles (i.e., those families in the highest and lowest 25th percentile) for MF and MS coalitions based on the global coalition scores. To begin this analysis, we consider the profile of mean frequencies of all of the behavior for all 40 families, which is given in the first column in Table 6.5. Most of the talk is between parents and the son, with the parents talking to the son more frequently than he talks to them. Analysis of positive and negative behaviors is more informative.

The profiles in Table 6.4 are accompanied by F tests from multivariate analyses of variance that tested whether the profile in one type of family was significantly different from that in another type of family (e.g., highest-quartile MF coalition families versus lowest-quartile MF coalition families). If the MANOVA test was significant at the 0.05

TABLE 6.4   Family Behavior Profiles With MANOVA Tests for
Coalition Quartiles (Highest and Lowest)

Speaker and Recipient	Positive Behavior				Negative Behavior			
	MF Coalition		MS Coalition		MF Coalition		MS Coalition	
	Low ($n = 10$)	High ($n = 12$)	Low ($n = 26$)	High ($n = 6$)	Low ($n = 10$)	High ($n = 12$)	Low ($n = 26$)	High ($n = 6$)
F → M	2.1*	3.3*	2.8	2.3	3.0	1.2	0.9***	5.8***
F → S	3.7*	1.3*	2.5	3.2	6.8*	14.8*	7.1	7.7
M → F	3.7	4.1	3.6	4.7	2.9	1.1	1.2***	5.3***
M → S	6.3**	2.7**	4.0	4.5	4.0*	17.1*	9.7	6.2
S → F	2.1	1.7	1.6	4.2	3.0	7.6	3.1*	6.3*
S → M	3.8**	1.3**	1.4	2.3	1.7***	8.0***	5.7	4.2
MANOVA F	3.86		1.01		4.01		8.29	
df	6		6		6		6	
P	0.01		0.44		0.01		0.0001	

*Univariate ANOVA test significant at the 0.05 level; **univariate ANOVA test significant at the 0.01 level; ***univariate ANOVA test significant at the 0.001 level.

level, we followed it up with univariate ANOVA tests to locate the source of the difference. Significant differences in the univariate ANOVA tests are indicated by asterisks in Table 6.4. To better meet the homogeneity of variance and distributional assumptions of analysis of variance, we applied the square root transformation before conducting the analysis. Values in Table 6.4, however, are the raw frequencies, for ease of interpretation.

Table 6.4 shows significant differences in the positive and negative behavior profiles in high and low MF coalition families. Both parents were much more negative toward the son in high MF coalition families, and the sons tended to attack the mothers. In high MF coalition families, both parents were less positive toward their son and more positive toward each other. These patterns are what would be expected given the definition of the MF coalition. However, they provide useful detail on how much behavior of what types, and behavior by whom toward whom, is involved in displaying an MF coalition during problem solving. These patterns also clarify the kind of parental behavior the son is exposed to during family problem solving. The son's elevated opposition toward mother but not father here, even though the father is almost as negative as the mother toward the child,

TABLE 6.5 Family Behavior Profiles With MANOVA Tests for Differences Between High and Low Problem-Solving Families and Families With the Most and Least Antisocial Child

Speaker and Recipient	All Behavior (n = 40)	Positive Behavior Problem Solving		Negative Behavior Antisocial Child	
		Low (n = 20)	High (n = 20)	Low (n = 20)	High (n = 20)
F → M	11.2	2.8	2.7	2.7	2.1
F → S	33.1	1.9+	2.9+	6.1+	12.4*
M → F	13.3	3.2	4.5	2.5	2.5
M → S	39.9	2.2**	5.7**	7.6*	13.0*
S → F	22.8	1.3	1.6	3.0	6.2
S → M	29.9	0.7***	3.1***	5.9	5.8
MANOVA F		2.79		2.36	
df		6		6	
P		0.03		0.05	

+Univariate ANOVA test significant at the 0.10 level; *univariate ANOVA test significant at the 0.05 level; **univariate ANOVA test significant at the 0.01 level; ***univariate ANOVA test significant at the 0.001 level.

is informative about how this coalition form is articulated. The pattern of children's tending to oppose mothers more than fathers has been found in other research (Vuchinich, 1987).

The articulation of MS coalitions was somewhat different. There were no profile differences for positive behavior. The negative profiles indicated that strong MS coalitions were largely articulated by high levels of mother-father conflict, though the son was also more likely to oppose the father. This result is consistent with the family therapy literature that links cross-generational coalitions with marital problems (e.g., Minuchin et al., 1978).

Table 6.5 gives the corresponding profiles when significant differences were found. It includes tests that compared families who had more effective family problem solving with the less effective families, and that compared families with antisocial sons with those having more normal sons. Regarding problem solving, there were no profile differences for negative behavior. But for positive-behavior parents, in the effective problem-solving families the parents were more positive toward the sons, and sons were three times as positive toward their mothers.

There were no profile differences for positive behavior across the high and low antisocial child families. However, negative-behavior parents with more antisocial sons were twice as negative toward the sons as the other families. More antisocial sons also were twice as negative toward their fathers as other sons, though this difference only approached significance ($p < 0.15$).

Sequential Analysis

Patterns in family behavioral rates may be generated in a number of ways. First, there may be a tendency for one family member to act a certain way (e.g., positive, negative) toward everyone. This would be found in the case of a hostile father, a happy-go-lucky mother, or a depressed son. Second, there may be tendencies for certain family members to act certain ways toward other specific family members. For example, the father and son may have a relationship that is usually conflictual, with the father frequently criticizing the son. Third, there may be tendencies for family members to respond to certain actions of other family members with given types of behavior. For example, all family members may have a strong tendency to reciprocate any negative comment. Fourth, there may be tendencies for a person to continue a type of behavior regardless of what other family members do. For example, a mother may tend to continue negative behavior once she gets started, regardless of what anyone else does. In order to distinguish whether these patterns are the basis for observed family behavior, we need to express them in more technical terms. *Individual base rates* are the baseline tendencies of family members (i.e., mother, father, son) to act in given ways. An individual base rate can be expressed as number of behaviors per unit of time or as the odds of the person doing the behavior rather than anything else. This base rate may differ according to who is being spoken to. Tests for such differences are easily done. Testing for reciprocity or responsiveness is somewhat more difficult, but is frequently done. Similarly, tests for whether individuals tend to extend their behaviors, known as autodependency, are well established (e.g., Gottman & Roy, 1990; Vuchinich et al., 1991).

Determining whether any of these specific patterns are the basis for family behavior can be very useful in attempting to change dysfunctional family interaction patterns. For example, if the high level of negative behavior in a family can be traced to a mother's consistent negative behavior, rather than, say, lack of father's positive responsiveness or mother's autodependency, getting the mother to reduce her negative thoughts might be a useful approach. On the other hand, if negative behavior in the family can be traced to a tendency for father and son to respond negatively and immediately to any negative behavior, then an approach that focuses on reducing the spirals of conflict that such negative reciprocity produces can be useful (Forgatch & Patterson, 1989; Robin & Foster, 1989). The same logic applies to locating the sources of positive behavior and developing strategies for increasing it. Our concern in this part of the analysis is to examine whether or not sequential patterns are associated with effective family problem solving.

Many sequential patterns are a normal part of social interaction. We tend to speak next if we are spoken to. If someone opposes us, we tend to oppose them next, and so on. We are interested in whether such contingencies are more likely in certain family types than in others. Such analysis has the important side benefit of allowing tests for differences in behavior rates that control for normal sequential patterns. Thus the sequential analysis may clarify patterns found in the above examination of family behavior profiles.

Our sequential analysis is organized to provide more precise tests for differences in positive and negative behavior that occur in different types of families (e.g., comparing those that are good at problem solving with those that are not). Although several different hypotheses about sequential patterns could be tested, we focus on testing whether there are disparate levels of positive and negative responsiveness in different types of families. As in the analysis discussed above, we consider family differences in terms of coalitions, problem-solving success, and the presence of an antisocial child. Sample size limitations preclude a unified analysis of all types, so comparisons will be done separately. Separate models will also be examined for positive and negative behavior.

For this analysis, the data that had been sequentially coded in terms of each person's behavior as positive, negative, or other was transformed into two separate formats. For examining positive responsiveness, the negative behaviors were collapsed into the "other" code, so that all behaviors were either positive or other. For the analysis of negative responsiveness, positive codes were collapsed into the "other" category (Kerig, Cowan, & Cowan, 1993; Vuchinich et al., 1991). For tests of differences between family types, the data for all families of one type were pooled together.

The raw sequential information was transformed into contingency table form with a three-slot "moving window" (Gottman & Roy, 1990, p. 16). Each of the three time slots represented in the contingency table could be one of six possible actions. In the analysis of negative behavior, the six behavior categories were *mother negative, father negative, son negative, mother other, father other,* and *son other.* The analysis began with a $6 \times 6 \times 6 \times 2$ contingency table. Following previous work (Gottman & Roy, 1990), we tested the data sequences for order (i.e., how many turns in a row were sequentially dependent) and stationarity (i.e., whether the sequential dependency changed over time). We found that the sequences depended only on the immediately prior turn and that sequencing was constant across the 10-minute session. Thus the analysis focused on $6 \times 6 \times 2$ contingency tables such as Table 6.6, which displays the frequencies of sequential transitions of negative behavior in high and low (highest and lowest quartiles) problem-solving families. In a turn-based coding system speakers cannot follow themselves (Gottman & Roy, 1990), so several of the cells are impossible by design and are treated as "structural zeros" (Bishop, Fienberg, & Holland, 1975; Gottman & Roy, 1990).

Such tables are analyzed using logit models (e.g., Agresti, 1990; Gottman & Roy, 1990; Vuchinich et al., 1991) that were estimated from the corresponding loglinear models (in the SAS Statistical Package using PROC CATMOD). These models were used to estimate whether family type or behavior in the prior turn influenced the odds of occurrence of each behavioral category in the second (or respondent) slot. For this analysis we focused on testing whether there was a difference in responsiveness across family type. This could be tested through a determination of whether the observed frequencies in the contingency table (such as Table 6.6) could be approximately reproduced with a logit model that did not include an effect for differential responsiveness across family type (Allison & Liker, 1982). If models

TABLE 6.6   Contingency Table for the Sequential Analysis of Negative
Reciprocity in High and Low Problem-Solving Families

Initial Speaker	Respondent					
	M–	F–	S–	Mo	Fo	So
Low problem-solving families						
M–	—	31	52	—	21	50
F–	41	—	51	31	—	68
S–	45	54	—	22	21	—
Mo	—	46	26	—	85	121
Fo	32	—	14	83	—	97
So	34	53	—	144	104	—
High problem-solving families						
M–	—	15	12	—	26	43
F–	12	—	18	36	—	29
S–	19	13	—	28	15	—
Mo	—	28	31	—	169	230
Fo	29	—	13	172	—	213
So	34	38	—	257	217	—

NOTE: M– = mother negative behavior, F– = father negative behavior, S– = son negative
behavior, Mo = mother other behavior, Fo = father other behavior, So = Son other behavior.

without that effect provide an adequate fit to the data (which is indicated by a likelihood ratio chi-square p value greater than 0.05), then responsiveness is the same in both groups.

We estimated models that included terms for an overall family type frequency difference, differential frequencies across the six behavior categories in the initiator and respondent slots, interaction terms for effects of family type on the initiator and respondent categories, and an interaction term for the effect of the category in the initiator slot on the category in the respondent slot. This is a hierarchical model (Gottman & Roy, 1990), which means that all lower-order effects had to be included, regardless of whether they had significant effects, before an interaction effect involving those variables could be included. If F represents family type, I represents initial slot, and R the respondent slot, then the loglinear model we estimated could be expressed in the following terms: F, I, R, F × I, F × R, I × R. Ideally, there would be enough data to include all four family types in one 6 × 6 ×

TABLE 6.7   Goodness-of-Fit Tests for Sequential Models Testing for
Family Reciprocity Effects

	Likelihood Ratio Chi-Square	p Value
Positive behavior		
Family effect tested		
problem-solving effectiveness	22.27	0.051
mother-father coalition	18.78	0.130
mother-child coalition	17.71	0.165
antisocial child	26.99	0.013
Negative behavior		
Family effect tested		
problem-solving effectiveness	21.30	0.067
mother-father coalition	16.68	0.214
mother-child coalition	29.38	0.006
antisocial child	20.59	0.082

NOTE: All these tests have 13 degrees of freedom.

$2 \times 2 \times 2 \times 2$ table, which would allow more detailed analysis. With the present sample size this was not feasible.

Table 6.7 gives the likelihood ratio chi-square goodness-of-fit statistic for the models for positive and negative behavior. For negative behavior there was evidence ($p = 0.006$) of a significant difference in negative responsiveness between high and low mother-son coalition families. For positive behavior there was evidence of a difference in positive responsiveness between families that had antisocial sons and those that did not ($p = 0.013$). Consideration of what these effects mean requires examination of the parameter estimates in the logit models. An extended interpretation of all the estimates in these models is beyond the scope of this report, but we will provide a general summary and give more detail on the logit models involving family problem solving.

Table 6.8 gives the most pertinent logit estimates for the differences between high and low problem-solving families from the positive and negative behavior logit models. The top part of this table presents the logits, which are logarithms of the odds, of the person in the row emitting a negative behavior in the family type represented by that column, rather than in the family type represented in the other col-

TABLE 6.8 Logit Model Coefficients and Corresponding Odds Effects for Differences Between High and Low Problem-Solving Families

| | Logit Effects Problem Solving | | Multiplicative Effect on the Odds of the Behavior Occurring[a] |
	Low	High	
Negative behavior			
As initiator			
mother	0.64***	−0.64***	3.6
father	0.40**	−0.40**	2.2
son	−0.50***	0.50***	0.4
As respondent			
mother	0.32**	−0.32**	1.9
father	0.62***	−0.62***	3.4
son	0.40**	−0.40**	2.2
Positive behavior			
As initiator			
mother	−0.12	0.12	0.8
father	−0.82***	0.82***	0.2
son	0.42***	−0.42***	2.3
As respondent			
mother	−.24	0.24	0.6
father	−0.14	0.14	0.7
son	−0.86***	0.86***	0.2

a. These values, which are odds ratios, express the difference in the odds of a type of behavior occurring (e.g., negative) in low problem-solving families compared with the odds of occurrence in high problem-solving families.

**Coefficient significant at the 0.01 level; ***coefficient significant at the 0.001 level.

umn. Because there are only two family types in each model, the logits for each person are of equal magnitude with opposite signs. The final column gives the multiplicative family type effect on the odds of negative behavior occurring. Thus being in a low problem-solving family multiplies the odds of the mother's emitting a negative behavior by a factor of 3.6.

The negative behavior estimates indicate that both mother and father are significantly less oppositional in high problem-solving families as initiators and respondents. Also in the high problem-solving families, sons are significantly more negative as initiators but less oppositional as respondents. This suggests that allowing sons to initiate more opposition is beneficial to the problem-solving process. This is consistent with the value of open expression of some negative emotion. Indeed, as respondents, sons are less oppositional in the effective families. These results are especially noteworthy because the analysis of behavior rates found no differences in negative behavior across high and low problem-solving families.

Consideration of the logit estimates in the positive behavior model shows a mirror image of the above effects for sons, with them being somewhat less prosocial as initiators but much more prosocial as respondents. The only significant effect for fathers is that they are more prosocial in the high problem-solving families. The other parent effects are not significant but are in this same direction.

The estimates for the other models (not shown) indicate that the mother was more negative in high MF coalition families and in families with more antisocial sons. This is consistent with the findings concerning the prominent role of mothers in creating these communication patterns of families. Fathers were more oppositional in the MS coalition families, which would be expected, given that the mother and son "gang up" on him. Sons were more prosocial in the high MS coalition group and less prosocial in the high MF coalition families. This suggests the buoyant emotional effect on the child of being part of a coalition as well as the sobering effect of having a coalition against him.

Given the substantial magnitude of these effects involving family type and responsiveness, it is clear that models that allow interaction effects involving different family types (e.g., MF coalition × problem-solving effectiveness) are needed if we are to estimate accurately the sequential patterns associated with effective family problem solving. Estimation of the sequential differences between family types indicated in Table 6.7 would be suspect unless more than one family type is taken into account. However, it is clear from Table 6.7 that significant differences in responsiveness are present. Further analysis is beyond the scope of this report.

SUMMARY

Overall, the results presented above clarify several aspects of how communication structures are related to problem solving in different types of families. The analysis demonstrates specific ways in which the three levels of family communication (i.e., behavior exchange, relationships, and family systems) are involved in generating important patterns of family communication. Our analysis is generally descriptive, but several specific findings are noteworthy. First, mother-father coalitions and mother-son coalitions can be reliably measured using independent observational methods. A simple global rating of these coalitions was reliably correlated with an elaborate sociometric measure of the same coalitions. Such global rating can greatly reduce the time and cost associated with assessing these types of coalitions. Convergent measures for a father-son coalition against mother were not obtained, but this may be a result of the absence of such coalitions in this context. Studies of father-son coalitions in stepfamilies in which fathers have custody and stepmothers are in residence would provide a better test of how well father-son coalitions can be measured.

Second, strong mother-father coalitions are associated with ineffective family problem solving and the presence of antisocial sons. This is consistent with a scapegoating process in which the parents draw close together to cope with the child's misbehavior. The etiology of this link is controversial. The present results from the analysis of rates and sequencing suggest that the pattern is driven by the parents, rather than by the son's behavior. For example, in this study the only behaviors distinguishing families with antisocial sons from those without them were the mothers' and fathers' negative behaviors toward the sons. The sequential analysis also shows that the parents' tendency to initiate negative behavior is associated with ineffective family problem solving. These patterns are consistent with those found by family therapy researchers who view pathological behavior by the son as a reaction to the parents and structured interactions in the family (e.g., Madanes, 1981). In this regard the mother-son relationship seems to be especially prominent based on the analysis of behavior rates.

Third, the sequential analysis adds important insights to family behavior and effective problem solving that are not apparent in the analysis of rates. Of special significance was the tendency of both parents to be less negative, and fathers to be more positive, in effective problem-solving families. Furthermore, in the more effective families sons were freer to initiate negative comments.

This analysis has several limitations. The sample was small and could not take potentially important interaction effects into account. The data were collected in one urban area, and so the results may not generalize to other samples. Other variables that might effect family problem solving, such as family income, gender of child, and family size, were not included in the analysis. Nonetheless, our analysis has sufficient statistical power to isolate some important correlates of family problem solving. We have been able to validate measures of family coalitions and to identify family processes that can be verified on other samples.

If replicated in other studies, these results have clear implications for work in the area of training families with preadolescent sons to solve problems more effectively. Our findings suggest that excessive mother-father coalitions should be avoided. Parents need to be consistent, but when carried too far such coalitions inhibit effective problem solving with preadolescent sons, who are typically seeking increased autonomy. Avoiding such coalitions can be especially difficult when a child is exhibiting behavior problems.

The results also suggest the importance of parents moderating their negative behavior during problem solving. This is consistent with social learning theory's emphasis on positive reinforcement (e.g., Forgatch & Patterson, 1989). The sequential results further show the value of allowing, or even encouraging, preadolescent sons to initiate some negative behaviors toward parents during problem solving. Although this too could be carried to extremes, it clearly distinguished the more effective problem-solving families from the less effective ones in our sample. This analysis contributes to ongoing efforts to improve behavioral family therapy and counseling (e.g., Miller & Prinz, 1990).

Our results have some important implications for future theory and research. First, they suggest that renewed efforts to study and understand intrafamily coalitions may be beneficial in practical and theoretical terms. Theories of family coalitions are well known. Better measures of these family subsystems, which are demonstrated here, may provide a more solid empirical base for advances in the theory of family systems in preadolescence and adolescence. Second, the comparative analysis of behavioral rates and sequencing suggests the importance of sequential analysis in the study of family interaction. Prior sequential analyses have focused on dyads (e.g., Gottman & Roy, 1990). The present study extended these methods to the analysis of family triads and found that sequential analysis can illuminate the analysis of family triads as well as it does for dyads (e.g., Gottman, 1987).

REFERENCES

Achenbach, T. M., & Edelbrock C. (1983). *Manual for the Child Behavior Checklist and Revised Child Behavior Profile.* Burlington, VT: University Associates in Psychiatry.

Agresti, A. (1990). *Categorical data analysis.* New York: John Wiley.

Allison, P. D., & Liker, J. K. (1982). Analyzing sequential categorical data on dyadic interaction. *Psychological Bulletin, 91,* 393-403.

Bakeman, R., & Dorval, B. (1989). The independence assumption and its effect on sequential analysis. *Behavioral Assessment, 11,* 31-38.

Bakeman, R., & Gottman, J. M. (1986). *Observing interaction: An introduction to sequential analysis.* New York: Cambridge University Press.

Baumrind, D. (1991). Effective parenting during the early adolescent transition. In A. Cowan & E. M. Hetherington (Eds.), *Family transitions* (pp. 111-164). Hillsdale, NJ: Lawrence Erlbaum.

Beavers, R. W. (1982). Healthy, midrange and severely dysfunctional families. In F. Walsh (Ed.), *Normal family processes* (pp. 101-123). New York: Guilford.

Bishop, Y. M., Fienberg, S. E., & Holland, P. W. (1975). *Discrete multivariate analysis.* Cambridge: MIT Press.

Brody, G. H., Stoneman, Z., McCoy, J. K., & Forehand, R. (1992). Contemporaneous and longitudinal associations of sibling conflict with family relationship assessments and family discussions about sibling problems. *Child Development, 63,* 391-400.

Bronfenbrenner, U. (1979). *The ecology of human development: Experiments by nature and by design.* Cambridge, MA: Harvard University Press.

Capaldi, D. M., & Patterson, G. R. (1989). *Psychometric properties of fourteen latent constructs from the Oregon Youth Study.* New York: Springer-Verlag.

Christensen, A., & Margolin, G. (1988). Conflict and alliance in distressed and nondistressed families. In R. A. Hinde & J. Stevensen-Hinde (Eds.), *Relationships within families: Mutual influences* (pp. 263-282). New York: Oxford University Press.

Cummings, E. M., Ballard, M., El-Sheikh, M., & Lake, M. (1991). Resolution and children's response to interadult anger. *Developmental Psychology, 27,* 462-470.

Forgatch, M. S. (1989). Effects of negative emotion on family problem solving. *Journal of Marriage and the Family, 51,* 115-124.

Forgatch, M. S., & Patterson, G. R. (1989). *Parents and adolescents living together: Family problem solving.* Eugene, OR: Castalia.

Gilbert, R., Christensen, & Margolin, G. (1984). Patterns of alliances in nondistressed and multiproblem families. *Family Process, 23,* 75-87.

Gottman, J. M. (1987). The sequential analysis of family interaction. In T. Jacob (Ed.), *Family interaction and psychopathology* (pp. 453-480). New York: Plenum.

Gottman, J. M., & Roy, A. K. (1990). *Sequential analysis.* New York: Cambridge University Press.

Grych, J. H., & Fincham, F. D. (1990). Marital conflict and children's adjustment. *Psychological Bulletin, 108,* 267-290.

Gurman, A. S., & Kniskern, D. P. (1981). *Handbook of family therapy.* New York: Brunner/Mazel.

Haley, J. (1964). Research on family patterns: An instrument measurement. *Family Process, 3,* 41-65.

Haley, J. (1976). *Problem solving therapy.* San Francisco: Jossey-Bass.

Jacob, T. (1987). *Family interaction and psychopathology.* New York: Plenum.

Kazdin, A. E., Siegel, T. C., & Bass, D. (1992). Cognitive problem-solving skills training and parent management training in the treatment of antisocial behavior in children. *Journal of Consulting and Clinical Psychology, 60,* 733-747.

Kerig, P. K., Cowan, P. A., & Cowan, C. P. (1993). Marital quality and gender differences in parent-child interaction. *Developmental Psychology, 29,* 931-939.

Madanes, C. (1981). *Strategic family therapy.* San Francisco: Jossey-Bass.

Mann, B. J., Borduin, C. M., Henggeler, S. W., & Blaske, D. M. (1990). An investigation of systemic conceptualizations of parent-child coalitions and symptom change. *Journal of Consulting and Clinical Psychology, 58,* 336-344.

Miller, G. E., & Prinz, R. J. (1990). Enhancement of social learning family interventions for childhood conduct disorders. *Psychological Bulletin, 108,* 291-307.

Minuchin, S., Rosman, B., & Baker, L. (1978). *Psychosomatic families.* Cambridge, MA: Harvard University Press.

Mishler, E. G., & Waxler, N. E. (1968). *Interaction in families.* New York: John Wiley.

Patterson, G. R., Reid, J. B., & Dishion, T. J. (1992). *Antisocial boys: A social interactional approach* (Vol. 4). Eugene, OR: Castalia.

Preli, R., & Protinsky, H. (1988). Aspects of family structures in alcoholic, recovered and nonalcoholic families. *Journal of Marital and Family Therapy, 14,* 311-314.

Rausch, H. L., Barry, W. A., Hertel, A. K., & Swain, M. A. (1974). *Communication, conflict, and marriage.* San Francisco: Jossey-Bass.

Reid, J. B. (1993). Prevention of conduct disorder before and after school entry: Relating interventions to developmental findings. *Development and Psychopathology, 5,* 243-262.

Reiss, D. (1981). *The family's construction of reality.* Cambridge, MA: Harvard University Press.

Robin, A. L., & Foster, S. L. (1989). *Negotiating parent-adolescent conflict.* New York: Guilford.

Schuham, A. I. (1970). Power relations in emotionally disturbed and normal family triads. *Journal of Abnormal Psychology, 75,* 30-37.

Seelig, W. R., Goldman-Hall, B. J., & Jerrell, J. M. (1992). In-home treatment of families with seriously disturbed adolescents in crisis. *Family Process, 31,* 135-149.

Selman, R. L., Beardslee, W., Schultz, L. H., Krupa, M., & Podorefsky, D. (1986). Assessing adolescent interpersonal negotiation strategies: Toward the integration of structural and functional models. *Developmental Psychology, 22,* 450-459.

Simmel, G. (1950). *The sociology of Georg Simmel* (K. H. Wolff, Trans.). Glencoe, IL: Free Press. (Original work published 1908)

Spanier, G. B. (1976). Measuring dyadic adjustment: New scales for assessing the quality of marriage and similar dyads. *Journal of Marriage and the Family, 38,* 15-28.

Steinberg, L. (1990). Interdependence in the family: Autonomy, conflict, and harmony in the parent adolescent relationship. In S. S. Feldman & G. L. Elliot (Eds.), *At the threshold: The developing adolescent* (pp. 255-276). Cambridge, MA: Harvard University Press.

Steinhauer, P. D. (1987). The family as a small group: The process of family functioning. In T. Jacob (Ed.), *Family interaction and psychopathology* (pp. 67-116). New York: Plenum.

Vuchinich, S. (1987). Starting and stopping spontaneous family conflicts. *Journal of Marriage and the Family, 49,* 591-601.

Vuchinich, S., Bank, L., & Patterson, G. R. (1992). Parenting, peers, and the stability of antisocial behavior in preadolescent boys. *Developmental Psychology, 28,* 510-521.

Vuchinich, S., Emery, R. E., & Cassidy, J. (1988). Family members as third parties in dyadic family conflict: Strategies, alliances and outcomes. *Child Development, 59,* 1293-1302.

Vuchinich, S., Hetherington, E. M., Vuchinich, R. A., & Clingempeel, W. G. (1991). Parent-child interaction and gender differences in early adolescents' adaptation to stepfamilies. *Developmental Psychology, 25,* 618-626.

Vuchinich, S., Vuchinich, R., & Wood, B. (1993). The interparental relationship and family problem solving with preadolescent males. *Child Development, 64,* 1389-1400.

7

Family Conflict, Divorce, and Children's Adjustment

SUSAN GANO-PHILLIPS
FRANK D. FINCHAM

At the beginning of the twentieth century, concerns about "problems of interpersonal relations in the family" (Burr, Hill, Nye, & Reiss, 1979) prompted the scientific study of families. Considerable discussion emerged regarding the continued existence of the family as a group (Bell & Vogel, 1960), reflecting, among other things, an awareness of increasing rates of separation and divorce. Combined with the emergence of childhood as a life stage distinct from adulthood and the recognition that child deviance was not sinful but a psychological problem amenable to rehabilitation (Empey, 1976), this awareness resulted in attention to the impact of marital distress and divorce on children. Particular attention was again given to this topic in the 1950s, when marriage and family life were idealized. Growing up in a single-parent family was viewed as a threat to the child's development, as divorce was thought to disrupt the nurturance and socialization of children (Cherlin, 1981). Bowlby's (1951) seminal work linking juvenile delinquency to parent-child separation and the disruption of attachments also fueled concern about the harmful effects of separation and divorce on children. During this period systematic research in psychology began on the relations among child deviance, marital problems, and parenting skills. As divorce rates climbed in the 1970s, increased efforts were made to document the impact of divorce on children.

A large body of literature now exists linking divorce to a variety of childhood problems, including externalizing disorders, internalizing disorders, difficulties in interpersonal relationships, academic problems, and increased use of mental health services (for reviews, see Amato & Keith, 1991a; Emery, 1988; Grych & Fincham, 1992). Although results are not uniformly consistent, small but reliable differences have been documented in the adjustment of children from divorced and intact families. As adults, children from divorced families, compared with those from intact families, show poorer psychological adjustment, lower economic attainment, and less marital stability (Amato & Keith, 1991b). The fact that nearly half of all children born in the 1980s will experience the divorce of their parents (Glick & Lin, 1986), a figure likely to rise to 60% for children born in the 1990s (Furstenberg & Cherlin, 1991), continues to prompt concern. However, it is becoming increasingly apparent that the impact of divorce on children may not be caused by divorce per se but rather by factors associated with divorce. Chief among these is interparental conflict, as research has accumulated evidence suggesting that the conflict accompanying divorce, rather than the breakup of the family, may be primarily responsible for the adjustment problems of children whose parents divorce (Amato, 1993; Emery, 1988; Cherlin et al., 1991; Long & Forehand, 1987). This is an important development, as it suggests that child adjustment in intact and divorced families may reflect the same underlying process, namely, interparental conflict.

In this chapter, therefore, we focus on conflict in attempting to further our knowledge of family distress, divorce, and children's adjustment. By doing so, we do not mean to imply that understanding conflict alone will yield a complete picture of the relations among family distress, divorce, and children's adjustment. Similarly, it is important to acknowledge that conflict processes may differ across family forms (e.g., intact nuclear families, extended families, gay or lesbian families, stepfamilies, single-parent families) even though space constraints prevent examination of such possible differences. Rather than provide a comprehensive review of the literature and all the relevant issues, we briefly review the findings from the psychological literature on conflict, divorce, and child adjustment and then highlight ways to increase our understanding of family conflict. Toward this end, we address three primary questions: What is family conflict? What do we know about the relationship between family conflict and children's adjustment? How might we gain a more complete understanding of family conflict? We turn now to the first of these questions.

DEFINING FAMILY CONFLICT

Although frequently studied, conflict is rarely defined in the psychological literature (Fincham, 1993). In fact, research on family conflict has been driven largely by empirical rather than theoretical concerns (Emery, 1992). There are at least two possible reasons for this oversight. First, the referent for the term *conflict* appears to be self-evident, a circumstance that most likely reflects the broad usage to which it lends itself (for the confusion this can cause, see Fincham & Bradbury, 1991). In its common sense usage, conflict refers to both physical and verbal confrontation as well as the psychological states of the parties in conflict even though no overt confrontation takes place. The most common definition of conflict in the psychological literature, perceived goal incompatibility between two or more individuals or groups (Boulding, 1962; Fincham, Bradbury, & Grych, 1990; Lewin, 1948; Shantz, 1987), is consistent with this usage. However, some scholars restrict the term to its use as a description of interactional behaviors of opposing parties (Emery, 1992; Fitzpatrick, 1988). Whether conflict is best construed to include intrapersonal phenomena or as strictly interpersonal is not clear. In this chapter we focus our attention on *interpersonal* conflict within the family setting.

The second reason conflict is rarely defined concerns the complex nature of the task when more than two parties are involved. Perhaps it is for this reason that most research has been limited to the study of dyads within families. For example, research on family conflict and child adjustment has focused on marital conflict and has tended to exclude other forms of family conflict that may accompany marital conflict. However, the systemic and interdependent aspects of family life suggest that conflict may not be easily maintained within specific dyads. Family systems theory suggests a number of mechanisms whereby conflict is transmitted across family subsystems (e.g., distressed parents may "detour" their conflict away from the marital relationship and onto others, particularly the children; Minuchin, 1985). Similarly, social learning theory suggests that through the processes of observation, imitation, and coercive family cycles, children may come to be involved directly in conflict within the family (Margolin, 1981). Once this occurs, a new level of analysis is needed because behavior at the level of the family group is not simply an extension of individual or dyadic behavior. Unfortunately, there are few reliable and theoretically meaningful measures for such family-level dynamics (Green, Kolevson, & Vosler, 1985) and the systemic, family level of analysis has garnered little attention in the empirical literature.

Family conflict differs from other forms of social conflict in at least three other respects (Emery, 1992). First, the close physical proximity and shared experiences of family members suggest that family conflict is frequent and difficult to escape. Unlike acquaintances who experience conflict and choose to terminate their relationship, biological relationships are ended only by death. Second, family relationships are dynamic and evolving, and conflict is a common consequence of individual development within the family. That is, conflict is a natural outgrowth of the developmental transitions that occur within families throughout the life span. Finally, because of the importance of the family as a context for social, emotional, and practical support in Western countries, family conflicts carry potentially significant consequences for individuals and make the stakes for successfully managing conflict within the family quite high.

There are several additional issues in defining family conflict that have not been adequately addressed in the research literature. Foremost among these is the extent to which a precise and explicit definition of conflict would aid or hinder attempts at understanding the relation between family conflict and child adjustment. Recently, Fincham and Osborne (1993) outlined how greater clarity in specifying the construct of marital conflict led to advances in understanding the marital conflict-child adjustment relationship. A similar analysis of family conflict is not yet possible, and it must suffice to note that in the literature *family conflict* represents a wide variety of phenomena, ranging from intrapersonal struggles to triadic and systemic characteristics (Emery, 1992; Minuchin, 1985; Vuchinich, Emery, & Cassidy, 1988).

Although conflict is inevitable in family relationships (Coombs, 1987), the consequences of family conflict vary tremendously. Conflict can be handled in a hostile, destructive manner or it can be resolved in healthy and constructive ways through compromise and cooperation (Deutsch, 1969). Given that conflict occurs in all families and most children do not develop adjustment problems, the critical task is to determine which aspects of conflict result in pathogenic child outcomes.

A necessary step in pursuing this task is to examine the full range of interpersonal relationships in which conflict may be experienced within the family. Interparental conflict is one type of conflict that has received significant empirical examination, but other less frequently examined types of family conflict may also serve important roles in helping us to understand individual and family functioning. These include parent-child conflict and sibling conflict. We therefore examine these three types of conflict in addressing the second question posed at the outset of this chapter: What do we know about the relationship between family conflict and children's adjustment?

FAMILY CONFLICT AND CHILD ADJUSTMENT: CURRENT STATUS

Whereas some types of family conflict have received relatively little theoretical or empirical examination, others have been studied in great detail as they relate to child adjustment. In this section, we examine evidence linking three types of dyadic conflict in families to child maladjustment (we discuss triadic and systemic conflict in a later section). Our goal within each domain is to highlight the major empirical approaches and findings in the psychological literature. We begin with the most frequently examined dyad—the mother-father relationship.

Interparental Conflict

Several recent reviews on the relation between interparental conflict and child adjustment are available (e.g., Fincham & Osborne, 1993;

Grych & Fincham, 1990; Jouriles, Farris, & McDonald, 1991; Reid & Crisafulli, 1990), so we offer only a brief overview here.

Early research demonstrated that marital conflict is more closely associated with child problems than is general marital dissatisfaction (e.g., Hetherington, Cox, & Cox, 1982). Moreover, this relation is most reliable when children are exposed to the conflict (Porter & O'Leary, 1980). As noted earlier, studies of marital conflict in both intact and separated/divorced families provide support for the hypothesis that child problems are related to marital conflict. In the divorce literature, interparental conflict has been related to a wide range of negative child outcomes, including low social and cognitive competence (Long, Forehand, Fauber, & Brody, 1987), conduct disorder and anxiety/withdrawal symptoms (Forehand et al., 1991; Wierson, Forehand, & McCombs, 1988), and aggression and failure to engage in prosocial behavior (Hetherington et al., 1982). Because marital conflict may both precede and follow divorce, it has been difficult to separate the effects of divorce per se from the effects on child adjustment due to interparental conflict. Cherlin et al.'s (1991) large-scale studies in the United States and Great Britain have shown that, at least for boys, child outcome following divorce is predicted largely by predivorce functioning, and hence research has continued to focus on interparental conflict rather than divorce alone in attempting to understand children's adjustment.

Most prior research has examined aggregate measures of marital conflict and child adjustment, yielding significant correlations but little explanation about the *processes* that underlie this relationship. Though it is often assumed that conflict is always experienced as stressful or harmful, this is not necessarily the case (Camara & Resnick, 1989); indeed, "exposure to some types of conflict may promote the development of constructive problem-solving or coping strategies" (Grych & Fincham, 1990, p. 268). The emphasis in this research area has thus moved from documenting a relation between marital conflict and child maladjustment to attempts to understand more specifically the nature of the relationship between these two complex multidimensional constructs and the processes that give rise to it. What features of conflict are pathogenic? What specific impacts do those pathogenic features of conflict have on child outcomes?

In an attempt to determine the features of conflict that are pathogenic for children, greater attention is being given to the identification
of *specific dimensions* of conflict related to child outcomes. This has
occurred in the correlational field studies that have always characterized this area of inquiry and in the experimental, analog studies
that have recently become more prevalent in this area. Several dimensions of conflict are now recognized as important for child outcomes.
Conflict is more closely related to child distress when it is frequent
(e.g., Cummings, Zahn-Waxler, & Radke-Yarrow, 1981), when it is
intense (e.g., Grych & Fincham, 1993), when it involves physical
aggression (e.g., Fantuzzo et al., 1991), when it is unresolved (e.g.,
Cummings, Ballard, El-Sheikh, & Lake, 1991), and when it concerns
child behavior (e.g., Grych & Fincham, 1993).

As regards processes that might account for the marital conflict-
child outcome association, a number of mechanisms have been suggested (e.g., modeling), but few have been systematically explored at
an empirical level. However, there is some evidence to suggest that
parental psychopathology (e.g., Downey & Coyne, 1990), antisocial
behavior (Capaldi & Patterson, 1991), parenting difficulties (Fauber,
Forehand, McCombs Thomas, & Wierson, 1990), family adversity
(Rutter, 1978), and extrafamilial support (Jenkins & Smith, 1990) may
partially mediate the relation between conflict and children's adjustment. In a recent addition to this literature, Grych and Fincham (1990)
argue that children's responses to interparental conflict are mediated
by the children's appraisals or understanding of the conflict. Grych
and colleagues found that children's reports of interparental conflict
predicted children's adjustment more consistently than did parent
reports of conflict (Grych, Seid, & Fincham, 1992) and that children's
coping responses to conflict were related to their appraisals of the
conflict (Grych & Fincham, 1993). Although designed to study a
mediating variable, this research also had the advantage of providing
multiple and independent sources of information regarding conflict
and adjustment. The significance of such data is emphasized by the
fact that 45 of 80 observations used in a meta-analysis of 33 studies in
this research area comprised data from a single (parental) source (Reid
& Crisafulli, 1990).

In summary, consistent relations exist between divorce and child adjustment difficulties as well as between interparental conflict and child difficulty. Progress has been made in identifying the pathogenic dimensions of conflict for children, and there are some, albeit limited, data on the processes that might account for the conflict-child outcome association. Perhaps the most salient of these concerns the parent-child relation, to which we now turn.

Parent-Child Conflict

Ecological theory and family systems theory support the idea that the quality of the marital relationship and that of the parent-child relationship are interdependent (Easterbrooks & Emde, 1988). Some scholars argue that the detrimental effects of interparental conflict are mediated through disrupted parenting behavior or perturbations in the parent-child relationship (e.g., Fauber & Long, 1991; Jouriles et al., 1991; for a rebuttal, see Emery, Fincham, & Cummings, 1992). A difficulty in testing this hypothesis is that parent behavior is, in part, a response to child behavior and is therefore always likely to covary more with child behavior than other factors that may also potentially explain child behavior (e.g., marital conflict) but are not necessarily direct responses to it.

There is some evidence that the effects of interparental conflict on parenting (inconsistent discipline, poor parent-child relationships) may be responsible for child adjustment problems. For example, Fauber et al. (1990), in research involving a sample of intact and divorced families, found that parental behavior (rejection/withdrawal and use of psychological or emotional controls as a way of securing strong alliances with a child) mediated the relation between marital conflict and children's internalizing problems. However, there have also been studies in which marital conflict has been found to account for unique variance in child adjustment after the effects of parenting were statistically controlled (e.g., Jenkins & Smith, 1990).

In contrast, little attention has been given to how parent-child conflict per se influences child outcomes (Osborne & Fincham, in press). Buchanan, Maccoby, and Dornbusch (1991) found that in divorced families, adolescents who experienced high levels of "feeling caught" between their divorced parents, in terms of either emotional or practical issues, had poorer adjustment. "Feeling caught" is relevant here because it is viewed as having a negative effect on parent-child interactions such that the child is either explicitly drawn into conflict or left to deal with emotional reactions (e.g., worry, fearfulness) about what impact a positive relationship with one parent may have on the child's relationship with the other parent. In a further study, sibling differences in reported parent-child conflict following divorce were associated with differences in adjustment. Specifically, greater parent-child conflict was associated with greater externalizing problems, even though siblings shared a similar home environment (Monahan, Buchanan, Maccoby, & Dornbusch, 1993).

In sum, although considerable attention has been given to parent-child relationships in the psychological literature (discipline styles, consistency of interactions, and so on), few studies have focused specifically on parent-child conflict. This is surprising, given that the task of socialization ensures that the immediate goals of parents and children will often be at odds, resulting in the potential for conflict. Yet no cohesive, identifiable literature has emerged on this topic, a circumstance that may reflect the belief that the imbalance of power between parents and children precludes the expression of true conflict. A recent attempt to address this topic by Osborne and Fincham (in press) provides a more detailed account of parent-child conflict.

Sibling Conflict

Sibling relationships are important because they are among life's most enduring relationships and can be important sources of conflict, support, and companionship (Minuchin, 1985; Vandell & Bailey, 1992). Because conflict with a sibling does not easily threaten the continuation of the relationship, children may be freer to engage in conflict with siblings than might otherwise be expected. Sibling conflicts provide a mechanism through which children may differentiate themselves from one another and achieve a variety of developmental tasks, such as learning to express and manage negative affect (Shantz & Hobart, 1989). On a practical level, sibling conflicts are one of the most frequent and persistent problems reported by parents (Kelly & Main, 1979). As a function of the amount of time spent together and the permanent familial tie between siblings, sibling conflict is an inevitable part of family life. Although inevitable, sibling conflicts vary tremendously across children, both in frequency and in terms of whether they are destructive or constructive. Destructive conflict is characterized by high negative affect, a spread from initial issues to broader issues, and an escalation to intrusiveness and coercion, whereas constructive conflict has lower affective intensity, focuses on the issues at hand, and is likely to be resolved through mutually acceptable negotiations (Vandell & Bailey, 1992). Greater involvement in conflict is believed to provide children with increased opportunities to experience some of the constructive outcomes associated with successful conflict resolution, so engagement in sibling conflict may be an important developmental task for young children.

Empirical evidence documents an association between sibling conflict and family functioning. For example, using a sample of 76 latency aged and early adolescent siblings, Brody, Stoneman, McCoy, and Forehand (1992) demonstrated that paternal equality of treatment, family harmony during family discussions, and parents' perceptions of family cohesiveness are associated with low levels of sibling conflict. The behavior of parents toward siblings in conflict is also related to the frequency of such conflict (Dunn & Munn, 1986; Brody, Stoneman, & Burke, 1987). There is some evidence that parental intervention increases sibling conflict (Dunn, 1988), so it is possible that the reduced parental attention (and hence reduced intervention) often accompanying divorce contributes to reduced sibling conflict among siblings in divorced families. Alternatively, differential treatment of children has been clearly implicated in increasing sibling conflict; in divorced families this often results in unusual parent-child alliances and in children feeling caught between their parents (Brody et al., 1987).

Two distinct sources of sibling conflict have been suggested. One involves parents' relationships with their children, and the other focuses on the individual temperaments and personalities of the siblings (Vandell & Bailey, 1992). We review below four ways in which sibling conflicts are thought to arise through parental interaction, particularly as they relate to family functioning during the divorce transition.

Differential treatment of children by a parent may involve extra attention or affection or, alternatively, a requirement for behavioral performance that differs between children. It is possible that differential treatment of children may have positive effects, especially when it reflects sensitivity to children's differing needs. However, differential treatment can also have negative effects on favored as well as unfavored children (Stocker, Dunn, & Plomin, 1989). The results of several observational studies suggest that parental inequities may result in increased conflict between children. Studies examining differential treatment of siblings often examine the transition during the birth of a new sibling, but it is clear that differential treatment may develop as a function of the life circumstances surrounding interparental conflict, separation, or divorce. For example, a mother may hold her eldest daughter responsible for more household and family management responsibilities as a function of having to head a single-parent household. Although this differential treatment of the eldest child is a practical necessity brought about by family circumstances, it may have a significant impact on sibling relations as well.

Sibling conflict may also arise from *inadequate or insufficient parental attention* (Monahan et al., 1993; Vandell & Bailey, 1992). This inadequate parental attention is portrayed in the literature as an absolute (rather than relative) failure to meet children's emotional needs. The best research linking inadequate attention or parental warmth to sibling conflict is found in the literature on infant attachment. No research has been conducted in divorcing families on this potential contributor to sibling conflict.

The *emotional climate of the family,* as a third mechanism for influencing sibling conflict, refers to the parents' psychological states, their relationship with one another, and global measures of family stress (Vandell & Bailey, 1992). MacKinnon (1989) examined the relations between marital relationships and sibling relationships in divorced and intact families and found that conflicted marital relationships were associated with conflict between siblings, whereas positive marital relationships were associated with more positive sibling relations. Thus family stress and conflict in other domains of the family are mirrored in sibling interactions.

Fourth, *poor parental modeling* suggests that children may imitate the types of interactions they have observed or have been part of with respect to their parents. For example, children who experience hostile or negative interactions with their parents may model or imitate this type of interaction in dealing with their siblings (Kendrick & Dunn, 1983). Furthermore, parents may respond inconsistently to sibling quarrels, thereby directly reinforcing the conflictual behavior by intermittently reinforcing the children's participation in it.

Although these four hypothesized mechanisms by which parents influence sibling conflict do not all relate directly to family conflict, it is easy to imagine how parental conflict may lead to individual changes in parents that may be reflected in their interactions with their children.

Very little is known about factors that influence the positive aspects of sibling relationships. Kempton, Armistead, Wierson, and Forehand (1991) suggest that siblings may either exacerbate or minimize the effects of divorce, depending on the relationship between siblings. They examined whether the presence of a sibling had a buffering effect on children who experienced parental divorce. In their sample of adolescents, children with no siblings appeared to have more externalizing problems following parental divorce than did adolescents with either older or younger siblings. Thus, their data support the hypothesis that siblings serve to buffer the impact of divorce for one another. Even so, it is difficult to predict what component of having a sibling is responsible for the buffering effect on children's adjustment to divorce.

Because of the need to satisfy assumptions of statistical independence, most research on divorce has not examined siblings' experiences of divorce (Kurdek, 1989). Instead, research has examined interfamilial differences in children's adjustment rather than intrafamilial patterns. What little is known about siblings' reactions to divorce suggests that considerable differences in adjustment to divorce are common, even among siblings who live in the same residence following parental divorce (Monahan et al., 1993). The literature on intact families is similarly unhelpful, as there have been virtually no studies on sibling differences in the experiences and effects of marital conflict.

In sum, although theories have been advanced to explain how sibling conflict arises, very little theory and very few data have accumulated to suggest how sibling conflict may be related to child adjustment. What theory does exist suggests that sibling conflict may be positively related to adjustment, as this conflict is seen as a normative developmental progression. Empirical findings within the divorce literature suggest that siblings may serve as sources of support rather than as sources of conflict during the divorce transition. Additional work is needed to clarify the mechanisms by which interparental conflict is related to sibling conflicts as well as the mechanisms by which sibling conflict influences other forms of conflict within the family.

TOWARD A MORE COMPLETE
UNDERSTANDING OF FAMILY CONFLICT

Our goal in this section is to raise four major issues that should advance our understanding of the relations among family conflict, divorce, and children's adjustment: the study of causal relations, the developmental level of the child as a background for viewing conflict, the unit of analysis in examining family conflict, and the role that the socioemotional environment plays in family conflict. We discuss ways in which each of these factors may help to clarify the relationship between family conflict and child outcomes.

Snapshots Versus Movies

Much of our knowledge concerning family conflict and child adjustment can be compared to snapshots taken from a single angle or point of view (e.g., the role of anger in children's experiences of parental conflict, the relevance of child- versus non-child-focused conflict). Although these snapshots provide useful information, they fail to capture sequential or temporal relations, and hence it is difficult to order the various pictures that have been taken. Consider the difference between still photographs and motion pictures: More meaning can be conveyed by observing the relationships between characters in a movie than by viewing a series of still photographs. The characters' actions, viewed in temporal order, allow us to make causal inferences and thereby increase our understanding.

There is a compelling need for researchers to integrate the various aspects of family conflict that have been examined to this point, and to study the temporal relations among them and child adjustment. Although causal relations are best inferred from experimental data, practical and ethical difficulties make it exceedingly difficult to collect experimental data on family conflict. However, *longitudinal research* on conflict and child adjustment can help provide a more complete picture of the mechanisms and processes by which conflict, divorce, and child adjustment are related (Amato, 1993). Prospective longitudinal studies have already begun to suggest that changes seen in children whose parents divorce can be attributed to parental conflict prior to divorce. However, longitudinal studies are still relatively rare in this area of research.

The urgent need to demonstrate that conflict *predicts* the development of children's emotional and social problems over time is also emphasized by the reliance on analogue studies in this domain. Analogue studies have been quite useful in identifying dimensions of conflict that produce stress in children. However, experimental controls in which naturally occurring covariates of conflict are randomly distributed may provide a distorted view of relations outside the laboratory. Moreover, the demonstration that various dimensions of conflict *can* cause distress among children in the laboratory does not necessarily reflect the extent to which conflict actually *does* cause children stress in the real world. Longitudinal field studies need to be integrated with laboratory research if we are to gain a more accurate picture of the causal relations among family conflict, divorce, and child adjustment.

Conducting longitudinal research on family conflict and child adjustment raises many difficult issues. Foremost among these are the issues of multiple and bidirectional causation. To address the former, a broader, more integrative theoretical position is needed to shift the focus from single-factor models of child adjustment to more realistic models involving multiple causation. When considering the breadth of the construct *child adjustment,* it is quite reasonable to suggest that multiple factors may play a causal role. As regards bidirectional causation, a family systems viewpoint suggests that reciprocal influences and circular causality are integral to understanding the functioning of individuals within the family. Given the complexity of family relationships, more sophisticated methodological and statistical procedures will be needed to begin to address questions of reciprocal influence and circular causality. Notwithstanding this need, researchers can make judicious use of existing technologies (e.g., lag sequential analysis, structural equation modeling) to address family members' reciprocal influences upon one another.

In sum, an understanding of sequential relations provides a window on causal mechanisms in the family conflict-child adjustment domain. Although costly and time-consuming, complex longitudinal designs are likely to provide a much more realistic and comprehensive picture of the relationship between conflict and child adjustment.

Black-and-White Versus Color Pictures

Black-and-white film, regardless of the manner in which it is processed, does not capture the bright hues and subtle shadings evident in color pictures. Much of the research on conflict and children's adjustment seems comparable to black-and-white pictures, in that richness is lost in the failure to consider children's *developmental levels* as a context for understanding the family conflict-child adjustment relationship.

Research has shown that children's affective and behavioral responses to conflict change with age. Some scholars have asserted that young children are more susceptible than older children to the influence of family conflict, as they are less familiar with it and have fewer coping responses to deal with their emotions (Maccoby, 1982). Alternatively, others have argued that older children, given their greater capacity to understand and process emotional expressions, are more likely to be adversely affected by family conflict (Emery, 1988). Although speculations of this nature are common, no single age group appears to be more adversely affected by conflict than other age groups (Cummings, Iannotti, & Zahn-Waxler, 1985; Cummings, Zahn-Waxler, & Radke-Yarrow, 1984). Children's awareness of conflict increases with age, and their ability to cope with stressful events and regulate their emotions and behavior also increases (Grych & Fincham, 1990). These findings suggest that future research needs to consider how developmental differences influence children's appraisals, their understanding of conflict, and their choice of coping behaviors (Grych & Fincham, 1993).

The need to investigate child appraisals has been echoed elsewhere. For example, Kurdek (1993) has recently criticized Amato's (1993) theoretical and empirical review of children's adjustment to divorce for failing to consider children's developmental levels in understanding their adjustment to divorce. More specifically, he argues that, "because the *appraisal* of stressful life events is more important than their mere *occurrence*, the meaning of divorce is likely to differ for infants, preschoolers, adolescents, and young adults" (p. 41). Pickles and Rutter (1991) have raised a similar concern regarding life transitions more generally: "It cannot be assumed that the transitions impinge similarly on everyone. Rather, the content or meaning of the transitions must be personalized in ways that go beyond their mere occurrence" (p. 135).

In addition to differences in perceptions of conflict at various developmental levels, there are normative changes in conflict patterns that occur as a function of children's changing development that need to be considered. For example, sibling conflict has been shown to decrease in frequency from the second year of life through adolescence (Vandell & Bailey, 1992). Similarly, parent-child conflicts increase during early adolescence in most families. Failure to recognize these normative and developmentally appropriate changes in conflict patterns within families may lead us to overlook aspects of the very phenomenon that we are using to predict child outcomes.

In sum, research on children's adjustment to conflict and parental divorce has often failed to consider the cognitive, social, and emotional development of the children in exploring relationships between conflict and adjustment. Although some progress has been made in considering the developmental implications of children's perceptions of interparental conflict, similar progress is needed in the examination of other forms of family conflict. Future research needs to consider how children's developmental levels influence their understanding of and coping with all types of conflict that occur within the family.

Telephoto Versus Wide-Angle Lens

A telephoto lens provides a window of observation that is intricate and detailed, in contrast to the panoramic, broad-spectrum view provided by a wide-angle lens. Much of the research on the relationship between family conflict and children's adjustment has utilized a telephoto lens, examining specific and detailed components of conflict and relating them to children's adjustment (e.g., Cummings et al., 1984, 1985; Grych & Fincham, 1993). The fact that research has focused on details of conflict raises two distinct questions. First, what is the appropriate *level of investigation* for this domain? Second, what is the appropriate *unit of analysis* for understanding the role of family conflict in children's adjustment?

Level of Investigation

Questions regarding the level of investigation center on the methodologies used to study conflict and child adjustment. There have been two primary approaches thus far. One consists of field studies that examine correlations among self-reports of within-family variables (e.g., levels of conflict, overall child adjustment, parenting style). Occasionally such studies may also include observational data or data coded from interviews. Typically, data from these studies reflect general levels of functioning rather than responses to specific events. A second approach has involved experimental analogue studies of conflict in which children are exposed to hypothetical or real conflict situations and are either observed or asked to report about their feelings and cognitions during the conflict. The level of analysis in this approach is therefore quite different from that of the first approach, as it focuses on responses to specific events rather than on general or aggregated levels of responding. Although data from studies using the first approach are not as microanalytic as those obtained using the second, neither provides a panoramic view of the family as a whole.

The two primary approaches have provided an impressive body of data but have yielded a limited perspective on family conflict, divorce, and child adjustment. There is a clear need to understand the relationship between these two levels of investigation, as we know very little about how children's immediate responses to conflict relate to the development of long-term adjustment difficulties (Fincham, Grych, & Osborne, 1993; Fincham & Osborne, 1993). In addition to integrating these two levels of analysis, there is also considerable scope for providing macroanalytic perspectives on the family that include its context within broader social units.

Unit of Analysis

The unit of analysis in this research refers to the component parts of the family and how they are studied independently or in combination with one another. Most research on family conflict and children's adjustment has been quite narrow (or telephoto) in its focus, with the vast majority focusing on dyadic conflict and how it is related to individual functioning. Although this approach has provided significant information, particularly concerning the relationship between interparental conflict and child adjustment, it falls far short of capturing family processes as a whole. In fact, very little research exists in which the level of analysis is commensurate with the views offered of families in systems theory (e.g., Minuchin, 1985).

Family theorists argue that the family is a system, a unit that is greater than the sum of its component parts. A systems perspective holds that individuals are interdependent and are affected not only by conflict in their own relationships but by conflict in the relationships between other family members. As participants in triadic and larger conflict situations, according to systems theory, individuals not only are affected by other family members' conflicts but also affect the processes and outcomes of those conflicts (Emery, 1992).

Applying a systems perspective to understanding family conflict requires some rethinking of the most appropriate unit(s) of analysis. Although the outcomes one seeks to predict may remain individual (each child's adjustment), triadic and systemic units of analysis may be warranted. Emery (1992), for example, suggests that conflict produces nonnormative family alliances, and it is these alliances that contribute to child maladjustment. This may involve a father and son allying together against a mother, for example. Although systemic approaches are intuitively appealing to many, very little research has been conducted from these perspectives, owing to the complexity of operationalizing and analyzing constructs such as alliances and boundaries. Some innovative approaches have recently been developed that begin to address methodological and analytic difficulties in addressing family systems. These include a triadic observational coding system that allows for identification of alliances, strategies used, and outcomes (Vuchinich et al., 1988) and the use of sequential interaction analyses to examine the spread of conflict across dyads within the family (Christensen & Margolin, 1988).

In sum, it is not possible to address all of the concerns and shortcomings of past research regarding levels of investigation and units of analysis in a single study or even a series of studies. However, it is important that researchers are cognizant of the limitations of past research and the need for new and creative designs to advance our understanding and to bring our research designs into accord with theoretical writings in this domain.

Drive-In Theaters Versus Modern, High-Tech Theaters

Old-fashioned drive-in theaters (with their monophonic speakers and blurry projected pictures) do not provide the full extent of experiences that modern movie theaters (with their sharp visual images and sophisticated sound systems) can provide. Most research on the conflict-child adjustment relationship can be compared to the experience of going to a drive-in theater, in that the studies rarely include the full range of variables that can enrich experiments to their fullest potential. In particular, research has failed to consider many variables concerning the broad socioemotional context of the family that may influence family and individual functioning.

These broad contextual variables may be important for moderating relations between family conflict and child adjustment. For example, how marital conflict is experienced by the child may depend on the emotional climate of the family; the conflict may be less upsetting in families characterized by warmth and openness than in families marked by tension and hostility. Such variables can be viewed as risk factors when they take certain forms (e.g., unsupportive family environment) and as protective factors when they take other forms (e.g., a supportive family environment). Although the importance of risk factors has been widely recognized in research on family conflict and child adjustment, protective factors have received less attention. Empirical studies of protective factors are limited, but the results are quite impressive. Rutter (1971), for example, demonstrated that children in conflictual homes who had a good relationship with one parent were less likely to show Antisocial disorder than were children who had poor relationships with both parents. Similarly, positive relationships with parents, siblings, and adults outside of the family have been shown to buffer children from the impact of high marital conflict (Camara & Resnick, 1988; Jenkins & Smith, 1990; Peterson & Zill, 1986).

It is unclear how risk and protective factors combine to influence children's adjustment, as empirical data on the combination of these types of contextual factors do not exist in research on family conflict. Within the divorce literature, calls to examine the interactions between stressors or risk factors and resources have recently been made. Amato (1993), for instance, notes that "future research on children of divorce needs to model interactions between stressors and resources; studying particular factors out of context, rather than trying to grasp the larger pattern, will probably only generate more findings that are inconsistent and contradictory" (p. 36). We concur with this imperative.

A further issue regarding contextual factors influencing children's adjustment concerns the boundary conditions under which the observed relationships between conflict and child adjustment hold. This is particularly relevant in the consideration of different family forms, as the observed relationships between conflict processes and child adjustment may differ across intact, divorced, and single-parent families. For example, children who have experienced parental divorce may interpret and respond to conflict in qualitatively different ways from children who have little history of interparental conflict (Grych & Fincham, 1993).

In sum, empirical findings from the family conflict-child adjustment literature suggest that broad contextual variables may contribute meaningfully to our understanding of how family conflict is related to child adjustment. Both risk and protective factors should be considered and measured in longitudinal designs attempting to understand the genesis of child adjustment problems.

CONCLUSION

In this chapter we have examined the association between family conflict and divorce and child adjustment. Because of recent evidence suggesting that the relation between parental divorce and children's adjustment may be spurious, and that interparental conflict may be responsible for producing both child problems and marital dissolution, we have focused primarily on family conflict.

Our review has shown that most research has examined family dyads (interparental, parent-child, and sibling) and that both the amount of research and the focus of the research on each dyad have differed. It is also apparent that relatively little is known about the *processes* that give rise to the observed associations between family conflict and child adjustment problems. In fact, the relations between children's immediate reactions to conflict and their long-term adjustment remain largely unexplored. Finally, the various forms of dyadic conflict have not been examined consistently in relation to one another, and conflict in the family as a whole is relatively unexplored.

Although considerable progress has been made in our understanding of the "problems of interpersonal relations in the family" and how they relate to child adjustment, it is equally apparent that much remains to be learned. We therefore have offered here some suggestions to advance understanding of family conflict and children's adjustment, emphasizing, in particular, the use of longitudinal research to examine causal relations, greater attention to the developmental level of the child, the integration of diverse levels of investigation (field research and microsocial analyses of conflict) and units of analysis (dyads, triads, and entire family systems) in examining family conflict, and the inclusion of the broader socioemotional environment of the family. Recent attention in the literature to several of these issues bodes well for the advancement of our understanding of the relationship between family conflict and child adjustment.

REFERENCES

Amato, P. R. (1993). Children's adjustment to divorce: Theories, hypotheses, and empirical support. *Journal of Marriage and the Family, 55,* 23-38.

Amato, P. R., & Keith, B. (1991a). Consequences of parental divorce for the well-being of children: A meta-analysis. *Psychological Bulletin, 110,* 26-46.

Amato, P. R., & Keith, B. (1991b). Parental divorce and adult well-being: A meta-analysis. *Journal of Marriage and the Family, 53,* 43-58.

Bell, N. W., & Vogel, E. F. (1960). *A modern introduction to the family.* Glencoe, IL: Free Press.

Boulding, K. E. (1962). *Conflict and defense: A general theory.* New York: Harper & Row.

Bowlby, J. (1951). *Maternal care and mental health: A report prepared on behalf of the World Health Organization as a contribution to the United Nations programme for the welfare of homeless children.* Geneva: World Health Organization.

Brody, G. H., Stoneman, Z., & Burke, M. (1987). Child temperaments, maternal differential behavior, and sibling relationships. *Developmental Psychology, 23,* 354-362.

Brody, G. H., Stoneman, Z., McCoy, J. K., & Forehand, R. (1992). Contemporaneous and longitudinal associations of sibling conflict with family relationship assessment and family discussions about sibling problems. *Child Development, 63,* 391-400.

Buchanan, C. M., Maccoby, E. E., & Dornbusch, S. M. (1991). Caught between parents: Adolescents' experience in divorced homes. *Child Development, 62,* 1008-1029.

Burr, W. R., Hill, R., Nye, F. I., & Reiss, I. L. (Eds.). (1979). *Contemporary theories about the family* (Vol. 1). New York: Free Press.

Camara, K. A., & Resnick, G. (1988). Interparental conflict and cooperation: Factors moderating children's post-divorce adjustment. In E. M. Hetherington & J. D. Arasteh (Eds.), *Impact of divorce, single parenting, and stepparenting on children* (pp. 169-195). Hillsdale, NJ: Lawrence Erlbaum.

Camara, K. A., & Resnick, G. (1989). Styles of conflict resolution and cooperation between divorced parents: Effects on child behavior and adjustment. *American Journal of Orthopsychiatry, 59,* 560-575.

Capaldi, D. M., & Patterson, G. R. (1991). Relation of parental transitions to boys' adjustment problems: I. A linear hypothesis. II. Mothers at risk for transitions and unskilled parenting. *Developmental Psychology, 3,* 489-504.

Cherlin, A. J. (1981). *Marriage, divorce, remarriage.* Cambridge, MA: Harvard University Press.

Cherlin, A. J., Furstenberg, F. F., Chase-Lansdale, P. L., Kiernan, K. E., Robins, P. K., Morrison, D. R., & Teitler, J. O. (1991). Longitudinal studies of effects of divorce on children in Great Britain and the United States. *Science, 252,* 1386-1389.

Christensen, A., & Margolin, G. (1988). Conflict and alliance in distressed and non-distressed families. In R. A. Hinde & J. Stevenson-Hinde (Eds.), *Relationships within families: Mutual influences* (pp. 263-282). Oxford: Oxford University Press.

Coombs, C. H. (1987). The structure of conflict. *American Psychologist, 42,* 355-363.

Cummings, E. M., Ballard, M., El-Sheikh, M., & Lake, M. (1991). Resolution and children's responses to interadult anger. *Developmental Psychology, 27,* 462-470.

Cummings, E. M., Iannotti, R. J., & Zahn-Waxler, C. (1985). Influence of conflict between adults on the emotions and aggression of young children. *Developmental Psychology, 21,* 495-507.

Cummings, E. M., Zahn-Waxler, C., & Radke-Yarrow, M. (1981). Young children's responses to expressions of anger and affection by others in the family. *Child Development, 52,* 1274-1281.

Cummings, E. M., Zahn-Waxler, C., & Radke-Yarrow, M. (1984). Developmental changes in children's reactions to anger in the home. *Journal of Child Psychology and Psychiatry, 25,* 63-74.

Deutsch, M. (1969). Conflicts: Productive or destructive. *Journal of Social Issues, 25,* 7-41.

Downey, G., & Coyne, J. C. (1990). Children of depressed parents: An integrative review. *Psychological Bulletin, 108,* 50-76.

Dunn, J. (1988). Sibling influences on childhood development. *Journal of Child Psychology and Psychiatry, 29,* 119-127.

Dunn, J., & Munn, P. (1986). Sibling quarrels and maternal intervention: Individual differences in understanding and aggression. *Journal of Child Psychology and Psychiatry, 27,* 583-595.

Easterbrooks, M. A., & Emde, R. N. (1988). Marital and parent-child relationships: The role of affect in the family system. In R. A. Hinde & J. Stevenson-Hinde (Eds.), *Relationships within families: Mutual influences* (pp. 83-103). Oxford: Oxford University Press.

Emery, R. E. (1988). *Marriage, divorce, and children's adjustment.* Newbury Park, CA: Sage.

Emery, R. E. (1992). Family conflicts and their developmental implications: A conceptual analysis of meanings for the structure of relationships. In C. U. Shantz & W. W. Hartup (Eds.), *Conflict in child and adolescent development* (pp. 270-298). New York: Cambridge University Press.

Emery, R. E., Fincham, F. D., & Cummings, M. (1992). Parenting in context: Systemic thinking about parental conflict and its influence on children. *Journal of Consulting and Clinical Psychology, 60,* 909-912.

Empey, L. T. (1976). The social construction of childhood, delinquency, and social reform. In M. Klein (Ed.), *The juvenile justice system* (pp. 143-168). Beverly Hills, CA: Sage.

Fantuzzo, J., DePaola, L. M., Lambert, L., Martino, T., Anderson, G., & Sutton, S. (1991). Effects of interparental violence on the psychological adjustment and competencies of young children. *Journal of Consulting and Clinical Psychology, 59,* 258-265.

Fauber, R., Forehand, R., McCombs Thomas, A., & Wierson, M. (1990). A mediational model of the impact of marital conflict on adolescent adjustment in intact and divorced families: The role of disrupted parenting. *Child Development, 61,* 1112-1123.

Fauber, R., & Long, N. (1991). Children in context: The role of the family in child psychotherapy. *Journal of Consulting and Clinical Psychology, 59,* 813-820.

Fincham, F. D. (1993). Introduction. In F. D. Fincham (Ed.), Marital conflict [Special issue]. *Clinical Psychology Review, 13,* 1-2.

Fincham, F. D., & Bradbury, T. N. (1991). Marital conflict: Towards a more complete integration of research and treatment. In J. Vincent (Ed.), *Advances in family intervention, assessment and theory* (Vol. 5, pp. 1-24). London: Jessica Kingsley.

Fincham, F. D., Bradbury, T. N., & Grych, J. (1990). Conflict in close relationships: The role on intrapersonal factors. In S. Graham & V. Folkes (Eds.), *Attribution theory: Applications to achievement, mental health, and interpersonal conflict* (pp. 161-184). Hillsdale, NJ: Lawrence Erlbaum.

Fincham, F. D., Grych, J. H., & Osborne, L. O. (1993, March). *Interparental conflict and child adjustment: A longitudinal analysis.* Paper presented at the annual meeting of the Society for Research on Child Development, New Orleans.

Fincham, F. D., & Osborne, L. N. (1993). Marital conflict and children: Retrospect and prospect. *Clinical Psychology Review, 13,* 75-88.

Fitzpatrick, M. A. (1988). *Between husbands and wives: Communication in marriage.* Newbury Park, CA: Sage.

Forehand, R., Wierson, M., McCombs Thomas, A., Fauber, R., Armistead, L., Kempton, T., & Long, N. (1991). A short-term longitudinal examination of young adolescent functioning following divorce: The role of family factors. *Journal of Abnormal Child Psychology, 19,* 97-111.

Furstenberg, F. F., & Cherlin, A. J. (1991). *Divided families.* Cambridge, MA: Harvard University Press.

Glick, P. C., & Lin, S. (1986). Recent changes in divorce and remarriage. *Journal of Marriage and the Family, 48,* 737-747.

Green, R., Kolevzon, M., & Vosler, N. (1985). The Beavers-Timberlawn model of family competence and the circumplex model of family adaptability and cohesion: Separate but equal? *Family Process, 24,* 385-398.

Grych, J. H., & Fincham, F. D. (1990). Marital conflict and children's adjustment: A cognitive-contextual framework. *Psychological Bulletin, 108,* 267-290.

Grych, J. H., & Fincham, F. D. (1992). Interventions for children of divorce: Towards greater integration of research and action. *Psychological Bulletin, 111,* 434-454.

Grych, J. H., & Fincham, F. D. (1993). Children's appraisals of marital conflict: Initial investigations of the cognitive-contextual framework. *Child Development, 64,* 1-17.

Grych, J. H., Seid, M., & Fincham, F. D. (1992). Assessing marital conflict from the child's perspective: The children's perception of interparental conflict scale. *Child Development, 63,* 558-572.

Hetherington, E. M., Cox, M., & Cox, R. (1982). Effects of divorce on parents and children. In M. E. Lamb (Ed.), *Nontraditional families: Parenting and child development* (pp. 233-288). Hillsdale, NJ: Lawrence Erlbaum.

Jenkins, J. M., & Smith, M. A. (1990). Factors protecting children living in disharmonious homes: Maternal reports. *Journal of the American Academy of Child and Adolescent Psychiatry, 29,* 60-69.

Jouriles, E. N., Farris, A. M., & McDonald, R. (1991). Marital functioning and child behavior: Measuring specific aspects of the marital relationship. In J. Vincent (Ed.), *Advances in family intervention, assessment and theory* (Vol. 5, pp. 25-46). London: Jessica Kingsley.

Kelly, F. D., & Main, F. O. (1979). Sibling conflict in a single-parent family: An empirical case study. *American Journal of Family Therapy, 7,* 39-47.

Kempton, T., Armistead, L., Wierson, M., & Forehand, R. (1991). Presence of a sibling as a potential buffer following parental divorce: An examination of young adolescents. *Journal of Clinical Child Psychology, 20,* 434-438.

Kendrick, C., & Dunn, J. (1983). Sibling quarrels and maternal responses. *Developmental Psychology, 19,* 62-70.

Kurdek, L. A. (1989). Siblings' reactions to parental divorce. *Journal of Divorce, 12,* 203-219.

Kurdek, L. A. (1993). Issues in proposing a general model of the effects of divorce on children. *Journal of Marriage and the Family, 55,* 39-41.

Lewin, K. (1948). The background of conflict in marriage. *Resolving social conflicts: Selected papers on group dynamics* (pp. 84-102). New York: Harper & Row.

Long, N., & Forehand, R. (1987). The effects of parental divorce and parental conflict on children: An overview. *Developmental and Behavioral Pediatrics, 8,* 292-296.

Long, N., Forehand, R., Fauber, R., & Brody, G. H. (1987). Self-perceived and independently observed competence of young adolescents as a function of parental marital conflict and recent divorce. *Journal of Abnormal Child Psychology, 15,* 15-27.

Maccoby, E. E. (1982). Social-emotional development and response to stressors. In N. Garmezy & M. Rutter (Eds.), *Stress, coping, and development in children* (pp. 217-234). New York: McGraw-Hill.

MacKinnon, C. E. (1989). An observational investigation of sibling interactions in married and divorced families. *Developmental Psychology, 25,* 36-44.

Margolin, G. (1981). Behavior exchange in distressed and nondistressed marriages: A family cycle perspective. *Behavior Therapy, 12,* 329-343.

Minuchin, P. (1985). Families and individual development: Provocations from the field of family therapy. *Child Development, 56,* 289-302.

Monahan, S. C., Buchanan, C. M., Maccoby, E. E., & Dornbusch, S. M. (1993). Sibling differences in divorced families. *Child Development, 64,* 152-168.

Osborne, L. N., & Fincham, F. D. (in press). Conflict between parents and their children. In L. Cahn (Ed.), *Conflict in personal relationships.* Hillsdale, NJ: Lawrence Erlbaum.

Peterson, J. L., & Zill, N. (1986). Marital disruption, parent-child relationships, and behavior problems in children. *Journal of Marriage and the Family, 48,* 295-307.

Pickles, A., & Rutter, M. (1991). Statistical and conceptual models of "turning points" in developmental processes. In D. Magnusson, L. R. Bergman, G. Rudinger, & B. Torestad (Eds.), *Problems and methods in longitudinal research: Stability and change* (pp. 133-165). Cambridge: Cambridge University Press.

Porter, B., & O'Leary, K. D. (1980). Marital discord and childhood behavior problems. *Journal of Abnormal Child Psychology, 8,* 287-295.

Reid, W. J., & Crisafulli, A. (1990). Marital discord and child behavior problems: A meta-analysis. *Journal of Abnormal Child Psychology, 18,* 105-117.

Rutter, M. (1971). Parent-child separation. *Journal of Child Psychology and Psychiatry, 12,* 233-260.

Rutter, M. (1978). Family, area, and school influences in the genesis of conduct disorders. In L. Hersov, M. Berger, & D. Shaffer (Eds.), *Aggression and antisocial behavior in childhood and adolescence* (pp. 95-114). Oxford: Pergamon.

Shantz, C. U. (1987). Conflicts between children. *Child Development, 58,* 311-335.

Shantz, C. U., & Hobart, C. J. (1989). Social conflict and development: Peers and siblings. In T. J. Berndt & G. W. Ladd (Eds.), *Peer relationships in child development.* New York: John Wiley.

Stocker, C., Dunn, J., & Plomin, R. (1989). Sibling relationships: Links with child temperament, maternal behavior, and family structure. *Child Development, 60,* 715-727.

Vandell, D. L., & Bailey, M. D. (1992). Conflicts between siblings. In C. U. Shantz & W. W. Hartup (Eds.), *Conflict in child and adolescent development* (pp. 242-269). New York: Cambridge University Press.

Vuchinich, S., Emery, R. E., & Cassidy, J. (1988). Family members as third parties in dyadic family conflict: Strategies, alliances, and outcomes. *Child Development, 59,* 1293-1302.

Wierson, M., Forehand, R., & McCombs, A. (1988). The relationship of early adolescent functioning to parent-reported and adolescent-perceived interparental conflict. *Journal of Abnormal Child Psychology, 16,* 707-718.

8

Postdivorce Relations

SANDRA METTS
WILLIAM R. CUPACH

Relationships between former spouses are sparsely researched and little understood. In general, efforts to understand divorce tend to focus on the disengaging process, taking the point of disjuncture known as the "breakup" as an end point. Thus models of relationship termination (e.g., Duck, 1982; Knapp, 1984) serve well to illuminate the process by which a state of relationship cohesion becomes a state of relationship disintegration, but offer less insight into the nature of relationships that continue after the initial state of disintegration.

The limitation of existing literature no doubt stems in part from the practical need to impose parameters on a potentially indefinite process and in part from the relatively greater incidence of truly terminated relationships among the college student (courtship) couples used frequently in research studies. A somewhat less obvious influence may also be the channelizing effect of a prevailing relationship metaphor that Conville (1991) refers to as the "life-cycle metaphor." According to Conville, much of our thinking about relationships originates in a fundamental view that relationships are organic, that they have "a beginning, middle, and end—that they grow and develop into maturity and eventually wither and die" (p. 104). For scholars this is a convenient metaphor, but for divorced couples it is very seldom an accurate depiction of a complicated and ongoing process of relationship redefinition.

Indeed, even the notion that marriage relationships are "redefined" may be a simplistic view. It implies that the definition of a relationship as "marriage" has some recognizable or discoverable corollary when a relationship is "nonmarriage" and a couple is "divorced." It implies that a culturally shared frame, script, or schema may be invoked to guide emotional response and expression, time and space coordination, frequency of interaction, tone of interaction, breadth and depth of topics, and so forth. Unfortunately, and in spite of the increasing frequency of divorce, postdivorce relationship definitions are remarkably idiosyncratic and emergent. For some couples, affective bonds dissolve long before the divorce; for others, long after. For some couples, structural interdependence is difficult to disentangle; for others, very easy. For some couples, hostility is an undercurrent in all important interactions; for others, sorrow is pervasive; and for still others, there is no affect at all. And, of course, for couples with children, changes in individuals' roles as spouses also entail adjustments in their roles as parents.

The fact that a reformulated configuration of interaction patterns emerges from and supplants the long-standing marriage configuration has important consequences for all involved. For example, the degree and quality of interaction between formerly married partners influence their personal adjustment (Isaacs & Leon, 1988) as well as their adjustment to new relationships (Gold, Bubenzer, & West, 1993). The degree and quality of interactions between divorced parents influence the adjustment of their children to the divorce (e.g., Hetherington, Cox, & Cox, 1976; Wallerstein & Kelly, 1980). Moreover, a supportive coparental relationship between ex-spouses seems to facilitate adjustment of the custodial parent (Hetherington, Cox, & Cox, 1982; Kurdek & Blisk, 1983; Wallerstein & Kelly, 1980) and to mitigate the noncustodial parent's estrangement from the children (Hess & Camera, 1979).

It is important, therefore, to understand the dynamics that contribute to a successful renegotiation of the relationship between former spouses when children are involved. And regardless of whether children are involved, relationships between ex-spouses can be a source of ongoing tension and/or satisfaction for the partners. Some postdivorce relationships may fulfill important attachment needs for some former spouses (e.g., Ahrons & Wallisch, 1987; Masheter & Harris, 1986). Thus the former spouse relationship merits scholarly inquiry not only because it is an unexplored context of relationship reformulation, but because the nature of that relationship has important consequences.

The purposes of this chapter are to characterize the nature and quality of postdivorce relationships and to identify factors that contribute to their formation. Toward this end, we explore the following research questions:

1. How much do ex-spouses interact with one another?
2. What is the content of interaction between ex-spouses?
3. What is the general quality of ex-spouse relationships?
4. What effect does the relationship between ex-spouses have on the individuals' current levels of happiness and life satisfaction?

In addition, because postdivorce relationships are negotiated most actively during the first few months after divorce, we also consider possible variations in the answers to these questions depending upon the length of time since divorce.

In order to provide answers to these questions, we summarize the existing literature that has examined postdivorce relationships. In addition, we augment this literature with the results of a telephone survey we conducted during the spring of 1993 with 41 recently divorced individuals. These individuals were identified from court records as having been granted divorces during the period from June 1988 to June 1993. They had been married on average approximately 11 years (ranging from 1 to 29 years) and had been divorced on average a little more than 2 years. The average age of the respondents was mid-30s (females, 34.4 years; males, 35.5) and most had children (68%). We asked these respondents to characterize their postdivorce relationships with their ex-spouses, particularly those features that would provide answers to the questions guiding this chapter. We turn now to a discussion of the first of these questions.

AMOUNT OF INTERACTION
BETWEEN FORMER SPOUSES

A rudimentary gauge of the existence of a relationship between people resides in the frequency of interaction between them. The expectation that communication will continue at some level minimally defines a relationship (Hinde, 1979). In this sense, most couples who dissolve the legal aspects of their unions do not concomitantly terminate their relationships. Research findings indicate that few couples simply cease all contact at the time of divorce. A more typical pattern is a gradual decrease in the quantity of interaction over time and decreased involvement in face-to-face communication, accompanied by greater reliance on mediated communication (i.e., communication via telephone). This trajectory is common in both parental and nonparental couples, but the slope is much greater for couples who do not have children.

For example, Masheter (1991) surveyed 265 individuals who had been divorced for two to two and a half years. She found that 50% reported at least monthly contact (telephone or face-to-face) with their former spouses, and another 25% reported at least weekly contact. The majority of couples with children (86%) as well as those without children (63%) indicated that they had at least occasional contact. Similarly, at least occasional contact was reported by 84% of couples in which neither partner had remarried, and 59% of couples in which one or both partners had remarried.

In a sample of former spouses who had been divorced for a little more than six years ($m = 6.2$ years), Ambert (1989) found much less contact, especially among nonparental couples. When asked how often they visited (face-to-face) with their ex-spouses, 83% of the nonparents reported rarely (once a year or less), if at all. In contrast, 44% of those ex-spouses who shared children saw each other frequently (once a month or more). Among coparents, 23% saw each other irregularly, whereas 34% visited with each other rarely.

Ambert also questioned respondents about how often they talked to their ex-spouses over the phone. As with visits, phone contact was more frequent for ex-spouses who had children (44% reporting frequent contact) versus those who did not have children (7.7% reporting frequent contact).

Ambert's earlier data from some of the same couples confirm that in general, the frequency of contacts between ex-spouses diminishes over time. In addition, when couples divorce late in life, even initial postdivorce contact is moderate, perhaps because the ex-spouses' child-care, financial, and employment obligations are less entangled (Goodman, 1993). Thus moderate contact in the early months leads to almost no contact at all in a very short time (although those who do have contact enjoy better mental health) (Goodman, 1993).

In our own interviews, we also inquired about the frequency of contact between former spouses, both face-to-face and over the telephone. In addition, in order to represent early phases of postdivorce reformulation, we asked about contact during the first few months after the divorce. For respondents who had been divorced longer than six months, we asked about their contact at the time of the interview (current contact).

We found that the early months following the divorce are characterized by frequent contact. Within the first two to three months following divorce, 80% of our respondents reported frequent telephone contact ("every other week" to "once a week or more"), and 70% reported frequent face-to-face contact ("every other week" to "once a week or more"). Interestingly, parental and nonparental couples differed very little in these early months: Frequent phone contact was reported by 78% of parental couples and 63% of nonparental couples; frequent face-to-face contact was reported by 68% of parental couples and 69% of nonparental couples.

However, consistent with previous research, we found that the frequency of contact declines over time, and most dramatically for nonparental couples. Although the majority reported both telephone and face-to-face contact at least once a month, talking once a week or more on the telephone decreased from 60% of the respondents during the first two to three months to 20% at later points in time. Face-to-face contact dropped from 40% of the respondents right after divorce to 10% at later points in time. It is important to note, moreover, that these figures represent only parental couples. Nonparental couples virtually ceased contact: 75% of the nonparental couples spoke on the telephone only "three to four times a year" or less, and 88% met face-to-face "three to four times a year" or less.

Clearly, parenting responsibilities tend to pull some divorced couples into relatively frequent contact for much longer periods than those reported by their nonparent counterparts. This does not necessarily mean, of course, that the relationships associated with frequent interactions are by any other measure superior to those associated with infrequent interactions. Frequency of interaction is but one way to characterize a relationship. Indeed, Masheter (1991) found that, although less frequent, the interactions of nonparental divorced couples were friendlier and less conflictual than those of divorced parental couples. We might speculate that in even the most amicable divorce, negotiating shared time with children is difficult, given its finite nature and the constraints of the school year. In less amicable divorces, couples may have stayed together because of the children longer than perhaps they should have and hostilities may involve issues that are merely complicated by the presence of children. Our data offer indirect support for such an assumption in that 64% of the nonparent respondents recalled their marriages as "somewhat" to "very happy," whereas only 46% of the parental respondents felt as positive. Likewise, only 15% of the nonparental respondents recalled their marriages as "somewhat" to "very unhappy," compared with 29% of the parental respondents. We turn now to a discussion of the content of the interactions for divorced couples with and without children, and subsequently to a discussion of the quality of those interactions.

CONTENT OF INTERACTIONS
BETWEEN FORMER SPOUSES

Very little is known about the specific content of interactions between former spouses. Presumably, those who share children engage in activities and talk that center on that common interest. Ahrons and Wallisch (1987) asked former spouses, all of whom had children, a series of 10 questions regarding how often they related to each other in areas such as making decisions affecting the children; discussing the children's personal, school, or medical problems; discussing child-rearing problems; and discussing finances related to the children. At one year postdivorce, about 21% of the couples reported a high degree of parental-focused interaction; that is, they "always" or "usually" discussed 7 or more of the 10 topics. Another 21% reported relatively little discussion of these topics, "rarely" or "never" discussing 7 or more. By far the greatest number (59%) shared at least a "moderate" amount of coparental interaction.

Following the same pattern as frequency of contact, the frequency of discussing parenting responsibilities declines over time. At three years following divorce, Ahrons and Wallisch found that "coparental interaction as a whole dropped off significantly, with only 9% of respondents reporting a continuing high degree of interaction and 24% a very low amount of interaction" (p. 278).

Ahrons and Wallisch also asked respondents about their "nonparental" interaction topics—that is, such areas as talking about old friends and relatives, about the past marriage or reasons for the divorce, and about personal problems or new experiences. Respondents were asked to recall how often over the past several months they had related in 13 specific areas, ranging from "never" to "once a week or more." At one year postdivorce, in contrast to the parental topics, only about 5% discussed nonparental topics often enough to feel involved in the current lives of their former spouses; only about 25% had even a moderate degree of interaction about these topics (at least once every few months in half or more of the areas they rated), whereas 80% of the respondents reported "little or no involvement" in the current lives of their former spouses (Ahrons & Wallisch, 1987, p. 282). The amount of nonparental interaction declined over time as well. The initial ratings fell after three years to only about 8% interacting at least every few months in half or more of the areas that were rated.

In an effort to extend Ahrons and Wallisch's (1987) findings to the early months of postdivorce adjustment, we asked our parental respondents who were still in the first six months of their divorce how often ("none," "some," or "a lot") they discussed the following topics with their former spouses: children's personal problems, children's medical or school problems, planning special events for the children, children's progress and accomplishments, child-rearing problems, how the children are adjusting to the divorce, and finances related to the children. Just following the divorce, all of these topics were discussed "a lot" by the vast majority of former spouses. The most frequently discussed among these topics was finances related to the children.

Consistent with the general pattern of declining frequency of inter-action, all of these topics were discussed less frequently by respon-dents who had been divorced longer than six months. Nevertheless, the majority of coparental respondents reported at least some "current" discussion about children's medical/school problems, planning special events for the children, children's progress and accomplishments, and finances related to the children, with finances clearly being the most frequently discussed topic by the greatest number of respondents.

Clearly, children constitute the focus of much discussion between coparental ex-spouses. But they are not the only basis for postdivorce interaction. Moreover, they are not even a topic available to nonpar-ental couples. Thus we asked all respondents, both those with chil-dren and those without, the extent to which they talked with their ex-spouses about the non-child-related topics used by Ahrons and Wallisch (1987). These included friends in common, their (past) mar-riage, new experiences, possible reconciliation, finances unrelated to the children, families (other than the children), personal problems, and why they got divorced. To clarify patterns among these topics, we reduced these eight topics to three general areas: *social network* (friends and families), *relationship issues* (past marriage, possible reconcili-ation, joint finances, and reasons for divorce), and *individual concerns* (new experiences and personal problems).

Comparison of nonparental and parental couples reveals an inter-esting pattern. During the first two to three months following divorce, nonparental couples exhibit a fairly even distribution across all three topic areas, with the one exception being a good deal of talk about the relationship (54% of the respondents talked about the relationship "a lot"). By contrast, parental couples exhibit greater variation, talking about the social network "some" of the time (54%), but not "a lot" (11 %), and talking about their individual concerns hardly at all (71% reported no discussion and only 7% reported "a lot" of discussion).

When considering the topics currently discussed by our former spouses, again it is apparent that there is a trend to interact less frequently and on fewer topics as time goes by. Ex-spouses have less in common to discuss as their lives become less entangled. Although some ex-spouses continue to interact and to communicate about issues other than their children, they avoid topics that are particularly face-threatening. The topics discussed most often are families and new experiences—relatively nonthreatening topics. Notably, the topics of reconciliation and why they got divorced drop off markedly after six months subsequent to the divorce. As time passes, individuals renegotiate what topics are permissible. Although there is still a shared relationship, the nature of what is shared changes drastically. Ambert (1989) indicates that her respondents "stressed the importance of avoiding personal topics such as dating, remarriage, and even feelings for each other" (p. 33). The data on "nonparental" interaction reported by Ahrons and Wallisch (1987) are consistent with this pattern:

> Even among those respondents who had a moderate to high amount of interaction, a large majority said they never talked about their marriage to each other or about why they had divorced, nor did they report continued dating of each other, physical contact, or discussions of reconciling. (p. 282)

Interestingly, when both former spouses remarry, the boundaries for what constitutes acceptable topics for discussion may become more permeable or flexible (Ambert, 1989). Our sample of remarried respondents was not large enough for us to explore this issue, but we speculate that when both partners remarry they are better able to facilitate redefinition of the previous relationship and, in that transformation, many topics become less taboo.

EVALUATIVE/AFFECTIVE DIMENSIONS OF FORMER SPOUSE RELATIONSHIPS

Just as postdivorce interactions exhibit a wide range in frequency and content, the relationships between formerly married partners exhibit a wide range of evaluative and affective dimensions. Four approaches to the affective landscape of the postdivorce relationship are reflected in the literature: (a) characterizations of the overall evaluative quality of contact (e.g., friendly), (b) characterizations of the overall evaluative quality of the "relationship" in ordinary language categories (e.g., friends), (c) characterizations of attitudes toward the partner, and (d) assessments of the positive and negative aspects (costs and rewards) associated with the postdivorce relationship. On all these measures, once again, time moderates intensity.

Quality of Contact

Although measures of interaction frequency and content diversity might provide indices of the activity, vitality, or enmeshment of the postdivorce relationship, they do not provide an evaluation of the affective tone of the relationship, particularly along the dimensions of warm to cold and friendly to hostile.

In our own sample, we found that approximately 44% of respondents reported that the quality of contact with their former spouse was cordial or friendly, 24% reported it was indifferent or distant, and about 32% reported that the relationship was generally unfriendly or hostile within the first two to three months of divorce. Thus overall assessments of interaction quality as amicable were slightly more common than assessments as acrimonious.

Over time, the intensity of the early months tends to lessen and more moderate feelings mark the interactions between ex-spouses. At points subsequent to the first six months, our respondents reported greater degrees of indifference in the interactions with their former spouses (from 24% to 33%), and even slight increases in friendliness (44% to 47%). They also reported corresponding decreases in hostility (32% to 20%).

Quality of the Relationship

To the extent that relationships are enacted during conversation, it is tempting to assume that quality of contact and quality of relationship are isomorphic. They are not. As one respondent divorced almost three years put it, "Our conversations are very often hostile but I think that's because we are still in love." More often than scholars have perhaps realized, former spouses make independent judgments concerning how they talk and how they feel. Interaction sequences depend critically upon the actions of the other person, whereas descriptions of relationship quality are more stable, global assessments.

In Ambert's (1989) sample, 27% of the respondents reported that they had *no* relationships with their former spouses. Whereas 20% agreed that the quality of their current relationships with their former spouses was very bad, another 20% indicated that the quality of their relationships was very good. It is important, therefore, not to assume that a singular profile or common trajectory adequately characterizes all or even most ex-spouse relationships.

When we asked our respondents how they would characterize their relationships with their ex-spouses currently, 27% reported that they had "almost no relationship." A surprising 15% reported that they were still in love, and 37% said they were good friends or friendly. Only about a fifth of the respondents (22%) indicated that they were uncomfortable being together or antagonistic toward one another.

When asked how happy they were with their relationships as they existed at present, 46% reported that they were somewhat or very happy with their current ex-spouse relationships, 29% were somewhat or very unhappy, and 24% said that they felt indifferent. Consequently, the majority of our respondents (54%) also reported that they would prefer "no change" in the status of their relationships. As might be expected, about 37% preferred their relationships to be more intimate or friendly.

Attitude Toward Partner

A third evaluative dimension used to describe postdivorce relationships is one's attitude toward a former spouse. Masheter (1991) surveyed ex-spouses two to two and a half years following their divorces. Drawing on Weiss's (1975) work, she employed several items to create a measure of "affect" regarding one's former spouse (i.e., friendly versus hostile feelings). Masheter found that 43% of her respondents were in the friendly range, 36% in the middle range (perhaps indifferent), and 21% in the hostile range.

Although it is generally true that the intensity of negative feelings toward an ex-spouse diminish over time, there is evidence that when divorce comes late in life, negative feelings linger. Wallerstein (1986) found that 10 years after her initial contact with divorced couples, 40%

of the women and 30% of the men said that they still felt anger. This was especially true for women who were 34 years old or older when they divorced.

Positive/Negative Aspects of Postdivorce Relationships

A fourth way to characterize postdivorce relationships is to identify aspects that are positive and aspects that are negative. Hobart (1991) asked former spouses to list the ways their relationships were positive and the ways they were negative. In general, positive aspects pertained chiefly to benefits to the children, and secondarily to a continuing positive relationship with the former spouse. The positive aspects most frequently cited by wives were mutual concern for the welfare of the children, having a friendly relationship, maintaining an agreeable neutral relationship for the children, having a trusting, communicative relationship, and having a relationship supportive of mutual concerns. For husbands, the most frequently cited aspects were mutual concern for the welfare of the children, having a friendly relationship, having a relationship supportive of mutual concerns, admiration of the former spouse as a good parent, and feeling it is good for the children to see the other parent.

Negative aspects of ex-spouse relationships generally involved continuing differences or ill feeling between the divorced partners and the complications accruing to coparenting. Specifically, the negative aspects of the ex-spouse relationship for wives included differing expectations regarding custody, visitation, child support, and the like; unacceptable traits in the former husband, such as jealousy or alcoholism; and lingering feelings of resentment. The negative aspects identified by husbands included tensions caused by differing expectations, lingering feelings of resentment, and interference with present marriage relationships and lifestyle.

Factors Contributing to Evaluative/Affective Dimensions of Former Spouse Relationships

As we have noted frequently in this chapter, the presence of children in the postdivorce relationship is an important influence on the character of that relationship. Children constitute an ongoing mutual concern, promoting interaction between ex-spouses and engendering intensity in the postdivorce relationship. In Ambert's (1989) study, ex-spouses who also coparented were more likely to report feelings of friendliness or feelings of anger and dislike, whereas ex-spouses who did not coparent were more likely to express feelings of indifference. As Ambert notes, however, the former marriages not involving children were also briefer in duration and entailed more financial independence. Still, the presence of children is likely to create a barrier force that often compels ex-spouses to communicate with one another, even when they would prefer not to.

Furthermore, the vagaries of coparenting under conditions of divorce are likely to create disputes between former spouses. Masheter (1991) assessed the frequency of conflict regarding six topics ranging from financial matters to mutual acquaintances and found that respondents with children quarreled more than did respondents without children.

Hobart (1991) attempted to identify factors in addition to children that might be associated with the perceived quality of relationships between former spouses. He found that for ex-wives, educational and occupational levels and number of wife's prior-marriage children were positively associated with perceived relationship quality, whereas wife's age and number of current-marriage (shared) children were inversely associated with perceived relationship quality. The results for ex-husbands were quite different. Their perceived relationship quality (with former spouse) was positively associated with their own age, duration of the current marriage, having friends among remarried families, and reporting a difficult current economic situation. Ex-husbands' perceived relational quality was negatively associated with occupational level, duration of the first marriage, and number of husband's prior-marriage children. These results seem to indicate "on the one hand, that the more difficult his relationship with the current spouse, the more positive it is with his former spouse, and on the other hand that the more prior marriage children he has, the more difficult is his relationship with their mother" (Hobart, 1991, p. 14).

In our study, we found that the length of marriage was positively correlated with the quality of contact ($r = .31$) and negatively related to how much the divorce was desired ($r = -.35$) during the first few months after divorce. At points later than the initial postdivorce months, the correlation with length of marriage was no longer significant, but the correlation with how much the divorce was desired was even higher ($r = -.38$).

POSTDIVORCE ADJUSTMENT

An important aspect of postdivorce relations is how such relations are associated with the well-being of the former spouses. Historically, it has been assumed that ongoing interaction between former spouses may reflect unhealthy attachment on the part of one of the former partners. Social stereotypes have perpetuated the view that continuing involvement between former spouses is inimical or quasi-pathological (Kressel, Lopez-Morillas, Weinglass, & Deutsch, 1979). Much of the available clinical literature reinforces this bias. "Clinicians tend to see only the difficult or problematic former spousal relationships, while well-functioning divorced families are less apt to seek professional intervention" (Ahrons & Wallisch, 1987, p. 273). Thus, based on her review of the scholarly literature on divorce, Masheter (1990) concludes that "most investigators have either assumed that divorce terminates the relationship or have associated continued postdivorce contact and feelings for the ex-spouse with poor adjustment to divorce" (p. 98).

Based on findings from nonclinical couples, however, Masheter (1991) argues that the global notion of attachment can have either negative or positive components. Thus she incorporated two distinct aspects of attachment in her study of ex-spouses: preoccupation with the ex-spouse (presumably dysfunctional) and "affect" (i.e., friendly versus hostile feelings toward the former spouse). She found that personal well-being was not significantly associated with the affect dimension of attachment, nor was it associated with the frequency of interaction between former spouses. Negative correlations were found, however, between well-being and preoccupation with the ex-spouse ($r = -.20$) and current frequency of conflicts with the ex-spouse ($r = -.14$).

We also assessed "current life happiness" among our ex-spouses and examined factors associated with it. We found that it was remarkably unrelated to aspects of the postdivorce relationship: It was not associated with either the quality of interaction with an ex-spouse or how much the respondent liked the current relationship with his or her ex-spouse. Interestingly, quality of interaction and liking the current relationship were correlated with each other ($r = .63$), but neither was associated with our respondents' current life happiness and sense of well-being. Apparently, interactions with former spouses can be of varying degrees and quality, but their significance to personal happiness decreases as the former partners adjust to the dissolution of their marriage and the redefinition of their relationship.

On the other hand, a number of factors related to the former marriage and the divorce were significantly associated with current life happiness among our respondents. Specifically, individuals currently were happier to the extent that they (a) wanted the divorce in the first place ($r = .62$), (b) felt that they were prepared for the divorce ($r = .45$), (c) currently had positive thoughts about the former marriage ($r = .68$), and (d) currently had negative thoughts about the former marriage ($r = .42$). In addition, length of marriage ($r = -.49$) and degree of happiness during the marriage ($r = -.56$) were negatively correlated with current life happiness. These correlations suggest that adjusting to divorce is most difficult for those ex-spouses who were in long-term, happy marriages and thus felt unprepared for divorces they did not want.

CONCLUSION

Divorce implies relationship dissolution, so there is a tendency to assume that "ex-spouses" have terminated their relational ties with one another. However, our data and the findings of previous studies tell us that at least some former spouses *do* continue to interact and share relationships with one another, albeit much more complicated and normless relationships than marriage. The legal trend toward joint custody of children of divorced couples suggests that more and more ex-spouses will find themselves in interdependent continuing relationships, if for no other reason than their coparental responsibilities. And in spite of the lack of institutionalized norms for how former spouses should comport themselves with one another (Burgoyne & Clark, 1984; Goode, 1956; Hobart, 1991), the empirical data suggest that ex-spouses continue to communicate, even those without children, about a variety of topics, in a generally friendly manner. This pattern, however, may be relatively short-lived, as new relationships and new experiences overlay the salience of the marriage ties and interaction becomes increasingly nonaffective and infrequent.

Ex-spouses are also able, overtime, to separate their current states of happiness from the quality of the interactions and the quality of the relationships with their former spouses. They do seem to be subject, however, to the lingering effects of how they perceived their marriages at the time of divorce—snapshot memory. Thus a self-evaluated good marriage that was unwillingly dissolved continues to constrain current happiness.

In sum, we believe that divorce is less usefully viewed as an ending and more usefully viewed as a "critical event" that necessitates psychological and behavioral adjustments in the interpersonal relationship between spouses (Price-Bonham & Balswick, 1980). To borrow from Conville's (1991) description of alienation, we propose that divorce be viewed as a "juncture, a cul-de-sac of transformation" where the relationship-as-previously-defined is rejected and new roles are crafted in order to create the relationship-to-be-defined. Beyond this juncture, according to Conville, "the relationship itself continues, but the peculiar configuration of role-taking that had marked the relationship as theirs-in-particular is re-formed" (p. 119), and, we might add, continually re-formed.

Researchers interested in the postdivorce relationship must begin to grapple with the dynamics of relationship transformation. Just as researchers have come to regard the development of a relationship as an ongoing process of formulation, negotiation, and evolution, we can conceptualize the redefinition of a relationship as a process of *re*formulation, *re*negotiation, and *re*volution. An important aspect of relationship definition is its connection to the identities of the respective partners. Consequently, we believe that an important facet of relationship redefinition is the reformulation of partner identities.

To the extent that relationship development (i.e., escalation of intimacy and interdependence) entails the enmeshment of personal identities, the disengagement of relationships entails the uncoupling of identities. More specifically, significant change in the status of a relationship must necessarily involve transformations in the identities of relational partners. Indeed, researchers have acknowledged that relationship breakdown and dissolution entail processes of identity transformation (e.g., Duck & Lea, 1983; Orbuch, 1992; Vaughan, 1986). Thus one key to understanding relationship redefinition between former spouses may be exploration of partners' relational identity transformation.

The difficulty an individual experiences in adjusting to relational change should be in direct proportion to the relative importance of the particular relational identity for that person. Orbuch (1992) explains:

> When individuals form a romantic dyad with another person, they occupy a socially defined position (role) as partner, lover, or spouse. Where individuals place this identity in their prominence hierarchy of identities depends on the gratification they achieve from the identity connected to the relationship; the degree of their self-commitment to that identity; the support others give to that identity; and the number of opportunities they have to engage in the role of partner. The higher the identity of partner is located on the hierarchy of identities, the more central and significant the identity is to the person's total self. (p. 196)

The more important any particular relational identity is to a person, the more difficult it should be for him or her to cope with relational change. In a study of premarital relationship terminations, Orbuch (1992) found that the importance of relational identity was positively associated with distress following the breakup. Furthermore, identity variables were more important in predicting distress than were investment variables (e.g., degree of self-disclosure, amount of time spent together, number of friends in common).

In general, a marital relationship figures prominently in a person's identity hierarchy. In fact, our own data from ex-spouses are consistent with Orbuch's findings. Current well-being of former spouses was positively associated with wanting the divorce and feeling prepared for it. These results suggest that the partner seeking marital dissolution gets a head start on identity transformation prior to informing the partner of the desire for a divorce (e.g., Vaughan, 1986). On the other hand, we found that length of marriage and degree of happiness during the marriage were inversely associated with current life happiness, suggesting that affective attachment to partner produces relational enmeshment that is relatively difficult to untangle. Continuing preoccupation with the former spouse is incommensurate with the de-escalated relationship, and hence is a dysfunctional form of attachment that adversely affects well-being (e.g., Masheter, 1991). In general, we speculate that both "push" (i.e., barriers inhibiting exit from the marriage) and "pull" (i.e., attractions and attachments to the marriage and partner) factors operate to impede gradual identity transformation necessitated by relationship change. It would be useful for future research to explore how such factors change over time, and to discern the extent to which such changes are associated with adjustment and well-being.

The effects of children on relationship redefinition can also be interpreted within the identity transformation framework. Generally, coparents have more conflict than do former spouses without children. The presence of children, and the concomitant coparental role that it entails, can sometimes bind former spouses together, making it difficult for them to disentangle the original marital identity. The coparenting role, which continues, gets confounded with the spouse role. The need to separate these roles makes negotiating relational change more difficult. Future research should examine such role complications and the mechanisms individuals use to disambiguate a relational identity in transition.

Finally, research may also shed light on relationships between former spouses by considering how relationship identity transformation is accomplished. One area of change is psychological. A focus here might call for assessments regarding how ruminations about the prior relationship change over time, and how thoughts about the current relationship correspond to definitions of the relationship. Relevant questions might include the following: In what ways do ambivalence and dissonance about the divorce affect transformation? Does reminiscing about the marriage help or hinder adjustment to the divorce?

A second area of change is behavioral, particularly communication patterns. It is clear that communication becomes less frequent and less intimate after divorce, but what qualitative changes occur? Given that the relationship role has changed, it is inevitable that some of the rules governing interaction change as well. For example, in a study of women in the process of divorce, Isaacs and Leon (1988) found that a "disputing" style of communication was associated with negative feelings about the marriage and current adjustment. More important, however, they found that a "practical discussing" style was related to adjustment and decreased physical symptoms of stress more than was a "personal discussing" style. This suggests that control of emotional expression (positive and negative) may be an important new rule negotiated by divorced couples. Dropping or making taboo certain types of personal idioms that occurred in the marriage may also become a new rule. Restricting play, refraining from telling shared narratives, and other changes might also be manifestations of new rules.

In short, a great deal remains to be done to discover the communicative mechanisms that help former partners to reify their new relational role. The process is made immensely more difficult by the influences of overlapping networks of children and friends, as well as the introduction of new relational partners. Despite the challenge, however, understanding these mechanisms is the key to understanding the metamorphosis of ex-spouse relationships.

REFERENCES

Ahrons, C. R., & Wallisch, L. S. (1987). The relationship between former spouses. In D. Perlman & S. Duck (Eds.), *Intimate relationships: Development, dynamics, and deterioration* (pp. 269-296). Newbury Park, CA: Sage.

Ambert, A. (1989). *Ex-spouses and new spouses: A study of relationships*. Greenwich, CT: JAI.

Burgoyne, J., & Clark, D. (1984). *Making a go of it: A study of stepfamilies in Sheffield*. London: Routledge & Kegan Paul.

Conville, R. L. (1991). *Relational transitions: The evolution of personal relationships*. New York: Praeger.

Duck, S. W. (1982). A topography of relationship disengagement and dissolution. In S. W. Duck (Ed.), *Personal relationships 4: Dissolving personal relationships* (pp. 1-30). London: Academic Press.

Duck, S. W., & Lea, M. (1983). Breakdown of relationships as a threat to personal identity. In G. M. Breakwell (Ed.), *Threatened identities* (pp. 53-73). New York: John Wiley.

Gold, J. M., Bubenzer, D. L., & West, J. D. (1993). Differentiation from ex-spouses and stepfamily marital intimacy. *Journal of Divorce and Remarriage, 19*, 83-95.

Goode, W. J. (1956). *Women in divorce.* New York: Free Press.

Goodman, C. C. (1993). Divorce after long-term marriages: Former spouse relationships. *Journal of Divorce and Remarriage, 20*, 43-61.

Hess, R. D., & Camera, K. A. (1979). Postdivorce family: Relationships as mediating factors in consequences of divorce for children. *Journal of Social Issues, 35*, 79-97.

Hetherington, E. M., Cox, M., & Cox, R. (1976). Divorced fathers. *Family Coordinator, 25*, 417-428.

Hetherington, E. M., Cox, M., & Cox, R. (1982). Effects of divorce on parents and children. In M. E. Lamb (Ed.), *Nontraditional families: Parenting and child development* (pp. 233-288). Hillsdale, NJ: Lawrence Erlbaum.

Hinde, R. A. (1979). *Towards understanding relationships.* London: Academic Press.

Hobart, C. (1991). Relationships between the formerly married. *Journal of Divorce and Remarriage, 14*, 1-23.

Isaacs, M. B., & Leon, G. (1988). Divorce, disputation, and discussion: Communicational styles among recently separated spouses. *Journal of Family Psychology, 1*, 298-311.

Knapp, M. (1984). *Interpersonal communication and human relationships.* Boston: Allyn & Bacon.

Kressel, K., Lopez-Morillas, M., Weinglass, J., & Deutsch, M. (1979). Professional intervention in divorce: The views of lawyers, psychotherapists, and clergy. In G. Levinger & O. Moles (Eds.), *Divorce and separation* (pp. 246-272). New York: Basic Books.

Kurdek, L. A., & Blisk, D. (1983). Dimensions and correlates of mothers' divorce experiences. *Journal of Divorce, 6*, 1-24.

Masheter, C. (1990). Postdivorce relationships between exspouses: A literature review. *Journal of Divorce and Remarriage, 14*, 97-122.

Masheter, C. (1991). Postdivorce relationships between ex-spouses: The roles of attachment and interpersonal conflict. *Journal of Marriage and the Family, 53*, 103-110.

Masheter, C., & Harris, L. M. (1986). From divorce to friendship: A study of dialectic relationship development. *Journal of Social and Personal Relationships, 3*, 177-189.

Orbuch, T. L. (1992). A symbolic interactionist approach to the study of relationship loss. In T. L. Orbuch (Ed.), *Close relationship loss: Theoretical approaches* (pp. 192-204). New York: Springer-Verlag.

Price-Bonham, S., & Balswick, J. O. (1980). The non-institutions: Divorce, desertion, and remarriage. *Journal of Marriage and the Family, 42*, 959-972.

Vaughan, D. (1986). *Uncoupling: How relationships come apart.* Oxford: Oxford University Press.

Wallerstein, J. (1986). Women after divorce: Preliminary report from a ten-year follow-up. *American Journal of Orthopsychiatry, 56*(11), 65-77.

Wallerstein, J., & Kelly, J. (1980). *Surviving the breakup.* New York: Basic Books.

Weiss, R. S. (1975). *Marital separation.* New York: Basic Books.

PART III

Extending Family Boundaries

In the past few decades, numerous social changes have caused us to reconsider our definitions of "the family." As researchers, we know that how we define the family limits what we study and how we study it. If we define the family as a mother, a father, and at least one minor child, then that is exactly the group we examine. Definitions of the family are often thinly veiled political or ideological statements rather than scientifically neutral views.

In their book *Communication in Family Relationships*, Noller and Fitzpatrick (1993) extensively discuss and elaborate upon the three distinctive classes of definitions of the family noted by Wamboldt and Reiss (1989). The first cluster of definitions is made up of *family structure definitions,* which delineate as members only those who have established biological or sociolegal legitimacy by virtue of shared genetics, marriage, or adoption. These definitions specify criteria for membership and particular hierarchies based on age and sex. The first part of this book may be taken as adopting this perspective on the family, because the contributors to Part I do not problematize the family as a unit.

Families can also be defined in terms of psychosocial tasks. *Psychosocial task definitions* view the family as a group that works toward mutual need fulfillment, as well as the nurturance and development of its members. Although these definitions help us to focus on the goals of family life, the various stages and types of families have markedly different goals. This multiplicity of goals that we study may delimit the usefulness of these types of definitions. Part II of this book, focusing as it does on various tasks of family life (e.g., becoming parents, problem solving, conflict, and renegotiating relationships) may be taken as adopting a psychosocial task definition of the family.

Finally, families can be defined in terms of transactional processes. *Transactional process definitions* see the family as a group of intimates who generate a sense of home and group identity, complete with strong ties of loyalty, emotion, and experience. Although these definitions are complex and contain many abstract concepts that themselves need to be defined (for a more elaborate treatment, see Noller & Fitzpatrick, 1993), they have two major advantages. First, they place great emphasis on family communication. Second, they can encompass the many forms of modern family life, because they depend on how families define themselves rather than on some set of predetermined sociolegal or genetic criteria.

The five chapters in this section employ a transactional process definition of the family. The chapters on dual-career marriages, stepfamilies, and homosexual couples extend the boundaries of the family beyond the structural definitions. For instance, in Chapter 9, Lawrence Rosenfeld, Gary Bowen, and Jack Richman distinguish among three different types of dual-career couples and discuss the demographic and communication characteristics of each. In Chapter 10, Nancy Burrell offers metaphors of stepfamily life and examines the issues that come up as stepfamily members negotiate roles, boundaries, and loyalty issues. Sara Steen and Pepper Schwartz, in Chapter 11, provide a stimulating analysis of the interaction patterns of homosexual couples. Using a case study method, these authors consider the origins of gender differences in communication and describe both the style and substance of homosexual couples' interaction. All three chapters, in short, focus on the manner in which groups of intimates use communication to develop their own sense of home and group identity and to forge ties of emotion and loyalty.

Marie-Louise Mares's contribution on the aging family in Chapter 12 is included in this section because it takes us out of individual family households to examine family relationships across time. Mares reviews a good deal of research and makes some very interesting points about how social changes have affected many of our family roles. Finally, Alan Sillars ends the book with an elegant statement about the relationship between communication and family cultures. Sillars reminds us of our pluralistic society and of the mosaic of alternative lifestyles, living arrangements, and family values that make the study of family communication an exciting and valuable enterprise.

REFERENCES

Noller, P., & Fitzpatrick, M. A. (1993). *Communication in family relationships.* Englewood Cliffs, NJ: Prentice Hall.

Wamboldt, F. S., & Reiss, D. (1989). Task performance and the social construction of meaning: Juxtaposing normality with contemporary family research. In D. Offer & M. Sabshin (Eds.), *Normality: Context and theory* (pp. 229-248). New York: Basic Books.

9

Communication in Three Types of Dual-Career Marriages

LAWRENCE B. ROSENFELD
GARY L. BOWEN
JACK M. RICHMAN

The number of marriages in which both partners maintain careers increases with each new survey (Pearson, 1993; Silberstein, 1992; Yogev, 1982). Historically, this trend parallels a variety of changes in the United States: (a) the dramatic increase of married women in the workforce since World War II (Hayghe, 1986; Kaplan, 1992; Teachman, Polonko, & Scanzoni, 1987; U.S. Bureau of the Census, 1989); (b) the increased importance of equity in husband and wife roles (Price-Bonham & Murphy, 1980); (c) the trend toward smaller families (Teachman et al., 1987); (d) the rise in an egalitarian ideology associated with the women's movement (Burke & Weir, 1976; McBroom, 1984; Thornton, 1989; Wood, 1994); (e) the increase in the number of women obtaining higher levels of education (Parker, Peltier, & Wolleat, 1981); (f) the increased necessity for both partners to hold full-time career positions if they are to reach their desired standard of living (Tryon & Tryon, 1982); and (g) the significant increase in the number of women in prestigious and high-paying positions traditionally occupied by men (Glick, 1989; Powell, 1988; Stewart & Clarke-Kudless, 1993). Although attitudes toward women working outside the home have changed rapidly (Furstenberg, 1980), wives in dual-work families still often lack support for their career pursuits, and find themselves in situations in which they must simultaneously fulfill the demanding role of wage earner and the equally demanding role of homemaker (Pearson, 1993).

The literature on dual-career marriages draws a careful distinction between *career* and *work*. A career typically is defined as a job sequence in the professional, technical, and managerial fields (Rice, 1979) that involves a high level of commitment and that has a developmental quality (Parker et al., 1981). Researchers often include spouses' commitment to each other and to family life when defining *dual-career marriage*; dual-career spouses have high levels of commitment to both career and family. Yet researchers often ignore the element of commitment to family when actually selecting couples for study (Ladewig & White, 1984; Pearson, 1993).

Because of their commitment to their marital relationship, family life, and the development of their careers, dual-career couples face many challenges (Gilbert & Rachlin, 1987; Heacock & Spicer, 1986; Pearson, 1993). Rapoport and Rapoport (1969), who pioneered the study of dual-career marriages and first introduced the term, discuss five such challenges (Rapoport & Rapoport, 1971; see also Silberstein, 1992). First, dual-career couples may experience disparity between their values and society's values. For example, a couple may place less value on having children than is "expected" of a couple in North American society. Next, partners may face identity issues and self-esteem concerns. The husband, for instance, may feel threatened by the career success of his wife. Third, couples may encounter social disapproval that arises from their dual-career status. For example, neighbors may perceive them as too involved with their work. Fourth, partners may face unusually high demands at particular points in the life cycle, such as juggling the high expectations of a career in its early stages with the high demands of young children. Finally, one or both partners may experience stress and strain owing to role overload and role conflict, for example, when the wife attempts to be "superwoman," trying to attend with equal attention to work and home responsibilities.

In addition to the challenges first enumerated by Rapoport and Rapoport, dual-career couples may face the challenge of "commuter marriage," in which partners attempt to fulfill their career and family roles and obligations while living apart for several days of each week or for several weeks at a time (Gertel & Gross, 1984; Gross, 1980;

Rhodes & Rhodes, 1984). Channels of communication may become limited as the partners lose daily face-to-face access to each other and attempt to substitute telephone conversations, letters, and faxes for intimate interaction.

Wood (1986) and Silberstein (1992) explain that many of the challenges faced by dual-career couples are the result of a lack of a clear framework on which to structure their relationship. For example, societal obstacles, such as inadequate day care and family leave opportunities, reflect the structure of families that have a single full-time wage earner and a single full-time homemaker. Challenges arise, however, not simply at the marital level, but at the sociohistorical level as well. To respond to these challenges, Wood suggests that dual-career couples utilize communication to define and enhance their relationships, including legitimating their relationships, promoting trust and flexibility, and providing opportunities for change. She also indicates that whereas society provides a normative framework for traditional marital relationships, dual-career couples must strengthen and undergird their own relationships by developing supportive internal structures.

As Wood (1986) suggests, partners in dual-career marriages may use communication in specific ways to address their unique situations and to respond to the challenges of their marital arrangements. For instance, Rosenfeld and Welsh (1985), differentiating between self-disclosure in dual-career and single-career marriages, found that wives and husbands in dual-career marriages were more responsive to each others' self-disclosures and were more willing to reciprocate them. Comparing dual-career couples' communication at home versus work, Steil and Weltman (1992) studied the use of influence strategies. Their findings indicate few relevant sex differences: Direct requests were the strategy most frequently used by both wives and husbands, regardless of context, and both wives and husbands reported using more indirect-bilateral (e.g., persuading) strategies at work and more indirect-unilateral (e.g., withdrawing) strategies at home. Although sex was a poor predictor of differences in strategy use, personality was useful: Low self-confidence was positively associated with the use of indirect-unilateral strategies.

In addition to context, time is another factor that may affect communication patterns of dual-career partners. Alger (1991) suggests that choosing to be committed to and balancing both family and career obligations limits the time that members of dual-career couples can spend together. These time constraints, which lead to diminished opportunities for partners to relate to each other as a couple, can lead to a reduction in intimacy and emotional contact.

Research focusing on decision-making communication indicates that partners in dual-career marriages differ from single-career couples in how they make decisions. Krueger (1986), for example, analyzed decision making specifically to determine whether there is greater equality of spousal roles within dual-career marriages. This equality was found to be present most of the time in about half of the nine dual-career couples studied (Krueger did not include any comparisons with single-career or other couple types). The couples who exhibited egalitarianism in their decision making employed various positive decision-making strategies, such as turn taking when speaking and listening, and compromising while discussing alternative solutions. These strategies may assist dual-career couples in their efforts to resolve numerous issues effectively and arrive at mutually acceptable decisions.

Although the findings of previous research may have potential for improving our understanding of dual-career couples, two problems affect our ability to draw meaningful generalizations from the studies that have been conducted. The first concerns controlling for the possible confounding effects of including a variety of occupations among the respondents' careers; the implicit assumption is that all dual-career marriages are alike. The second problem concerns the development of a meaningful way to distinguish among dual-career couple types, which includes considering the interaction and interdependence of work and family for dual-career couples, as well as the necessity to adapt to both environments.

The question typically ignored by research in the area of dual-career marriages is, Are all dual-career marriages alike? The answer to this question is the primary focus of the investigation reported here. The purpose of our investigation was to gather evidence from which we could develop a typology of dual-career marriages. Further, we aimed to distinguish among the types with respect to their communication—

specifically, how the couples communicate within their marriages and the extent to which spouses experience communication apprehension when communicating with people outside their families.

CONTROLLING FOR THE CONFOUNDING EFFECTS OF NONCOMPARABLE CAREERS

Careers represented in a typical study of dual-career marriage differ *between* spouses (that is, spouses in each marital dyad have different occupations) and *among* couples (that is, spouses' occupations differ from marital dyad to marital dyad). According to Pearson (1993), it is important to account for intracouple career differences—variables such as career type, status, earning potential, and part-time versus full-time employment. For example, wives in dual-career relationships who see themselves as lower in professional success and income than their husbands report greater marital satisfaction than do other wives, and husbands who see themselves as higher in professional success and income than their wives report greater marital satisfaction than do other husbands. The assumption in most dual-career research seems to be that within-marriage career differences are irrelevant—for example, that communication in a marriage in which the husband is a stockbroker and the wife is an elementary school teacher is similar to communication in a marriage in which these occupations are reversed, with the wife a stockbroker and the husband an elementary school teacher.

Just as the literature on dual-career marriages ignores within-marriage career differences, it also generally ignores differences among couples in a sample.[1] When researchers fail to control for the careers represented in their samples—assuming that all dual-career couples are of one type and can be combined in comparisons with other couple types, such as single-career and career-work marriages—they conduct analyses on what may be considered confounded samples. A number of studies exemplify this point. For example, Rapoport and Rapoport's (1971) seminal study of five couples included (a) a wife research manager and husband in marketing, (b) a wife and husband architect team, (c) a wife television drama director and a husband architect, (d) a wife and husband who were both senior administrative-class civil servants, and (e) a wife fashion designer and a husband managing director of a marketing company.

Attempting to add some measure of control, Steffy and Ashbaugh (1986) studied 118 dual-career couples who consisted of a wife who was a registered nurse employed by a psychiatric hospital and a husband "who worked full time" (p. 116). Controlling for the wife's career, and having only wives complete the packet of measuring instruments, prompted the researchers to comment, "It is felt that such a homogeneous sample is particularly advantageous, because so much of the career research has been across multiple sites and multiple occupations" (p. 116). Unfortunately, the careers of the nurses' spouses, which were not controlled for, may have affected responses to questions concerning "spouse support," "dual-career planning," "job stress," and several other variables measured.

Hoping to control for both wives' and husbands' careers, Steil and Weltman (1992) selected 60 couples on the following basis: "Both partners had to be employed full-time outside the home in a supervisory capacity. 'Supervisory' was defined as responsible for delegating work to another or actually supervising another at work" (p. 71). In addition to problems associated with the comparability of "supervisors" representing different organizations and careers, relying on a snowball effect (in which one subject provides the researchers with potential recruits) resulted in the recruitment of several subjects through professional women's organizations and alumni from a postdoctoral program in psychology.

When within- and between-couple career differences are uncontrolled, the assumption seems to be that the communication observed in all dual-career couples is similar because of their shared dual-careerness. Is it reasonable to assume that communication in a marriage in which, for example, the wife is a lawyer and the husband is a teacher is similar to communication in a marriage in which the husband is an electrical engineer and the wife a nurse? Why should dual-careerness exert such an overpowering force—a force more powerful than within-couple and between-couple career differences?

DISTINGUISHING AMONG DUAL-CAREER COUPLES

Much of the research on dual-career couples defines dual-career-ness as a function of each partner's commitment to family and work, with the archetypal dual-career family one in which both spouses are highly committed to their marriage, family, and careers (e.g., Heacock & Spicer, 1986, Ladewig & White, 1984; Pearson, 1993; Price-Bonham & Murphy, 1980). Yet the measurement of commitment varies across studies and in many cases has questionable validity. For example, Rosenfeld and Welsh (1985), using a method typical of research in the area, operationalized commitment as an inherent aspect of an occupation. Based on the argument by Rapoport and Rapoport (1976) and Rice (1979) that advanced educational degrees represent a "high level of commitment," the assumption is that occupations that are full-time, have a developmental quality, and require advanced degrees may be assumed to have high levels of commitment. Much as Rosenfeld and Welsh *imply* respondent commitment in the occupations they define as careers, Steffy and Ashbaugh (1986) also imply respondent commitment in their selection of nurses and their full-time employed spouses as respondents (although it is difficult to understand how "full-time employment" constitutes commitment). As Ladewig and White (1984) point out, "If commitment to work roles is viewed as the critical variable affecting the work-family relationships, merely inferring commitment from job title or degree earned probably is inadequate" (p. 345).

In addition to the problem of trying to assess commitment from job titles, occupation, and education, most conceptualizations of commitment ignore the link between career and family life. There can be and often is a reciprocal relationship between events, satisfaction, and stressors within marriage and events, satisfaction, and stressors in the work environment (Bowen, 1988; Burke & Bradshaw, 1981; Burke & Greenglass, 1987; Steffy & Ashbaugh, 1986; Voydanoff, 1980). Voydanoff (1980) suggests that although society often functions with the belief that family and work are separate and independent spheres, families must adapt to the work environments of their members, socialize them to be competent workers, and support and nurture them so that they are capable of and motivated to work each day. According to Gilmer (1971), "The man [woman] at work, be he [she] executive or a laborer, does not function alone in his [her] industrial environment. It is almost inevitable that his [her] problems of work are shared with his [her] family, and the feedback from family life affects his [her] work" (p. 341). When the man or woman in this situation is a member of a dual-career relationship, the impact of home on work, the impact of work on home, and the reciprocity of home and work are certain to be greatly heightened. Although the time individuals spend at work is usually separate from the time they spend with their marital partners, these two spheres interrelate and have impacts on each other, particularly for occupations with strong organizational cultures, such as the military (Orthner, Bowen, & Beare, 1990).

A potentially more heuristic perspective than "commitment" to assess dual-careerness considers the family's and each family member's *adaptability*—the ability of the family, as a whole, and each family member, specifically, to cope with and adjust to family demands and the demands of the environment in which the family operates (Lavee & McCubbin, 1985). Bowen (1993; Bowen, Orthner, Zimmerman, & Bell, 1993) describes how a family adapts at two levels: First, family members adapt in their relationships to one another and to demands generated from within the family system itself (internal adaptation); second, they adapt in their relationships to the environment outside the family and its requisite demands (external adaptation), of which work is a primary microsystem for employed adult members.

The requirements for external adaptation may be even more powerful in institutional-type organizations that permeate almost every aspect of a person's life through a combination of occupational demands and supports (Orthner et al., 1990). Melson (1983) suggests that adaptation is the family working to create and maintain a good "fit" between internal and external levels. Bowen (1993) emphasizes this family adaptation as an active interchange between the family and work environments. The aim, according to Burke and Greenglass (1987), is for dual-career couples to ensure that their time is flexible so they can respond to unexpected changes in work or family.

TYPOLOGIES OF DUAL-CAREER COUPLES

Working from the assumption that not all dual-career marriages are the same, except for their shared dual-careerness, researchers have developed typologies describing different dual-career configurations. For example, more than a decade ago, Hall and Hall (1980) concluded from their review of the literature that "there is no single dual-career family role structure" (p. 246). They propose four dual-career couple types: "accommodators," where one spouse has high work involvement and the other has low work involvement, and one has high home involvement and the other has low home involvement; "adversaries," where both have high work involvement and low home involvement (with both valuing a well-ordered home); "allies," where both are high in work involvement and low in home involvement, or both are low in work involvement and high in home involvement (with neither valuing a well-ordered home); and "acrobats," where both spouses have high work involvement and high home involvement.

Jones and Jones (1980) developed another early typology; they describe five dual-career marriage types: the "liaison marriage," in which the husband keeps his work and family lives separate, and the wife is subordinate to the husband; the "marriage of state," in which both spouses are more committed to their work than to their family, and in which family responsibilities are shared; the "morganatic marriage"—traditionally, the name for a marriage arranged between a member of royalty and someone of lesser status—in which both spouses are professionals, but one agrees to allow her or his career to take second place to the other's; the "love match marriage," in which both spouses place family above work; and the "magnetized marriage," in which both spouses are highly committed to work and family (i.e., similar to Hall & Hall's acrobats).

Gilbert (1985) found three marital types in a study of men in dual-career marriages: "traditional" (the wife maintains all her parenting and household responsibilities and adds career obligations to her role); "participant" (spouses share child-rearing responsibilities, but the primary obligation for household duties resides with the wife); and "role-sharing," the most egalitarian (both parents are involved in parenting and household duties).

Like many researchers, those who posit typologies of dual-career marriages describe their classification systems and develop hypotheses to test for differences among the types, but often fall short of providing the data necessary to test their hypotheses (Burke & Bradshaw, 1981; Olson, 1981). For example, the Jones and Jones (1980) typology describes five dual-career marriage types based on the emphasis of career versus private lives, the Hall and Hall (1980) typology describes four couple types along with a model of stress as it affects each type, and the Gilbert (1985) typology emphasizes variations in parenting and household responsibilities, yet all these typologies are logically rather than empirically derived. The result is a variety of dual-career marriage typologies that are rich in description but the discriminant and predictive validity of which remain untested.

RESEARCH GOALS

Paralleling the work of Snyder and Smith (1986), who developed "an empirically based classification system of marital relationships" (p. 138), and Fitzpatrick (1988), who developed an empirical scheme of marriage in which couples shared a large number of characteristics in common, our first purpose in this investigation was to develop an empirically based classification system of dual-career marriages, employing a multidimensional approach to conceptualizing husbands' and wives' internal and external adaptation. Once we had developed this classification system, our second purpose was to describe differences among the couple types with regard to their communication (i.e., marital communication openness and communication apprehension) and demographic characteristics.

METHOD

Source of Data

Because of problems inherent in drawing conclusions from research comparing dual-career couples with any other couple type (e.g., single-career, career-work, and work-work), where "career" is uncontrolled and samples are small, we focused this investigation on respondents for whom there was little within- or between-couple variation in career and confined comparisons to different types of dual-career couples within this population group.

Dual-career respondents included in this investigation were taken from a pool of 928 randomly selected married couples (n = 1,856) in which one or both spouses was serving in the U.S. Air Force. These 928 couples were located across nine bases in the United States, eight in Asia, and seven in Europe. Couples were randomly selected at each base from lists of personnel provided by the Air Force Management and Personnel Center. Military couples, although younger on the average than civilian couples, share many similarities with their civilian counterparts, such as current trends in marriage and divorce, dual-career patterns, and voluntary childlessness (Bowen & Orthner, 1989). They also endure many of the same pressures as other American families, including inadequate finances, changing definitions of husband and wife roles, and high mobility (Bowen, 1985; Hunter, 1982; Kaslow & Ridenour, 1984).

Participants were interviewed in private by professionally trained interviewers using a structured questionnaire. To qualify for inclusion in the study, both the husband and wife had to agree to separate interviews. More than two-thirds (69%) of those contacted agreed to participate. The majority of those who declined did so because of problems in scheduling the one-hour interview (e.g., short-term assignments away from the base location).

Couples in which both wives and husbands were serving in the Air Force were selected as the dual-career sample for this investigation. Of the 928 couples, 148 (16%) indicated that both spouses were members of the Air Force. Table 9.1 presents a demographic profile of the 148 dual-career Air Force couples and a profile of the remainder of the sample of couples interviewed.

Measures

External Adaptation

Three variables were used to operationalize external adaptation for each spouse. Two of these were single-item variables: (a) satisfaction with the partner's career (measured on a 5-point scale, with 0 = *very*

TABLE 9.1	Demographic Characteristics of Dual-Career Air Force Versus Other Air Force Couples

	Dual-Career Air Force (n = 148)	Other Air Force Couples (n = 780)
Mean age		
husband	35.5	33.1
wife	32.5	31.7
Mean number of years in current marriage	4.9	9.2
Percentage previously married		
husband	34.3	15.5
wife	19.7	12.7
Mean years of school completed		
husband	14.3	14.8
wife	13.7	13.1
Family life cycle		
percentage childless	53.4	19.5
percentage youngest child under 6	35.2	46.6
percentage youngest child 6 or older	11.4	33.9
Race		
husband		
percentage white	83.9	85.0
percentage other	16.1	15.0
wife		
percentage white	74.5	74.1
percentage other	25.5	25.9

satisfied and 4 = very dissatisfied) and (b) feelings about one's own military career (measured on a 3-point scale, with 0 = one of the least satisfying careers and 2 = only career that could satisfy me).

The third variable was multi-item, developed to assess job morale. This variable included six items that were sum averaged; questions included the following: "How important is the job you do for the Air Force?" "To what extent does your Air Force job match your interests?" "To what extent do you enjoy your day-to-day job activities?" Each item was measured on a 5-point scale, from 0 = very little extent to 4 = very great extent. Alpha reliability for this variable was .84 for husbands and .82 for wives.

Taken together, the multidimensional assessment of job morale, satisfaction with one's military career, and satisfaction with one's partner's military career (i.e., the interaction of the spouses in this domain of adaptation) constitute a variable much broader and more inclusive than more commonly used unidimensional measures of "job satisfaction."

The three variables—the scores for the two single-item variables and the single score for the job morale variable—were coded from low to high and sum averaged to obtain a measure of external adaptation. For husbands, alpha reliability (standardized) for the external adaptation measure was .60, the mean was 2.26, and the standard deviation was .64 (minimum was .33 and maximum was 3.22). For wives, alpha reliability (standardized) for the external adaptation measure was .73, the mean was 1.91, and the standard deviation was .74 (minimum was .17 and maximum was 3.33).

Internal Adaptation

Four single- and multi-item variables were used to operationalize internal adaptation for each spouse: (a) physical expressions of affection, such as feelings about the physical love and sex relations experienced with the spouse (4 items; alpha reliability was .70 for husbands and .77 for wives); (b) agreement on marital issues, such as handling family finances (12 items; alpha reliability was .74 for husbands and .82 for wives); (c) general marital satisfaction, such as the frequency of arguments (6 items; alpha reliability was .76 for husbands and .87 for wives); and (d) desire for the marriage to succeed (1 item). All of the scales and items have been demonstrated in prior research efforts to be valid and reliable indicators of the internal adaptation of spouses in marriage (Bowen, 1987; Locke & Williamson, 1958; Spanier, 1976).

Taken together, the multidimensional assessment of marital satisfaction, marital adjustment, aspects of marital interaction, and marital agreement (the latter two of which relate to the interaction of the spouses in this domain of adaptation) constitute a variable much broader and more inclusive than more common unidimensional measures of "marital satisfaction."

The four variables were sum averaged to obtain a measure of internal adaptation and coded such that the higher the score, the higher the internal adaptation. For husbands, alpha reliability (standardized) for the internal adaptation measure was .63, the mean was 1.25, and the standard deviation was .40 (minimum was .42 and maximum was 2.65). For wives, alpha reliability (standardized) for the internal adaptation measure was .74, the mean was 1.26, and the standard deviation was .52 (minimum was .40 and maximum was 3.33).

The Relationship Between External and Internal Adaptation

An examination of the relationship between the two levels of adaptation for Air Force husbands and Air Force wives in the present investigation indicated that, for husbands, internal and external adaptation correlated −.0004; for wives, the correlation was .40. The spouses' internal adaptation scores correlated .40, and their external adaptation scores correlated .20. Also, husbands' internal and wives' external adaptation scores correlated .19, and wives' internal and husbands' external adaptation scores correlated −.055. Not all the correlations were statistically significant, and the variance accounted for by even the largest correlation was only 16%, indicating relatively independent dimensions of adaptation for the respondents in the present investigation.

To assess the independence of the two dimensions of adaptability further, we employed factor analysis, using alpha extraction and varimax rotation. Table 9.2 presents the results of the analysis for wives and the analysis for husbands, both of which support the conclusion that external and internal adaptation are separate dimensions.

Criterion Measures

Dual-career couple types were compared with respect to two aspects of their communication (each spouse's reported openness with the other and each spouse's reported apprehension about communication outside the marriage) and with respect to their demographic characteristics.

TABLE 9.2 Family Adaptation: Factor Analysis

	Factor 1	Factor 2
Air Force husbands		
physical expressions of intimacy	.58	.18
marital agreement	.78	−.03
marital satisfaction	.61	−.08
desire for marriage to succeed	.40	−.05
job morale	−.08	.42
satisfaction with own career	.03	.77
satisfaction with spouse's career	.05	.55
Air Force wives		
physical expressions of intimacy	.84	−.02
marital agreement	.50	.06
marital satisfaction	.86	.02
desire for marriage to succeed	.52	.07
job morale	.09	.58
satisfaction with own career	−.05	.82
satisfaction with spouse's career	.07	.72

Marital Communication Openness. Marital communication openness was measured using nine items selected from Powers and Hutchinson's (1979) Personal Report of Spouse Communication Apprehension, each relating only to spouse-spouse interaction. Husbands and wives responded to each of the marital communication items using a 5-point interval scale: 0 = *strongly agree*, 1 = *agree*, 2 = *mixed feelings*, 3 = *disagree*, and 4 = *strongly disagree*. The items were as follows: "I don't hesitate to tell my spouse exactly how I feel"; "I am hesitant to develop a 'deep' conversation with my spouse"; "I look forward to expressing my opinion to my spouse on controversial topics"; "I look forward to evening talks with my spouse"; "Usually I try to work out problems myself instead of talking them over with my spouse"; "I usually come right out and tell my spouse exactly what I mean"; "I never hesitate to tell my spouse my needs"; "Even in casual conversations with my spouse, I feel I must guard what I say"; and "I feel I am an open communicator in my marriage."

The items were selected based on high factor loadings (.50 and above) on a factor identified by Powers and Hutchinson as "spouse communication apprehension" and found by Orthner and Bowen

(1982) to have high face validity and adequate variance in the pretest of their survey instrument. Powers and Hutchinson (1979), Bowen (1987), and Rosenfeld and Bowen (1991) present validity and reliability information that argues for the usefulness of the instrument. Powers and Hutchinson report unidimensionality for the items selected, and factor analysis for the 148 dual-career couples in the present study (using generalized least squares extraction, varimax rotation, and a loading cutoff of .50) essentially confirmed the unidimensional structure (see Rosenfeld & Bowen, 1991). Alpha reliability for the nine items was .86 for husband interviewees and .84 for wife interviewees in the present investigation.

Communication Apprehension. Communication apprehension was measured using six items from McCroskey's (1970, 1978, 1986; Richmond & McCroskey, 1992) Personal Report of Communication Anxiety (PRCA). The PRCA, and recent versions of it, such as the PRCA-24, is the most commonly used measure of communication anxiety (Leary, 1988); it has a 20-year history of published research supporting its validity and reliability (see, for example, Daly & McCroskey, 1984; Levine & McCroskey, 1990; McCroskey, Beatty, Kearney, & Plax, 1985), including its applicability to cross-cultural contexts (Fayer, McCroskey, & Richmond, 1984). High communication apprehension adversely affects social, academic, and work performance. For example, workers who suffer from high communication apprehension are less apt to receive pay increases and promotions (Daly & McCroskey, 1984).

Items from the PRCA used in this study, and also used by Powers and Hutchinson (1979) in their study of communication apprehension in marriage, were as follows: "While participating in a conversation with a new acquaintance, I feel very nervous"; "I look forward to expressing my opinions at meetings"; "I am tense and nervous when participating in group discussions"; "I feel that I am more fluent when talking to people than most other people are"; "Conversing with people who hold positions of authority causes me to be fearful and tense"; and "I feel relaxed and comfortable when speaking." Each item was presented with five response categories, ranging from *strongly agree* to *strongly disagree*. Alpha reliability for the six items was .81 for husband interviewees and .74 for wife interviewees in the present investigation. Marital communication openness and communication apprehension were found, for the most part, to be independent. The correlation between husbands' marital openness and communication apprehension was .41; for wives, it was .31. Although statistically significant ($p < .05$), the shared variance is only 16.8% and 9.6%, respectively. Paralleling the findings of Rosenfeld and Bowen (1991), the correlation between husbands' and wives' marital communication openness was a nonsignificant .05, and between their communication apprehension it was a nonsignificant .03.

Demographic Variables

The following demographic data were collected for wives and husbands in each couple: (a) the age of each spouse, (b) the number of years of the current marriage, (c) whether or not each spouse was married previously, (d) years of education completed by each spouse, (e) stage in the family life cycle (based on the age of the youngest child or if the couple is childless), and (f) the race of each spouse.

Analysis Plan

To develop an empirically based classification system of dual-career marriages based on husbands' and wives' internal and external adaptation, and to describe differences among the couple types derived from the classification system, we needed to make two decisions. First, we had to decide what level of analysis (e.g., couple or individual) we would employ to create couple types. Second, we needed to determine what analytic procedure would be most useful for distinguishing among couple types with respect to their communication.

Development of the Dual-Career Typology. The study of dual-career couples can take any of several different approaches, each of which provides different information. Analyses can be conducted at the level of the dyad or couple (e.g., averaging spouses' internal adaptation scores to derive a "couple score"), at the level of the individual (e.g., each spouse's internal adaptation score is considered separately), or a combination of individual and dyad (e.g., each spouse's internal adaptation score is entered separately into an analysis that considers both direct and interaction effects). Evidence exists to support the importance of the separate contributions of husband and wife perceptions to marital outcomes (Chelune, Rosenfeld, & Waring, 1985; Gruen, Folkman, & Lazarus, 1987; Rosenfeld & Bowen, 1991; Snyder & Smith, 1986).

Given the first goal of this investigation, we used cluster analysis to create an empirically derived typology of dual-career marriage. Cluster analysis is a method for classification that makes no assumptions about differences within a population; that is, it is a purely inductive technique (Gerard, 1957). Like other types of segmentation research, cluster analysis "is designed to identify groups of entities (people, markets, organizations) that share certain common characteristics (attitudes, purchase propensities, media habits, etc.)" (Punj & Stewart, 1983, p. 135). The object is to create clusters with couples similar to each other and, at the same time, different from couples in other clusters (Anderberg, 1973).

For this investigation, we used each spouse's internal and external adaptation score—four variables—to create clusters. These variables provide each spouse's perceptions of the extent to which she or he is adapted to both the work and family domains of activity, as well as perceptions of aspects of husband-wife interaction relevant to each domain—for example, each spouse's perception of the other's career, and each spouse's perception of the couple's agreement on marital issues.

As recommended by Punj and Stewart (1983), the clustering procedure we employed in the present investigation was Ward's minimum variance method. Found to be superior to other methods, Ward's method generates clusters that minimize within-cluster variance.

Comparisons Among Dual-Career Marriage Types. Because of the independence of the comparison variables, we conducted four analyses of variance (ANOVAs) to distinguish among the dual-career types with respect to their communication. In each analysis, "dual-career couple type" was the independent variable and communication was the dependent variable (wife's marital communication openness, husband's marital communication openness, wife's communication apprehension, and husband's communication apprehension). Significant *F*-test results were followed with the least significant difference (LSD) multiple comparison procedure (Games, 1971); also, significant *F* ratios were converted to eta-squared to assess their effect size (Cohen, 1977; Rosenthal, 1991).

RESULTS

The first purpose of this investigation was to develop an empirically based classification system of dual-career marriages by employing assessments of each husband's and wife's internal and external adaptation. Cluster analysis of 137 dual-career Air Force couples (11 of the original pool of couples were missing one or more variables used to measure internal and/or external adaptation) revealed three dual-career couple types. We employed analysis of variance to evaluate the differences in internal and external adaptation of the three couple types and, therefore, to begin to describe them.

Table 9.3 and Figure 9.1 present the results of the cluster analysis and follow-up comparisons among the three groups. Table 9.3 presents a summary of the *F*-test comparisons of the means, and Figure 9.1 presents a graph of the standardized mean levels of internal and external adaptation for each spouse in each dual-career couple type.

The *F*-test result for *husband's internal adaptation* was statistically significant: $F(2, 136) = 23.99, p < .001$. Standardized means for the three groups were +.067, −.422, and +.398, respectively. Results of the LSD follow-up multiple comparison procedure (Games, 1971) indicated that all three groups were statistically significantly different from each other.

The *F*-test result for *wife's internal adaptation* was statistically significant: $F(2, 136) = 17.67, p < .001$. Standardized means for the three groups were −.505, −.020, and +.387, respectively. LSD results indicated that all three groups were statistically significantly different from each other.

The *F*-test result for *husband's external adaptation* was statistically significant: $F(2, 136) = 57.58, p < .001$. Standardized means for the three groups were −.850, +.232, and +.359, respectively. LSD results indi-

TABLE 9.3   Internal and External Adaptation of Three Dual-Career Couple Types

| | Internal Adaptation | | External Adaptation | |
Couple Type	Husband	Wife	Husband	Wife
Collapsing marriage	moderate	low	low	low
Work-directed marriage	low	moderate	high	high
Traditional role marriage	high	high	high	low

cated that the first group differed from the other two, which did not differ from each other.

The F-test result for *wife's external adaptation* was statistically significant: $F(2, 136) = 47.60$, $p < .001$. Standardized means for the three groups were $-.380$, $+.735$, and $-.371$, respectively. LSD results indicated that the second group differed from the other two, which did not differ from each other.

The first couple type ($n = 35$; 25.5% of the total sample) we call the dual-career *collapsing marriage* (CM), based on the observation that neither the wife nor the husband in this type of marriage was even moderately adapted externally, the wife was poorly adapted internally, and the husband was only moderately adapted internally. The second couple type ($n = 47$; 34.3% of the total sample) we call the dual-career *work-directed marriage* (WDM), based on the observation that both the wife and husband were well-adapted externally and neither was well-adapted internally (the husband was poorly adapted internally, and the wife was only moderately adapted internally). The third couple type ($n = 55$; 40.1% of the total sample) we call the *traditional role marriage* (TRM), based on the observation that both wife and husband were well-adapted internally, the husband was well-adapted externally, and the wife was poorly adapted externally.

With regard to the demographic profile of each of the three dual-career couple types, WDM and TRM couples appear similar on all the variables measured. CM couples, however, have a unique profile:

- CM couples have younger husbands ($M_{age} = 33.2$) than the other two dual-career couple types ($M_{age} = 38.4$), which do not differ from each other—$F(2, 135) = 6.11$, $p < .003$.

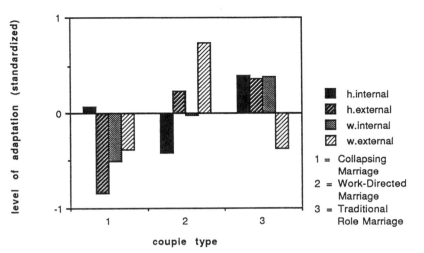

Figure 9.1. Adaptation in Three Dual-Career Couple Types

NOTE: h.internal = husband's internal adaptation score, w.internal = wife's internal adaptation score, h.external = husband's external adaptation score, w.external = wife's external adaptation score.

- CM couples have been married approximately two years less than have the other couple types, 3.4 versus 5.5 years (although the F result was not statistically significant at a usual alpha level—$F[2, 136] = 2.32, p <$ .10—LSD comparisons revealed CM and TRM couples significantly different at $p < .05$).
- A smaller percentage of CM husbands have been married previously (22.9% versus 38.7%)—$\chi^2(3, N = 137) = 17.42, p < .001$.
- Although the highest proportion of childless couples are in the CM type (65.7% versus 48.7%), differences are not statistically significant—$\chi^2(3, N = 137) = 4.16, p < .20$.

No differences among the three dual-career couple types, or between CM couples and other couples, were found for (a) wives' mean age, (b) percentage of wives previously married, (c) husbands' and wives' mean years of school completed, (d) stage in the family life cycle, or (e) racial composition.

Our second purpose in undertaking this investigation was to describe differences among the three dual-career couple types with regard to their communication. Only one of the four ANOVAs was statistically significant. The three nonsignificant ($p > .05$) findings were for (a) husband's marital communication openness, $F(2, 135) = 1.41, p > .24$; (b) husband's communication apprehension, $F(2, 135) = .07$, $p > .92$; and (c) wife's communication apprehension, $F(2, 132) = 1.12$, $p > .32$. The one statistically significant finding was for wife's marital communication openness, $F(2, 135) = 5.82, p < .004$. The eta-squared correlation associated with this F result was .08 (indicating that 8% of the variance of the differences among the marriage types is accounted for by the F result), which, according to Cohen (1977), is a small effect size. Results of the LSD follow-up comparisons indicated that CM wives reported significantly lower marital communication openness than did wives in either WDM or TRM couples, who were not different from each other. The means for each dual-career marriage type (higher means indicate less marital communication openness) were TRM = 7.98, WDM = 9.13, and CM = 11.74.[2]

DISCUSSION

Three primary shortcomings of previous investigations of dual-career couples provided the impetus for the study reported here. First, research attempting to compare dual-career couples with other couple types has tended to ignore the possible confounding effects of within-couple and between-couple career differences. Typically, researchers cast all dual-career couples together into a single group, assuming that all that matters is the couples' shared dual-careerness. Second, prior typologies of dual-career couple types often have lacked empirical support; therefore, as appealing as their descriptions are—including couple types that "have it all," both well-functioning and highly satisfactory home and work lives—their validity is, at least, open to question. And third, the notion of commitment—to work, to family, to one's spouse—presumed to be a defining characteristic of dual-careerness, has been operationalized in several bewildering and dubious ways, including the level of education required for a job and the job title itself. Indeed, most researchers appear to have ignored altogether the notion of commitment to one's spouse and one's family.

We responded to these shortcomings in the investigation reported above in an effort to provide a more valid typology and description of dual-career couple types. First, our respondents were 137 couples in which both spouses are members of the U.S. Air Force. This effectively controlled for between-couple and within-couple career differences. Second, rather than explicate a typology without empirical support, we allowed a typology to emerge from data analysis. The result is a typology grounded in the reality of the couples studied, and not imposed on them. Finally, we replaced the concept of "commitment" with the concepts of internal and external adaptation. This change provided broader consideration of individual-to-environment fit, with greater conceptual and empirical support.

Typology of Dual-Career Couples

Three dual-career couple types, distinguished with respect to each spouse's internal and external adaptation, emerged from the cluster analysis employed in this study. The three couple types are the collapsing marriage, the work-directed marriage, and the traditional role marriage.

The collapsing marriage couple type is distinguished from the others by its low external adaptation for both spouses, low internal adaptation for the wife, and moderate internal adaptation for the husband. Poorly adapted to her marriage and work life, the wife also is less open with her husband. Only 25% of the couples studied were classified as this type, perhaps because of a high divorce rate (the mean number of years married was lowest for this group, indicating, perhaps, that spouses in this group do not remain together long before either divorcing or reconfiguring their relationships). What holds this type of marriage together? The glue may be the husband, with his moderate level of internal adaptation.[3]

The CM couple is unrepresented in the Hall and Hall (1980) and Jones and Jones (1980) dual-career marriage typologies. These two typologies work from the assumption that at least one of the spouses has high work involvement/commitment or, in the event that neither does, at least one assuredly has a high involvement with/commitment to the family. The empirical evidence is clear: Dual-career marriages exist in which the couples have low external adaptation and no more than moderate internal adaptation—marriages, perhaps, on the verge of collapse.

The work-directed marriage couple is distinguished from the others by high external adaptation for both spouses, moderate internal adaptation for the wife, and low internal adaptation for the husband. This couple type, slightly more than a third of the couples studied, has a husband whose internal adaptation is lower than that of husbands in the other dual-career couple types, and a wife whose internal adaptation is higher than that of CM wives and close to that of TRM wives. Wives in work-directed marriages report being as open with their marital communication as wives in traditional role marriages, although, given their high external and moderate internal adaptation, it may be that topics of conversation about which they are open concern work. Of the three dual-career couple types, the WDM couple is perhaps the most "positive" for the wife, given her high external and moderate internal adaptation. In each of the other two couple types, the wife has low internal and/or low external adaptation.

The work-directed marriage is well represented in two of the three typologies, albeit in slightly varying forms. For example, Hall and Hall's (1980) "adversaries," where both spouses have high work involvement and low home involvement, are similar to WDM couples, except that the latter have wives with moderate home involvement; and Jones and Jones's (1980) "marriage of state," in which spouses are more committed to their work than their home and both share family responsibilities, is similar to the work-directed marriage except the husband in the work-directed marriage either shares household duties and is not happy about it (Rosenfield, 1992, found that as sharing domestic labor increases, husbands' mental health decreases), or does not share them at all.

The traditional role marriage couple—the largest percentage of the couples in our study—is distinguished from the others by both spouses' high internal adaptation, the high external adaptation of the husband, and the low external adaptation of the wife. The high proportion of this type of dual-career couple in the sample may reflect the effects of the strong masculine culture in the military, which might implicitly encourage women to accommodate their careers to their husbands'

(Segal, 1989). In a traditional role marriage the wife has high internal and low external adaptation, indicating she may be adhering to traditional perspectives of the "woman's role" as homemaker first and career woman second.[4] This also fits with the finding that wives in TRM couples report the highest level of marital communication openness (although not statistically significantly different from wives in WDM couples). Just as the work-directed marriage is, perhaps, the most "positive" type for the wife, the traditional role marriage is, perhaps, the most "positive" one for the husband: In no other couple type is husband's internal and external adaptation higher.

Although one may interpret the wife's accommodation to work and family as the "sacrifice" of her external adaptation for internal adaptation,[5] our results support Burke and Greenglass's (1987) conclusion that "the notion of tradeoffs . . . becomes particularly important when both partners are pursuing careers" (p. 299). There is just so much time and energy, and "the more a person invests in and identifies with his or her career role, the less time and energy there is to invest in the roles of parent, partner, or keeper of the house" (p. 299). The wife in the traditional role marriage, by exhibiting a low level of external adaptation, probably enhances her own and her husband's high levels of internal adaptation, and perhaps makes possible her husband's high level of external adaptation. The cost may or may not be too high—it depends on the wife's perspective.

The Hall and Hall (1980) and Jones and Jones (1980) dual-career marriage typologies describe "acrobats" and "magnetized marriage" partners for whom there is both high work and high home commitment—high internal and external adaptation. We found no such dual-career type in this investigation (at least not in sufficient numbers to create a fourth type in the cluster analysis).[6] Perhaps, as Burke and Greenglass (1987) suggest, it cannot exist.

Maybe the closest to the ideal that reality can offer for the husband is the traditional role marriage (see Jones & Jones's, 1980, "morganatic marriage"), where the wife trades off external for internal adaptation. However, there is no inherent reason this trade-off needs to be the wife's "sacrifice"; this dual-career couple type may be just as rewarding for the wife if it is her husband who "sacrifices" external for internal adaptation. Maybe the closest to the ideal that reality can offer for the wife is the work-directed marriage, where she has high external adaptation and moderate internal adaptation. The "sacrifice" in this couple type appears to be the husband's; he "gives up" a "traditional" wife in the couple's mutual pursuit of their careers.

The typology empirically derived in this investigation, together with the characterization of dual-career marriage types on the basis of their communication, may provide a more realistic and accurate portrayal of dual-career marriages than those typologies based on nonempirically based conceptualizations. The good news is this: Without the confounding effects of representing myriad careers in the dual-career couples studied, and the uncertainties raised by failing to operationalize commitment as the defining aspect of career, three dual-career couple types become evident. The bad news is that, except for a small number of couples, no one couple type seems to work best for both wives and husbands. For most, the dream of a dual-career couple with both spouses involved in/committed to/satisfied with/mutually supportive of their work and family lives may be just that, a dream. The reality is that "dual-career couples of today are a transition generation who live without a clear precedent. It is as much a challenge for them to manage their lives as it is for researchers to study them" (Yogev, 1982, p. 603).

FUTURE RESEARCH

Although the investigation reported in this chapter attempted to solve several of the problems associated with previous research on dual-career couples (e.g., the sample of Air Force dual-career couples helped control for the effects of noncomparable careers), our empirically derived typology requires further examination. Although intuitively appealing, the discriminant validity of the typology is generally weak, generating significant between-group differences in only one of the four comparisons involving the two criterion communication measures. With larger samples, we recommend that researchers not only attempt to verify the three-cluster pattern, but also examine its stability within different population subgroups, including comparisons of couples with and without children in the home. For example, the traditional role marriage may result from an accommodation by wives to having children in the home, especially if wives in this couple type are more likely than wives in other couple types to define parenting as highly salient to their identities. It may be that a fourth type of dual-career marriage that has been discussed in the literature will emerge among childless couples: husbands and wives who share both high internal and high external adaptation.

It is also important for researchers to experiment with different indicators of internal and external adaptation. As a secondary analysis, the present investigation was limited to variables that had been included on the survey of Air Force families. In particular, we recommend that the specification of external adaptation include not only job- and career-related variables, but general indicators of family adaptation to career demands. The inclusion of such external dimensions should result in measures of external adaptation that more fully capture the interface between the couple and the environmental system. Although the testing of different indicators of internal and external adaptation may result in some inconsistency among studies in the conceptualization of these variables, such experimentation may result in clusters that have greater discriminant validity while maintaining the general integrity of the distinction between internal and external adaptation in defining couple types. It is this general distinction between the two dimensions of family adaptation that we believe will be heuristic to further research that attempts to identify and examine the predictive validity of dual-career couple types.

NOTES

1. A notable exception to this trend is a recent study by Tesch, Osborne, Simpson, Murray, et al. (1992), in which women in dual-career physician marriages ($n = 91$) were compared with women physicians whose partners were not physicians ($n = 156$). Findings indicated that, while in training, women in both types of dual-career marriages were similar with respect to the egalitarian division of household labor; however, there were several differences between practicing respondents. For example, practicing women with physician husbands were more likely than those without physician husbands to assume responsibility for household chores and to interrupt their careers for their husbands' careers.

2. Originally, we conducted analyses of covariance (ANCOVA) to include an assessment of the effects of three variables known from prior research to contribute to marital processes. The first, length of marriage, was added as a covariate because of its relationship to communication, particularly self-disclosure, in married couples (Komarovsky, 1967; Rice, 1979; Rosenfeld & Welsh; 1985). For example, Burke, Weir, and Harrison (1976) found that communication openness decreased with increasing length of marriage. The second covariate was created by subtracting the Air Force rank of the wife from that of her husband. Differences in rank, which denote differences in authority and income, may affect marital interaction, an aspect of internal adaptation. For example, role homophily theory (Simpson & England, 1981) argues that marital solidarity increases when husband and wife share similar roles (i.e., rank differences approach zero) because it enhances their communication and companionship; Parsons's (1942, 1949, 1955) sex role differentiation theory, on the other hand, argues that when the wife and husband share similar work roles they become competitors, and that marital outcomes are positive only to the extent that the wife's occupation is secondary to her husband's and he is the primary wage earner (i.e., rank differences are positive). The third covariate was whether or not the couple had any children (either 0 for none or 1 for one or more children). A summary of research on the effects of children on family life indicates, for example, that the presence of children can increase stress levels and decrease marital satisfaction, both aspects affecting internal adaptation (Pearson, 1993). Results indicated that none of the three variables was a significant covariate in any of the four analyses.

3. Analysis of the gender role preferences of spouses in each dual-career marriage type indicated that the husband in the collapsing marriage is more modern, as opposed to traditional. He probably perceives his wife's problems in adapting—both at home and at work—and is aware of her low level of internal adaptation (regarding marital satisfaction). He responds, perhaps, by assuming responsibility for household chores that traditionally are viewed as the wife's responsibility. With his willingness to take on family and home responsibilities, he can adapt—at least moderately—to his marriage.

4. Analysis of the gender role preferences of spouses in each dual-career marriage type indicated that the husband in the traditional role marriage is more traditional as opposed to modern. His preferences include having his wife assume primary responsibility for homemaking and ensuring that his career comes before hers.

5. Karambayya and Reilly (1992) found that the wives in their study of dual-earner couples adapted their work behavior to fit their families and their spouses more frequently than did the husbands.

6. Although the cluster analysis revealed three distinct types of dual-career marriages, we conducted some post hoc data snooping to see if we could identify any couples with both spouses high in internal and external adaptation (i.e., standardized means above zero). Of the 137 dual-career couples, we found 16 (11.7%) who were likely to fit the classification of "acrobats" or "magnetized marriage partners." The standardized means for couples in this group were wives' internal adaptation = .41 (SD = .34), wives' external adaptation = .74 (SD = .45), husbands' internal adaptation = .65 (SD = .52), and husbands' external adaptation = .45 (SD = .38). It is likely that the 16 couples did not form a fourth dual-career

marriage type in the cluster analysis because of their similarity to the TRM couples. Comparisons of the means for this group of 16 couples with those for the three dual-career types indicate (a) the husband is better adapted internally than in any of the three dual-career couple types, (b) the husband is no better adapted externally and the wife is no better adapted internally than in the traditional role marriage type, and (c) the wife is as well adapted externally as the wife in the work-directed marriage type.

REFERENCES

Alger, I. (1991). Marital therapy with dual-career couples. *Psychiatric Annals, 21,* 455-458.

Anderberg, M. R. (1973). *Cluster analysis for applications.* New York: Academic Press.

Bowen, G. L. (1985). Families in blue: Insights from Air Force families. *Social Casework, 66,* 459-466.

Bowen, G. L. (1987). Changing gender-role preferences and marital adjustment: Implications for clinical practice. *Family Therapy, 14,* 17-33.

Bowen, G. L. (1988). Corporate support for the family lives of employees: A conceptual model for program planning and evaluation. *Family Relations, 37,* 183-188.

Bowen, G. L. (1993). *Family adaptation to relocation in the U.S. Air Force: Toward a conceptual model* (Task Report 2). Washington, DC: U.S. Department of the Air Force.

Bowen, G. L., & Orthner, D. K. (Eds.). (1989). *The organization family: Work and family linkages in the U.S. military.* New York: Praeger.

Bowen, G. L., Orthner, D. K., Zimmerman, L. I., & Bell, D. B. (1993). *Family adaptation: Contributions to the work and personal adjustments of soldiers and their spouses.* Alexandria, VA: U.S. Army Research Institute for the Behavioral and Social Sciences.

Burke, R. J., & Bradshaw, P. (1981). Occupational and life stress and the family. *Small Group Behavior, 12,* 329-375.

Burke, R. J., & Greenglass, E. R. (1987). Work and family. In C. L. Cooper & I. T. Robertson (Eds.), *International review of industrial and organizational psychology 1987* (pp. 273-320). New York: John Wiley.

Burke, R. J., & Weir, T. (1976). Relationship of wives' employment status to husband, wife, and pair satisfaction and performance. *Journal of Marriage and the Family, 38,* 279-287.

Burke, R. J., Weir, T., & Harrison, D. (1976). Disclosure of problems and tensions experienced by marital partners. *Psychological Reports, 38,* 531-542.

Cohen, J. (1977). *Statistical power analysis for the behavioral sciences* (rev. ed.). New York: Academic Press.

Chelune, G. J., Rosenfeld, L. B., & Waring, E. M. (1985). Spouse disclosure patterns in distressed and nondistressed couples. *American Journal of Family Therapy, 13,* 24-32.

Daly, J. A., & McCroskey, J. C. (Eds.). (1984). *Avoiding communication: Shyness, reticence, and communication apprehension.* Beverly Hills, CA: Sage.

Fayer, J. M., McCroskey, J. C., & Richmond, V. P. (1984). Communication apprehension in Puerto Rico and the United States I: Initial comparisons. *Communication, 13*, 49-66.

Fitzpatrick, M. A. (1988). *Between husbands and wives: Communication in marriage.* Newbury Park, CA: Sage.

Furstenberg, F. F. (1980). Reflections of remarriage. *Journal of Family Issues, 1*, 4.

Games, P. A. (1971). Multiple comparisons of means. *American Educational Research Journal, 7*, 531-565.

Gerard, R. W. (1957). Units and concepts of biology. *Science, 125*, 429-433.

Gertel, N. R., & Gross, H. E. (1984). *Commuter marriage: A study of work and family.* New York: Guilford.

Gilbert, L. A. (1985). *Men in dual-career families: Current realities and future prospects.* Hillsdale, NJ: Lawrence Erlbaum.

Gilbert, L. A., & Rachlin, V. (1987). Mental health and psychological functioning of dual-career families. *Counseling Psychologist, 15*(1), 7-49.

Gilmer, B. V. H. (1971). *Industrial and organizational psychology.* New York: McGraw-Hill.

Glick, P. C. (1989). The family life cycle and social change. *Family Relations, 38*, 123-129.

Gross, H. E. (1980). Dual-career couples who live apart: Two types. *Journal of Marriage and the Family, 42*, 567-576.

Gruen, R. J., Folkman, S., & Lazarus, R. S. (1987). Dyadic response patterns in married couples, depressive symptoms, and somatic dysfunction. *Journal of Family Psychology, 1*, 168-186.

Hall, D. T., & Hall, F. S. (1980). Stress and the two-career couple. In C. L. Cooper & R. Payne (Eds.), *Current concerns in occupational stress* (pp. 243-266). Chichester: John Wiley.

Hayghe, H. (1986). Rise in mothers' labor force activity includes those with infants. *Monthly Labor Review, 109*, 43-45.

Heacock, D., & Spicer, C. H. (1986). Communication and the dual-career couple: A literature assessment. *Southern Speech Communication Journal, 51*, 260-266.

Hunter, E. J. (1982). *Families under the flag.* New York: Praeger.

Jones, W., & Jones, R. (1980). *Two careers, one marriage.* New York: AMACOM.

Kaplan, L. F. (1992, May 10). Mother's work is truly never done. *Fort Collins Coloradoan*, p. C-1.

Karambayya, R., & Reilly, A. H. (1992). Dual earner couples: Attitudes and actions in restructuring work for family. *Journal of Organizational Behavior, 13*, 383-601.

Kaslow, F. W., & Ridenour, R. I. (Eds.). (1984). *The military family.* New York: Guilford.

Komarovsky, M. (1967). *Blue-collar marriage.* New York: Random House.

Krueger, D. L. (1986). Communication strategies and patterns in dual-career couples. *Southern Speech Communication Journal, 51*, 274-284.

Ladewig, B., & White, P. N. (1984). Dual-earner marriages: The family social environment and dyadic adjustment. *Journal of Family Issues, 5*, 343-362.

Lavee, Y., & McCubbin, H. I. (1985, November). *Adaptation in family stress theory: Theoretical and methodological considerations.* Paper presented at the Theory Construction and Research Methodology Workshop at the meeting of the National Council on Family Relations, Dallas.

Leary, M. R. (1988). Socially-based anxiety: A review of measures. In C. H. Tardy (Ed.), *A handbook for the study of human communication: Methods and instruments for observing, measuring, and assessing communication processes* (pp. 365-384). Norwood, NJ: Ablex.

Levine, T. R., & McCroskey, J. C. (1990). Measuring trait communication apprehension: A test of rival measurement models of the PRCA-24. *Communication Monographs, 57,* 62-72.

Locke, H. J., & Williamson, R. C. (1958). Marital adjustment: A factor analysis study. *American Sociological Review, 23,* 562-569.

McBroom, W. H. (1984). Changes in sex-role orientations: A five year longitudinal comparison. *Sex Roles, 11,* 583-592.

McCroskey, J. C. (1970). Measures of communication-bound anxiety. *Speech Monographs, 37,* 269-277.

McCroskey, J. C. (1978). Validity of the PRCA as an index of oral communication apprehension. *Communication Monographs, 45,* 192-203.

McCroskey, J. C. (1986). *An introduction to rhetorical communication* (5th ed.). Englewood Cliffs, NJ: Prentice Hall.

McCroskey, J. C., Beatty, M. J., Kearney, P., & Plax, T. G. (1985). The content validity of the PRCA-24 as a measure of communication apprehension across communication contexts. *Communication Quarterly, 33,* 165-173.

Melson, G. F. (1983). Family adaptation to environmental demands. In H. I. McCubbin & C. R. Figley (Eds.), *Stress and the family I: Coping with normative transitions.* New York: Brunner/Mazel.

Olson, D. H. (1981). Family typologies: Bridging family research and family therapy. In E. E. Filsinger & R. A. Lewis (Eds.), *Assessing marriage: New behavioral approaches* (pp. 74-89). Beverly Hills, CA: Sage.

Orthner, D. K., & Bowen, G. L. (1982). *Families in blue: Insights from Air Force families in the Pacific.* Greensboro, NC: SRA.

Orthner, D. K., & Bowen, G. L., & Beare, V. G. (1990). The organization family: A question of work and family boundaries. *Marriage and Family Review, 15*(3/4), 15-36.

Parker, M., Peltier, S., & Wolleat, P. (1981). Understanding dual-career couples. *Personnel and Guidance Journal, 60*(1), 14-18.

Parsons, T. (1942). Age and sex in the social structure of the United States. *Family Coordinator, 28,* 604-616.

Parsons, T. (1949). The social structure of the family. In R. Ashen (Ed.), *The family: Its function and destiny.* New York: Harper & Row.

Parsons, T. (1955). The American family: Its relations to personality and to the social structure. In T. Parsons & R. F. Bales (Eds.), *Family, socialization, and interaction process* (pp. 3-33). New York: Macmillan.

Pearson, J. C. (1993). *Communication in the family: Seeking satisfaction in changing times.* New York: HarperCollins.

Powell, G. N. (1988). *Women and men in management.* Newbury Park, CA: Sage.

Powers, W. G., & Hutchinson, K. (1979). The measurement of communication apprehension in the marriage relationship. *Journal of Marriage and the Family, 41,* 89-95.

Price-Bonham, S., & Murphy, D. C. (1980). Dual-career marriages: Implications for the clinician. *Journal of Marital and Family Therapy, 6,* 181-188.

Punj, G., & Stewart, D. W. (1983). Cluster analysis in marketing research: Review and suggestions for application. *Journal of Marketing Research, 20,* 134-148.

Rapoport, R., & Rapoport, R. N. (1969). The dual-career family: A variant pattern and social change. *Human Relations, 22,* 3-30.

Rapoport, R., & Rapoport, R. N. (1971). *Dual-career families.* Harmondsworth: Penguin.

Rapoport, R., & Rapoport, R. N. (1976). *Dual-career families revisited.* New York: Harper & Row.

Rhodes, J. P., & Rhodes, E. L. (1984, June). Commuter marriage: The toughest alternative. *Ms.,* pp. 44-48.

Rice, D. G. (1979). *Dual-career marriage: Conflict and treatment.* New York: Free Press.

Richmond, V. P., & McCroskey, J. C. (1992). *Communication: Apprehension, avoidance, and effectiveness* (3rd ed.). Scottsdale, AZ: Gorsuch Scarisbrick.

Rosenfeld, L. B., & Bowen, G. L. (1991). Marital disclosure and marital satisfaction: Direct-effect versus interaction-effect models. *Western Journal of Speech Communication, 55,* 69-84.

Rosenfeld, L. B., & Welsh, S. M. (1985). Differences in self-disclosure in dual-career and single-career marriages. *Communication Monographs, 52,* 253-263.

Rosenfield, S. (1992). The costs of sharing: Wives' employment and husbands' mental health. *Journal of Health and Social Behavior, 33,* 213-225.

Rosenthal, R. (1991). *Meta-analytic procedures for social research.* Newbury Park, CA: Sage.

Segal, M. W. (1989). The nature of work and family linkages. In G. L. Bowen & D. K. Orthner (Eds.), *The organization family: Work and family linkages in the U.S. military* (pp. 3-36). New York: Praeger.

Silberstein, L. R. (1992). *Dual-career marriage: A system in transition.* Hillsdale, NJ: Lawrence Erlbaum.

Simpson, I. H., & England, P. (1981). Conjugal work roles and marital solidarity. *Journal of Family Issues, 2,* 180-204.

Snyder, D. K., & Smith, G. T. (1986). Classification of marital relationships: An empirical approach. *Journal of Marriage and the Family, 48,* 137-146.

Spanier, G. B. (1976). Measuring dyadic adjustment: New scales for assessing the quality of marriage and similar dyads. *Journal of Marriage and the Family, 38,* 15-28.

Steffy, B. D., & Ashbaugh, D. (1986). Dual-career planning, marital satisfaction and job stress among women in dual-career marriages. *Journal of Business and Psychology, 1*(2), 114-123.

Steil, J. M., & Weltman, K. (1992). Influence strategies at home and at work: A study of sixty dual career couples. *Journal of Social and Personal Relationships, 9,* 65-88.

Stewart, L. P., & Clarke-Kudless, D. (1993). Communication in corporate settings. In L. P. Arliss & D. J. Borisoff (Eds.), *Women and men communicating: Challenges and changes* (pp. 142-152). Fort Worth, TX: Harcourt Brace Jovanovich.

Teachman, J. D., Polonko, K. A., & Scanzoni, J. (1987). Demography of the family. In M. B. Sussman & S. K. Steinmetz (Eds.), *Handbook of marriage and the family* (pp. 3-36). New York: Plenum.

Tesch, B. J., Osborne, J., Simpson, D. E., Murray, S. F., et al. (1992). Women physicians in dual-career relationships compared with those in other dual-career relationships. *Academic Medicine, 67,* 542-544.

Thornton, A. (1989). Changing attitudes toward family issues in the United States. *Journal of Marriage and the Family, 51,* 873-893.

Tryon, G. S., & Tryon, W. W. (1982). Issues in the lives of dual-career couples. *Clinical Psychology Review, 2*(1), 49-65.

U.S. Bureau of the Census. (1989). *Earnings of married-couple families: 1987* (Current Population Reports, Series P-60, No. 165). Washington, DC: Government Printing Office.

Voydanoff, P. (1980). *The implications of work-family relationships for productivity.* Scarsdale, NY: Work in America Institute.

Wood, J. T. (1986). Maintaining dual-career bonds: Communicative dimensions of internally structured relationships. *Southern Speech Communication Journal, 51,* 267-273.

Wood, J. T. (1994). *Gendered lives: Communication, gender, and culture.* Belmont, CA: Wadsworth.

Yogev, S. (1982). Happiness in dual-career couples: Changing research, changing values. *Sex Roles, 8,* 593-605.

10

Communication Patterns in Stepfamilies

Redefining Family Roles, Themes, and Conflict Styles

NANCY A. BURRELL

Although the divorce rate remains consistent in the United States, more than 40% of marriages each year are remarriages (Coleman & Ganong, 1990). Whereas a first marriage represents the joining of two families, a second marriage signifies the intertwining of three, four, or more families (McGoldrick & Carter, 1989). In addition, 8.8 million children under the age of 18 live in stepfamilies (Schwebel, Fine, & Renner, 1991). Thus, remarriages involve not only the relational partners but often also children from one or both prior marriages. As McGoldrick and Carter (1989) note, "So complex is the process whereby the remarried-family system stabilizes and regains its forward developmental thrust that we have come to think of this process as adding another whole phase to the family life cycle for those involved" (p. 399).

When stepfamilies are formed, the enormous tasks of reorganizing households, adjusting to one another, and renegotiating family roles must be undertaken. Compounding this adjustment is the issue that many of these "family" relations begin as unchosen or involuntary for some or most family members, although legal relationships may exist between stepparents and stepchildren (Cissna, Cox, & Bochner, 1990;

Einstein, 1985; Galvin & Brommel, 1991; Galvin & Cooper, 1990; Papernow, 1984, 1987; Visher & Visher, 1988).

My purpose in this chapter is to describe the stereotypes of stepfamilies, metaphors of stepfamily life, conflict in stepfamilies, and new directions for stepfamily research. There is little available communication research to guide theorists, researchers, counselors, and families in ways to investigate and formulate stepfamilies. I use the terms *blended family, reorganizing family, remarried family,* and *stepfamily* synonymously here. Cissna et al. (1990) employ the terms *blended family* and *stepfamily* to denote cases in which "two adults are providing continuing care for at least one child who is not the biological offspring or originally adoptive child of at least one of the adults" (p. 59). A more complex version of the stepfamily might involve two remarried partners, both with children, or even additional children from previous marriages. Over time, these same partners might have a child together. Noller and Fitzpatrick (1993) aptly describe this membership complexity as "yours, mine and ours" (p. 238).

STEPFAMILY STEREOTYPES

The majority of family research centers on intact first families (Burrell & Mitchell, 1993; McGoldrick & Carter, 1989). Berardo (1990) notes that stepfamily research "still contains a number of critical inconsistencies and methodological shortcomings" along with biases, stereotypes, and myths that have inhibited investigation in this area (p. 7). One such myth that has hindered research on stepfamilies concerns comparisons between blended and intact families; there appears to be an inherent predisposition to view intact families as positive, natural, and normative. This chapter is based on the premise that stepfamilies deserve to be studied in their own right. Until recently, stepfamilies have been studied only in terms of how they differ from intact families, with the assumption often made that members of stepfamilies are somehow deficient in comparison with intact family members simply because of their family structure (Coleman & Ganong, 1990).

This negative view may be fueled by common stereotypes in perceptions of stepfamilies (Fine, 1986). For example, in a study of 175 college students (90 from continuously intact families, 55 from single-parent families, and 30 from stepfamilies) Fine (1986) found that, overall, stepparents were rated more negatively than biological parents on dimensions such as hateful/affectionate, unfair/fair, unloving/loving, and good/bad. A feasible conclusion is that biological parents are considered better equipped with traditional parental characteristics than are stepparents for assuming the parenting role. Even in the educational system an unbiased view of stepfamilies is sadly lacking. Of the 28 most widely used texts in U.S. college courses dealing with family living, none includes the possible strengths associated with the stepfamily structure; all delineate only the potential problems (Coleman, Ganong, & Ginrich, 1985).

As Mitchell (1992) notes, positive aspects of stepfamily life for children might include opportunities to know new people, to have fresh experiences, to be exposed to positive models of marriage and intimacy, to have increased access to adults, and to learn cooperation, flexibility, and sharing. Unfortunately, unless the positive sides of divorce and remarriage begin to be appreciated, stepfamilies will remain "second best" in a society that values the picture-perfect intact family. The negative stereotypes of stepfamilies are even more astonishing given that fewer and fewer families fit the intact/ideal family form. In fact, it has been projected that by the year 2000, the number of stepfamilies and single-parent families will exceed the number of intact nuclear families (Bryan, Ganong, Coleman, & Bryan, 1985). Given this projection, it is not surprising that in the late 1980s researchers started calling for a more normative view of stepfamilies (Coleman & Ganong, 1990), one that would allow stepfamilies to be studied as a distinct phenomenon, separate from intact families and negative comparisons. In addition, therapists now recognize that treatment for dysfunctional stepfamilies should be based on typical structural patterns found in functional stepfamilies rather than intact families. As Anderson and White (1986) assert, "Armed with only a nuclear model of family functioning, the therapist may select inappropriate or even destructive goals for treatment" (p. 420).

TABLE 10.1 Stepfamily Characteristics

Characteristic	Illustration
History of "natural" family loss	The family has experienced divorce or death.
Past family history	The family has memories of celebrations, rituals, family traditions.
Parent-child relationships that predate the marital union	The level of concern, lines of authority, discipline routines, and expectations for behavior have been established.
Biological parental influence	Regardless of who is the primary caretaker, both parents have impact on their children's development.
Children's functioning as members of more than one household	Depending on the number of times biological parents remarry and the activeness of parents' roles, children may be members of two or three households.
Complex extended family networks	Children of remarriages may have several sets of grandparents, aunts, uncles, and cousins, depending on the size of each "new" family.
Strong triangles involving biological parents and stepparents	Children may be used as weapons to sabotage a newly formed/ reorganizing family.
No legal relationship between stepparent and stepchildren	Adoption may not be an option for stepparents.

SOURCE: Stepfamily characteristics are drawn from Galvin and Brommel (1991).

In sum, the trend in current theory and research is to consider stepfamily communication as a phenomenon deserving of study in its own right, without comparison to other family systems. As Miller and Soper (1982) note, given that the stepfamily form seems to be deeply rooted in our society, it "needs to be understood and supported" (p. 715). Table 10.1 presents eight characteristics of stepfamilies that have been discussed by scholars. To further facilitate understanding of stepfamilies, metaphors of stepfamily life as they apply to family members' attempts to negotiate new roles, boundaries, and loyalty issues are discussed in the following section.

METAPHORS OF STEPFAMILY LIFE

Spangle (1991) suggests several advantages of using metaphors as a research tool to study family communication. First, metaphors present collective representations of group energies and patterns. Second, images convey significant aspects of attitude, meaning, and emotional connotations in the family experience. Third, family metaphors reflect the presence or absence of family cohesion. Thus "a single metaphor can reveal how an individual relates to and is valued by the family as a whole" (Spangle, 1991, p. 3). Metaphoric analysis enables researchers to uncover perceptions of how individuals approach and manage family life. These images reveal the ways in which family members see and experience daily interactions, because one sure indicator of conscious and unconscious worldviews is linguistic choice.

Metaphor is defined as a figure of speech in which "the qualities of one object are carried over or transferred to another object, with the result that the second object receives the qualities of the first. In the process, the second object becomes transformed" (Norton, 1989, p. 3). Because of this transformational process, metaphors function to create reality, supply means of conceptualizing different realities, indicate shifts in social change prior to social movements, offer vocabulary for thoughts and feelings that may be difficult to articulate, and provide implicit philosophies of life and coping mechanisms for dealing with life events (Hart, 1990; Lakoff & Johnson, 1980; Morgan, 1986; Norton, 1989; Tsousakas, 1991). A metaphor can be our means of having or knowing a reality (Foss, 1989).

Metaphors offer vocabulary for comprehending experience in such a way that some elements become more germane to individuals than others. Metaphors are expressions cast in digital language, but their importance exists in their implied analogies (Bochner, 1978). Because metaphors position some aspects in sharper relief, other elements become less prominent and may fail to influence behavior significantly. Family-created and -justified metaphors can control conscious and unconscious behaviors of family members and thus privilege one version of reality over another. In short, metaphors generated by relational partners provide descriptions of stepfamily life that the partners perceive as salient and reveal underlying issues about the reorganizing process. In this section I explore how relational partners in stepfamilies characterize their family lives (both past and present) through metaphors. Assumptions underlying the discussion are that explicit metacommunication is involved in developing the new blended family and that metaphors provide one index of shared or overlapping psychological realities among family members.

In a recent study, a colleague and I examined spouses' perceptions about stepfamilies to gain knowledge about the reorganizing process and to extend our understanding of stepfamilies by identifying the metaphors that characterize both individual and shared worldviews in family systems (Burrell & Buzzanell, 1992). Consider the following exchange, which took place when we asked one couple what stepfamily life was like in both the past and present.

WIFE: To be perfectly honest with you, we never thought about being a blended family. . . . We both told each other that I'm a package deal, if you want me, the kid comes along . . .

HUSBAND: So . . .

WIFE: We were just looking after our own little wants and needs at that time. We were both much younger at the time.

HUSBAND: It would be like a pepperoni pizza that's half eaten . . .

WIFE: Oh, where'd you get that one? Explain this one.

HUSBAND: I don't know, I just thought I'd throw it out there and you could finish it.

WIFE: Um, what were we like? Like it was kind of stormy.

HUSBAND: It's always been stormy. It's always like . . .

WIFE: We haven't had a calm day, I mean. What do I say at work? Life is rough. We don't have a normal family. We probably make a wonderful sitcom or soap opera out of it. Our life is like a . . .

HUSBAND: It's dirty laundry. It eventually gets cleaned.

WIFE: Yeah!

HUSBAND: And then it gets dirty again.

WIFE: Yeah, it's a never-ending cycle.

HUSBAND: It's a roller coaster.

WIFE: It's definitely a roller coaster and you never get off.

This example illustrates a highly interactive exchange between partners. The wife initiates the exchange, but the husband actually creates the first metaphor by comparing their family life with a pepperoni pizza. He describes the pizza as "half eaten," creating the impression that there must be some unresolved issues or ambiguity within the family. Perhaps family members are experiencing some stressors or life transitions. The wife is amused and challenges her partner to explain the metaphor. In response to the challenge, he implicitly requests that she continue the verbal game when he replies, "I just thought I'd throw it out there and you could finish it." Essentially, he is reminding her that it is her turn to extend or embellish his family metaphor. The wife characterizes the family as "stormy," and the husband agrees with this description. She then extends the metaphor by describing family life as never having "a calm day," as "not normal," and as a "sitcom" or "soap opera."

All of these metaphors convey a perception of family life as unpredictable, uncontrollable—perhaps even threatening. Not to be upstaged, the husband picks up on the phrase "soap opera" and compares family life with dirty laundry that "eventually gets cleaned." The wife banters back that family life is a "never-ending cycle," playing off the laundry image. Finally, the husband forwards the "roller coaster" metaphor and both agree that their family life is a continuous cycle, perhaps even an adventure, with its ups and downs, strengths and weaknesses, positives and negatives. Clearly, these marital partners enjoy verbal exchange and collaborative word play.

In contrast, other couples were not as open about exploring, developing, interpreting/assessing, and integrating their family life metaphors. Consider the following exchange:

INTERVIEWER: When you first became a blended family, life was like . . . ?

HUSBAND: Well, let's see. Life was like turmoil.

WIFE: Yeah, yeah, that's a good one.

This couple's responses illustrate a minimal interactive exchange between partners. The husband offers a metaphor and there is no further development, extension, or discussion of early family life.

Some partners characterized family life as a process (e.g., their living situations were fluctuating and ever changing, with the potential for influencing outcomes): "When we first became a blended family, life was like looking for a corner in a circle," or family life was like a "car that needed a tune-up real bad. . . . There was so much new stuff going on at the beginning, there was a lot of rattling and shaking." In contrast, other partners viewed family life as unchanging, with little variation, or statelike: Family life was like a "broken teacup," or "When we first became a blended family, life was like Pandora's Box."

Some marital partners demonstrated solidarity in their family metaphors: "And *we* seem to be finding more time for each other, occasionally" (emphasis added). Other couples distanced themselves from the reorganizing process: "*It* is not like the Brady Bunch. *It*'s just . . . *it* isn't under the best of circumstances, and under the worst of circumstances, *it* can be horrible" (emphasis added). Other marital partners' perceptions of stepfamily life could be seen in their use of first-person pronouns: "*I*'d say family life was like a spring. There was always fresh water coming out" (emphasis added).

Finally, some stepfamily metaphors illustrated more affect or emotion than others through use of intensifiers, superlatives, and vivid words and phrases. For example, the metaphor, "Family life was like a war in the Middle East because it was a pretty violent home. There were a lot of up and downs and it was very intense," was considered highly emotive/affective based on the descriptors/qualifiers ("pretty," "very," "a lot of") and vivid word choices ("war," "violent," "intense"). Typically, a family that is reorganizing, that is negotiating new membership roles, should experience a full range of emotions. The following metaphor, for example, displays strong affect, with its use of intensifiers and vivid language:

> Our family life is like a bay. Our life is an extremely safe harbor where you have a lake that when the wind comes up and the storms come up and the waves come up and smash the outer rocks and things that they put up to block the violent storm. The harbor itself stays very calm, cool, and smooth most of the time . . . quite a bit of the time.

On the other hand, some family metaphors reflected low affect/intensity based on their matter-of-fact phrasing. Descriptions of family life as "a nice boat ride" or "the Rocky Mountains" are examples of metaphors using straightforward, unembellished language, with minimal affect/emotion.

Overall, findings from the Burrell and Buzzanell (1992) investigation of stepfamily metaphors indicated four metaphoric themes depicting blended family life: (a) an *adventure* (e.g., "Family life was like photographing an African safari . . . exciting, frustrating, exhilarating."); (b) a *journey* (e.g., "My family life is just smooth sailing, like an airplane ride with no clouds."); (c) *unpredictable* (e.g., "My family is like the NFL draft. . . . It's inconsistent because in the draft you pick players based on their college records and you never know if they'll last playing pro ball or become superstars."); and (d) an *opportunity for growth* (e.g., "My family life is like a plant ready to blossom. My kids are finding out what they want in their lives.").

As previously stated, we asked the stepparents in our sample to describe their family lives, both past and present (Burrell & Buzzanell, 1992). When some stepfamilies were first organizing, partners described life as unpredictable. For example, a wife reported, "When we first got together, we never knew how our children would react emotionally to things. . . . Yeah, it was kind of rocky." This depiction of a newly formed stepfamily is not really surprising. Galvin and Brommel (1991) note that "for newly formed stepfamilies, boundaries may be biologically, legally, and spatially unclear. Members may be confused about family membership and norms for behavior" (p. 259). Thus relational partners' metaphors may reflect the newness of their stepfamilies and/or the point of departure blended families use to distinguish their new families from prior families and "intact" families. In contrast, in describing current family life, some partners spoke of opportunities for growth. For example, a husband suggested that his stepfamily was like milk, "because milk's homogenized and you have these three separate individuals that are blended together to create one." This metaphoric theme reflects sharing, acceptance, a merger or blending of ideas, giving, and caring. It appears that metaphoric themes of stepfamily life as unpredictable and as an opportunity for growth reflect spouses' past and present perceptions, respectively, whereas metaphoric themes of stepfamily life as adventure and journey may be used interchangeably to depict both past and present perceptions (see Burrell & Buzzanell, 1992). To summarize, metaphoric analyses help to illustrate how relational partners characterize family life through communication. Findings suggest that many relational partners are uncertain about the reorganizing process, but over time view stepfamily life as an opportunity to nurture and blend shared realities. Verification of shared metaphors provides data about how language is used within the family system, in addition to how language functions for that system.

CONFLICT IN STEPFAMILIES

Stepfamily integration is a process that may take up to five or six years to complete, or that may never fully occur (Visher & Visher, 1990), so ongoing conflict is not unlikely. In addition, many scholars agree that stepfamilies experience unique stressors, such as distant or conflictual relationships with stepchildren; financial difficulties; disruptive interactions with ex-spouses over such issues as child rearing, finances, and legalities; discrepant life-cycle stages between relational partners; and varying levels of conflict with biological children living outside the home (Cherlin, 1978; Fishman, 1983; Furstenberg & Spanier, 1984; Schwebel et al., 1991). According to McGoldrick and Carter (1989), there are certain "predictable emotional issues" in remarriage, including role ambiguity, boundaries, and loyalty conflicts. These family issues are discussed below in terms of their effects on stepfamily integration. Although the issues are discussed separately, it is important to keep in mind that many of them may overlap, further complicating the reorganization process for stepfamilies.

Undoubtedly, the reorganization of family roles that take place when families merge causes conflict among individual members. All couples or families experience areas of conflict, for instance, concerning resource management, child-rearing practices, or in-laws (Goldberg, 1987), but these and other conflicts are intensified whenever two separate families merge. Change in a family system often triggers uneasiness and conflict (Galvin & Brommel, 1991).

Scholars agree that it is through communicative behavior that the family system is regulated and maintained (Crocker, 1977; Galvin & Brommel, 1991; Noller & Fitzpatrick, 1993). In family life, we develop a perceptual frame through which to experience and interpret various events within our world (Spangle, 1991). Thus membership in a family influences what an individual values and what he or she does not. In other words, individual family members' cognitive representations interact with perceptions, resulting in a shared social reality. These perceptual combinations and holistic frameworks are salient in stepfamilies because the individuals involved consciously negotiate their roles on dyadic and family levels simultaneously. This intentional reorganizing is accomplished through explicit metacommunication in which individuals actively and consciously negotiate roles. However, the current blended family must also deal with the intrapersonal concepts of past and future families, self-perception, and connectedness with others (Trost, 1990).

Role ambiguity occurs when people are unsure of what actions they are expected to take in given situations—that is, the emotions and/or behaviors they are expected to exhibit. In the context of stepfamilies, remarried individuals lack normative models for their new families (Cherlin, 1978; Keshet, 1989; Walker & Messinger, 1979). Contrary to myth, the stepfamily is not "just like" the intact family (Juroe & Juroe, 1983). When stepfamily members expect and attempt to behave similarly to members of intact families, they can hinder the integration process, which can create numerous problems (McGoldrick & Carter, 1989; Visher & Visher, 1990). For example, the observation of traditional gender roles, which place the responsibility for the emotional well-being of the family on females, may cause competition between stepmother and stepdaughter as they vie for the caregiver role (McGoldrick & Carter, 1989).

To make matters worse, because of the complexity of the stepfamily, those entering it are faced with the possibility of gaining several new roles at once (McGoldrick & Carter, 1989). For example, upon marrying, a single, childless adult may become a wife and the stepmother of four. To be sure, inexperience with parenting, coupled with the absence of norms for stepparenting, can cause intense role ambiguity. Some stepparents fall victim to "super stepparent syndrome," over-extending themselves for their stepchildren in attempts to gain affection and approval. The intense energy this requires, however, cannot be sustained, and such stepparents ultimately feel emotionally abused (Nadler, 1983). Stepchildren may also resent stepparents who try to fill the role of a biological parent, especially when that role is already occupied (Kent, 1980).

Boundary issues/problems may also occur. Many scholars use systems theory to frame their research on families (Galvin & Brommel, 1991; Noller & Fitzpatrick, 1993). In brief, a family system is made up of members developing interdependent relationships, creating rules, establishing limitations or boundaries, setting goals, accomplishing tasks, and functioning in a variety of hierarchical roles. Moreover, research addressing issues associated with remarriage must take a family systems approach (Kent, 1980), because old family members do not disappear simply because a "new" family is formed. "Members of the original family, including both former spouses, still function as a self-regulating system, although the characteristics (e.g., rules, roles, functions, etc.) have been altered" (Goldsmith, 1980, p. 19). Thus the formation of the new system will be affected by feelings, behaviors, and so on, of the old system. Family boundary issues include such concepts as membership, space, authority, and time (McGoldrick & Carter, 1989).

Loyalty issues will also have to be addressed in the reorganizing process. This is especially true for children. For example, a custodial parent may forbid his or her children from expressing positive feelings about the divorced parent (Kent, 1980). Or a child may feel guilt about loving a stepparent, making it especially difficult for the stepparent to establish a friendly/loving relationship with him or her. Even the seemingly simple decision of what to call each other may cause competition—for instance, a biological father may not want to hear his son call his ex-wife's new husband "Dad."

A number of triangles may develop as a result of remarriage. Triangles are apparent in many family systems when two members are close and one is distant (McGoldrick & Carter, 1989). One such triangle involves the husband, his second wife, and the husband's children (or wife, second husband, and wife's children). Often the stepparent describes his or her position as peripheral to and experiences alienation from the parent-child dyad (Kent, 1980; Nadler, 1983). Biological parents feel caught in the middle. On the one hand, they want to support their new spouses; on the other hand, they feel the need to overprotect their children as a result of guilt associated with the divorce (Nadler, 1983).

Although scholars warn stepparents about becoming disciplinarians before they become friends to their stepchildren (Kent, 1980; Visher & Visher, 1990), it seems that parent and stepparent's presenting a unified front to the children regarding the marital relationship helps foster acceptance of the new partner (Cissna et al., 1990). Only after the marriage is legitimate in the eyes of the stepchildren will the stepparent be able to fill the disciplinarian role, thus propelling the stepfamily toward successful reorganization (Cissna et al., 1990).

In any marriage or family, conflict is inevitable. The stepfamily context, however, increases the dimensions of marital conflict. Stepfamilies face types of conflict that are different from those found in traditional families. Not only must stepfamily members deal with "expected" areas of family conflict (children, money, in-laws, and so on), which are often heightened by their situation, they must deal with conflicts that arise out of their unique family structure (e.g., acceptance of the stepparent as an authority figure). Furthermore, in situations where blended families have been formed as a result of divorce and remarriage, it can be assumed that at least one partner in the current marital dyad has experienced enough conflict with a former spouse to end the previous relationship. Such a conflict history will inevitably influence an individual's attitudes and expectations concerning conflict in his or her present marriage (Burrell & Fitzpatrick, 1990).

In two recent investigations, 30 marital dyads from stepfamilies completed questionnaires about partners' perceptions of conflict and the effects of those perceptions on how conflict was enacted, either verbally or nonverbally (Burrell & Mitchell, 1993; Mitchell, 1992). In addition, the couples participated in hour-long interviews that addressed potential problems unique to stepfamilies. The survey results indicated that these partners tended to have either extremely negative or slightly positive views of conflict. Furthermore, high agreement existed between relational partners' perceptions of self and other's conflict style. In other words, when one partner viewed his or her conflict style as nonconfrontational (avoided), solution oriented (problem solved), or controlling (confronted aggressively), his or her spouse agreed with that perception.

More revealing, however, were the results from the interviews with these stepfamily spouses. The findings support the stepfamily literature, in that the issues described in the literature were to some extent discussed by the relational partners (Burrell & Mitchell, 1993; Mitchell, 1992). Almost everyone interviewed made reference to one of the four types of boundary issues discussed by McGoldrick and Carter (1989). Not surprisingly, the two mentioned most often were authority and membership. Cissna et al.'s (1990) investigation of the relational dialectics at work in blended families has shown that these two issues are intertwined throughout the reorganization process. A large number of couples from this investigation reported that the biological parent felt it necessary to back up the stepparent in situations concerning discipline. Respondents emphasized the importance of presenting a united front to the children in aiding stepchildren's acceptance of stepparents as both family members and disciplinarians. One spouse noted: "We've been real lucky because in disciplining the kids, he never contradicts me in front of the kids. I never contradict him in front of the kids. If I'm not happy with a punishment . . . we'll discuss it."

In addition, almost 75% of the spouses brought up role-oriented issues. Specifically, spouses discussed the problems associated with entering the role of stepparent, whether they were results of negative cultural stereotypes or simply lack of knowledge pertaining to stepparenting responsibilities. One stepparent who clearly wanted to resolve his role as a "new" parent remarked: "Oh, I'd say the first year and a half the kids tested me. See what they can get away with. And they played the game, 'You're not my dad,' or 'Our dad wouldn't do that.' We resolved that when I explained that I wasn't trying to replace their dad. I always helped to make their dad more active than he was." Approximately half of the stepparents were comfortable in the roles they had created for themselves, although the types of roles they assumed varied. Some saw themselves as parents, whereas others viewed themselves as secondary parents or friends to their stepchildren.

Finally, almost half of the couples brought up loyalty issues as problems experienced in the reorganization process. Several types of triangles emerged from the interview transcripts. As described earlier, a triangle exists in a family system when two members are close and one is distant. More than half of the triangles identified included the noncustodial parent, the biological child, and either the stepparent or the custodial parent. These triangles can be particularly difficult on the children, who may try to fight feelings of affection they have for stepparents for fear of betraying absent biological parents. One wife suggested, "The kids feel, uh, because he is their father, they feel a sense of loyalty to him and therefore sometimes, um, are a little distant to Elmo." This illustrates that children may have trouble accepting additional adult figures in their lives, and caution should be taken not to rush the process of relational development between stepparent and stepchild.

In another case the triangle was brought about by the jealousy of the biological mother over the affection her children showed their stepmother. One stepmother pointed out a particular situation: "The kids were at our home for the weekend, and one of them would give me a hug or kiss, then when the kids got home, she [the biological mother] would be angry with one of them. They would say, well, Beth gave Karen a hug. And they would get punished for that." It is clear that biological parents can hinder the merging process through denial of the new marital dyad and family unit. Feelings such as those this woman described are indicative of the degree to which adults can hamper the reorganization process, because acceptance of all family members is important to successful reintegration (Burrell & Buzzanell, 1992).

The other major triangle that was present involved the biological parent, the child, and the stepparent. One stepmother was frustrated because her stepchildren would try to play the spouses against each other when they were both present, but would be responsive to her when she was alone with them. She reported: "Their interaction with me would be totally different when their dad was not around. They respected me, we laughed, we had a good time. . . . And Gary would come back, and they would totally shut me out again." In this exam-ple, as in almost half of the couples identified as having triangles including the stepparent, the biological parent, and the stepchild, the stepparent also reported not being accepted as a legitimate family member. Another stepparent observed: "I think the biggest problem from my standpoint is trying to find out where I stand on the priority totem pole as opposed to the rest of the family members." These two examples support Cissna et al.'s (1990) argument that the first step toward reintegration is the acceptance of the new married couple.

What is encouraging is that the couples interviewed did not report only the difficulties they faced concerning these issues, but the positive aspects as well. For example, relational partners expressed satisfaction at being members of larger family networks with more adult role models present in the children's lives. A stepfather reported: "The joy is instead of waiting to have a kid, you already have a kid, and they're grown up, and you get to work with her through her teenage years. I don't know, helping her with homework, and eating as a family, and all of us just doing stuff together." Another positive example of stepfamily living was forwarded by a stepmother: "I've gained two children. Two very special children. Um, and the fact that I had crummy, crummy relationships with men and I don't have that anymore. We're very happy with who we are, where we've been, and where we're going." Clearly, these stepparents have experienced some of the dramatic and positive changes available to reorganizing families.

FUTURE RESEARCH

Before discussing possible future directions for stepfamily research, a brief summary of what we know is appropriate. First, there currently exist several negative stereotypes about stepparents. Stepparents are often characterized as less effective at parenting, at expressing love and affection, and at being judicious when compared with biological parents. It is important that we overcome these stereotypes, given the growing numbers of single-parent families and stepfamilies. Because the divorce rate remains constant, it is probable that increasing numbers of individuals will divorce and remarry, becoming stepparents as they combine/blend families. Second, it is important to understand stepfamily members' psychological realities. Metaphoric analysis provides a useful method for accessing the perceptions of stepfamily members concerning their family lives. Common metaphoric themes of reorganizing or blending families include anticipating an adventure, experiencing a journey, feeling a lack of control/predictability, and observing an opportunity for growth. Third, conflict in stepfamilies occurs as family members experience role ambiguity, address boundary issues, and develop new loyalties/bonds in the reorganizing process.

Scholars, researchers, and practitioners need to consider the permeability of family boundaries. At the family level, members (especially children) should feel free to participate in multiple family celebrations, functions, and day-to-day routines (such as going to the ball park with aunts, uncles, or cousins). For example, parents, ex-spouses, and stepparents should allow and even encourage the maintenance of family and extended family relationships by following custody and visitation agreements. Built into this family system are ever-changing social support networks that should be observed/tracked for their obvious influence on the reorganizing family as it moves through its life span.

In addition, future research should focus on the various types of stepfamilies to increase our ability to predict which family types will be able to integrate/adjust most easily. In the stepfamily interviews described above, different stepfamily types emerged, in addition to several variables that appear to influence family functioning (Burrell & Buzzanell, 1992; Burrell & Mitchell, 1993; Mitchell, 1992). First, the ages of the children at the time families merge are apparently a factor in family dynamics. An additional factor that may affect stepfamily integration is whether or not there are children from both spouses entering the family, or whether the newly married couple has additional children. Third, the extent to which noncustodial parents are active in children's lives also appears to affect family development, especially in reference to the children's relationship with stepparents. Finally, whether the family is formed as a result of death or divorce is an important factor.

Researchers and practitioners must recognize that viewing all stepfamilies in reference to one model is too simplistic, because several factors have impacts on family functioning. For example, we need to revise our thinking about traditional gender roles. As McGoldrick and Carter (1989) note, "Such traditional roles, rigidly applied, are one of the most serious flaws in the currently unstable structure of first marriages" (p. 400). Many new stepmothers are not equipped immediately to manage a household, nurture stepchildren, and continue to operate at the same level of productivity in the workplace. Clearly, the issues faced during family reorganization will depend somewhat on a variety of situational factors. Research should attempt to separate stepfamilies into types, because judging all stepfamilies against one standard is as misleading as judging them against the intact family form.

In sum, it is my hope that this chapter will encourage future research in which the stepfamily is studied as a separate family form. The strengths, not just the weaknesses, of stepfamilies need to be explored; stepfamilies must be recognized as different, but not necessarily dysfunctional. Metaphoric analysis can provide a starting point for future research to examine how relational partners communicate and negotiate difficult issues when reorganizing their families.

One stepfather interviewed in the study discussed above had this to say about the positive side of stepfamily life: "There's just a lot of love to be had that wasn't in the air of my previous marriage . . . a lot more communication and openness and that's something we hadn't experienced before, my daughters and I. And also it's good for them to see that although one relationship has dissolved that it is possible to move on and to meet somebody and to fall in love again." It is my hope that this chapter has increased awareness of the ongoing shift in family form from intact to blended. With the increase in the numbers of stepfamilies, the concept of family is not being abandoned—rather, it is being defined differently. It is time to stop focusing on the stepfamily as an inferior family form and to realize that for millions of people, blended families offer opportunities for new beginnings.

REFERENCES

Anderson, J., & White, G. (1986). An empirical investigation of interaction and relationship patterns in functional and dysfunctional nuclear families and stepfamilies. *Family Processes, 25*, 407-420.

Berardo, F. M. (1990). Trends and directions in family research in the 1980s. *Journal of Marriage and the Family, 52*, 809-817.

Bochner, A. P. (1978). On taking ourselves seriously: An analysis of some persistent problems and promising directions in interpersonal research. *Human Communication Research, 4,* 179-191.

Bryan, S. H., Ganong, L., Coleman, M., & Bryan, L. (1985). Brief reports: Counselors' perceptions of stepparents and stepchildren. *Journal of Counseling Psychology, 32,* 279-282.

Burrell, N. A., & Buzzanell, P. M. (1992, October). *Looking for a corner in a circle: A metaphoric analysis of stepfamily images.* Paper presented at the annual meeting of the Speech Communication Association, Chicago.

Burrell, N. A., & Fitzpatrick, M. A. (1990). The psychological reality of marital conflict. In D. Cahn (Ed.), *Intimates in conflict: A communication perspective* (pp. 167-185). Hillsdale, NJ: Lawrence Erlbaum.

Burrell, N. A., & Mitchell, A. K. (1993, May). *The definitional impact on conflict styles as stepfamilies reorganize.* Paper presented at the 43rd Annual Conference of the International Communication Association, Washington, DC.

Cherlin, A. (1978). Remarriage as an incomplete institution. *American Journal of Sociology, 84,* 634-650.

Cissna, K., Cox, D., & Bochner, A. (1990). The dialectic of marital and parental relationships within the stepfamily. *Communication Monographs, 57,* 44-61.

Coleman, M., & Ganong, L. H. (1990). Remarriage and stepfamily research in the 1980s: Increased interest in an old family form. *Journal of Marriage and the Family, 52,* 925-940.

Coleman, M., Ganong, L. H., & Ginrich, R. (1985). Stepfamily strengths: A review of popular literature. *Family Relations, 34,* 583-589.

Crocker, C. (1977). The social function of rhetorical forms. In J. D. Sapir & J. C. Crocker (Eds.), *The social use of metaphor* (pp. 33-66). Philadelphia: University of Pennsylvania Press.

Einstein, E. (1985). *The stepfamily.* Boston: Shambhala.

Fine, M. (1986). Perceptions of stepparents: Variation in stereotypes as a function of current family structure. *Journal of Marriage and the Family, 48,* 537-543.

Fishman, B. (1983). The economic behavior of stepfamilies. *Family Relations, 32,* 359-366.

Fitzpatrick, M. A. (1988). *Between husbands and wives: Communication in marriage.* Newbury Park, CA: Sage.

Foss, S. K. (1989). *Rhetorical criticism: Exploration and practice.* Prospect Heights, IL: Waveland.

Furstenberg, F. F., Jr., & Spanier, G.B. (1984). *Recycling the family: Remarriage after divorce.* Beverly Hills, CA: Sage.

Galvin, K., & Brommel, B. (1991). *Family communication: Cohesion and change* (3rd ed.). New York: HarperCollins.

Galvin, K., & Cooper, P. (1990, March). *Stepfamily communication: Developmental and interpersonal issues.* Paper presented at the meeting of the Illinois Council on Family Relations, Moline.

Goldberg, M. (1987). Patterns of disagreement in marriage: Six areas of interaction determine marital success or failure. *Medical Aspects of Human Sexuality, 21,* 42-52.

Goldsmith, J. (1980). Relationship between former spouses: Descriptive findings. *Journal of Divorce, 4,* 1-20.

Hart, R. P. (1990). *Modern rhetorical criticism*. Glenview, IL: Scott, Foresman.

Juroe, D., & Juroe, B. (1983). *Successful stepparenting*. Old Tappan, NJ: G. H. Renell.

Kent, M. O. (1980). Remarriage: A family systems perspective. *Social Casework, 61*, 146-153.

Keshet, J. (1989). Cognitive remodeling of the family: How remarried people view stepfamilies. *American Journal of Orthopsychiatry, 60*(2), 196-202.

Lakoff, G., & Johnson, M. (1980). *Metaphors we live by*. Chicago: University of Chicago Press.

McGoldrick, M., & Carter, B. (1989). Forming a remarried family. In B. Carter & M. McGoldrick (Eds.), *The changing family life cycle: A framework for family therapy* (2nd ed., pp. 402-429). Needham Heights, MA: Allyn & Bacon.

Miller, M., & Soper, B. (1982). An emerging contingency, the stepfamily: Review of literature. *Psychological Reports, 50*, 715-722.

Mitchell, A. K. (1992). *Definitional impact on conflict style in blended families and issues embedded in the reorganization process*. Unpublished master's thesis, University of Wisconsin—Milwaukee, Department of Communication.

Morgan, G. (1986). *Images of organization*. Newbury Park, CA: Sage.

Nadler, J. (1983). Effecting change in stepfamilies: A psychodynamic/behavioral group approach. *American Journal of Psychotherapy, 37*, 100-112.

Noller, P., & Fitzpatrick, M. A. (1993). *Communication in family relationships*. Englewood Cliffs, NJ: Prentice Hall.

Norton, C. S. (1989). *Life metaphors: Stories of ordinary survival*. Carbondale: Southern Illinois University Press.

Papernow, P. (1984). The stepfamily cycle: An experimental model of stepfamily development. *Family Relations, 33*, 335-363.

Papernow, P. (1987). Thickening the middle ground: Dilemmas and vulnerabilities of remarried couples. *Psychotherapy, 24*, 630-639.

Schwebel, A. I., Fine, M. A., & Renner, M. A. (1991). A study of perceptions of the stepparent role. *Journal of Family Issues, 12*, 43-57.

Spangle, M. (1991, November). *Shared metaphors: A reflection of family world views*. Paper presented at the annual meeting of the Speech Communication Association, Atlanta, GA.

Trost, J. (1990). Do we mean the same by the concept of family? *Communication Research, 17*, 431-443.

Tsousakas, H. (1991). The missing link: A transformational view of metaphors in organizational science. *Academy of Management Review, 16*, 566-585.

Visher, E. B., & Visher, J. S. (1988). *Old loyalties, new ties: Therapeutic strategies and stepfamilies*. New York: W. W. Norton.

Visher, E. B., & Visher, J. S. (1990). Dynamics of successful stepfamilies. *Journal of Divorce and Remarriage, 14*, 3-11.

Walker, K., & Messinger, L. (1979). Remarriage after divorce: Dissolution and reconstruction of family boundaries. *Family Process, 18*, 185-192.

Communication, Gender, and Power

Homosexual Couples as a Case Study

SARA STEEN
PEPPER SCHWARTZ

In the recent past, intense interest has been generated concerning research on gender differences in communication. This research has suggested, among other things, that men and women have different attitudes toward conversation, different approaches to decision making, and different methods of responding to others' concerns (Peplau, 1983; Tannen, 1990; Thorne & Henley, 1975). According to Deborah Tannen (1990), a popularizer of this kind of work, women view conversation as a means of creating intimacy, whereas men take it as an opportunity to demonstrate their status and to compete with their conversational partners. Women feel it is essential to keep conversation going, which they do by encouraging other speakers, filling silences, and asking questions. Men, on the other hand, view such supportive devices as weak, and prefer to use strong tactics such as making statements and interrupting other speakers. Gendered patterns of decision making and problem solving stem from these broader views of the purpose of communication. Women seek consensus in making decisions, because their primary objective is to maintain the emotional link between partners. Men seek to make decisions more expeditiously, with the more powerful person deciding the outcome. In responding to others' concerns or problems, men are likely to suggest solutions or possible actions, whereas women are more likely to express sympathy by sharing similar feelings or experiences, thus creating the intimacy that is women's goal in conversation.

Kollock, Blumstein, and Schwartz (1985) summarize this research by suggesting that, in cross-sex conversations, men tend to play a dominant role, whereas women tend toward a supportive role. We use this motif throughout our analysis because we feel that it accurately captures the dominant strain of research in this area. The obvious question arising out of this research is, Where do these conversational differences come from? Do they arise out of gender differences, either biological or socialized, or out of power differentials between two individuals? Further, are they a necessary by-product of intimate communication, or are they a result of mixing two genders whose communicative styles are different? Our central focus in this chapter, then, is the role of gender in determining the style and substance of communication in intimate relationships. Most recent research has focused on differences between men and women (intergroup variation) rather than on differences among men or among women (intragroup variation) (Wright, 1988). To avoid some of the dangers of doing this (such as stereotyping by gender or failing to explore fully the implications of gender as a subject variable), we will look at research on heterosexual couples about intergroup variation and at research on homosexual couples about intragroup variation. We apply the ideas that dominate this field of study (although, of course, there are studies that contradict this research, such as that by Marche & Peterson, 1993) to homosexual couples in an effort to test some of the basic ideas underpinning this research. By removing one gender from the equation, we hope to meet three specific goals: (a) to set forth a preliminary argument about the origins of gender differences in communication, (b) to illuminate communication in homosexual couples, and (c) to suggest and encourage further research to these ends.

Our guiding question in this analysis is whether the pattern of dominance and support identified in heterosexual couples carries over into homosexual couples. This question has several possible answers, each of which suggests something different about the origins of the dominant-supportive pattern. If the pattern exists in virtually all gay and lesbian couples, then we would hypothesize that it serves a necessary function and is a natural by-product of two individuals' communicating with one another in an intimate relationship. If we see the dominant-supportive pattern in some homosexual couples but not all, we would ask the further question, What differentiates couples in which the pattern is evident from those in which it is not evident? It could be that the dominant-supportive pattern exists only in those relationships where one partner tends to take on the "male" role and the other the "female" role, which would point to gender identities as a causal factor. It is also possible that the pattern shows up only in those couples in which an imbalance of power exists. If, in such cases, the more powerful partner tends to take on a dominating conversational style and the less powerful a supporting style, we would argue that power is the most important causal factor in determining conversational roles. A third possible outcome is that both men in a gay couple may display dominant tendencies, whereas both women in a lesbian couple may display supportive tendencies, suggesting that the pattern is a product either of gender (biological characteristics) or of gender socialization. Finally, the pattern could be found to be nonexistent in homosexual couples, which would suggest that in heterosexual couples, one partner becomes dominant and one supportive as a result either of mixing genders or of unequal power between men and women in our society.

Each of the possible causes (biological gender, socialization, being in an intimate relationship, and power) has some theoretical support. The sociobiological argument is that gender differences are caused by biologically different societal functions. Because of their primary function as childbearers and caretakers, women are biologically inclined to nurture (Davis, 1985). They nurture conversations by supporting their partners just as they nurture their children. Men, on the other hand, are biologically designed to protect. They are inclined to defend territory, including abstract conversational territory. They control conversations because of their innate tendencies toward protection and dominance.

A more widely held argument is that gender differences in conversation arise because of differential socialization of men and women. Many people argue that females are socialized to be cooperative, whereas males are socialized to be competitive (Tannen, 1990). Males and females develop both different goals and different means of attaining those goals. Women support conversations because they are taught to be supportive, and men control conversations because they are encouraged to compete and dominate.

It is, of course, possible that homosexuals and heterosexuals go through somewhat different socialization processes, in which case they may acquire different conversational goals and styles. Silverstein (1981) argues, for example, that many homosexual males are separated out early on as "sissies," and as such are treated as girls. Young males with this kind of personal background are likely to develop (perhaps reluctantly) more feminine self-identities than other boys, which could mean that they are more likely to be supportive and nurturing as adults. A similar argument could be made about lesbians, who may grow up as "tomboys," and as a result develop self-identities as competitive and unemotional. The acquisition of gender identities through childhood socialization could affect adult conversational strategies.

A third argument is that the division of conversational labor is necessary to sustain an intimate relationship. The classical Parsonian argument posits that the division of labor, both physical and emotional, by sex serves to reduce the struggle for dominance between partners, and to make more efficient the workings of the relationship. The creation and maintenance of clear expectations regarding what each partner is to do reduces or eliminates confusion, which in turn leads to greater efficiency. The dominant-supportive pattern, according to this perspective, serves a necessary function in intimate relationships by establishing distinct conversational roles for each partner.

Finally, there is the potential impact of power on communication. Conversational roles may evolve from unequal distribution of power within a relationship. The person who has more power outside of a relationship (owing to such elements as income, education, and employment) may be inclined to replicate his or her power on the micro level through personal relationships (Drass, 1986). The more powerful individual often feels that he or she has the right (or, sometimes, the responsibility) to control conversations by defining what the couple will talk about, when they will talk, and who will do the talking. According to this perspective, men are likely to control communication because they generally hold more powerful positions in our society than do women. Whether power plays the same role in homosexual relationships will be one of the central questions in our analysis.

In any discussion of homosexuals, it is important to bear in mind the different conditions they face in our society relative to heterosexuals. Homosexuality is "unscripted" in the dominant culture; there are no guidelines or norms of appropriate conduct for homosexuals to follow. This forces homosexuals to determine for themselves how they will behave. Having few role models against which to measure their behavior, they have to create their own norms and define their own roles. One of the central issues they must solve is the distribution of power. Because they cannot use gender, or traditional marital roles, as a guide, they must decide for themselves how power will be apportioned in their relationships. A couple may decide to allocate power in a conscious and egalitarian manner, or may attempt individually to dominate one another, or may avoid power issues by operating as autonomously as possible. Homosexual couples of today have largely abandoned their version of the heterosexual relationship, the butch-femme model, wherein one partner acts as the powerful male, the other as the supportive female. Currently, the more popular model for homosexuals is one based on friendship (Harry & DeVall, 1978; Peplau & Cochran, 1990), which suggests that both partners should treat each other as equals. This is, of course, more easily said than done. Partners have different advantages over each other, and there is often only lip service to equality—even among those deeply and truly committed to equal partnership, dialogue about the equitable distribution of privileges and privileged behavior creates issues and infiltrates everyday communication.

METHOD OF ANALYSIS

To begin to answer the question of where the dominant-supportive pattern comes from and whether it exists in homosexual couples, we have divided communication into two parts: *how* couples communicate (style) and *what* they communicate about (substance). In the section below on conversational style, we look at whether specific indicators of dominance and support (such as interruptions and questions) are present in communication between homosexual partners, and, if they are, how they affect homosexual relationships. We then turn to a discussion of the substantive issues homosexual couples face, and how differences in hierarchy (dominance and support) affect communication about these issues. Although homosexual and heterosexual couples face similar issues, we focus on the unique problems (and advantages) of same-sex partners.

To examine these issues, we have explored the literature and will present both an overview of what has been written and a critical analysis of the state of research in the area. In writing this chapter, we have drawn from three different literatures. We rely heavily on the literature on communication between heterosexual partners in looking for dominance and support patterns that may or may not derive from gender. We then attempt to draw comparisons with homosexuals, looking at both the literature on homosexual communication specifically (of which there is very little) and the literature about homosexual couples more generally. We have been hampered, to some extent, by a paucity of specific studies on homosexual communication; it is our hope that this chapter will suggest heuristic directions for future research.

STYLE: HOW COUPLES COMMUNICATE

Overview

Many researchers have argued that men and women view communication differently. Men see communication as a means of conveying information and demonstrating status, whereas women see it as a means of interacting and establishing emotional ties (Tannen, 1990; Thorne & Henley, 1975). Different styles of conversation become a primary means of achieving these disparate goals of status and connection. Tannen (1990), in her book *You Just Don't Understand,* states that the combination of the different goals and different styles of men and women complicates heterosexual attempts at communication, resulting in anger, confusion, frustration, and, occasionally, extinguished relationships.

Communication styles that vary by gender also create problems for homosexual couples. Although same-sex couples may be less likely to obfuscate messages because of different communication styles, there are skills that are, for the most part, held by only one gender, thus creating a deficit (or an excess) when only one gender is present. For example, gay male couples may have difficulty reaching satisfactory agreement about how to solve a problem because both men are anxious to "win" the dispute, neither takes on the "mediator" role, and a situation arises in which neither partner is willing to give in (Berzon, 1988). Lesbian couples may also have trouble with efficient problem solving. If both women are committed to reaching complete consensus, discussions may go on interminably, erupting in anger when frustrated partners cannot reach mutual agreement. Understanding the use of conversational support and dominance helps illuminate why same-sex couples might have some advantages—and some disadvantages—in communicating and resolving differences.

Conversational Support

Questions

Asking a question is one way to encourage, or support, conversation. Questions naturally elicit responses, thereby prompting another person to speak. Questions are often used as conversation starters, such as, "How was your day?" They are also a means of encouraging a speaker to elaborate on what he or she has said (e.g., "What do you mean by that?"). Questions can be used by a person who has been speaking to encourage commentary from the listener, as when a speaker ends a statement with a question (e.g., "What do you think?"). This can occur when one person feels he or she is dominating the conversation and wishes to give the listener an opportunity to speak. When a speaker uses a question to weaken the impact of a statement, such as "don't you think?" it is called a tag question (we separate questions and tag questions because of their different conversational functions). Asking questions is one way of acting in a supportive manner by encouraging one's conversational partner to speak and showing interest in what he or she has to say.

A pattern of one partner doing most of the talking (dominating) while the other encourages the speaker with questions (supporting) has been shown to exist in heterosexual couples (Fishman, 1983). Men rely heavily on statements, leaving their partners with the responsibility of maintaining the conversation either by responding with another statement or by asking the speaker a question about what he has said. In Fishman's (1983) study, women asked many more questions than men, both in response to their partners' statements and at the ends of their own statements. These findings show an active concern on the part of women that conversations be supported.

If these differences are caused by gender, one might expect conversation to be disastrous in gay male couples, with both partners concerned about making statements and neither being truly concerned about keeping the conversation flowing. In a study of heterosexual and homosexual couples, however, Kollock et al. (1985) found that, in cross-sex couples, asking questions was positively correlated not with gender, but with an individual's power in the relationship, with the more powerful partner asking significantly more questions. This finding also held true for gay male couples, whereas in lesbian couples there was no significant difference between partners in number of questions asked. The authors argue that this distinctive finding can be accounted for through an examination of the different uses of questions in different situations. They agree with Fishman (1983) that questions serve as a conversation-maintenance device, but argue that they also are used to elicit opinions or suggestions. In looking at who asks more questions, it is important to look also at the substance of the questions being asked. The questions recorded in Kollock et al.'s study were questions oriented toward completing the tasks at hand (such as deciding where to go for vacation), as the conversations analyzed for this study were task oriented. If the conversations had been more relationship oriented, the findings may have been significantly different.

Regardless of the situation, however, it is instructive that Kollock et al. found power to be a significant determinant of conversational style in heterosexual and gay male couples, but not in lesbian couples. This finding suggests that in those relationships where a male is present, clout is more important than gender in determining the use of questions. The impact of power differentials appears to influence interactions with men in them, perhaps because men are more likely to acknowledge rank and its privileges and feel free to compete for their "rightful" conversational territory. Lesbian couples, in which both partners asked an equal number of questions in the Kollock et al. (1985) study, appear to use conversational devices to maintain a balance of power in their relationships.

Tag Questions

When a person is unsure of or uneasy about making a statement, he or she will often end that statement with a tag question, such as "don't you think?" Like other types of questions, tag questions encourage the listener to speak, thereby supporting the conversation. A tag question weakens the impact of a statement and gives conversational power to the listener. It conveys a sense of deference to the listener by suggesting that the questioner is uncomfortable with what he or she has said, and is willing to retract the statement if the listener disagrees. Women in heterosexual relationships use tag questions more often than do their male partners (Lakoff, 1975).

Kollock et al. (1985) found that in heterosexual couples, the less powerful partner used more tag questions. This was also true in lesbian couples, but not as dramatically. This finding suggests, once again, that lesbian couples, although they are influenced by power to a certain degree, make a conscious effort to avoid conversational devices that grant power to one partner over the other. The opposite finding appeared in gay male couples, with the more powerful partner using more tag questions. This may be evidence that gay male couples feel uncomfortable when there is an imbalance of power in the relationship. In this case, the less powerful male is unwilling to take on the burden of conversational support because he resents being dominated. Likewise, the more powerful partner tries to bring his partner into the conversation by attempting to decrease the role division created by inequality. Both partners use conversational techniques to encourage a more equal distribution of power in their relationship.

Minimal Responses

One way of filling conversational gaps is to respond to a partner's statement with a minimal utterance such as *uh-huh* or *mhm*. This type of response may be indicative of support, agreement, or boredom. Maltz and Borker (1982) argue that women and men use minimal responses to mean different things. Women use them to show that they are listening and understanding what their partners are saying, whereas men use them to indicate agreement. Others argue that, particularly when used by men, minimal responses are simply a lazy way to take a conversational turn (see, e.g., Kollock et al., 1985). In this case, the listener has little interest in what the speaker has said, but wishes to avoid the conflict that would arise if no response at all were made.

In their comparative study of heterosexual, gay, and lesbian couples, Kollock et al. (1985) found greater use of minimal responses in gay male couples than in either lesbian or heterosexual couples. Both men in gay partnerships, regardless of their power position, used minimal responses more than people in other types of couples. The study also showed that in heterosexual relationships men were more likely to use minimal responses than were women. The authors conclude that minimal responses are a sign of conversational lassitude, and are less an indicator of power in a relationship than a general conversational privilege assumed by males.

The greater incidence of minimal responses in gay male couples might suggest that their conversations are more difficult to maintain (if responses are often passive and disinterested rather than active and interested, conversations might be cut off). Gay males, however, are likely less offended by such responses than are lesbians (because they accept them as an ordinary part of conversation), and therefore are more likely to continue conversation even if their partners are responding only minimally. If this is true, then we would posit that minimal responses are problematic only in heterosexual couples, where the conversational partners have different feelings about them.

Sharing Feelings

Sharing feelings with one's partner is a form of conversational, and relational, support. Self-disclosure is a very vulnerable form of communication; it shows trust in one's conversational partner and occurs only when the speaker is willing to give up some control over the conversation. One way to maintain control in a conversation is to reveal only certain pieces of information. By sharing personal feelings, an individual asks for reciprocity, or at least acceptance, which may be refused; gives information that may potentially be used against him or her; and, in general, creates an intimacy that puts the self up for scrutiny.

Men and women tend to differ in the area of self-disclosure, with women preferring greater self-disclosure, both from themselves and their partners, than men. Sharing personal feelings creates an intimate bond between two people, which is often the goal of conversation for women. Men, on the other hand, feel it is important to maintain a position of advantage in conversation, and are therefore more likely to share only their strengths (Peplau, 1983). Gay men, who tend to be competitive as opposed to consultative (Blumstein & Schwartz, 1983), may share feelings less readily than lesbians or couples with a female partner. On the other hand, for those gay men who are critical of heterosexual models of maleness, vulnerability and exposure are goals, and counternormative emotional styles are positively reinforced.

Many gay men do hold intimacy as a primary goal. It may not, however, play a vital role in relationship satisfaction. Reece and Segrist (1981) compared gay men in ongoing relationships that had dissolved, and found that self-disclosure was not significantly correlated with relationship longevity. This suggests that sharing feelings is not vitally important to the maintenance of a gay male relationship. Silverstein (1981) hypothesizes that intimacy has differing importance in different types of gay male couples. Some couples, whom he labels "home builders," are more intent than those he calls "excitement seekers" on attaining intimacy within a primary relationship. For these men, sharing feelings is of utmost importance, whereas for others it is more optional. In some relationships (such as those of "excitement seekers"), the development of emotional intimacy may even cause a breakup if the men involved are uncomfortable with or afraid of this type of intimacy.

Lesbian couples have a strong desire for intimacy, and they are fairly successful at attaining this goal. This should not be surprising, as women are socialized to think and talk about feelings and to be concerned with how others are feeling (Gilligan, 1982). Lesbians are in the fortunate situation of having a good chance that both partners will be skillful at communicating feelings. This concern for sharing feelings, however, also creates some problems for lesbian couples. Women tend to focus on their relationships and spend a lot of time and energy working to improve them. Having two partners scrutinizing the relationship often means that they want to discuss their feelings constantly, which is emotionally exhausting and may have deleterious effects on the relationship (nitpicking, overanalyzing, feeling claustrophobic, and so on). Further, lesbians often have very high expectations of their partners, which include expectations that they should always want to hear about feelings. Coolness may be associated with disinterest or, worse, an attempt to insert role-playing and/or dominance behaviors into the relationship. On the other hand, a common theme of lesbian relationship books is "implosion"—the fear that the desire for intimacy will become suffocating and struggles for identity separation will result (Andrews, 1990; Clunis & Green, 1988; Sang, 1984).

Clearly, here is a place where gendered approaches to intimacy create problems for the same-sex couple. But the hesitancy to engage in self-disclosure may be related more to sex-role identity than to sex itself. In a study of married and cohabiting heterosexuals and gay and lesbian couples, Kurdek and Schmitt (1986) found that couples in which one or both partners viewed their roles as androgynous or feminine reported the highest relationship satisfaction, whereas couples in which one or both partners were undifferentiated or masculine reported the lowest relationship satisfaction. The authors attribute this to expressiveness, which was part of their measurement of sex role types (feminine and androgynous couples had high levels of expressiveness; masculine and undifferentiated couples had low levels). We would extend this conclusion further to argue that couples in which neither partner views him- or herself as masculine are likely to experience more effective and satisfying communication, as one or both partners are concerned with conversational support (Blumstein & Schwartz, 1983). Turning now to the other half of the conversational cadence, we address dominance strategies.

Conversational Dominance

Interruptions

One good indicator of the allocation of power within a relationship is the use of interruptions. Interruptions are evidence of which partner has the power to take over the direction of a conversation successfully, and also which partner has the power to resist interruption successfully. Interrupting carries with it the implication that what the speaker is saying is less important than what the interrupter has to say. In cross-sex conversations, men have been shown to do virtually all the interrupting (Zimmerman & West, 1976). Further, women have been shown to be much more likely than men to allow interruptions (Thorne & Henley, 1975). Interruptions seem to be part of an overall verbal strategy used to achieve and maintain control over the direction and content of a conversation.

Kollock et al. (1985) found that the use of interruptions is connected to power, not gender, in both homosexual and heterosexual relationships. In all types of relationships studied, the partner with more power was found to interrupt his or her partner a great deal more than the weaker partner. Further, allowing interruptions to be successful was associated with weakness, with the weaker partner being much more likely to be interrupted successfully. Again, however, male couples show a distinctive pattern, showing far fewer successful interruptions (but not fewer attempts) than either heterosexual or lesbian couples. Men likely feel that their status is on the line in conversations, and that by allowing themselves to be interrupted, they "lose." Because of this, they work hard to protect themselves from interruptions. Lesbian couples experience a rate of attempted interruptions lower than that of heterosexual couples, which demonstrates their distaste for dominating conversational devices. They are likely to feel that interrupting goes against norms of cooperation and support, and therefore hesitate to show power or control in this fashion.

In a study of same-sex interactions, Drass (1986) found that the use of interruptions was associated with gender identity, with individuals who considered themselves more "male-like" being more likely to interrupt the other speaker. This is not inconsistent with the findings of Kollock et al. (1985), as power may lead an individual to acquire a masculine self-identity. The findings of both studies suggest that the use of interruptions is more likely to be unequal in couples who are power imbalanced or in which the partners have very different gender identities. The more similar partners are, then, the more likely they are to have similar views and usage of interruptions, and the less likely such devices are to be seen as destructive to the relationship.

Challenges

Challenging another person's statements can be seen as either a conversational stimulus or a personal assault on the speaker. Men are much more comfortable with challenges than are women (Tannen, 1990), as they tend to view this conversational device as a necessary component of the status negotiation that occurs during conversations. They are more likely than women to challenge the authority of a speaker, whether male or female, as a way of demonstrating status (Leet-Pellegrini, 1980). Women are likely to view challenges as personal attacks and therefore try to avoid them as much as possible. For women, communication is ideally a cooperative, not competitive, enterprise, and challenging others is an uncooperative form of communication.

The tendency of lesbians to avoid challenging one another is likely to make communication generally more congenial. However, it also means that problems will go unacknowledged if one partner fears hurting the other. Lesbians avoid expressing differences because they worry about losing one another's support (Clunis & Green, 1988). Women not only wish to avoid confrontation, they also lack the skills necessary for confrontation, as they are socialized to be peacemakers. The inability to confront one another in an assertive manner often means that lesbians discuss a problem superficially, resolve it quickly, then have to face the same problem again later because it was never truly resolved the first time (Clunis & Green, 1988). The inability and unwillingness to challenge one another clearly makes problem solving difficult for lesbian couples.

Gay men face an entirely different problem. In conversation, both partners may be so intent on challenging each other that neither really listens to what his partner is saying. Again, this will create difficulties when the couple is trying to work through a problem. If both partners are intent on "winning," there is small likelihood of compromise. If a high level of agreement is present, gay conversation may be especially instrumental and efficient; if there is disagreement, however, this style of rushing to resolve conflict without exchanging or trying to understand feelings can create or prolong conflict.

Gay men work on conversing without competing, whereas lesbians see confrontation on disagreements as a relationship goal. Couples who have been together for many years usually find ways of resolving these conversational problems. McWhirter (1984) suggests that competition between gay male partners is highest during the first five years or so of a relationship, after which each partner becomes more comfortable establishing independence from his partner and allowing his accomplishments to stand on their own without constant comparison to his partner. Lesbian couples find it difficult to learn to confront problems head-on; however, Clunis and Green (1988) suggest that as lesbian relationships develop and each partner becomes more aware of her needs and desires in the relationship, both partners are more likely to be able to express their feelings openly, even if those feelings are negative. There are, of course, many lesbian and gay male couples who are never able to get beyond dominance or support to achieve truly effective communication, but this is true in all types of relationships.

SUBSTANCE: WHAT COUPLES COMMUNICATE ABOUT

Overview

We turn now to a discussion of the substantive issues homosexual couples have to communicate about. What a couple discusses is clearly as important as how they discuss it in defining overall communication. Throughout this section, we stay with our theme of dominance and support, looking at how power determines relationship outcomes, and how different definitions and styles of conversation affect the ways in which issues are resolved. For example, we will examine such questions as, How does structural power affect decision making about issues such as housework and parenting? What effect does having two partners socialized to be supportive have on the sexual activity of lesbian couples? We divide the substantive issues faced by homosexual couples into two subsections: power and responding to the outside world. The first, which includes those issues we feel to be most affected by power, covers work, money, housework, and sex. The second subsection includes coming out (making one's homosexuality known to others), family concerns (the "in-law" issue), and children.

Power

Work

In the traditional heterosexual division of labor, the husband earns a living and the wife takes care of the home and children. As more women join the workforce, both by choice and out of financial necessity, fewer couples fit this traditional mold. Such a division of labor is even rarer in the homosexual world, in which dual-career couples overwhelmingly form the rule rather than the exception. Having two paychecks helps to create both financial stability and a sense of equality in a relationship. Gay males, like most men, have grown up expecting to work, so gay couples are not usually conflicted about whether or not both partners will have jobs. Conflict and stress occur instead when one partner does not or cannot work. Men gain much of their identity from their work, and a partner who does not have a job often suffers from self-esteem problems in addition to worrying that he is not doing his fair share in making a financial contribution to the relationship. Often he feels such a loss of status and power that it affects the relationship's stability. Blumstein and Schwartz (1983) have noted that among gay couples a low-earning or nonearning partner is more likely to leave a relationship than is a high-earning partner.

The members of lesbian couples, although not necessarily socialized to have careers, quickly realize that both partners must work, partly because no male provider exists and partly because they desire both independence and equality within their relationships. Lesbians are wary of financial dependence, which they equate with the dynamics of heterosexual husbands' subordination of their wives. Like most women, lesbians understand the power that money confers on the high earner, and they attempt to equalize power imbalances by minimizing dependence. According to Blumstein and Schwartz (1983), however, sensitivities about carrying an appropriate economic load are felt more intensely by the *higher*-earning partner in a lesbian couple, who is more likely to leave the relationship than is the less-advantaged partner. Blumstein and Schwartz speculate that this may be related to the fact that women do not expect ever to assume the provider role in a relationship, and are uncomfortable doing so. In the final analysis, however, both members of a lesbian couple are likely to work, because the lower wage structure of women's jobs generally makes it necessary for both partners to work to ensure financial survival or an adequate level of comfort.

Although homosexual couples begin with the assumption of two working partners, there are still the problems of allocating time for jobs and of whether or not one job will be given priority insofar as jobs affect couple choices and planning. Traditional heterosexual couples expect that the man's career will have priority over the woman's career. If the man is transferred to or finds a better job in another city, the woman is expected to quit her job (if she has one) and move with her husband (thus granting the husband the dominant role and the wife the supportive role). Homosexual couples have no such norm to guide them, so job conflicts require more complex negotiation. Questions of commitment, fairness, the best interests of the couple, and individual ambition surface, and are not solved merely by invoking a husband's breadwinner role—or his obvious ability to earn a higher salary—entitling him to determine where the couple should live or how their time needs to be allocated. In a same-sex male couple, both men, regardless of income level, may feel the need to protect their work—first, because their jobs are such important parts of their identities, but also because partners often judge their own success by weighing their achievements against the other partner's achievements (Blumstein & Schwartz, 1983) and are unwilling to lose status within the relationship. The opportunity or necessity to move for one's work creates a crisis, as it is beginning to do more frequently in heterosexual dual-career couples, because there is no easy way to determine how to choose one partner's career path over the other's.

The major complaint lesbian couples have about work is that it cuts too deeply into time that could be spent on their relationships (Blumstein & Schwartz, 1983; Clunis & Green, 1988). Although this happens also in heterosexual relationships, the fact that both partners, not just the wife, are frustrated makes this a core relationship issue among lesbians. Although competition does not appear to be a central issue for most lesbians (Blumstein & Schwartz, 1983), if one woman works longer hours or enjoys her work more than the other, the less satisfied partner is likely to feel that she is carrying the burden of maintaining the relationship alone (Clunis & Green, 1988; Sang, 1984). The more satisfied partner may also wish that she had more time to devote to the relationship, but often feels that her work is necessary for the couple's financial well-being. A lesbian who is intensely committed to her work and takes a big chunk of couple time to fulfill her ambitions comes up against strong norms of putting her relationship first.

The struggle to avoid using employment to grant one partner a dominant role and the other a supportive role clearly causes complications in both lesbian and gay male couples. However, if both partners in a relationship have the same attitude toward work (either giving it top priority or agreeing that it will be secondary to the relationship), they will be better able to understand each other's feelings and will be able to avoid much of the frustration experienced by heterosexual couples when they discover that their priorities are different (McWhirter, 1984). If both partners have the same occupation, as many homosexual couples do, this adds further to conversational compatibility.

Money

Money, like employment, has a strong effect on power relations in a couple. The extent of such influence differs for gay male and lesbian couples. In gay male couples, money problems center on equality of contributions and dominance in decision making (Berger, 1990).

Financially successful men feel they have earned the right to exercise control or at least to predominate in decision making if they bring home a majority of the couple's earnings (Blumstein & Schwartz, 1983). The partner with a higher income heavily influences the decision-making process in the couple, which leads to feelings of resentment on the part of the other partner. The partner who wields the power often perceives the other partner as weak, whereas the partner with less power resents the control the other has over him and over their relationship (McWhirter, 1984). Men are expected to earn money, and if one partner is unemployed, or underemployed, for a lengthy period, the other partner feels that he is being taken advantage of financially, and may lose respect for his partner. The exceptions to this are found among the minority of gay men who "role-play" and enjoy being breadwinner and homemaker, and the gay man who enjoys fulfilling the provider role—happily fulfilling the norm of provider, even without the "provided for" role of a female partner. However, in this case, even though the high-earning partner is happy supporting his partner, the low-earning partner is conflicted about his dependency and often unwilling to adopt a "supportive" role (Blumstein & Schwartz, 1983).

Money does not appear to be as centrally related to the balance of power in lesbian couples (Blumstein & Schwartz, 1983). This is because of a conscious decision by lesbians to undercut the traditional use of money in heterosexual relationships. This effort to be egalitarian causes an enormous amount of discussion and microaccounting. Lesbians continually assess the impacts of economic inequality, which means that the high-earning partner is always open to accusations of high-handedness and efforts to be dominant. This is exacerbated by the fact that lesbian couples operate within the constraints of relatively low income; of the four types of couples Blumstein and Schwartz (1983) studied—heterosexual married couples, cohabitors, gay couples, and lesbian couples—lesbians were the poorest and gay males the wealthiest. However, economic issues proliferate for reasons beyond sheer lack of money. Literature on the workplace and on stress indicates that the single greatest cause of anxiety and other forms of mental distress is lack of control over working conditions (Waldron, 1980). Lesbians, like other working women, are concentrated in blue-

and pink-collar jobs that allow for little personal autonomy. The interaction of low control and low income presents an especially intense problem for a large number of female same-sex couples.

Housework

In heterosexual married couples, even those who claim to hold egalitarian standards, women do most of the housework (Berk & Berk, 1979; England & Farkas, 1986). Gender norms play an important role in defining which tasks get done by whom. Because such norms are nonexistent for homosexual couples, and because housework is a stigmatized form of labor, these couples must make conscious and delicate decisions regarding who does what chores. Gay male couples, for example, must allocate chores traditionally defined as "women's work" without role imputation. Moreover, men, both heterosexual and homosexual, feel they should be exempted from doing such work if they are the primary financial providers in their relationships (Blumstein & Schwartz, 1983). One way that couples resolve this issue is by dividing the tasks equally between partners, with each partner doing those things he enjoys doing, and splitting equally the tasks neither enjoys (McWhirter, 1984). Occasionally, one partner will take on the role of "housewife," doing the majority of the cooking and cleaning, because he enjoys doing these things, but this occurs only in a small number of male couples (Blumstein & Schwartz, 1983; McWhirter, 1984). Even this solution, however, can be problematic, as the partner who does most of the work often expects something in return—at the very least, gratitude. If his partner has grown up having someone else do chores for him, he is not likely to realize the amount of work his partner has taken on, and will therefore be less grateful than his partner expects. Moreover, this division of labor is not supposed to confer hierarchy or help establish dominance; however, the similarity to heterosexual traditions of dominance and support roles make egalitarian interactions tricky.

There are other ways of resolving the issue of housework. In dual-career couples, neither partner is likely to have the time or the energy to devote to extensive housework. To avoid both the unpleasantness of the chores and the conflict involved in allocating them, an affluent couple may choose to hire someone to do the housework for them. This happens much more frequently among gay men than among lesbians, partly because gay men are likely to be better off financially, and partly because some lesbians have ideological objections to having someone else (usually a woman) do their housework (Blumstein & Schwartz, 1983). On the other hand, each woman is likely to refuse too large a share of the "dirty work" because of the history of women's entrapment by household duties and the lower status implied by having too central a homemaking role. This is one area in same-sex couples' lives where the support role is studiously and ideologically avoided. Given the politicized nature of housework, lesbian couples are more likely to decide to ignore housework and allow their homes to remain somewhat disorderly than to hire someone to do housework for them. Of course, there is a limit to which an issue can be resolved by neglect, and home maintenance remains a sensitive area among lower-earning lesbians.

Sex

Because sexuality is heavily scripted by gender in our society, same-sex couples have to be innovative about establishing expectations and roles. For example, women in this society are often less comfortable than men about stating their sexual desires and preferences. Men often take the role of "sexual guide" in heterosexual relationships, establishing sexual parameters and customs. Lesbians have no apparent "guide" and may be ideologically opposed to the idea of one. If both women are reticent about stating what they want, the development of a sexual relationship becomes uncertain and difficult. In the following discussion, we look at the consequences of having a sexual relationship that requires self-discovery and role innovation in the context of the avoidance of hierarchy and the "politicization" of patterns of dominance and support.

Initiation and Refusal Patterns. In heterosexual relationships, initiation of sexual activity is traditionally the male's responsibility. This sexual norm requires negotiation and often causes problems in both gay and lesbian couples, because it encourages each gay man to claim initiation as his right, and makes it hard for either lesbian to initiate at all (Blumstein & Schwartz, 1983). Competition arises between gay male partners over who has the role of sexual initiator (Blumstein & Schwartz, 1983). Both men compete for the role, both because it is viewed as the more masculine role and because the alternative role may be seen as too passive, too "female." Furthermore, it is counternormative for men to say no too often. A more male way to control sex is to be able to decide whether or not to initiate. Conversely, in lesbian couples, the problem is not competition for the role of initiator, but rather hesitation to take on such a role. Initiating sex can be seen as aggressive, "male," and unconsensual, all of which go against values of lesbian life. The difficulty of ensuring consensual sex and equal initiation contributes to a decrease in sexual frequency, which is an issue for many lesbian couples (Rosenzweig & Lebow, 1992).

To manage either competition for or avoidance of sexual initiation, same-sex partners must confront the historical designation and valuation of gender roles during sex. Who is entitled to do what can require actual dialogue, instead of just serendipitous behavior. Such communication is likely made easier by the fact that most same-sex couples are committed to changing old gender role inhibitions or privileges. Further, sexual communication in general may be easier because same-sex partners have more familiarity with a partner's desires and body than do opposite-sex partners. Many people argue that a man knows better how to please a man (and a woman knows better how to please a woman) because of empathy and intuition (Bressler & Lavender, 1986). There has been no study conducted to compare directly relative knowledge and ability between heterosexual and homosexual couples, but it is certainly a theoretically powerful idea. Particularly among gay men, who are more likely to be explicit about what they want from each other, and in general have a wide repertoire of sexual acts (Blumstein & Schwartz, 1983), communication skills and familiarity may interact to create well-understood and well-acted-out sexual scenarios. A vocal wing of radical feminist lesbian writers and activists have as one political goal the repudiation of traditional female sexual conduct. Writers such as Vance (1984) have created a new dialogue in lesbian literature about creating straightforward and adventurous sexual attitudes and behavior, including validating such

heretofore taboo possibilities as nonmonogamy, sex without commitment or love, and even dominance and submission (including mild
sadomasochism) in lesbian relationships.

Sex Roles. A second issue related to sex is whether or not a couple
will adopt traditional sex roles in the relationship. Taking on "butch"
and "femme" roles was popular among homosexuals in the nineteenth
and early twentieth centuries (D'Emilio & Freedman, 1988), but it
appears that most homosexual couples today try to avoid adopting
these gendered roles because they carry the inheritance of dominance
and submission patterns of male-female relationships (Harry & DeVall,
1978; McWhirter, 1984). This may be an especially salient issue in gay
male couples when one partner is the "insertor" and the other the
"insertee" in anal sex, or when one person only gives, or only receives,
oral sex. Such roles carry with them heavy cultural meanings, with
the insertor being seen as dominant (and male) and the insertee as
submissive (and female). Some gay men are able to ignore the labels
and just do what pleases them—others actively enjoy the sexual
fantasy of male-female roles—but a substantial number of gay men
become resentful about a consistent lack of reciprocity. Many gay men
choose to avoid the conflict that frequently arises over the issue by
avoiding anal sex if there is no reciprocity in roles, and by consciously
trading roles during oral sex. By doing so, they avoid defining one
partner as "masculine" and the other as "feminine," or one as dominant and the other as submissive. These same issues occur for women.
Although reciprocity in oral sex is by far the norm, occasionally only
one woman will claim the "right" to perform oral sex. This lack of role
exchange is almost always an issue, because the dominance inferences
are inescapable.

Monogamy. Homosexuals, particularly gay men, have redefined the
meaning and terms of monogamy. For the most part, gay male couples
define monogamy and commitment not in terms of sexual fidelity, but
in terms of emotional commitment (McWhirter, 1984). Gay male
partners who are successful at maintaining a nonmonogamous relationship are likely able to isolate outside sex from their emotional

commitment to one another. To be successful, such couples are clear and specific negotiators. They create rules for outside sex, most often emphasizing that sex outside the relationship is to remain casual (Blumstein & Schwartz, 1983), but also including items such as when and with whom the partners will be allowed to have sex, and whether they will share their experiences with one another (McWhirter, 1984). The process of creating such rules necessitates honest and direct communication, and can be particularly difficult for those couples in which one partner is more interested in establishing an open relationship than the other. There has in the past been little support in the gay world for gay men who desire monogamy, and such men have had an extremely difficult time negotiating monogamous contracts or finding like-minded partners (Blumstein & Schwartz, 1983).

Even before the advent of the AIDS epidemic, however, monogamy was gaining increasing normative support in the gay male community, probably because of the aging of the baby boom generation, the eventual surfeit of experimentation, and the subsequent search for security and settling down (Siegel & Glassman, 1989). But still, until the mid-1980s, a vast majority of gay male couples were nonmonogamous (Blumstein & Schwartz, 1983). In a recent study, however, most of the gay men (96.4%) interviewed defined their relationships as monogamous (Berger, 1990), suggesting that AIDS has definitely had a significant impact on gay male sexuality. The epidemic made nonmonogamous sex life threatening, and the vast majority of male homosexuals drastically revised their sex lives. Couples negotiated monogamy, nonmonogamy with condoms, or "safer sex" techniques, such as using telephone sex services or other kinds of sexual titillation that do not allow intromission or exchange of body fluids.

The nature of lesbian relationships both encourages and discourages monogamy. Women are taught that sex should be tied to emotional commitment. This would seem to encourage monogamy in lesbian relationships, but this same attitude may lead women to be nonmonogamous, because lesbian communities often consist of networks of women in very close friendships. The emotional attachments that are formed between lesbians often lead to sexual attraction and, subsequently, affairs (Clunis & Green, 1988). Thus, if lesbians do choose to have sex with someone other than a primary partner, the person is much more likely to be a close friend than a stranger. Nonmonogamy may therefore be more problematic for lesbians than for gay men because outside sex is more likely to be an "affair" that can truly threaten the woman's primary relationship. A woman whose partner is engaged in an affair is likely to feel betrayed and insecure about the loss of control over her partner and the future of her relationship. Even though certain schools of feminist philosophy encourage or accept nonmonogamy as another way of defying heterosexual models of female sexuality, there is no indication that this makes the management of emotions any easier. Lesbians who take exception to traditional female sexual norms may feel that monogamy is a part of the repressive nature of married life and consciously choose to reject it (Clunis & Green, 1988). This view is not, however, acted upon by the majority of lesbians; only 28% of the lesbians surveyed by Blumstein and Schwartz (1983) were nonmonogamous, a proportion only slightly higher than that found for heterosexual married women (21%), and significantly lower than that of gay men (82%).

Competition and Jealousy. Competition for sexual partners is a uniquely homosexual phenomenon. Unlike heterosexuals, homosexuals choose their sexual partners from the same pool of individuals, either male for gay men or female for lesbians. Thus partners may find themselves competing for the attention of the same person (McWhirter, 1984). This is most likely in social meeting places, such as gay bars, where the possibilities for sexual interest are enhanced. If one partner consistently gets more attention than the other, the unattended partner is likely to feel unattractive and rejected. This kind of competitive resentment is difficult to talk about and may result in withdrawal from social situations (Silverstein, 1981) or unconstructive, petulant displays of temper. In many couples, particularly gay male couples, physical beauty is a major component of power, and when one partner is deemed less attractive than the other, he is likely to feel uncomfortable with his partner's dominant status (Blumstein & Schwartz, 1983).

Responding to the Outside World

Coming Out

There are different levels of self-revelation and exposure in the coming out process. An individual can come out to him- or herself, to a sexual partner, to the homosexual community, to his or her family, to employers, to friends, or any combination thereof. The amount each individual in a homosexual relationship is out affects how open the partners can be as a couple. For example, one partner in a lesbian relationship could be out to all of her friends, family members, and fellow employees, whereas the other partner could be out only to herself and her partner. Not only does the partially closeted individual have to present him- or herself quite differently in different situations (Bell & Weinberg, 1978), but the couple will have to adjust their social life to accommodate the closeted partner (McWhirter, 1984; Sang, 1984). If they are living together, they will have to pretend to be roommates whenever anyone comes over. They may feel uncomfortable going to social gatherings because one partner may want to show her affection for the other, whereas the other is trying to hide the fact that she is lesbian. Problems arise, then, not only because of disagreements over what information to share with outsiders and whose definition of the relationship will predominate, but because of the stress involved in trying to hide the relationship (Berger, 1990).

The question of coming out is powerful because it brings into serious question a person's commitment to being homosexual or being in a homosexual relationship and/or a homosexual community. Some homosexuals who believe that homosexuality is inherently political feel that it is their duty to be involved in feminist or gay liberation movements. If only one partner feels this way and the other is more comfortable either living a closeted lifestyle or simply not becoming involved in political issues, major conflicts can arise. On the other hand, mutual agreement on this question often binds the couple together: They may be open, and see it as a brave mutual political act, or they may be closeted, and perceive their relationship as a small, bonded, secret society. Whose preference predominates provides another interesting insight into how power is shared in the relationship.

Family

Families can be a major cause of stress for all couples, but same-sex couples have additional management and affiliation problems. Even if parents accept their own adult child's homosexuality, they may be unsupportive or cruel about the child's partner and relationship. Some families accept a member's homosexuality philosophically, but are unable to face the reality of it (McWhirter, 1984). This makes any situation in which the family and the homosexual family member's partner have to interact very uncomfortable for the partner, whom the family often blames (either consciously or subconsciously) for the member's homosexuality (Berzon, 1988; Clunis & Green, 1988). Lack of support from family members is disturbing and stressful both to the homosexual individual and to his or her partner (Berger, 1990). If the family does not like the partner or refuses to give him or her a chance, the individual is forced to choose between partner and family at the least for holidays and family get-togethers; at worst, he or she may sever family relations as an act of solidarity and love. When this happens, loyalty to family is in direct opposition to the individual's identity and love for his or her partner (Clunis & Green, 1988). No decision in such a situations is emotionally uncomplicated.

Children

Children affect many homosexual couples in two ways. First, especially among lesbians, one partner may come into the relationship with children, often from a previous heterosexual marriage. The personal and legal complications that result significantly affect dominance and support patterns within a relationship. Child custody is frequently problematic following a heterosexual divorce, and courts tend to side with the nonhomosexual parent (Lewin, 1984; Wolf, 1979). Even if custody is granted to the homosexual parent, there is a great deal of pressure on him or her not to make mistakes that a motivated and angry nonhomosexual parent could use to reopen the custody issue. Homosexual parents who desire custody of their children after a divorce often choose to conceal their homosexuality out of fear that it will influence the custody decision adversely (de Monteflores &

Schultz, 1978). Lifestyle choices—including how one may live with one's partner—become circumscribed by assessment of custodial vulnerability.

The question also arises of what role the parent's partner should play in relation to the child. This is a role barely defined in the heterosexual world, and much less so among homosexual couples. The biological parent is most often assumed to have primary parenting responsibilities and privileges, whereas his or her partner plays a supportive role, not interfering in the large decisions (Clunis & Green, 1988; Moore, Blumstein, & Schwartz, 1993). It is easy to see how power could become unbalanced in such a situation, as one partner shares in the everyday work of caring for the child but has no real power in decision making. To avoid conflict, the biological parent learns to share the child's affections and the responsibilities involved in raising him or her. However, the biological parent may both preserve and increase dominance in the relationship by keeping "ownership" over the child's life and loyalties. Children are valued by lesbians, as by most women, and, contrary to the research on heterosexuals, custody confers power on the biological parent (Moore et al., 1993).

The language of parenting—of competence and awareness of children's needs—is more common among women, and thus there are possibilities for good communication among lesbians on this issue. Gay male couples, however, may have a more awkward time making the nonbiological parent comfortable with a parenting role. This difference between gay and lesbian couples is heightened by organizational supports for lesbians with children (lesbian mothers' groups and newsletters), whereas the fewer males in this situation are more isolated.

The second issue that arises for some homosexual couples occurs when they decide to adopt and/or have biological children. Couples who make this decision face many potential difficulties. Lesbian couples have to decide which partner will become pregnant and what method (artificial insemination, intercourse) will be used. If both women are biologically capable and desire to become mothers, the couple will have to decide who will be the biological mother. This decision has important implications, as the biological mother is likely to feel that the child is more hers than her partner's, and her partner may be inappropriately disenfranchised. Both women may want a primary identity as mother, and this can cause competition for the child's love and attention. Unresolved difficulties of this sort are now starting to show up in family courts, with nonbiological mothers suing their previous companions for custodial or visitation rights.

DISCUSSION

Homosexual partners, like heterosexual partners, are in complex, changing relationships. There is no "typical" gay or lesbian couple. There are differences in the issues that homosexual couples face, the ways the partners respond to similar issues, and the styles of communication they use in everyday life. Because of this, a parsimonious conclusion about dominance and supportive patterns cannot completely explain the complex conversational patterns of these couples. We do believe, however, that we can make some statements based on this review of communication in same-sex couples that elucidate the causes and consequences of a dominant-supportive conversational pattern.

To begin, it is clear that the functional argument that a dominant-supportive pattern is necessary to sustain an efficient working relationship is incorrect. Many same-sex couples do not utilize this pattern of interaction. Further, we have shown that lesbians are not restricted to communicating in supportive ways and gay men are not restricted to dominant ways, which suggests that biological gender is not ultimately determinant of conversational style.

We found considerable support for socialization, gender identities, and power as important factors in determining conversational patterns. The effects of socialization on communication in homosexual couples come through most clearly in conversational goals of lesbians and gay men. Tannen's (1990) assertion that men are socialized to be competitive and women cooperative is supported by the fact that gay male couples are much more likely to compete for dominant conversational position than are women. Power has a greater effect on gay male couples because they have been socialized to believe that power is important and are more likely to be in competitive work environments. Further, men learn that they are expected to control others, and to expect others (typically women) to do the necessary support work. Thus we see gay men taking conversational privileges (such as minimal responses) for granted, whereas lesbians rarely take advantage of such devices.

Definitions of conversational goals by gender are again apparent in the differential use of challenges and interruptions by lesbians and gay men. Lesbians view both devices as uncooperative, and are much less likely to use them than are gay men, who view them as a necessary component of the competition inherent in conversation. Whereas challenges and interruptions are disparaged by lesbians, gay men may find them not only necessary, but enjoyable. Thus gay men not only challenge and interrupt one another at a higher rate than do lesbians, they are also less bothered by challenges and interruptions from their partners.

Gender identity is a good device to use to differentiate between certain gay male couples and certain lesbian couples. We have shown that many homosexuals have a distaste for the gender roles the dominant culture has shaped for them. Many gay men feel uncomfortable competing with one another for power, just as many lesbians feel it is harmful to protect themselves by avoiding confrontation. When gender norms are challenged, demonstrable changes occur in conversation. For example, gay men who are critical of the macho man image are much more likely to be willing and able to share their feelings with their partners, and lesbians often experience deeply satisfying communication by talking openly about their disagreements and conflicts.

Finally, the effects of power on conversational style are highly significant, although often in the direction opposite of that expected (that is, we often see the more powerful partner taking on less powerful conversational techniques). Throughout our analysis, we have seen many instances in which structural power correlated with both dominant conversational techniques and decision-making power within the relationship. However, we have also seen that homosexual couples are often critical of the role power can play in shaping a relationship, and that conversational techniques are often used as a way of balancing power within homosexual relationships.

It is not surprising that no consistent pattern of communication emerges from our discussion of homosexual couples. They are, after all, in the unique position of having to create relationships in two different cultures—that of mainstream society (based on heterosexual couples) and that of homosexual culture. The conversational styles that we see emerging in homosexual couples are in large part dependent on the various issues they have to discuss. For example, because so many substantive issues bring up questions of power, and because homosexuals lack cultural guidelines as to how power is to be allocated within their relationships, homosexual couples tend to be highly sensitive to conversational techniques that demonstrate hierarchy and dominance. Thus particularly those gay and lesbian couples who are critical of the heterosexual model of dominance and support will be much more aware of their conversational styles than are most people in our society.

There are numerous issues that homosexual couples have to handle without the guidance of cultural expectations and norms. This lack of guidelines means that direct communication and patient negotiation are vitally important for the achievement of satisfying relationships. Homosexual couples who are able to be flexible in the roles they adopt and to compromise some of the gender-specific expectations they grew up with are likely to achieve something many heterosexual couples would envy—relationships based on desires and preferences rather than on culturally dictated roles and norms. As heterosexual couples move away from traditional sex roles, they could learn a great deal by looking at how some homosexual couples have resolved the issues raised by dual-career relationships and the struggle for equitable distribution of power. Homosexual couples have wrestled with these issues for years, and it would be to the benefit of heterosexual couples to try to identify some of the mechanisms homosexual couples have used to create satisfying relationships without having the safety net of traditional male/female roles.

We have designed this chapter, as we stated at the outset, more to raise questions than to answer them. Our hope is that, by laying out previous research done on communication of homosexual couples, we have inspired others to do further research on those issues for which we have only very tentative answers. Possible research directions include examining how homosexual couples define their conversational goals and styles, how they define their relational goals (e.g., gay men may define intimacy in some way other than self-disclosure), and how decisions are made about issues such as whose career is followed, what rules will be enforced to cope with non-monogamy, how partners share parenting privileges and duties, and how children affect partners' support for one another. We strongly believe that further research done to these ends will be beneficial to *all* couples as they face constantly changing roles and challenges in an era of massive redefinition of what makes a relationship satisfying and durable.

REFERENCES

Andrews, C. (1990). *Closeness and satisfaction in lesbian relationships*. Unpublished master's thesis, University of Washington, Seattle.

Bell, A. P., & Weinberg, M. S. (1978). *Homosexualities: A study of diversity among men and women*. New York: Simon & Schuster.

Berger, R. M. (1990). Men together: Understanding the gay couple. *Journal of Homosexuality, 19*(3), 31-49.

Berk, R. A., & Berk, S. F. (1979). *Labor and leisure at home*. Beverly Hills, CA: Sage.

Berzon, B. (1988). *Permanent partners: Building gay and lesbian relationships that last*. New York: E. P. Dutton.

Blumstein, P., & Schwartz, P. (1983). *American couples: Money, work, sex*. New York: William Morrow.

Bressler, L. C., & Lavender, A. D. (1986). Sexual fulfillment of heterosexual, bisexual, and homosexual women. *Journal of Homosexuality, 12*(3/4), 109-122.

Clunis, D. M., & Green, G. D. (1988). *Lesbian couples*. Seattle: Seal.

Davis, K. (1985). The meaning and significance of marriage in contemporary society. In K. Davis (Ed.), *Contemporary marriage* (pp. 1-24). New York: Russell Sage Foundation.

D'Emilio, J., & Freedman, E. B. (1988). *Intimate matters: A history of sexuality in America*. New York: Harper & Row.

de Monteflores, C., & Schultz, S. J. (1978). Coming out: Similarities and differences for lesbians and gay men. *Journal of Social Issues, 34*, 59-71.

Drass, K. A. (1986). The effect of gender identity on conversation. *Social Psychology Quarterly, 49*, 294-301.

England, P., & Farkas, G. (1986). *Households, employment, and gender*. New York: Aldine de Gruyter.

Fishman, P. (1983). Interaction: The work women do. In B. Thorne, C. Kramarae, & N. Henley (Eds.), *Language, gender, and society* (pp. 89-101). Rowley, MA: Newbury House.

Gilligan, C. (1982). *In a different voice: Psychological theory and women's development.* Cambridge, MA: Harvard University Press.

Harry, J., & DeVall, W. B. (1978). *The social organization of gay males.* New York: Praeger.

Kollock, P., Blumstein, P., & Schwartz, P. (1985). Sex and power in interaction: Conversational privileges and duties. *American Sociological Review, 50,* 34-46.

Kurdek, L. A., & Schmitt, J. P. (1986). Interaction of sex role self-concept with relationship quality and relationship beliefs in married, heterosexual cohabiting, gay and lesbian couples. *Journal of Personality and Social Psychology, 51,* 365-370.

Lakoff, R. (1975). *Language and woman's place.* New York: Harper & Row.

Leet-Pellegrini, H. M. (1980). Conversational dominance as a function of gender and expertise. In H. Giles, W. P. Robinson, & P. M. Smith (Eds.), *Language: Social psychological perspectives* (pp. 97-104). Oxford: Pergamon.

Lewin, E. (1984). Lesbianism and motherhood: Implications for child custody. In T. Darty & S. Potter (Eds.), *Women-identified women* (pp. 163-184). Palo Alto, CA: Mayfield.

Maltz, D. N., & Borker, R. A. (1982). A cultural approach to male-female miscommunication. In J. J. Gumperz (Ed.), *Language and social identity* (pp. 196-216). Cambridge: Cambridge University Press.

Marche, T. A., & Peterson, C. (1993). The development and sex-related use of interruption behavior. *Human Communication Research, 19,* 388-408.

McWhirter, D. P. (1984). *The male couple: How relationships develop.* Englewood Cliffs, NJ: Prentice Hall.

Moore, M., Blumstein, P., & Schwartz, P. (1993). *Motherhood as a resource.* Manuscript submitted for publication.

Peplau, L. A. (1983). Roles and gender. In H. H. Kelley, E. Berscheid, A. Christensen, J. H. Harvey, T. L. Huston, G. Levinger, E. McClintock, L. A. Peplau, & D. R. Peterson (Eds.), *Close relationships* (pp. 220-264). New York: W. H. Freeman.

Peplau, L. A., & Cochran, S. D. (1990). A relationship perspective on homosexuality. In D. P. McWhirter, S. A. Sanders, & J. M. Reinisch (Eds.), *Homosexuality/heterosexuality: Concepts of sexual orientation* (pp. 321-346). New York: Oxford University Press.

Reece, R., & Segrist, A. E. (1981). The association of selected "masculine" sex-role variables with length of relationship in gay male couples. *Journal of Homosexuality, 7*(1), 33-44.

Rosenzweig, J. M., & Lebow, W. C. (1992). Femme on the streets, butch in the streets? Lesbian sex roles, dyadic adjustment, and sexual satisfaction. *Journal of Homosexuality, 23*(3), 1-20.

Sang, B. (1984). Lesbian relationships: A struggle toward partner equality. In T. Darty & S. Potter (Eds.), *Women-identified women* (pp. 51-66). Palo Alto, CA: Mayfield.

Siegel, K., & Glassman, M. (1989). Individual and aggregate level change in sexual behavior among gay men at risk for AIDS. *Archives of Sexual Behavior, 18,* 335-348.

Silverstein, C. (1981). *Man to man: Gay couples in America.* New York: William Morrow.

Tannen, D. (1990). *You just don't understand: Women and men in conversation.* New York: Ballantine.

Thorne, B., & Henley, N. (Eds.). (1975). *Language and sex: Difference and dominance.* Rowley, MA: Newbury House.

Vance, C. S. (1984). *Pleasure and danger: Exploring female sexuality.* Boston: Routledge & Kegan Paul.

Waldron, I. (1980). Employment and women's health: An analysis of causal relationships. *International Journal of Health Services, 10,* 435-454.

Wolf, D. G. (1979). *The lesbian community.* Berkeley: University of California Press.

Wright, P. H. (1988). Interpreting research on gender differences in friendship: A case for moderation and a plea for caution. *Journal of Social and Personal Relationships, 5,* 367-373.

Zimmerman, D. H., & West, C. (1976). Sex roles, interruptions and silences in conversation. In B. Thorne & N. Henley (Eds.), *Language and sex: Difference and dominance* (pp. 105-127). Rowley, MA: Newbury House.

The Aging Family

MARIE-LOUISE MARES

What happens to a family as its members get older? How does the inexorable movement from childhood into adulthood, and on to old age, affect the types of family relationships an individual has and the experience of those relationships? This chapter is a review of social scientific literature relevant to these questions. Much of the research reviewed here was designed to address specific policy questions— How much care can and do children give their aging parents? How much help do parents offer children? Other research has focused on the phenomenology of aging relationships. How do spouses feel about one another after 40 years of marriage? How do middle-aged sons and daughters feel about their relationships with their elderly parents?

In this chapter, I try to pull together these studies to examine various roles of elderly family members. The approach used here is to examine each relationship separately (spouse, sibling, parent, grandparent) because that is the way the research is most commonly done. However, it is important to recognize the strong probability that each relationship varies as a function of the number and quality of other relationships. Unfortunately, this interaction between roles is infrequently addressed.

ELDERLY SPOUSES

During the 1980s, most adults over 60 years old were or had been married. Of men ages 65 to 74, 82% were married. For women, the

figure was 49%. Most adults over 60 had been married a long time—
an average of 43 years (Grambs, 1989). This section addresses some of
the characteristics of such long-term relationships.

Historical Context of Marriage

The character of the relationship between spouses in a long-term
marriage appears to depend in part on the historical context of the
relationship (for an extended discussion of this point, see Mares &
Fitzpatrick, in press). For example, couples formed during the 1920s
or earlier have been found to place less emphasis on communication
and shared activities with one another than do couples formed during
the 1960s and 1970s (Caplow, Bahr, Chadwick, Hill, & Williamson, 1982).
Other relevant changes include decreased emphasis on marriage as
the normative lifestyle for women (Faver, 1984) and increased expectations for egalitarian decision making in the couple (Holahan, 1984).
    A final historical change is the prevalence of divorce. Women who
are over 60 today grew up when divorce was considered a shameful
admission that one had failed at marriage or had been unwise in
selecting a mate (Grambs, 1989). Statistics from the U.S. Bureau of the
Census in 1984 indicate that only 5% of those aged 65 to 74 and 3% of
those over age 75 at that time had ever been divorced. Of women born
between 1910 and 1930 who married, 81% married once and never
divorced (U.S. Senate Special Committee on Aging, 1986). Future
cohorts are more likely to divorce and to redivorce after remarriage
(Goldscheider, 1990; Heaton, 1991; Norton & Moorman, 1987).

Levels of Satisfaction

One of the most common reports about marital satisfaction over
time is that there is a U-shaped trend, with satisfaction dipping in the
middle years of the relationship and increasing again in later years.
The dip in ratings of the relationship has frequently been argued to be
a function of the "family life cycle," which, put simply, means that the
middle years for most couples involve child rearing, which may have
negative effects on the husband-wife relationship (Burr, 1970; Rhyne,
1981; Rollins & Cannon, 1974). However, as Vaillant and Vaillant

(1993) point out, the studies that have presented these findings have all been cross-sectional, which means that different cohorts were compared, and the older sample did not include those who had divorced.

Longitudinal research seems to indicate that for many couples, levels of satisfaction with the relationship stay consistently high. Unhappy couples are more likely to divorce than to stay in their relationships (Vaillant & Vaillant, 1993; Weishaus & Field, 1988). The repeated findings of a dip in marital satisfaction may be chiefly an artifact of cross-sectional research methods.

Communication Patterns

What characterizes communication in couples who have many years of shared environmental experiences? One repeated finding is that long-term couples (who, as noted above, report feeling happy with their marriages) typically move toward a disengaged style of communication. Levels of conflict are relatively low, but so is the amount of involvement.

Swenson, Eskew, and Kohlhepp (1981) found that the older couples they studied reported lower levels of self-disclosure and higher levels of unexpressed feelings than did younger couples. It was unclear whether this was a pattern that had prevailed throughout their marriages or was related to the length of the marriage. Similarly, Rollins and Feldman (1970) found that younger couples reported being more likely to discuss their relationships, whereas older couples reported discussing more impersonal topics, such as religion and home repairs.

Zietlow and Sillars (1988) investigated differences in marital conflict resolution among individuals ranging in age from 23 to 83 years. Couples first ranked a series of potential problems in the relationship, and then were asked to discuss together these problematic issues in their marriages. Their conversations were coded for different conflict resolution strategies. Young couples showed fairly high levels of engagement (e.g., openly and directly dealing with problematic issues), regardless of whether or not they rated an issue as a problem for them. When discussing important issues, middle-aged adults moved toward an analytic style of discussion (problem-solving and solution-orientation remarks) with low levels of confrontative remarks (e.g., blaming and disparaging).

Older adults showed a different pattern. Their conversations were typified by a noncommittal style—they tended to use abstract and hypothetical remarks, statements that were irrelevant to any conflict issue, unfocused questions, and procedural remarks. Zietlow and Sillars characterize this as a low-risk, low-disclosure style of communication, which is much like casual conversation or small talk. They attribute the prevalence of this style to the fact that most problems were not particularly salient to the elderly (for discussion of this research, see Sillars & Wilmot, 1989).

Zietlow and VanLear (1991) studied the relational control behaviors and interaction patterns of 51 couples ranging in age from 24 to 77 years. The couples filled out Spanier's (1976) Dyadic Adjustment Scale and discussed a variety of topics on tape. Their discussions were then coded. The researchers found that, compared with younger couples, long-term couples (married at least 40 years) showed more deference (defined as willingness to relinquish some behavioral option to the other while maintaining some choice, e.g., simple agreement or requesting information). Long-term couples who used most deference were most satisfied (as measured by the Dyadic Adjustment Scale), whereas those who used more structuring (attempts to control the interaction and limit the partner's options) were least satisfied.

In addition, Zietlow and VanLear note that although couples married during the 1930s and 1940s are usually viewed as operating under a hierarchical, husband-dominant power structure, there were no significant sex differences found between long-term husbands' and wives' use of control. Further, the complementarity that one would expect in a husband-dominated marriage (husband one-up, wife one-down) occurred below chance, whereas the rates of symmetry found were higher than expected.

Overall, elderly adults report relatively high, stable levels of marital satisfaction yet appear to have moved toward a rather disengaged style of communication.

Changes in the Long-Term Marriage

Despite the above rather peaceful image of long-term marriages, there are a variety of changes that may affect or disrupt these relationships. Some of these changes are normative; for example, almost everyone who works eventually retires, and most people retire at the much the same age. Other changes, such as divorce or widowhood, may be less predictable. I address below the research on the effects of some of these changes.

Effects of Retirement

Lee (1988) surveyed 2,327 respondents over age 55 and found that although retirement was unrelated to men's assessment of their marriages, it affected women's perceptions. Wives had higher levels of marital satisfaction when they themselves were unemployed (whether through retirement or continuing to be housewives) and their husbands were employed. Wives who worked after their husbands had retired had the lowest levels of satisfaction. One reason that has been offered for this pattern is that couples may expect a more equitable division of household labor upon the husband's retirement but subsequently find that the wife continues to do the majority of the work (Ballweg, 1967; Brubaker & Hennon, 1982; Keating & Cole, 1980; Rexroat & Shehan, 1987; Szinovacz, 1980). As Brubaker (1990) concludes, most couples continue to follow patterns established earlier in their relationship—with disparity in time spent on housework and gender-stereotyped division of tasks.

Keating and Cole (1980) interviewed 400 recently retired teachers (men aged 63-68) and their wives (who had previously stayed home alone). In addition to finding that the husband's retirement did not result in more egalitarian division of household tasks, they found that for some wives, their husbands' retirement was associated with an increase (rather than a reduction) in demands upon their time, because their husbands required companionship and entertainment (see also Ward, 1993).

Loss of Spouse

One change in the marital relationship that can be predicted yet continues to be unexpected is the illness and eventual death of a spouse (Grambs, 1989). The average age at which individuals are widowed has increased: In 1900 the median age for widows was 51. In 1979 the median age for widows was 68 (for widowers the median age was 71). Because most women marry men who are older than themselves, they are more likely to be caretakers of ailing spouses, tend to be widowed earlier, and spend a larger proportion of their life spans following the deaths of their spouses. Two-thirds of all women over age 75 who have ever married will be widows (U.S. Senate Special Committee on Aging, 1984).

How do couples cope when a spouse falls ill? Data from the 1982 National Long-Term Care Study indicate that women provide considerable amounts of care to ailing husbands (Stone, Cafferata, & Sangl, 1987). The U.S. Senate Special Committee on Aging (1988) has reported that in 1982 more than one-third of elderly men living at home and needing care were cared for by their wives; only 1 in 10 elderly disabled women were cared for by their husbands. This discrepancy may be largely a result of the fact that men may have fallen ill or died before their wives required help. In reviewing the literature, Brubaker (1990) concludes that when husbands are available they tend to provide as much care as wives. Husbands and wives are equally as likely to quit paid jobs to care for their spouses, and both have the same patterns of assistance.

There is evidence that women find the role of caretaker more stressful and more damaging to relational satisfaction than do men. Zarit, Todd, and Zarit (1986) found that the caregiving wives in their sample initially reported more subjective burden than did caregiving husbands. Men reported approaching the daily caregiving activities in an instrumental, detached manner, whereas wives expressed difficulty in distancing themselves emotionally. However, when reinterviewed two years later, the wives no longer reported feeling as burdened (see also Fitting, Rabins, Lucas, & Eastham, 1986).

What happens to widowed spouses after their partners die? Is a death that is expected, following prolonged illness, less traumatic for the remaining partner? Hill, Thompson, and Gallagher (1988) interviewed 95 widows (aged 55 years and older) at two months, six months, and one year after the deaths of their spouses. They found that, contrary to their hypotheses, anticipation of the spouse's death was not related to adjustment to bereavement. Women who had known that their husbands would die did not adjust more successfully following their husbands' deaths.

Remarriage after divorce or widowhood is typical for young adults. In contrast, most women who find themselves single after age 50 are likely to remain so for the rest of their lives (Grambs, 1989). The probability of remarriage declines with age, and this decline is faster for women than for men. In 1977 the U.S. Census Bureau reported that "over three-quarters of women who lose their spouses prior to age 30 remarry, but only 6.4 percent of those aged 50-75 do so" (cited in Morgan, 1979). Men are much more likely to remarry; the remarriage rate for widowed men is about seven times higher than that for widowed women (U.S. Senate Special Committee on Aging, 1988).

Summary

Research indicates that recent and current elderly couples show high levels of satisfaction with their relationships. They report fewer salient problems with their relationships than do young couples and display a more disengaged, congenial manner of interaction. Retirement does not appear to have positive effects on long-term marriages—if anything, it appears to increase dissatisfaction with the distribution of household tasks. Finally, historical increases in life expectancy mean that the length of the marital relationship has also increased (among those not divorced). However, this increase also means that a greater part of the relationship is spent in illness and caregiving.

SIBLING RELATIONSHIPS

In contrast to spouses, we do not choose our siblings. Accidents of birth produce what are typically the longest relationships of many people's lives. The majority of elderly adults have at least one living sibling (Scott, 1983), yet after the intimacy of shared childhood, the normative rules of contact and obligation become less clear. What typifies this relationship?

Levels of Contact Between Siblings

In her pioneering work on familial relationships in old age, Shanas (1973) notes that sibling ties are strong. Approximately 40% of the individuals in her cross-national sample had seen at least one of their siblings within a week prior to the survey. Similarly, Scott (1983) found that about 10% of his sample saw a sibling weekly or more; about 20% talked to the most contacted sibling monthly, and about 16% phoned several times a year (see also Cicirelli, 1985).

Goetting (1986) argues that levels of contact between siblings change over time. In early and middle adulthood, she suggests, sibling contact is voluntary. The relationship is increasingly mediated by marriage, parenthood, jobs, and geographic distance, so the ties are looser and more diffuse. It is often the need to take care of frail elderly parents or the need to dismantle dead parents' households that reactivates the relationship. By old age, the relationship is less mediated by children and jobs, and spouses may no longer be alive. Perhaps because of this, elderly adults are more likely to report feeling close and compatible with siblings than are younger adults (Cicirelli, 1985; Scott, 1983). Nonetheless, Goetting (1986) describes the relationship as a "reserved form of companionship and socioeconomic support" (p. 709) expressed chiefly through the sharing of ritual occasions and brief visits.

A number of factors that can predict sibling contact in old age have been identified; these are discussed in turn below.

Proximity. One important predictor of contact is distance. Cicirelli (1980) found that more than one-fourth of her sample of individuals over age 65 had the most contact with siblings who lived in the same city, and more than 50% had the most frequent contact with siblings who lived within 100 miles (for similar results, see Connidis, 1989; Kivett, 1985a; Lee, Mancini, & Maxwell, 1990).

Family Size. A second predictor of the nature of relationships with specific siblings is the overall size of the family. Connidis (1989) found that the larger the family, the greater the likelihood an individual may differentiate among siblings, considering some close friends and others not. The elderly adults in Connidis's study who had one sibling were most likely to report having no sibling they considered a close friend. Overall, the larger the number of siblings in a family, the lower the percentage of all siblings who were considered friends and the higher the probability that at least one sibling was considered a close friend.

Sex of Siblings. Sisters engage in more contact than do sister-brother or brother-brother pairs. Gold (1989) interviewed 65 elderly siblings and found that sisters reported more support exchanges than brothers. Gold also found that brother-brother dyads reported more resentment and lower levels of acceptance than other pairings (sister-sister, sister-brother) (see also Cicirelli, 1980, 1985; Lee et al., 1990; O'Bryant, 1987; Spitze & Logan, 1991; compare Scott, 1983).

Presence of Other Relationships. Sibling relationships often seem to be compensatory. In the presence of other relationships, siblings may be quite uninvolved; in the absence of other relationships, the sibling relationship may become more intense. Connidis (1989) found that sibling pairs in which at least one member was single were in more frequent contact than were married pairs. Anderson (1984) found that widows were more likely to report feeling close emotional attachment to siblings and to report confiding in a sibling than were married elderly adults (see also Martin-Matthews, 1987; Shanas, 1973). Lee and Ihinger-Tallman (1980) analyzed data from 870 questionnaires conducted with adults over 65 and found that men without spouses or children relied more heavily on siblings than did married men or those with living children. Rosenberg and Anspach (1973) found that divorced or separated adults were more likely to interact with siblings than were those who were "maritally intact."

Ethnicity. A final predictor of sibling contact is the race or ethnic background of the family. There is some evidence from interviews conducted by Gold (1989) that black elderly siblings may have closer, less conflicted relationships than elderly whites. In contrast, Suggs (1989) compared black and white elderly siblings in rural North Carolina and found marked similarity in the types of activities shared and the patterns of aid. For both groups, the most important predictor for association was the amount of mutual helping behaviors. Johnson (1982) conducted research on Italian American families and found higher levels of sibling solidarity among them than among white Protestant families or Italian Americans who had married outside the group.

Functions of Sibling Relations

What roles do elderly siblings play for one another? Goetting (1986) has suggested that the single most important functions for elderly siblings may be reminiscence and perceptual validation. Cicirelli (1980) found that elderly adults were more likely to report discussing "old times" with siblings than with their adult children. Moreover, as old age progresses, psychological involvement with siblings appears to become increasingly important (Gold, 1989; see also Ross & Milgram's 1982 exploratory study).

The role of siblings in providing aid during old age appears to be less significant than the socioemotional role of reminiscence. Scott (1983) found that less than 40% of his sample had received assistance from the most contacted sibling—most aid received came from children. Kivett (1985a) found similar results in a rural sample: Siblings and siblings-in-law provided less care than did children, about the same as grandchildren (see also Cicirelli, 1982; McGloshen & O'Bryant, 1988; Suggs & Kivett, 1986). O'Bryant (1987) found that when sibling aid existed, it typically came from unmarried sisters. Brothers and brothers-in-law were seldom mentioned as sources of help (half as frequently as sisters).

It is worth noting again that there may be ethnic and geographic differences in levels of aid provided by siblings. Research by Taylor and associates suggests that siblings' contributions in black families may exceed levels of assistance in white families (Chatters, Taylor, & Jackson, 1986; Taylor, Chatters, & Mays, 1988). Chatters, Taylor, and Neighbors (1989) used data from the National Survey of Black Americans, a nationally representative cross section of blacks over age 18, and found geographic differences in patterns of aid. Blacks residing in the South were more likely to list sisters, friends, and neighbors as helpers than were blacks living in the Northeast and in north-central states. Chatters and associates suggest that the tendency of southern-ers to select sisters and "nonkin" may be a result of specific cultural values or of black migration patterns in the South depleting immedi-ate family resources.

Effects of Siblings on Morale

What effect does contact with siblings have on morale and well-being among elderly adults? Despite the research suggesting that siblings provide a source of shared reminiscence, a number of studies have shown no effect (or mildly negative effects) of sibling contact on reported well-being (Argyle & Furnham, 1983; Essex & Nam, 1987; Lee & Ihinger-Tallman, 1980). In comparison, research on interactions with friends and age peers has found that such interaction correlates positively with measures of emotional well-being among the elderly (Adams, 1971; Arens, 1982; Larson, 1978).

A number of variables may contribute to the effect on morale. First, Stoller (1985) found that the exchange of aid among siblings had negative effects on morale if it was perceived as inequitable. In her study, the inability to reciprocate aid led to lower levels of morale and satisfaction. Second, there may be gender differences in the effects of sibling contact on well-being (Brubaker, 1990). McGhee (1985) studied rural elderly adults and found that the availability of a sister was second only to physical mobility in predicting life satisfaction of women. There were no effects of sibling availability for men. Third, the presence of other relationships alters the effect of sibling contact. Research on widows found that although sibling support was not related to positive affect in the whole sample, among childless widows receipt of support from sisters was positively related to well-being (McGloshen & O'Bryant, 1988; O'Bryant, 1987).

Summary

Siblings provide the most enduring of family ties. Research indi-cates that the sibling relationship is typically rather low-key, despite fairly high levels of contact. Siblings provide each other with oppor-tunities to reminisce about shared experience; they also give one another aid when it is not available from other sources. Nonetheless, there is little evidence that contact between siblings has a positive effect on morale, although there may be more positive effects for sisters.

PARENT-CHILD RELATIONSHIPS

One reason parents give for having children is that it will benefit them in old age. The benefits they foresee include a sense of fulfillment, companionship, continuation of themselves into the future, and economic security. What does research show about the relationship between parents and children in old age?

Historical Changes

As with marital relationships, historical changes in life expectancy have had important effects on parent-child relationships. As life expectancy increases, so does the length of the parent-child relationship. Children may themselves be elderly before their parents die. In 1980, 10% of all people age 65 or older had children over the age of 65 (Brody, 1985). This has important implications for levels of contact and patterns of aid.

Levels of Contact

Shanas (1973) found that 80% of the elderly in one study were in regular contact with at least one of their children. A national survey follow-up in 1975 produced similar results (Shanas, 1980). About half of the elderly respondents who had children had seen one of them on the day of the interview or the day before (for similar results, see Aldous, 1987; Cicirelli, 1983). A number of variables appear to affect levels of contact, some of which are discussed below.

Gender of the Child. Spitze and Logan (1990) analyzed national data with a final sample size of 8,516 adults over age 65. They found that having at least one daughter was important for three kinds of support:

phoning, visiting, and helping. It was the presence of one daughter, rather than the number of daughters, that made the difference. Number of sons was unrelated to the amount of parent-child contact.

Geographic Proximity. Bengtson and Roberts (1991) have noted that proximity is one of the strongest predictors of contact. In fact, in their sample, the effect of proximity was twice the size of the effect of older parents' positive affect for their adult children.

Levels of Affect. As noted above, Bengtson and Roberts (1991) found that older parents' positive affect for their adult children was associated with greater contact, although the effect was not large. The relationship between child's affect for the parent and parent-child association was also significant, although its impact was less than half that of parental affection.

Level of Need. Aldous (1987) found that the parents she studied tended to divide their energy and attention among their children based on their perceptions of the children's needs. The children perceived to be most needy included those who were single or divorced. Aldous also found that parental choosiness carried over to the children parents sought out for comfort when they themselves were upset. These adult children were the ones parents had been most successful in socializing, as indicated by the similarity in values across the generations. Children who served as confidants tended to be married daughters with children of their own.

As noted before, patterns of contact and aid change as life expectancy increases. Brody (1985) argues that long-term parent care has become a normative experience—expectable, though usually unexpected.

Patterns of Caregiving to Parents

Brody (1985) notes that families, not the formal health care system, provide 80% to 90% of medically related and personal care, household tasks, transportation, and shopping for elder adults. Daughters (and sometimes daughters-in-law) tend to be the principal caregivers.

Brody also points out that parent care is not a single "stage" that can be fitted neatly into an orderly sequence of life events. The dependencies associated with old age appear with great variability over a wide time span. In addition, the timing of the marriages and parenthood of both parent and child influences the ages and life stages of adult children when their parents need help.

Care of a particular parent at a particular time may be only one of several caregiving relationships. In Brody's various samples of women providing care, she found that almost half had helped an elderly father before his death and one-third of them had helped other elderly relatives. Moreover, given the discrepancy in life expectancy for men and women, it was inevitable that many of those women would also eventually be called upon to care for their dependent husbands.

Brody (1985) found that although large majorities of all generations reported valuing equal roles for men and women, all age groups expected working daughters rather than working sons to adjust their work schedules for parent care. Some 28% of the nonworking women had quit their jobs because of their elderly mothers' needs for care. A similar proportion of the working women were considering giving up their jobs for the same reason, and some had already reduced the number of hours they worked. Despite this, three-fifths of the women said that "somehow" they felt guilty about not doing enough for their mothers, and three-fourths agreed that nowadays children do not take care of their elderly parents as was the case in the "good old days" (see also Boyd, 1989; Brody & Schoonover, 1986; Kivett, 1985a).

Effects of Parent-Child Relationship on Children

Baruch and Barnett (1983) interviewed women ages 35 to 55 about their relationships with their mothers. They found that psychological well-being (measured by sense of mastery and pleasure) was significantly correlated with the degree to which adult daughters felt close to their mothers. They also found that the relationship between rapport and well-being was stronger for women who were not mothers themselves. Similarly, Barnett, Kibria, Baruch, and Pleck (1991) found that the better a daughter's relationship with her mother or father, the fewer symptoms of anxiety and depression she reported.

This pattern changes when children become primary caregivers. Cicirelli (1983) found that 52% of adult children in his sample reported experiencing some degree of strain in connection with help to elderly parents, and 34% reported substantial strain. Feeling physically worn out, emotionally exhausted, and that the parent was not satisfied no matter what the child did were the most frequently reported stresses. Children also reported feeling tied down in their daily schedules by their parents' needs and having to give up their own social and recreational activities. A total of 51% reported substantial negative feelings toward their parents, such as frustration, impatience, and irritation. Personal strains and negative feelings seemed to be more strongly related to perceived parental dependency than to actual amount of help provided to the parents: Some adult children reported feeling stressed when they were providing little or no help.

Effects of the Parent-Child Relationship on Parents

What about the effects of contact on parents' morale? Pillemer and Suitor (1991) found that the effects of contact depended in part on how much the parent had to worry about the child. They conducted a telephone survey of noninstitutionalized elderly in Canada and found that parents who reported that their children had any physical or mental problems had higher depression scores than did their counterparts who reported no such problems in their children. Conflict with children was also positively related to depression but did not reduce the effect of children's problems. Children's financial dependence did not affect parents' levels of depression—nor, interestingly enough, did the amount of emotional support offered by the child to the parent.

In fact, there is some research indicating that adult children have relatively little positive impact on parents' morale. Glenn and McLanahan (1981) analyzed interview data with 1,500 adults from the 1973-1978 General Social Surveys and found that middle-aged and elderly couples without children were just as satisfied and happy as couples with children. Keith (1983) surveyed elderly adults (aged 72 and older) in small rural towns and found that an equal proportion (35%) of childless elderly adults and parents reported feeling lonely.

Similarly, Kivett and Lerner (1980) examined couples in rural towns and found that although childless couples had fewer social contacts, they did not report feeling any more lonely or being less likely to have confidants than did elderly parents.

Rempel (1985) found that parental status made relatively little difference in most aspects of life. Elderly parents had larger networks of friends, were more integrated into their neighborhoods, and were more likely to own their own homes, but childless elderly adults were in better health. There were no significant differences between parents and nonparents in reported life satisfaction.

Summary

Parent-child relationships now frequently continue into the children's old age. Daughters appear to play a critical role in maintaining these relationships and in providing care to elderly parents. Overall, these relationships have positive effects on children's morale, except when caregiving causes stress. In contrast, there is relatively little evidence that contact with children has positive effects on elderly adults' morale.

GRANDPARENTING

The chances of having a living grandparent are higher today than at any previous time. As of 1981, as reported by Serow, there were approximately 48 grandparents per 100 parents. At the beginning of the twentieth century, there were only 14 grandparents per 100 parents.

Troll (1983) reports that the modal age of becoming a grandparent is around 49-51 for women and 51-53 for men. However, this seems to vary considerably by population (Brubaker, 1990). One study of black families placed the median age of black grandmothers at 32 years and the median age of great-grandmothers at 56 years (Burton & Bengtson, 1985). In comparison, Thompson and Walker (1987) surveyed college students and found that most of the students' grandmothers were 60 years old or older.

Historical Changes in Grandparenting Norms

Hagestad (1988) describes two recent changes in grandparenting. First, the transition from grandparenthood into great-grandparenthood and great-great-grandparenthood has become more common, particularly for women. Second, the reduction in age at which women finish their childbearing (because of smaller families) makes it less likely than in the past that women will experience overlaps between active parenting and grandparenting. For men the trends are less clear, because there is greater variability in ages of fathers than of mothers. A third change in grandparenting, not discussed by Hagestad, has been caused by the increase in divorce and remarriage: More and more grandparents have stepgrandchildren.

Normative Styles of Grandparenting

In a classic study, Neugarten and Weinstein (1964) interviewed 70 middle-class grandparent couples in order to assess grandparents' attitudes toward their role and the ways in which they played out that role. They found that the majority reported finding comfort, satisfaction, and pleasure in being a grandparent, although approximately a third acknowledged some negative aspects, such as conflict with the parents about rearing the grandchild.

Based on their interviews, Neugarten and Weinstein developed a grandparenting typology. The first style of grandparenting they label *formal*: Grandparents in this style like to provide special treats for their grandchildren and even baby-sit occasionally, but they also maintain a clear line between parenting and grandparenting and are careful not to offer advice on child rearing. The second style is the *fun seeker*: Grandparents of this sort join their grandchildren specifically to have fun. They derive pleasure from interacting with the children and consider authority lines irrelevant. The third style is the *surrogate parent*: These are grandparents (usually grandmothers) who take on much of the parenting role, frequently because the grandchildren's mother works. Fourth is the *reservoir of family wisdom*: This is typically the grandfather who represents an authoritative older figure who dispenses lessons on special skills or resources. Fifth is the *distant figure*: These are grandparents who have contact with their grandchildren only on holidays and ritual occasions. According to Neugarten and Weinstein, the two most common types of grandparents are fun seekers and distant figures (for a similar typology, see Cherlin & Furstenberg, 1986).

Cherlin and Furstenberg (1986) found that among several activities rated by grandparents in their sample, the most common performed by grandparents were joking with their grandchildren, giving the grandchildren money, and watching television with the children. The least common were teaching the grandchildren new skills or games and helping to settle disagreements between grandchildren and their parents.

Nonnormative Grandparenting Roles

Grandparents as Primary Caretakers

Although the majority of grandparents express little interest in acting as parents to their grandchildren, there are situations in which grandparents are called upon to act as primary caretakers. As Troll (1983) argues:

> Probably few grandparents wish to return to parenting with their grandchildren . . . but they do remain alert to what goes on. If they think all is well, they prefer to remain formal and distant or indulgent grandparents, visiting their children and grandchildren as one part of their regular life activities but otherwise enjoying their own life. It is more interesting to be with their peers than helping out with needy children. . . . If there is trouble, however, they have to give up much of their personal, nonfamily life to meet the needs of the family. (pp. 66-67)

The U.S. Census Bureau estimates that in 1991 approximately 3.3 million children in the United States lived with grandparents (cited in Jendrek, 1993). In approximately half of these cases, the mother was present in the home; in 28% of these cases, no parent was present. Black children were much more likely to live in a grandparent's home than were white children or children of Hispanic origin; the proportions were 12.3%, 3.7%, and 5.6% for black, white, and Hispanic children, respectively (Jendrek, 1993).

"Divorced" Grandparents

More than 60% of divorcing couples have at least one minor child (Spanier & Glick, 1981). The effect of divorce on the grandparenting relationship seems to differ depending on whether the grandparents are biologically linked to the custodial parent. Johnson and Bahrer (1987) interviewed 50 parent-grandmother dyads in which the parent was divorced for less than three years. The grandmothers were reinterviewed an average of 16 months later. The researchers found that when the mother was biologically linked to a grandparent, that grandparent's family network contracted, dropping out the former son-in-law. Formal aid was offered to the daughter, presumably to facilitate care of the child. However, when the father was biologically linked and the mother was the grandparent's former daughter-in-law, the network typically expanded. The grandparent worked hard to maintain contact with the former daughter-in-law (who typically had custody of the grandchildren) as well as taking on a new daughter-in-law through the son's remarriage.

Matthews and Sprey (1984) conducted exploratory interviews with 18 couples who had at least one divorced adult child. They found that maternal grandparents were in a much better position to maintain relationships with their grandchildren than were paternal grandparents (presumably because mothers were more likely to get custody of the children). Maternal grandparents were much more likely to be called upon by their children for financial and emotional support. Similarly, Cherlin and Furstenberg (1986) found that divorce often leads to an intensification of bonds with grandparents on the "custodial" side but a weakening of bonds with the "noncustodial" grandparents.

Stepgrandparenting

As their adult children divorce and then remarry, parents may suddenly find themselves grandparents to new sets of children. In addition to maintaining links with biologically linked grandchildren who may now reside with former daughters-in-law or sons-in-law, grandparents are faced with the task of developing relationships with stepgrandchildren.

Visher and Visher (1979) describe a number of differences between stepfamilies and "intact" families: In stepfamilies, (a) there is a biological parent elsewhere, (b) members have sustained a primary relationship loss, (c) the parent-child relationship predates the current marriage, (d) children are members of more than one household, and (e) the stepparent is not legally related to the child. How do stepgrandparent-stepgrandchild relationships develop in the face of such ambiguity?

Cherlin and Furstenberg (1986) found that the age of the stepgrandchild affects the development of the stepgrandparenting relationship. The older the stepgrandchild at the time his or her parent remarries, the less emphasis stepgrandparents place on the new stepgrandparent role.

Sanders and Trygstad (1989) had 125 college students describe their relationships with their grandparents and 54 college students describe their relationships with their stepgrandparents. Comparisons between the two groups' descriptions indicated that grandchildren desired and had more contact with their grandparents than stepgrandchildren did with their stepgrandparents. The mean reported amount of contact for grandchildren was about once per month, but for stepgrandchildren the amount was between several times per year and once per year. Grandchildren also rated the relationship as more important.

Variables Affecting the Grandparenting Relationship

As Cherlin and Furstenberg (1986) point out, relationships are far from static, and they depend on a variety of variables that may be subject to change. Below are brief discussions of some of the variables that have been found to affect relationships between grandparents and their grandchildren.

Age of Grandchild and Grandparent

Kahana and Kahana (1970) found age differences in reasons given for liking grandparents. The youngest children in their sample (ages 4-5) discussed grandparents in egocentric and concrete terms—what grandparents gave the children in love, food, and presents. The middle age group (ages 8-9) focused on mutuality in the relationship, such as going to ball games together. Children in the oldest group (ages 11-12) were least likely to express preferences for particular grandparents, but when they did, they mentioned indulgent, treat-giving grandparents.

Neugarten and Weinstein (1964) found that younger grandparents were more likely to have either distant or fun-seeking relationships with their grandchildren. In contrast, older grandparents had formal relationships with their grandchildren. Cherlin and Furstenberg (1986) found a similar pattern, but they argue that it may be best explained by the ages of the grandchildren rather than by the ages of the grandparents. They point out that it is far easier to play with a young child than with an adolescent and suggest that some grandparents may move from a fun-seeking style to a more formal style as their grandchildren grow up and seek more independence.

Other work suggests that there are distinct perceptions about the age at which people should become grandparents and that these perceptions can have powerful effects. McGreal (1983, cited in Hagestad, 1988) interviewed individuals who were about to become grandparents and found that men and women who were entering grandparenthood at the expected time felt more prepared to be involved with their grandchildren than did individuals who felt "off time." Hagestad and Burton (1986) also found effects of perceptions about the "right time" to become grandmothers. Black women whose grandchildren arrived "too early" (the women were between 25 and 38 years old) reported lacking preparation for the role, having little peer support, and wanting to reject the role. Compared with other black women who became grandmothers at a more expected or "on-time" age (42-57), early grandmothers were more likely to report that the role was in conflict with education, parenting, work, and friendships.

Gender of the Grandparent

Kahana and Kahana (1970) interviewed white children ages 4 to 12 about their attitudes toward their grandparents and found that the majority of the children expressed preferences for their maternal grandmothers. Crawford (1981) argues that women view grandparenting as a source of biological renewal, whereas men value the opportunity to share information or financial resources, or to take pride in grandchildren's accomplishments (see also Neugarten & Weinstein, 1964).

In a study of three-generation families, Hagestad (1985) found that the grandfathers attempted to influence young adult grandchildren only in instrumental matters (e.g., jobs, finances), whereas grandmothers attempted to influence grandchildren's interpersonal and instrumental activities. These influence patterns were most pronounced in same-sex grandparent-grandchild dyads.

Thomas (1986a, 1986b; same data set in both articles) found a small but significant gender difference in levels of satisfaction with grandparenting: Grandmothers had slightly higher levels of satisfaction than did grandfathers. Thomas (1986b) also reports some gender differences in predictors of satisfaction. For women in Thomas's sample, perceived responsibility for helping grandchildren and providing care positively predicted satisfaction. For men, both these variables were significant positive predictors, but, in addition, men who were themselves relatively old and who had relatively young grandchildren were more likely to express high levels of satisfaction.

Kivett (1985b) interviewed 99 grandfathers living in a rural transitional area and had them rank their 4 "top roles in life today" out of 10 possible categories. She found that more than half her sample ranked grandparenting as their third most important role; only 5% ranked it as their most important role. Church participant and "leisure user" were both more likely than grandparenting to be picked as the most important role. Kivett concludes that her data show the grandfather role to be of little relative importance, despite the fact that the older men had relatively high expectations for assistance from grandchildren in times of need.

Geographic Proximity

Harris and associates (1975, cited in Troll, 1983) surveyed Americans over the age of 65 and found that three-fourths of them had living grandchildren, and that three-quarters of those who had living grandchildren saw them at least once every week. However, as with siblings, levels of contact seem largely dependent upon proximity. Cherlin and Furstenberg (1986) found that geographic distance alone counted for 62% of the variance in frequency of contact (see also Kivett, 1985b; Whitbeck, Hoyt, & Huck, 1993).

The possibility of indirect effects of distance on the quality of the relationship is suggested by Matthews and Sprey's (1985) finding that college students' reports of their relationships with their grandparents were predicted by the number of interactions during childhood. Those who visited at least three times a year were more likely than those who did not to describe their relationships as close.

Parent-Grandparent Relationship

The amount of contact and the quality of the relationship between grandchildren and grandparents seems to depend considerably on the relationships between children's parents and grandparents. As Whitbeck et al. (1993) describe it, parents set the conditions and provide the emotional context for the grandparent-grandchild interaction. Because of this, the relationship is typically described as indirect and as mediated by the relevant parent (Robertson, 1975).

Cherlin and Furstenberg (1986) found that where grandparents reported emotionally close relationships with their daughters, the grandparents saw their grandchildren about twice as often as those who viewed their relationships with their daughters as "fairly close" or "not very close."

Whitbeck et al. (1993) found that although geographic proximity was a strong predictor of levels of contact, it was a much weaker predictor of the quality of the grandparent-grandchild relationship than the relationship between the child's parent and the child's grandparent. In particular, parents' recollections of negative childhood interactions with their own parents (the grandparents in this study) were consistently negatively related to the quality of the grandparent-grandchild relationship. Matthews and Sprey (1985) report similar findings. In addition, they found that mothers' relationships with their mothers-in-law were an important predictor of contact between grandchildren and grandparents.

Finally, Thompson and Walker (1987) found that grandmothers' feelings for college-age granddaughters were indistinguishable from their feelings for their daughters. When grandmothers felt positively about their daughters, they also reported feeling positively about their granddaughters. Interestingly, granddaughters' feelings for their grandmothers were also mediated by their attitudes toward their mothers. The more grandchildren liked their mothers, the more they liked their grandmothers.

Great-Grandparenting

As Hagestad (1988) notes, it is increasingly common for adults to make the transition from being grandparents to being great-grandparents or even great-great-grandparents. Shanas (1980) reports that 50% of all people age 65 and over with living children are members of four-generation families. What characterizes relationships between great-grandparents and their great-grandchildren?

Wentowski (1985) conducted an exploratory study using in-depth interviews with 19 great-grandmothers ranging in age from 66 to 92 years. The most frequent comment among her subjects was that being a great-grandmother was "just like being a grandmother." However, the women in her study reported that they were not involved with great-grandchildren to the same degree that they had been with their grandchildren. Their direct social involvement with great-grandchildren was limited by diminished physical strength and/or geographic distance. About a third of the 19 great-grandmothers felt that the infrequency of visits with great-grandchildren might be a blessing in disguise, because the visits were too tiring. Finally, Wentowski notes, the women reported thinking of themselves first as mothers and grandmothers, and second as great-grandmothers.

Doka and Mertz (1988) conducted interviews with 40 great-grandparents recruited from senior centers and organizations in New York

City and New Jersey. They found that 93% of the great-grandparents in their sample reported feeling very favorable about being a great-grandparent and finding great emotional satisfaction in the role. There were three common themes in the interview responses: (a) that being a great-grandparent provides a sense of personal and familial renewal, (b) that great-grandchildren provide diversion—there are new things to do and new places to go as a result of having a great-grandchild, and (c) that becoming a great-grandparent feels like a milestone, a mark of longevity.

Interestingly, Doka and Mertz also report that although virtually all the great-grandparents they surveyed had very positive feelings about their role, 78% maintained a remote style in which there was limited and ritualistic contact with great-grandchildren. As in Wentowski's study, these respondents reported lacking the patience and energy to deal with young children for prolonged periods. The remaining 22% of these great-grandparents maintained a close style in which they reported seeing their great-grandchildren at least once a month, baby-sitting, taking the children shopping or on trips, and attending the children's sports and leisure events.

Summary

Not only are children today more likely than those of the past to have living grandparents, current social trends have brought about a new variety of grandparenting styles. In particular, increases in divorce and remarriage have changed the nature of grandparenting. A number of factors affect the relationship between grandparents and their grandchildren, including geographic proximity and the nature of the grandparent-parent relationship.

CONCLUSION

Such are the family ties that bind us in old age. The results of numerous studies suggest that elderly people remain closely attached to family members and that there are considerable exchanges of aid. Interestingly, much of the research also suggests that family relationships, though they may be strong and meaningful, play limited roles in determining an individual's morale in old age. In contrast, there is considerable evidence that interactions with friends and age peers correlate positively with measures of emotional well-being among the elderly (for reviews, see Adams, 1971; Larson, 1978). It is well worth investigating further the social networks of the elderly and the differences between family and peer interactions.

REFERENCES

Adams, D. L. (1971). Correlates of satisfaction among the elderly. *The Gerontologist, 11*, 64-68.

Aldous, J. (1987). New views on the family life of the elderly and the near-elderly. *Journal of Marriage and the Family, 49*, 227-234.

Anderson, T. B. (1984). Widowhood as a life transition: Its impact on kinship ties. *Journal of Marriage and the Family, 46*, 105-114.

Arens, D. A. (1982). Widowhood and well-being: An examination of sex differences within a causal model. *International Journal of Aging and Human Development, 15*, 27-40.

Argyle, M., & Furnham, A. (1983). Sources of satisfaction and conflict in long-term relationships. *Journal of Marriage and the Family, 45*, 481-493.

Ballweg, J. A. (1967). Resolution of conjugal role adjustment after retirement. *Journal of Marriage and the Family, 29*, 277-281.

Barnett, R. C., Kibria, N., Baruch, G. K., & Pleck, J. H. (1991). Adult daughter-parent relationships and their associations with daughters' subjective well-being and psychological distress. *Journal of Marriage and the Family, 53*, 29-42.

Baruch, G. K., & Barnett, R. C. (1983). Adult daughters' relationships with their mothers. *Journal of Marriage and the Family, 45*, 601-606.

Bengtson, V. L. & Roberts, R. E. L. (1991). Intergenerational solidarity in aging families: An example of formal theory construction. *Journal of Marriage and the Family, 53*, 856-870.

Boyd, C. J. (1989). Mothers and daughters: A discussion of theory and research. *Journal of Marriage and the Family, 51*, 291-301.

Brody, E. M. (1985). Parent care as a normative family stress. *The Gerontologist, 25*, 19-29.

Brody, E. M., & Schoonover, C. B. (1986). Patterns of parent-care when adult daughters work and when they do not. *The Gerontologist, 26*, 372-381.

Brubaker, T. H. (1990). Families in later life: A burgeoning research area. *Journal of Marriage and the Family, 52*, 959-981.

Brubaker, T. H., & Hennon, C. B. (1982). Responsibility for household tasks: Comparing dual-earner and dual-retired marriages. In M. Szinovacz (Ed.), *Women's retirement: Policy implications of recent research* (pp. 205-219). Beverly Hills, CA: Sage.

Burr, W. R. (1970). Satisfaction with various aspects of marriage over the life cycle: A random middle class sample. *Journal of Marriage and the Family, 32*, 29-37.

Burton, L. M., & Bengtson, V. L. (1985). Black grandmothers: Issues of timing and continuity of roles. In V. L. Bengtson & J. F. Robertson (Eds.), *Grandparenthood* (pp. 61-80). Beverly Hills, CA: Sage.

Caplow, T., Bahr, H. M., Chadwick, B. A., Hill, R., & Williamson, M. H. (1982). *Middletown families: Fifty years of change and continuity.* Minneapolis: University of Minnesota Press.

Chatters, L. M., Taylor, R. J., & Jackson, J. S. (1986). Aged blacks' choices for an informal helper network. *Journal of Gerontology, 41,* 94-100.

Chatters, L. M., Taylor, R. J., & Neighbors, H. W. (1989). Size of informal helper network mobilized during a serious personal problem among black Americans. *Journal of Marriage and the Family, 51,* 667-676.

Cherlin, A. J., & Furstenberg, F. F. (1986). *The new American grandparent: A place in the family, a life apart.* New York: Basic Books.

Cicirelli, V. G. (1980). Sibling relationships in adulthood: A lifespan perspective. In L. W. Poon (Ed.), *Aging in the 1980s* (pp. 455-462). Washington, DC: American Psychological Association.

Cicirelli, V. G. (1982). Sibling influence throughout the lifespan. In M. E. Lamb & B. Sutton-Smith (Eds.), *Sibling relationships: Their nature and significance across the lifespan* (pp. 267-284). Hillsdale, NJ: Lawrence Erlbaum.

Cicirelli, V. G. (1983). Adult children and their elderly parents. In T. H. Brubaker (Ed.), *Family relationships in later life* (pp. 31-46). Beverly Hills, CA: Sage.

Cicirelli, V. G. (1985). The role of siblings as family caregivers. In W. J. Sauer & R. T. Coward (Eds.), *Social support networks and the care of the elderly* (pp. 93-107). New York: Springer.

Connidis, I. A. (1989). Siblings as friends in later life. *American Behavioral Scientist, 33,* 81-93.

Crawford, M. (1981). Not disengaged: Grandparents in literature and reality, an empirical study in role satisfaction. *Sociological Review, 29,* 499-519.

Doka, K. J., & Mertz, M. E. (1988). The meaning and significance of great-grandparenthood. *The Gerontologist, 28,* 192-197.

Essex, M. J., & Nam, S. (1987). Marital status and loneliness among older women: The differential importance of close family and friends. *Journal of Marriage and the Family, 49,* 93-106.

Faver, C. A. (1984). *Women in transition: Career, family, and life satisfaction in three cohorts.* New York: Praeger.

Fitting, M., Rabins, P., Lucas, M. J., & Eastham, J. (1986). Caregivers for dementia patients: A comparison of husbands and wives. *The Gerontologist, 26,* 248-252.

Glenn, N., & McLanahan, S. (1981). The effects of offspring on the psychological well-being of older adults. *Journal of Marriage and the Family, 43,* 409-421.

Goetting, A. (1986). The developmental tasks of siblingship over the life cycle. *Journal of Marriage and the Family, 48,* 703-714.

Gold, D. T. (1989). Generational solidarity: Conceptual antecedents and consequences. *American Behavioral Scientist, 33,* 19-32.

Goldscheider, F. K. (1990). The aging of the gender revolution: What do we know and what do we need to know? *Research on Aging, 12,* 531-545.

Grambs, J. D. (1989). *Women over forty: Visions and realities* (rev. ed.). New York: Springer.

Hagestad, G. O. (1985). Continuity and connectedness. In V. L. Bengtson & J. F. Robertson (Eds.), *Grandparenthood* (pp. 31-48). Beverly Hills, CA: Sage.

Hagestad, G. O. (1988). Demographic change and the life course: Some emerging trends in the family realm. *Family Relations, 37,* 405-410.

Hagestad, G. O., & Burton, L. (1986). Grandparenthood, life context, and family development. *American Behavioral Scientist, 29,* 471-484.

Louis Harris & Associates. (1975). *The myth and reality of aging in America.* Washington, DC: National Council on Aging.

Heaton, T. B. (1991). Time-related determinants of marital dissolution. *Journal of Marriage and the Family, 53,* 285-295.

Hill, C. D., Thompson, L. W., & Gallagher, D. (1988). The role of anticipatory bereavement in older women's adjustment to widowhood. *The Gerontologist, 28,* 792-796.

Holahan, C. K. (1984). Marital attitudes over 40 years: A longitudinal and cohort analysis. *Journal of Gerontology, 38,* 49-57.

Jendrek, M. P. (1993). Grandparents who parent their grandchildren: Effects of lifestyle. *Journal of Marriage and the Family, 55,* 609-621.

Johnson, C. L. (1982). Sibling solidarity: Its origin and function in Italian-American families. *Journal of Marriage and the Family, 44,* 155-167.

Johnson, C. L., & Bahrer, B. M. (1987). Marital instability and the changing kinship networks of grandparents. *The Gerontologist, 27,* 330-335.

Kahana, B., & Kahana, E. (1970). Grandparenthood from the perspective of the developing grandchild. *Developmental Psychology, 3,* 98-105.

Keating, N. C., & Cole, P. (1980). What do I do with him 24 hours a day? Changes in the housewife role after retirement. *The Gerontologist, 20,* 84-89.

Keith, P. M. (1983). A comparison of the resources of parents and childless men and women in very old age. *Family Relations, 32,* 403-409.

Kivett, V. R. (1985a). Consanguinity and kin level: Their relative importance to the helping networks of older adults. *Journal of Gerontology, 40,* 228-234.

Kivett, V. R. (1985b). Grandfathers and grandchildren: Patterns of association, helping, and psychological closeness. *Family Relations, 34,* 565-571.

Kivett, V. R., & Lerner, R. M. (1980). Perspectives on the childless rural elderly: A comparative analysis. *The Gerontologist, 20,* 708-716.

Larson, R. (1978). Thirty years of research on the subjective well-being of older Americans. *Journal of Gerontology, 33,* 109-125.

Lee, G. R. (1988). Marital satisfaction in later life: The effects of nonmarital roles. *Journal of Marriage and the Family, 50,* 775-783.

Lee, G. R., & Ihinger-Tallman, M. (1980). Sibling interaction and morale: The effects of family relations on older people. *Research on Aging, 2,* 367-391.

Lee, T. R., Mancini, J. A., & Maxwell, J. W. (1990). Sibling relationships in adulthood: Contact patterns and motivations. *Journal of Marriage and the Family, 52,* 431-440.

Mares, M. L., & Fitzpatrick, M. A. (in press). The aging couple. In J. Nussbaum & J. Coupland (Eds.), *Handbook of communication and aging research.* Hillsdale, NJ: Lawrence Erlbaum.

Martin-Matthews, A. (1987). Support systems of widows in Canada. In H. Z. Lopata (Ed.), *Widows* (Vol. 2, pp. 225-250). Durham, NC: Duke University Press.

Matthews, S. H., & Sprey, J. (1984). The impact of divorce on grandparenthood: An explanatory study. *The Gerontologist, 24,* 41-47.

Matthews, S. H., & Sprey, J. (1985). Adolescents' relationships with grandparents: An empirical contribution to conceptual clarification. *Journal of Gerontology, 40*, 621-626.

McGhee, J. L. (1985). The effects of siblings on the life satisfaction of the rural elderly. *Journal of Marriage and the Family, 47*, 85-91.

McGloshen, T. H., & O'Bryant, S. L. (1988). The psychological well-being of older, recent widows. *Psychology of Women Quarterly, 12*, 99-116.

McGreal, C. E. (1983, August). *Transition to grandparenthood: Significance of the role to "expectant" grandparents*. Paper presented at the annual meeting of the American Psychological Association, Anaheim, CA.

Morgan, L. A. (1979). Problems of widowhood. In P. K. Ragan (Ed.), *Aging parents* (pp. 66-82). Los Angeles: University of Southern California Press.

Neugarten, B. L., & Weinstein, K. K. (1964). The changing American grandparent. *Journal of Marriage and the Family, 26*, 199-204.

Norton, A. J., & Moorman, J. E. (1987). Current trends in marriage and divorce among American women. *Journal of Marriage and the Family, 49*, 3-14.

O'Bryant, S. L. (1987). Sibling support and older widows' well-being. *Journal of Marriage and the Family, 50*, 173-183.

Pillemer, K., & Suitor, J. J. (1991). "Will I ever escape my child's problems?" Effects of adult children's problems on elderly parents. *Journal of Marriage and the Family, 53*, 585-594.

Rempel, J. (1985). Childless elderly: What are they missing? *Journal of Marriage and the Family, 47*, 343-348.

Rexroat, C., & Shehan, C. (1987). The family life cycle and spouses' time in housework. *Journal of Marriage and the Family, 49*, 737-750.

Rhyne, D. (1981). Bases of marital satisfaction among men and women. *Journal of Marriage and the Family, 43*, 941-955.

Robertson, J. F. (1975). Interaction in three generation families, parents as mediators: Toward a theoretical perspective. *International Journal of Aging and Human Development, 6*, 103-110.

Rollins, B. C., & Cannon, K. L. (1974). Marital satisfaction over the family life cycle: A reevaluation. *Journal of Marriage and the Family, 36*, 271-282.

Rollins, B. C., & Feldman, H. (1970). Marital satisfaction over the family life cycle. *Journal of Marriage and the Family, 32*, 20-28.

Rosenberg, G. S., & Anspach, D. F. (1973). Sibling solidarity in the working class. *Journal of Marriage and the Family, 35*, 108-113.

Ross, H. G., & Milgram, J. I. (1982). Important variables in adult sibling relationships: A qualitative study. In M. E. Lamb & B. Sutton-Smith (Eds.), *Sibling relationships: Their nature and significance across the lifespan* (pp. 225-249). Hillsdale, NJ: Lawrence Erlbaum.

Sanders, G. F., & Trygstad, D. W. (1989). Stepgrandparents and grandparents: The view from young adults. *Family Relations, 38*, 71-75.

Scott, J. P. (1983). Siblings and other kin. In T. H. Brubaker (Ed.), *Family relationships in later life* (pp. 47-62). Beverly Hills, CA: Sage.

Serow, W. J. (1981). Population and other policy responses to an era of sustained low fertility. *Social Science Quarterly, 62*, 323-332.

Shanas, E. (1973). Family-kin networks and aging in cross-cultural perspective. *Journal of Marriage and the Family, 35*, 505-511.

Shanas, E. (1980). Older people and their families: The new pioneers. *Journal of Marriage and the Family, 42,* 9-15.

Sillars, A. L., & Wilmot, W. W. (1989). Marital communication across the life span. In J. Nussbaum (Ed.), *Lifespan communication* (pp. 225-253). Hillsdale, NJ: Lawrence Erlbaum.

Spanier, G. B. (1976). Measuring dyadic adjustment: New scales for assessing the quality of marriage and similar dyads. *Journal of Marriage and the Family, 38,* 15-28.

Spanier, G. B., & Glick, P. C. (1981). Marital instability in the United States: Some correlates and recent changes. *Family Relations, 30,* 329-338.

Spitze, G., & Logan, J. R. (1990). Sons, daughters, and intergenerational social support. *Journal of Marriage and the Family, 52,* 420-430.

Spitze, G., & Logan, J. R. (1991). Sibling structure and intergenerational relations. *Journal of Marriage and the Family, 53,* 871-884.

Stoller, E. P. (1985). Exchange patterns in the informal support networks of the elderly: The impact of reciprocity on morale. *Journal of Marriage and the Family, 47,* 335-342.

Stone, R., Cafferata, G. L., & Sangl, J. (1987). Caregivers of the frail elderly: A national profile. *The Gerontologist, 27,* 616-626.

Suggs, P. K. (1989). Predictors of association among older siblings: A black/white comparison. *American Behavioral Scientist, 33,* 70-80.

Suggs, P. K., & Kivett, V. R. (1986). Rural/urban elderly and siblings: Their value consensus. *International Journal of Aging and Human Development, 24,* 149-159.

Swenson, C. H., Eskew, R. W., & Kohlhepp, K. A. (1981). Stage of family life cycle, ego development, and the marriage relationship. *Journal of Marriage and the Family, 43,* 841-853.

Szinovacz, M. E. (1980). Female retirement: Effects on spousal roles and marital adjustment. *Journal of Family Issues, 1,* 423-440.

Taylor, R. J., Chatters, L. M., & Mays, V. M. (1988). Parents, children, siblings, in-laws, and non-kin as sources of emergency assistance to black Americans. *Family Relations, 37,* 298-304.

Thomas, J. L. (1986a). Age and sex differences in perceptions of grandparenting. *Journal of Gerontology, 41,* 417-423.

Thomas, J. L. (1986b). Gender differences in satisfaction with grandparenting. *Psychology and Aging, 1,* 215-219.

Thompson, L., & Walker, A. J. (1987). Mothers as mediators of intimacy between grandmothers and their young adult granddaughters. *Family Relations, 36,* 72-77.

Troll, L. (1983). Grandparents: The family watchdogs. In T. H. Brubaker (Ed.), *Family relationships in later life* (pp. 63-74). Beverly Hills, CA: Sage.

U.S. Senate Special Committee on Aging. (1984). *Aging America.* Washington, DC: U.S. Department of Health and Human Services.

U.S. Senate Special Committee on Aging. (1986). *Aging America.* Washington, DC: U.S. Department of Health and Human Services.

U.S. Senate Special Committee on Aging. (1988). *Aging America.* Washington, DC: U.S. Department of Health and Human Services.

Vaillant, C. O., & Vaillant, G. E. (1993). Is the U-curve of marital satisfaction an illusion? A 40-year study of marriage. *Journal of Marriage and the Family, 55,* 230-239.

Visher, E. B., & Visher, J. S. (1979). *Stepfamilies: A guide to working with stepparents and stepchildren.* New York: Brunner/Mazel.

Ward, R. A. (1993). Marital happiness and household equity in later life. *Journal of Marriage and the Family, 55,* 427-438.

Weishaus, S., & Field, D. (1988). A half century of marriage: Continuity or change? *Journal of Marriage and the Family, 50,* 763-774.

Wentowski, G. J. (1985). Older women's perceptions of great-grandmotherhood: A research note. *The Gerontologist, 25,* 593-596.

Whitbeck, L. B., Hoyt, D. R., & Huck, S. M. (1993). Family relationship history, contemporary parent-grandparent relationship quality, and the grandparent-grandchild relationship. *Journal of Marriage and the Family, 55,* 1025-1035.

Zarit, S., Todd, P., & Zarit, J. (1986). Subjective burden of husbands and wives as caregivers: A longitudinal study. *The Gerontologist, 26,* 260-266.

Zietlow, P. H., & Sillars, A. L. (1988). Life-stage differences in communication during marital conflicts. *Journal of Social and Personal Relationships, 5,* 223-245.

Zietlow, P. H., & VanLear, C. A. (1991). Marriage duration and relational control: A study of developmental patterns. *Journal of Marriage and the Family, 53,* 773-785.

Communication and Family Culture

ALAN L. SILLARS

The contemporary family is marked, as much as by anything else, by pluralism (Hareven, 1982). Even what we refer to as "mainstream culture" is really a mosaic of alternative lifestyles, living arrangements, and family values. Cultural differences greatly enrich this mixture, which complicates description of families but also provides a way of gaining perspective on family diversity. Ethnic and national cultures magnify the contrasts that distinguish families in general. This serves to highlight qualities that distinguish all families as relationship cultures.

Relationship culture is a metaphor used to describe communication in close relationships, both family and otherwise (see Baxter, 1987; Montgomery, 1992; Wood, 1982). The implication of the metaphor is that people establish their own moral and social order within close relationships, including private codes and unique sets of rules for interacting. Ironically, this use of the term *culture* reveals a cultural bias, as it highlights uniqueness and privacy of close relationships over other cultural values, such as interdependence, tradition, obligation, and loyalty. This emphasis obscures one of the main factors distinguishing culturally diverse families, namely, the varying degrees and forms of autonomy versus connection between intimate relationships and larger collectivities (Montgomery, 1992). Still, the metaphor of relationships as cultures is worth holding on to, albeit in expanded form. The strength of the metaphor is that, by emphasizing the plurality of relationship definitions, it avoids simplistic and idealized notions of "communication quality," "intimacy," "normalcy," and other such concepts, which recent critics have repeatedly thrashed for their ideological treatment within communication research (e.g., Brown & Rogers, 1991; Montgomery, 1988; Stafford & Dainton, 1994).

In this chapter I draw upon culture in the macro sense—that is, ethnicity, national culture, and social class—in order to clarify cultural processes affecting all families. Specifically, my intent is to explore associations involving family structure/ideology and family communication. A similar interest in family structure and communication has driven research on family types, although this research has not had an intercultural focus.

As a focus of investigation, family communication is distinct from family structure; however, it can be very misleading to isolate these topics. Communication is embedded within a matrix of beliefs and patterns that give rise to communication and, in turn, are maintained or redefined through the exchange. Yet we often talk about communication in families without considering the surrounding matrix. For example, of the many studies that have considered communication and marital satisfaction or distress, only a small number have considered how cultural orientations contribute to the meaning of communication patterns.

In the forthcoming discussion I first take up structural characteristics that distinguish culturally diverse families. Later, I consider the relevance of these structural considerations to various functions of communication.

STRUCTURAL CHARACTERISTICS
OF FAMILY CULTURES

I use the term *family structure* to refer simultaneously to characteristics of family organization (e.g., authority or kinship structure) and ideology (e.g., values pertaining to hierarchy, autonomy, privacy). Although it is possible to separate organization and ideology analytically (Schwartz, 1990), the two levels are too thoroughly confounded for us to distinguish their implications for communication. Nor are the structural characteristics of families, in any strict sense, independent of one another. Although there are many potential combinations of family or cultural traits, the traits do not occur together at random but rather tend toward overall coherence. Thus the number of empirical family types is far fewer than purely mathematical combinations of traits would permit.

Centrality of Family

Familism, or the centrality of the family, is closely related to cultural collectivism-individualism and to equivalent concepts in the family literature. A familistic orientation is associated with collectivist values, such as sharing, cooperation, unity, loyalty, respect, and restraint, as well as behavioral norms pertaining to mutual assistance, family obligations, subordination of individual needs to family needs, and preservation of family honor or dignity. Cultural collectivism reflects the primacy of group goals versus individual goals (Schwartz, 1990; Triandis, 1986). Virtually the same distinction appears in the family literature under near synonyms such as togetherness-separateness, integration-differentiation, and autonomy-interdependence. This is perhaps the fundamental dimension distinguishing individual families, as shown by the prominence of collectivist and individualist themes in theoretically based family typologies (e.g., Fitzpatrick, 1988; Kantor & Lehr, 1975; McLeod & Chaffee, 1972; Olson, Sprenkle, & Russell, 1979; Reiss, 1981). Collectivism at the societal level tends to mirror interdependence at the family level, because collectivist cultures emphasize strong mutual obligations within extended primary groups, especially the family (Schwartz, 1990).

Many American ethnic minority groups are notable for the centrality of the family. The family is clearly important in mainstream culture as well, but there individual pursuits compete on a more equal footing with family obligations. By contrast, family is *the* fundamental orientation among a variety of ethnic groups (Staples & Mirande, 1980; Wilkinson, 1987). Ethnic identification and familism are mutually reinforcing, because ethnic patterns are learned and lived through family interactions. Conversely, ethnic traditions, celebrations, and rituals add to the richness and distinctiveness of family interactions, thereby strengthening the collective identity of family members.

Individual Autonomy

Although interdependence-autonomy is often depicted as a continuum, some family cultures stress high interdependence *and* high autonomy. Schwartz (1990) explains that certain individualist values (e.g., hedonism, achievement, social power) do not present any necessary conflict with group goals and may coexist with a predominantly collectivist value system. Various combinations of familism and autonomy are therefore possible. Whereas Anglo-Americans tend to subordinate the group to the individual, East Asians tend to subordinate individual expression to group or family interests (Kitano, 1988; Shon & Ja, 1982). African Americans and Native Americans, on the other hand, place considerable stress on the autonomy and uniqueness of the individual, but within a familistic model that also emphasizes values such as sharing, group cooperation, spirituality, and respect for the elderly and the past (Attneave, 1982; Hanson, 1980; Hines & Boyd-Franklin, 1982; McAdoo, 1993).

External Boundaries

A familistic orientation is further associated with clear delineation of external family boundaries. Triandis (1986) observes that collectivist cultures differentiate sharply between in-group and out-group situations. This tendency may be revealed by the use of a different code of conduct in family versus nonfamily or public versus private settings, by the maintenance of family secrecy, and by a tendency to keep dirty linen and family problems within family walls (Rotunno & McGoldrick, 1982; Shon & Ja, 1982; Wong, 1988). Concern for boundaries reflects the central importance of family reputation and loyalty in familistic cultures. In highly familistic cultures, an individual's identity and place in society may be defined more by family than by individual achievement (Falicov, 1982; Squier & Quadagno, 1988). Thus familistic cultures often demonstrate a marked tendency to limit the psychological accessibility of the family to outsiders.

Internal Boundaries

The most widely noted quality of many American ethnic family cultures is the high degree of interdependence among extended family. In their traditional form, family groups may have resided in extended multigenerational households, as in the case of Chinese and Mexican families (Falicov, 1982; Wong, 1988), or as clusters of separate dwellings with fluid family boundaries, as in the case of African and Native American villages (Attneave, 1982; Sudarkasa, 1988). Although vestiges of these traditional structures remain, ethnic American families now are more typically "semiextended," consisting of separate nuclear households in close proximity, with strong emotional ties and mutual assistance (Sanchez-Ayendez, 1988; Staples & Mirande, 1980; Wong, 1988).

Sociologists and family theorists have long noted the profound influence of kin networks on family interactions, with some authors emphasizing the positive functions of kin networks in providing social support (e.g., Milardo, 1988) and others noting the interventions of kin networks in intimate and personal matters (e.g., Bott, 1971; Morgan, 1986). Extended kin networks stabilize family relationships by providing instrumental and emotional support and by transmitting cultural knowledge about how relationships are expected to work. Extended networks also promote communal and traditional norms that foster consensus about family attitudes and values (Cohler & Geyer, 1982) and strengthen family and ethnic identity. At the same time, the intrusions of extended kin restrict the autonomy of individuals and dyadic relationships. Extended families are more likely to be conformist (Cohler & Geyer, 1982) and to encourage adoption of traditional sex roles (Bott, 1971; Richards, 1980).

Where extended family ties are strong, conjugal relationships tend to be correspondingly less exclusive, less private, and, in a certain sense, less "intimate." As Gadlin (1977) notes, intimacy presumes independence of the conjugal pair from intrusive social controls, primarily, having the ability to choose one's mate freely and to establish individualized relationship patterns based on personal preference. Thus the contemporary American view of intimacy, based on the ideal of expressive individualism (Bellah, Maddsen, Sullivan, Swidler,

& Tipton, 1985), evolved simultaneously with the decline in influence of extended family and community over family matters (Gadlin, 1977; Montgomery, 1992).

Role Structure

Hierarchy

The role structure of American ethnic families has received heavy comment, reflecting sociologists' concern with family power. This literature largely distinguishes between family cultures that are more egalitarian and those that are hierarchically structured. For example, traditional Hispanic and Asian families are subject to age and sex grading, whereby the "old order the younger, and the men the women" (Becerra, 1988; Shon & Ja, 1982; Staples & Mirande, 1980; Van Tran, 1988). Strong sex differentiation and male dominance are traditional norms in many ethnic cultures, a notable exception being African American families, which are more often characterized by egalitarianism or slight male dominance, in the same manner as Anglo-American families (Hines & Boyd-Franklin, 1982; McAdoo, 1993; Sudarkasa, 1988).

Family role structure has an obvious, even circular, relation to interactional processes in areas such as decision making, relational control, conflict, and socialization. The relation is more confounding than it would initially appear, however, because ideological beliefs about family power do not necessarily correspond with the exercise of influence. Despite the perception of male dominance in Hispanic families, egalitarianism is the dominant pattern observed in studies of marital decision making in such families (Cromwell & Cromwell, 1978; Staples & Mirande, 1980). A number of authors have commented that the subordinate power position of mothers in ethnic families is more apparent than real (Becerra, 1988; Falicov, 1982; Sanchez-Ayendez, 1988; Shon & Ja, 1982) and that female submissiveness occurs more in public than in private contexts (Kourvetaris, 1988).

Scripted Versus Negotiated Roles

Aside from the degree of hierarchy, a further aspect of role structure important to communication is the extent to which roles are *scripted* versus *negotiated.* Roles may be scripted either in the sociological sense of a traditional pattern learned from reference groups (Scanzoni & Szinovacz, 1980) or in the psychological sense of an overlearned sequence that, through repetition, ceases to be an object of conscious attention (Langer, 1978). In part because of the emphasis on conjugal privacy, Anglo-American couples typically begin their relationships with less scripted knowledge than do couples who proceed from a more tradition-bound and familistic outlook. However, during extended periods of relationship stability, all couples and families have the potential to achieve the functional equivalent of traditional culture—that is, an extensive store of unspoken agreements, although along lines that may have been subject to negotiation at an earlier time (Sillars & Kalbfleisch, 1989).

COMMUNICATION CHARACTERISTICS OF FAMILY CULTURES

Family communication patterns represent strategies for addressing basic issues of family definition and are part of a coherent configuration of family traits. The main interactional problems of families are suggested by the functions of communication addressed most often in family research: information, companionship, emotional expression, control, socialization, and identity. Although it is safe to say that each of these functions is addressed in some way during the interactions of all families, the issues they represent are not universally salient, nor are the solutions to interactional problems equivalent across family cultures.

Information

Communication in different family cultures is distinguished, first, by the presumed instrumentality of talk. For example, families in mainstream American culture frequently operate by the principle that it is important to put thoughts into words. This emphasis emanates from broader cultural themes, such as the tendencies to view relationships analytically (Deetz & Mumby, 1985), to see communication as "work" (Katriel & Phillipsen, 1981), and to expect individuals to think and behave uniquely. Within such a framework, extensive communication is required first to know another person and then to maintain understanding and coordination of action. Others are not expected to know what one is thinking without explanation, and "mind reading" is considered presumptuous, even (or especially) among intimates.

Thus one dominant way of thinking about communication is in terms of an information conduit between divergent perspectives. Alternatively, words may be appreciated more for their figurative, expressive, or defensive functions and less for their potential to transmit literal information (Rotunno & McGoldrick, 1982). Thus communication in some cultures (e.g., among Arabs, Italians, Irish) is verbally expressive but characteristically indirect (Galvin, 1982; Gudykunst & Ting-Toomey, 1988; McGoldrick, 1982).

It is also the case that words are sometimes unnecessary to achieve understanding, particularly in homogeneous cultures where roles and meanings are heavily scripted. In fact, Lebra (1993) comments that the greater problem for Japanese is being overly transparent rather than being inadequately expressive. To paraphrase the theories of Bernstein (1973) and Hall (1977), where role structures are relatively open and flexible and meanings are assumed to be idiosyncratic and ambiguous, messages tend to be more verbally explicit and elaborated. Where roles and meanings are collectively understood, there is less need to articulate meanings explicitly, so messages may appear cryptic, relying heavily on nonverbal communication and taken-for-granted knowledge. Interactions may be characterized by allusion (Falicov, 1982), ritual, idiomatic or metaphoric speech (Shon & Ja, 1982), incomplete utterances (Niyekawa, 1984), and meaningful silences (Basso, 1970).

Couples and families have been found to adopt more or less implicit styles of communication based partly on the stability and homogeneity of their relationships (Sillars & Kalbfleisch, 1989). For example, traditionalism among American couples tends to increase alignment of expectations concerning marital roles, thus fostering the adoption of "silent arrangements" (Scanzoni & Szinovacz, 1980) and use of "pragmatic codes," in which linguistic relations and individual experiences are relatively implicit and undifferentiated (Ellis & Hamilton, 1985; Fitzpatrick, 1988, p. 228). Ellis and Hamilton (1985) suggest that, because of the homogenizing effect of traditional role expectations, there is less need for talk and the talk that does occur "does more work." Families may also fluctuate between periods of more or less explicit talk over the course of time. In mainstream American culture, communication patterns may progress from a maximal reliance on explicit talk in courtship and early marriage to increasing reliance on unspoken understandings later on, except where this momentum is upset by periods of relationship instability and redefinition (Reiss, 1981; Sillars & Wilmot, 1989).

Companionship and Intimacy

Within mainstream culture, the privacy and exclusivity of marriage, along with the emphasis on emotional intimacy, raise the justificatory burden on communication. A spouse is expected to be, as much as anything else, a good conversational partner. This represents an idealization, but the expectation affects satisfaction in marriage. For example, research suggests that satisfied married couples, compared with less satisfied couples, spend more time talking regardless of topic (Kirchler, 1989), self-disclose more to one another (Burke, Weir, & Harrison, 1976), and spend more time "debriefing" one another about the events of the day (Vangelisti & Banski, 1993). A decline in the quantity or quality of conversation may be construed as disengagement or stagnation. Both wives and husbands cite the lack of interesting conversations with their spouses as one of their chief complaints (Birchler, 1979).

The cultural emphasis on frequent and open communication in marriage seems partly attributable to the exclusivity of intimacy in mainstream American culture. In extended families, on the other hand, adult siblings, parents, and others are a frequent source of reciprocal disclosure, emotional support, and advice. Where these close confidants exist outside the spousal relationship, there tends to be less emphasis on emotional intimacy within marriage (Bott, 1971). A family orientation or child-centered orientation may supersede the marital dyad, creating a less intense and more pragmatic form of marital attachment (e.g., Falicov, 1982). Ting-Toomey (1991) observes that romantic love is a solution to the disconnection of individuals within society. Kinship supports lessen this sense of disconnection and reduce uncertainty, thereby diffusing the intensity of romantic attachments.

To a large extent, modern society has seen an increased emphasis on romantic intimacy across cultures, but this value is more long-standing and firmly entrenched in some cultural contexts than in others. For example, Ting-Toomey (1991) found that individuals pro-fess stronger feelings of love toward heterosexual partners in indi-vidualist versus collectivist countries. Other studies indicate that love and companionship are important in collectivist cultures, but these values do not predominate over instrumental and social values to the same extent as in individualist cultures. Buss, Abbott, Angleitner, et al. (1990) found that mutual love and attraction are valued highly in nearly all cultures. However, individuals from collectivist cultures in Africa, Asia, and Latin America placed higher priority on mate char-acteristics that reflect social standing and instrumental role perform-ance (e.g., chastity, desire for home and children, good cook and housekeeper, good financial prospects, favorable social status) than did respondents in samples from individualist societies. Similarly, Kamo (1993) found that pragmatic considerations (i.e., income) pre-dicted marital satisfaction in a Japanese but not an American sample, whereas companionship (i.e., dining together, having mutual friends) was important in both cases.

Although Kamo maintains that Japanese marriages are more instru-mental and less expressive than marriages in the United States, she also notes an increased emphasis on romantic intimacy within recent generations in Japan (see also Kitano, 1988). A change of this nature within traditionally collectivist cultures necessitates some redefini-tion of extended family relations and is a likely source of frequent intergenerational conflicts. Such conflicts appear to be common in Japan. A frequent story line for family dramas on Japanese television involves the resistance of adult children to the traditional influence of parents over mate selection and other intimate matters (Niyekawa, 1984).

Emotional Expression

Emotional expressivity versus restraint is one of the most vivid areas of contrast between family cultures. Qualitative accounts of American families have provided memorable illustrations, for example, Hess and Handel's (1959) account of the "Littleton" family, where everyone speaks in muted voice with steady posture, minimal gesturing, and "an evenness of tone that extends into the physical surroundings," including the plastic coverings on the conventional furniture. This contrasts with the shrieking children, sudden laughter, and raucous play of Kantor and Lehr's (1975) "random" family.

The general level of emotionality is independent of the degree of emotional intimacy expected in marriage, because family cultures may dramatize feelings but maintain a degree of reserve in the spousal relationship (Herz & Rosen, 1982; Squier & Quadagno, 1988). Generally, we assume that a family's emotional well-being rests on the members striking an appropriate balance between expressivity and restraint. However, from a cultural standpoint, saying what represents an "appropriate" balance proves to be exceedingly tricky, because family cultures establish widely varying emotional baselines and tolerances (e.g., Hanson, 1980; Herz & Rosen, 1982).

Given that family cultures establish different expectations for emotionality, it follows that the relation between emotionality and family well-being should be affected by culture. In research conducted mainly with middle-class American couples, negativity in communication has been consistently associated with marital dissatisfaction and distress (Montgomery, 1988). However, in family cultures where there is a higher base rate of negativity, there appears to be a weaker relation between negativity and satisfaction. Studies have documented higher base rates of negativity among German versus Australian couples (Halford, Hahlweg, & Dunne, 1990), Israeli Jewish versus American Jewish couples (Winkler & Doherty, 1983), and blue-collar versus white-collar couples (Krokoff, Gottman, & Roy, 1988). In each case, the relation between negativity and marital dissatisfaction was attenuated when the base rates were higher. Given the near universality of emotional meanings and signals, the relation between negativity and marital distress is undoubtedly more robust than most presumed effects of communication. However, emotional tolerances appear to be calibrated against normal or expected levels of expressivity within particular family cultures.

Conflict and Control

As in the case of emotionality, cultures have dramatically varying tolerances for the expression of confrontation, dissent, and disharmony. These contrasts reflect the interaction of internal family organization and external boundary maintenance. Reiss (1981), in particular, points out that a family's orientation to the external environment depends on the internal organization of the family. In some cases, families attempt to act as a buffer between external problems and members by establishing mutually supportive, harmonious relations based on social obligations, conformity, and concern for others. In part, this represents a familistic outlook in which the concern for group cohesion overrides individual expression and disagreement. In these instances, family interactions amplify the experience of family membership but may reinforce isolation from sources of information in the broader community (Reiss, 1981). Other families may attempt a more active form of intervention by discussing, debating, analyzing, and "resolving" problems, thereby amplifying information flowing into the family from the environment. An illustration is suggested by the analytic and active style of persuasion adopted by Anglo-American and Mormon couples relative to Navaho couples in Strodtbeck's (1951) research.

Although Reiss was largely concerned with the interface of family and environment, the contrast between active versus passive/indirect mediation of problems typifies all instances of family decision making and conflict. Among other things, a family's dominant response to conflict seems to rest on the degree of homogeneity of expectations, role clarity, and stability (i.e., the distinction between scripted versus negotiated roles).

The standard functionalist position on conflict argues that conflict is a continuous state and that confrontation is generally preferable to conflict suppression. However, these assumptions also presume a particular type of relationship structure. In family relationships characterized by role ambiguity and change, negotiation necessarily plays an essential part in the adjustment and coordination of expectations. In such cases, conflict is frequent if not continuous. The ubiquitous nature of conflict may, however, help to insulate family members from the negative effects of conflict. Frequent conflict encourages tolerance for expressed tensions and provides practice in conflict management. Where relationships are heavily scripted, this situation is essentially reversed. In this case, there is less need for ongoing discussion to maintain coordination, therefore family members may rely on passive and indirect conflict strategies (e.g., note the comparison of conflict within elderly and young couples in Sillars & Zietlow, 1993). However, where conflict does occur, it is potentially explosive. As Ting-Toomey (1985) observes, in cultural settings marked by homogeneous normative standards, there is less tolerance for conflict and an increased perception of conflict as inherently personal rather than issue oriented. There is also an additional perplexing aspect to the conflicts of intercultural marriages or traditional families in the midst of cultural change. In these cases, scripted knowledge is an inadequate basis for clarifying family rules, yet the individuals may be predisposed by cultural background to rely on implicit relationship knowledge rather than on verbal negotiation of relationships.

Socialization

Adult-child communication in the context of socialization is affected by cultural assumptions of both relational and developmental natures. Relational assumptions specify a child's expected position within the family structure, for example, the centrality of children to family life, the diffusion of parental responsibilities, and the expected role distance between adults and children. Developmental assumptions are concerned with the maturation process: what is expected at a given age, what behaviors are seen as indicators of maturity, how the family environment is thought to affect developmental progress. The two sets of assumptions are closely interrelated, because maturation is determined by a child's ability to function within a system of relationships. Thus a parent's communication, whether characterized by reasoning or by strict discipline, is designed to encourage adaptation to and, ultimately, to reproduce cultural definitions of relationships.

The cultural ideal for adult-child communication in Western, middle-class society is suggested by Baumrind's concept of "authoritative" parenting (see Maccoby & Martin, 1983). The authoritative parent is both demanding (in the sense of setting limits, encouraging achievement) and responsive (i.e., attentive, democratic, flexible, and communicative). This style is congruent with middle-class, Anglo-American values, such as competence, individuality, and egalitarianism, and it reflects the view that family relationships are mediated by explicit communication. Closely related is the concept of "person-centered" messages (Applegate, Burleson, & Delia, 1992; Bernstein, 1973), which draw attention to the psychological antecedents and consequences of behavior rather than to assigned status (i.e., "positional" messages). Person-centered messages are seen as fostering the child's development of psychological constructs, often regarded as the key to social competence (Applegate et al., 1992). However, as Bernstein (1973) points out, person-centered communication primarily enables one to function in an open role system, where meanings are ambiguous and individualized. Person-centered messages do not foster social competence within a closed role system, where roles and meanings are based on culturally scripted knowledge.

The most obvious counterpoint to the authoritative, person-centered parent is the "authoritarian" parent (Maccoby & Martin, 1983), who emphasizes parental authority, tradition, obedience, strict discipline, and one-way communication. This description matches, to some extent, the description of parental control in hierarchical family cultures. However, the term *authoritarian* conjures up a rather cold vision of parental authority in these families, neglecting as it does the nurturance, warmth, and mutual concern often found as well (e.g., Falicov, 1982; Shon & Ja, 1982; Squier & Quadagno, 1988).

Interestingly, although Japanese culture places considerable importance on compliance with parental authority, Japanese parents may employ an indulgent, child-centered style of interaction (i.e., *amae*) and avoid more intrusive and directive forms of control, such as authority appeals or external rewards and punishments. Although both Japanese and American parents rely on verbal techniques to gain compliance, such as commands and explanations, Americans are more likely to supplement these with punishments (Kobayashi-Winata & Power, 1989). According to Kobayashi-Winata and Power (1989), this reflects the fact that American parents expect children to be independent and therefore to resist compliance. Japanese mothers, on the other hand, may encourage a strong sense of dependence on others through a particularly supportive and responsive relationship with young children, which Americans might see as "spoiling" children (i.e., interfering with the development of independence).

At the other end of the continuum from authoritarian styles of adult-child interaction, Native Americans may appear laissez-faire by Anglo-American standards. Socialization within Native American families is influenced by the norm of "noninterference," which represents a deep respect for innate forces within the individual (Attneave, 1982). Parental efforts at gaining compliance are often subtle, as children are expected to learn from the natural consequences of behavior. Thus they may receive far greater latitude to make decisions and assume responsibilities than do Anglo-American children at similar ages. Further, uncles and aunts often have disciplinary responsibilities toward young children, thus freeing parents for a looser and more pleasure-oriented association (Attneave, 1982).

Studies that consider the consequences of parent-child interaction for child development provide a strong case for the superiority of authoritative parenting over authoritarian, indulgent, and laissez-faire styles (Maccoby & Martin, 1983). However, the cultural generalizability of this conclusion is uncertain, particularly because outcome measures (e.g., child self-esteem, independence, cognitive complexity) tend to reflect individualist values and assume an open (negotiated) role system.

Individual and Family Identity

Quite obviously, norms pertaining to self-expression and self-presentation presume a particular understanding of the self. The "self" that is most familiar to mainstream American culture is a deep reservoir of private experience that is relatively stable, independent, internally consistent, and consciously available (Brown & Rogers, 1991;

Markus & Kitayama, 1991). From this frame of reference, self-expression is valued as an affirmation of individuality as well as a means of overcoming the threat of social isolation.

By implication, the American family is seen as a constellation of separate personalities kept in dynamic equilibrium through continual (verbal) negotiation of relationships. In contrast, the Japanese self is more fundamentally relational. For example, there are few references to *I* or *you* in Japanese conversation. This contrasts with American couples, where the choice of individual or joint self-reference (e.g., *I*, *you*, *us*) is an indicator of couple ideology (i.e., more separate versus connected) and cohesion (Acitelli, 1993; Ellis & Hamilton, 1985; Fitzpatrick, 1988; Sillars & Zietlow, 1993). Among Japanese, self- and other reference is always relational and is largely scripted (Lebra, 1993). Japanese self-reference reflects the "interdependent" nature of the Japanese self, in which self is expressed, not suppressed, through the individual's fitting in and cooperating with the group (Markus & Kitayama, 1991).

Paradoxically, the emphasis on individuality in mainstream American culture heightens the need for social validation of the self, owing to lack of institutionalized and ritualized forms of validation. In their seminal analysis of the social construction of reality in marriage, Berger and Kellner (1964) argue that marriage has a privileged status among validating relationships because of the privacy and intimacy of topics and the emotional importance of marriage. Marriage leads to a unique but fragile social reality (because it is shared by only two people) that is sustained through endless conversations "from bed to breakfast table" (p. 226). Although Berger and Kellner do not directly consider cultural differences, their argument is clearly based on isolated nuclear families. By extension, a more diffuse, subtle, and stable process of social validation should take place in familistic cultures, where self-identity is defined to a much greater extent by the individual's participation in a network of extended family relations.

The communication mechanisms may vary by family culture, but all families require some means of bridging individual and family identities. By constructivist accounts, the creation of family identity is primarily unconscious, indirect, and implicit in everyday discourse. Recent authors have focused particularly on the role of narrative speech (or accounts) in coordinating individual identities around common themes (e.g., Burnett, McGhee, & Clarke, 1987). There is a symbiotic relationship between the narrative transmission of family and ethnic culture, because family stories are often heavily laden with ethnic themes. In fact, Stone (1988) notes that ethnic identification, in the case of mixed loyalties, sometimes comes down to which side of the family has the more colorful and evocative stories.

Individually authored narratives usually show consistency and coherence, accomplished through great selectivity in reporting, interpreting, and embellishing events. However, the highly selective nature of individual accounts compounds the difficulty of reconciling individual stories. Thus the construction of coherent, jointly authored family narratives is a notable accomplishment, indicating considerable interdependence. Gergen and Gergen (1987) point out that the production of a coherent joint narrative is especially problematic in Western society, given the emphasis on independent self-identity and cultural preference for individual over collective accounting. Thus the successful coconstruction of coherent accounts also reflects relationship structure. Sillars, Burggraf, Yost, and Zietlow (1992) found that the comments of different speakers in more psychologically interdependent and conventional marriages often "blended" to form a unified account. Structurally, these conversations were characterized by a high degree of interspeaker continuity and by mutual reference to abstract, primarily communal themes. This contrasted with a style of speaking termed "differentiating," observed among highly autonomous spouses, in which speakers alternated in making loosely synchronized remarks about individual behaviors and personalities, somewhat like the "his and her" accounts noted by Mansfield and Collard (1988).

The tensions between individual and family identity are, in some respects, less problematic in collectivist and familistic cultures, however, this is the case primarily within homogeneous, traditional groups. In traditional cultures, ethnicity represents a way of living that is fully integrated with individual and family identity. Ethnicity is not a lifestyle "choice," but rather a taken-for-granted part of cradle-to-grave existence. Where this sort of ethnicity still persists, the cultural patterns have considerable moral force. Within complex modern societies, however, individuals are members of different cultures at different levels of social organization, including, but not limited to, the national culture, ethnic subculture, and family culture. In many cases, differing loyalties to traditional patterns produce a schism within families and ethnic communities (Staples & Mirande, 1980). Thus ethnic and family identity must be preserved more as a matter of conscious choice and effort in heterogeneous modern societies than in traditional cultures. The resulting tensions among individual, family, and cultural identities are managed in a variety of ways, including through maintenance of a traditional lifestyle, abandonment of all ethnic pretenses, "symbolic" ethnicity (Gans, 1985), and alternation between cultural patterns depending on the situation (Kitano, 1993).

CONCLUSIONS AND IMPLICATIONS

Despite the enormous diversity of contemporary families and great interest in the subject, we are not entirely reconciled with the implications of cultural diversity in the study of family communication. Although we all recognize that communication is cultural, our academic distinctions lead us to regard culture as a separate area of study (i.e., cross-cultural research) or paradigm (i.e., cultural perspectives). Thus family research often generates culturally specific knowledge of communication, which requires retrofitting to accommodate diverse families. A more efficient path would be to coordinate the study of family organization, ideology, and communication from the outset.

The metaphor of relationships as cultures is a promising heuristic, if broadly construed to cover the varying degrees of autonomy versus connectedness among individuals, dyads, families, cultures, and societies. There are a few general implications of this metaphor for research on family communication.

First, the forms and functions of communication are best understood in terms of how messages act out or act upon operative relationship structures. There is a tendency in some circles to speak of relationship structure in singular terms, for example, sexual intimacy and marriage as a unique, closed universe of meaning maintained through continuous conversation. This vision suggests a structure in which there is a precarious, negotiated balance between unique individuals, loose coupling with extended primary groups, and permeable boundaries with respect to the wider community and society. In such cases, frequent talk may be a necessary (although insufficient) condition for managing coordination, control, conflict, and identity. Similarly, person-oriented messages in adult-child communication socialize children to interact in a context where there is considerable autonomy, role ambiguity, and need for explicit communication.

On the other hand, we have noted a variety of ways that family structures interact with communication, our more central observations being the following:

1. Where relationship expectations are more scripted, stable, and homogeneous, there is less need for continual briefing to maintain the relationship, so the instrumental functions of communication may be accomplished more subtly, indirectly, and unconsciously. Role hierarchies are only one mechanism through which this occurs.

2. Extended family structures may diffuse the intensity of marital and parental communication by reducing the exclusive demands on these relationships. Extended family ties also increase homogeneity of expectations, promote a more family-centered form of intimacy, and stabilize individual and family identities.

3. In familistic cultures, deep sensitivities to relational concerns establish the limitations on acceptable communication and simplify the achievement of family coordination and coherence. However, expressive behaviors are proscribed only to the extent that they conflict with family identity, so one familistic group may enforce restraint and another permit considerable airing of strong emotions and differences.

4. The mixing of cultural models for intimacy and family within traditionally familist and collectivist cultures entails redefinition of relations with extended family, raises issues regarding family and ethnic loyalty, and creates role ambiguity for which there may be no well-established negotiation mechanism.

A second implication of relational culture is that families have their own comfort zone for many of the message variables that concern researchers—disclosure, negativity, criticism, punishment, relationship talk, "mind reading," and so forth. The effort to connect these behaviors to family well-being or distress runs into the obvious yet vexing problem that the behaviors mean different things in different families. Even nonverbal affect, which is as nearly universal as any aspect of communication, has a complex relation to compatibility based upon cultural norms for expressivity. Attempts to link messages directly with family outcomes in other areas are at least as likely to find that cultural orientations influence the findings.

There are at least two alternatives to the search for direct message effects that might accommodate cultural differences more readily. One strategy would be to explore connections between communication and family well-being that are integrated with and contingent upon specification of relationship structure. Preliminary thrusts in this direction are reflected in the writings of several authors (e.g., Bernstein, 1973; Fitzpatrick, 1988; Montgomery, 1988). A further alternative would be to pursue higher-order interaction concepts (e.g., coherence, congruence, confirmation, resilience, nurturance, synchrony) that are flexible enough to accommodate varied lower-order behaviors and sequences. This is essentially the strategy taken by systems theorists, however, many of the higher-order concepts from this perspective (e.g., complexity, variety, growth, open system) are ideologically tainted in their usual application.

Third, the conservation of family culture is accomplished partly through the regulation of external boundaries (Reiss, 1981), in terms of both the reproduction of external images within the family and the representation of family images externally. This regulation process is likely to affect what we see in research. The mere fact that families consent to be studied is a sign of permeable boundaries and/or strong communication orientation. Thus considerable homogenization of samples may occur inadvertently in communication research. Further, there is a likely interaction between family culture and reactivity to the research setting. In all studies there are questions about the validity of observations owing to the tendency of families to censor and otherwise modify their behavior in the presence of outsiders. However, it is especially difficult to read the observed behavior of familist/collectivist cultures because of the often sharp distinctions drawn between public and private behavior and between intimate and nonintimate behavior.

Finally, cultural models affect not only families, but family researchers as well. For example, most family and relational communication research has a dyadic focus, with sexual intimacy or marriage as the crux relationship. There has been recent attention to other parts of the network, but these relations are seen culturally as optional and tend to be studied by researchers as potential support for marital or romantic pairs, rather than as compelling relationships in their own right. Further, the cultural emphasis on emotional intimacy in marriage tends to narrow the choice of interaction and outcome measures; for example, marital satisfaction or an equivalent concept is usually the sole measure of relationship quality. The positive association usually found between satisfaction and intimate or open communication is unsurprising, given that the variables are so profoundly connected by the dominant relationship ideology of those sampled (Montgomery, 1988). To accommodate alternative relationship cultures, it is necessary to consider expanded indicators of family functioning, potentially including such things as general well-being or life satisfaction, contentment, stability, commitment, family identification, loyalty, and mutual support.

REFERENCES

Acitelli, L. (1993). You, me, and us: Perspectives on relationship awareness. In S. Duck (Ed.), *Understanding relationship processes: Vol. 1. Individuals and relationships* (pp. 144-174). Newbury Park, CA: Sage.

Applegate, J. L., Burleson, B. R., & Delia, J. G. (1992). Reflection-enhancing parenting as an antecedent to children's social-cognitive and communicative development. In I. E. Sigel, A. V. McGillicuddy-DeLesi, & J. J. Goodnow (Eds.), *Parental belief systems: The psychological consequences for children* (Vol. 2., pp. 3-39). Hillsdale, NJ: Lawrence Erlbaum.

Attneave, C. (1982). American Indians and Alaska native families: Emigrants in their own homeland. In M. McGoldrick, J. K. Pearce, & J. Giordano (Eds.), *Ethnicity and family therapy* (pp. 55-83). New York: Guilford.

Basso, K. (1970). "To give up on words": Silence in western Apache culture. *Southwestern Journal of Anthropology, 26,* 213-230.

Baxter, L. A. (1987). Symbols of relationship identity in relationship cultures. *Journal of Social and Personal Relationships, 4,* 261-280.

Becerra, R. M. (1988). The Mexican American family. In C. H. Mindel, R. W. Habenstein, & R. Wright (Eds.), *Ethnic families in America* (3rd ed., pp. 141-159). New York: Elsevier.

Bellah, R. N., Maddsen, R., Sullivan, W. M., Swidler, A. & Tipton, S. M. (1985). *Habits of the heart: Individualism and commitment in American life.* New York: Harper & Row.

Berger, P., & Kellner, H. (1964). Marriage and the construction of reality. *Diogenes, 46,* 1-24.

Bernstein, B. (1973). *Class, codes and control*. London: Routledge & Kegan Paul.

Birchler, G. R. (1979). Communication skills in married couples. In A. S. Bellack & M. Hersen (Eds.), *Research and practice in social skills training* (pp. 273-315). New York: Plenum.

Bott, E. (1971). *Family and social network*. New York: Free Press.

Brown, J., & Rogers, L. E. (1991). Openness, uncertainty, and intimacy: An epistemological reformulation. In N. Coupland, H. Giles, & J. M. Wiemann (Eds.), *"Miscommunication" and problematic talk* (pp. 146-165). Newbury Park, CA: Sage.

Burke, R., Weir, T., & Harrison, D. (1976). Disclosure of problems and tensions experienced by marital partners. *Psychological Reports, 38*, 531-542.

Burnett, R., McGhee, P., & Clarke, D. D. (Eds.). (1987). *Accounting for relationships: Explanation, representation and knowledge*. London: Methuen.

Buss, D., Abbott, M., Angleitner, A., et al. (1990). International preferences in selecting mates: A study of 37 cultures. *Journal of Cross-Cultural Psychology, 21*, 5-47.

Cohler, B., & Geyer, S. (1982). Psychological autonomy and interdependence within the family. In F. Walsh (Ed.), *Normal family processes* (pp. 186-228). New York: Guidion.

Cromwell, V., & Cromwell, R. (1978). Perceived dominance in decision making and conflict resolution among black and Chicano couples. *Journal of Marriage and the Family, 40*, 749-759.

Deetz, S., & Mumby, D. (1985). Metaphors, information, and power. *Information and Behavior, 1*, 369-386.

Ellis, D., & Hamilton, M. (1985). Syntactic and pragmatic code choice in interpersonal communication. *Communication Monographs, 52*, 264-278.

Falicov, C. J. (1982). Mexican families. In M. McGoldrick, J. K. Pearce, & J. Giordano (Eds.), *Ethnicity and family therapy* (pp. 134-163). New York: Guilford.

Fitzpatrick, M. A. (1988). *Between husbands and wives: Communication in marriage*. Newbury Park, CA: Sage.

Gadlin, H. (1977). Private lives and public order: A critical view of the history of intimate relations in the United States. In G. Levinher & H. Raush (Eds.), *Close relationships: Perspectives on the meaning of intimacy* (pp. 33-72). Amherst: University of Massachusetts Press.

Galvin, K. M. (1982). *Pishogues and paddywhackery: Transmission of communication patterns and values through three generations of an extended Irish-American family*. Paper presented at the annual meeting of the Speech Communication Association, Louisville, KY.

Gans, H. H. (1985). Symbolic ethnicity: The future of ethnic groups and cultures in America. In N. R. Yetman (Ed.), *Majority and minority* (4th ed., pp. 429-442). Boston: Allyn & Bacon.

Gergen, K. J., & Gergen, M. (1987). Narratives as relationships. In R. Burnett, P. McGhee, & D. C. Clarke (Eds.), *Accounting for relationships* (pp. 269-315). London: Methuen.

Gudykunst, W. B., & Ting-Toomey, S. (1988). *Culture and interpersonal communication*. Newbury Park, CA: Sage.

Halford, K. W., Hahlweg, K., & Dunne, M. (1990). The cross-cultural consistency of marital communication associated with marital distress. *Journal of Marriage and the Family, 52*, 487-500.

Hall, E. T. (1977). *Beyond culture*. Garden City, NY: Anchor.

Hanson, W. (1980). The urban Indian woman and her family. *Social Casework, 61*, 476-483.

Hareven, T. K. (1982). American families in transition: Historical perspectives on change. In F. Walsh (Ed.), *Normal family processes* (pp. 446-465). New York: Guidion.

Herz, F. M., & Rosen, E. J. (1982). Jewish families. In M. McGoldrick, J. K. Pearce, & J. Giordano (Eds.), *Ethnicity and family therapy* (pp. 364-392). New York: Guilford.

Hess, R. D., & Handel, G. (1959). *Family worlds: A psychosocial approach to family life*. Chicago: University of Chicago Press.

Hines, P. M., & Boyd-Franklin, N. (1982). Black families. In M. McGoldrick, J. K. Pearce, & J. Giordano (Eds.), *Ethnicity and family therapy* (pp. 84-107). New York: Guilford.

Kamo, Y. (1993). Determinants of marital satisfaction: A comparison of the United States and Japan. *Journal of Social and Personal Relationships, 10*, 551-568.

Kantor, D., & Lehr, W. (1975). *Inside the family*. New York: Harper & Row.

Katriel, T., & Phillipsen, G. (1981). "What we need is communication": "Communication" as a cultural category in some American speech. *Communication Monographs, 48*, 301-317.

Kirchler, E. (1989). Marital happiness and interaction in everyday surroundings: A time-sample diary approach for couples. *Journal of Social and Personal Relationships, 5*, 375-382.

Kitano, H. H. L. (1988). The Japanese American family. In C. H. Mindel, R. W. Habenstein, & R. Wright (Eds.), *Ethnic families in America* (3rd ed., pp. 258-275). New York: Elsevier.

Kitano, H. H. L. (1993). Japanese American values and communication patterns. In W. B. Gudykunst (Ed.), *Communication in Japan and the United States* (pp. 122-146). Albany: State University of New York Press.

Kobayashi-Winata, H., & Power, T. (1989). Child rearing and compliance: Japanese and American families in Houston. *Journal of Cross-Cultural Psychology, 20*, 333-356.

Kourvetaris, G. A. (1988). The Greek American family. In C. H. Mindel, R. W. Habenstein, & R. Wright (Eds.), *Ethnic families in America* (3rd ed., pp. 76-108). New York: Elsevier.

Krokoff, L. J., Gottman, J. M., & Roy, A. K. (1988). Blue-collar and white-collar marital interaction and communication orientation. *Journal of Social and Personal Relationships, 5*, 201-221.

Langer, E. (1978). Rethinking the role of thought in social interaction. In J. H. Harvey, W. J. Ickes, & R. F. Kidd (Eds.), *New directions in attribution research* (Vol. 2, pp. 35-58). Hillsdale, NJ: Lawrence Erlbaum.

Lebra, T. S. (1993). Culture, self, and communication in Japan and the United States. In W. B. Gudykunst (Ed.), *Communication in Japan and the United States* (pp. 51-87). Albany: State University of New York Press.

Maccoby, E. E., & Martin, J. A. (1983). Socialization in the context of the family: Parent-child interaction. In P. H. Mussen (Ed.), *Handbook of child psychology: Vol. 4. Socialization, personality, and social development* (pp. 1-101). New York: John Wiley.

Mansfield, P., & Collard, J. (1988). *The beginning of the rest of our life: A portrait of newly-wed marriage.* London: Macmillan.

Markus, H. R., & Kitayama, S. (1991). Culture and the self: Implications for cognition, emotion, and motivation. *Psychological Review, 98,* 224-253.

McAdoo, J. L. (1993). Decision making and marital satisfaction in African American families. In H. P. McAdoo (Ed.), *Family ethnicity: Strength and diversity* (pp. 109-119). Newbury Park, CA: Sage.

McGoldrick, M. (1982). Irish families. In M. McGoldrick, J. K. Pearce, & J. Giordano (Eds.), *Ethnicity and family therapy* (pp. 310-339). New York: Guilford.

McLeod, J. M., & Chaffee, S. H. (1972). The construction of social reality. In J. T. Tedeschi (Ed.), *The social influence processes* (pp. 50-99). Chicago: Aldine-Atherton.

Milardo, R. M. (Ed.). (1988). *Families and social networks.* Newbury Park, CA: Sage.

Montgomery, B. M. (1988). Quality communication in personal relationships. In S. W. Duck (Ed.), *Handbook of personal relationships* (pp. 343-359). New York: John Wiley.

Montgomery, B. M. (1992). Communication as the interface between couples and culture. In S. A. Deetz (Ed.), *Communication yearbook 15* (pp. 475-507). Newbury Park, CA: Sage.

Morgan, (1986). Personal relationships as the interface between social networks and social cognitions. *Journal of Social and Personal Relationships, 3,* 403-422.

Niyekawa, A. M. (1984). Analysis of conflict in a television home drama. In E. S. Krauss, T. P. Rohlen, & P. G. Steinhoff (Eds.), *Conflict in Japan* (pp. 61-84). Honolulu: University of Hawaii Press.

Olson, D. H., Sprenkle, D., & Russell, C. (1979). Circumplex model of marital and family systems I: Cohesion and adaptability dimensions, family types and clinical application. *Family Process, 18,* 3-28.

Reiss, D. (1981). *The family's construction of social reality.* Cambridge, MA: Harvard University Press.

Richards, E. F. (1980). Network ties, kin ties, and marital role organization: Bott's hypothesis reconsidered. *Journal of Comparative Family Studies, 11,* 139-151.

Rotunno, M., & McGoldrick, M. (1982). Italian families. In M. McGoldrick, J. K. Pearce, & J. Giordano (Eds.), *Ethnicity and family therapy* (pp. 340-363). New York: Guilford.

Sanchez-Ayendez, M. (1988). The Puerto Rican American family; the Cuban American family. In C. H. Mindel, R. W. Habenstein, & R. Wright (Eds.), *Ethnic families in America* (3rd ed., pp. 173-195). New York: Elsevier.

Scanzoni, J., & Szinovacz, M. (1980). *Family decision-making: A developmental sex role model.* Beverly Hills, CA: Sage.

Schwartz, S. H. (1990). Individualism-collectivism: Critique and proposed refinements. *Journal of Cross-Cultural Psychology, 21,* 139-157.

Shon, S. P., & Ja, D. Y. (1982). Asian families. In M. McGoldrick, J. K. Pearce, & J. Giordano (Eds.), *Ethnicity and family therapy* (pp. 208-228). New York: Guilford.

Sillars, A. L., Burggraf, C. S. Yost, S., & Zietlow, P. H. (1992). Conversational themes and marital relationship definitions: Quantitative and qualitative investigations. *Human Communication Research, 19,* 124-154.

Sillars, A. L., & Kalbfleisch, P. J. (1989). Implicit and explicit decision-making styles in couples. In D. Brinberg & J. Jaccard (Eds.), *Dyadic decision making* (pp. 179-215). New York: Springer-Verlag.

Sillars, A. L., & Wilmot, W. W. (1989). Marital communication across the life-span. In J. F. Nussbaum (Ed.), *Life-span communication: Normative processes* (pp. 225-253). Hillsdale, NJ: Lawrence Erlbaum.

Sillars, A. L., & Zietlow, P. H. (1993). Investigations of marital communication and lifespan development. In N. Coupland & J. F. Nussbaum (Eds.), *Discourse and lifespan identity* (pp. 237-261). Newbury Park, CA: Sage.

Squier, D. A., & Quadagno, J. S. (1988). The Italian American family. In C. H. Mindel, R. W. Habenstein, & R. Wright (Eds.), *Ethnic families in America* (3rd ed., pp. 109-137). New York: Elsevier.

Stafford, L., & Dainton, M. (1994). The dark side of "normal" family interaction. In W. R. Cupach & B. H. Spitzberg (Eds.), *The dark side of interpersonal communication* (pp. 259-280). Hillsdale, NJ: Lawrence Erlbaum.

Staples, R., & Mirande, A. (1980). Racial and cultural variations in American families: A decennial review of the literature on minority families. *Journal of Marriage and the Family, 42,* 887-903.

Stone, E. (1988). *Black sheep and kissing cousins: How family stories shape us.* New York: Penguin.

Strodtbeck, F. L. (1951). Husband-wife interaction over revealed differences. *American Sociological Review, 16,* 468-473.

Sudarkasa, N. (1988). Interpreting the African heritage in Afro-American family organization. In H. P. McAdoo (Ed.), *Black families* (2nd ed., pp. 27-43). Newbury Park, CA: Sage.

Ting-Toomey, S. (1985). Toward a theory of conflict and culture. In W. Gudykunst, L. Stewart, & S. Ting-Toomey (Eds.), *Culture and organizational processes: Conflict, negotiation, and decision-making* (pp. 71-86). Newbury Park, CA: Sage.

Ting-Toomey, S. (1991). Intimacy expressions in three cultures: France, Japan, and the United States. *International Journal of Intercultural Relations, 15,* 29-46.

Triandis, H. C. (1986). Collectivism vs. individualism: A reconceptualization of a basic concept in cross-cultural psychology. In C. Bagley & G. Verma (Eds.), *Personality, cognition, and values: Cross-cultural perspectives of childhood and adolescence.* London: Macmillan.

Vangelisti, A. L., & Banski, M. A. (1993). Couples' debriefing conversations: The impact of gender, occupation, and demographic characteristics. *Family Relations, 42,* 149-157.

Van Tran, T. (1988). The Vietnamese American family. In C. H. Mindel, R. W. Habenstein, & R. Wright (Eds.), *Ethnic families in America* (3rd ed., pp. 276-299). New York: Elsevier.

Wilkinson, D. (1987). Ethnicity. In M. B. Sussman & S. K. Steinmetz (Eds.), *Handbook of marriage and the family* (pp. 183-210). New York: Plenum.

Winkler, I., & Doherty, W. J. (1983). Communication style and marital satisfaction in Israeli and American couples. *Family Process, 22,* 221-228.

Wong, M. G. (1988). The Chinese American family. In C. H. Mindel, R. W. Habenstein, & R. Wright (Eds.), *Ethnic families in America* (3rd ed., pp. 230-257). New York: Elsevier.

Wood, J. (1982). Communication and relational culture: Bases for the study of human relationships. *Communication Quarterly, 30,* 75-83.

Index

About the Editors

Mary Anne Fitzpatrick is Professor and Chair of the Department of Communication Arts at the University of Wisconsin—Madison. She is author of *Between Husbands and Wives* and coauthor, with Patricia Noller, of *Communicaiton in Family Relationships*. She is also the coeditor, with Patricia Noller, of *Perspectives on Marital Interaction*. She has written and edited four books and more than 75 chapters and articles on communication in social and personal relationships. Her research has been funded by NIMH, NIH, WARF, and the Spencer Foundation. As a tribute to her outstanding contribution to communication research, she is a Fellow of the International Communication Association as well as a past president of that association. She has given numerous addresses and symposia around the world on communication and is frequently sought as a communication consultant to other universities, governments, and businesses in the United States and abroad.

Anita L. Vangelisti is Assistant Professor at the University of Texas at Austin. She is interested in interpersonal communication among family members and between romantic partners. Her research focuses on the associations between communication, affect, and socially-based interpretive processes. Her work has appeared in such journals as *Communication Monographs, Human Communication Research, Journal of Personality and Social Psychology, and Journal of Social and Personal Relationships*. She is coauthor, with Mark L. Knapp, of *Interpersonal Communication and Human Relationships*.

About the Contributors

Joseph Angelelli has an M.S. in human development and family studies from Oregon State University. He is currently a doctoral student in gerontology/public policy at the Andrus Gerontology Center, University of Southern California. He continues to pursue his interests in communications at USC's Annenberg School for Communication.

James L. Applegate (Ph.D., University of Illinois at Urbana-Champaign, 1978) is Professor in the Department of Communication at the University of Kentucky. He is author of more than 50 book chapters and journal articles, and his research interests include factors affecting the development of communication abilities, with special emphasis on the social-cognitive correlates and cultural antecedents of communication skills. He is coeditor of *Communication by Children and Adults: Social-Cognitive and Strategic Foundations* and is currently completing another book integrating recent research on communication competence. He has served as President of the Southern States Communication Association and was recently appointed a Fellow of the American Council on Higher Education.

Marguerite Stevenson Barratt (Ph.D., Department of Psychology, University of Wisconsin—Madison, 1978) is Professor of Child and Family Studies at the University of Wisconsin—Madison. She is a developmental psychologist interested in infant social interactions, particularly parent-child interactions. Through her affiliation with the Waisman Center on Mental Retardation and Human Development at the University of Wisconsin, she examines issues of perinatal and environmental risk. She is currently investigating how reciprocal exchange is affected by characteristics of the mother through a statewide study of adolescent and adult single mothers and their interactions with their children. Through her affiliation with Osaka University, Japan, she has conducted cross-cultural microanalyses of interactions between mothers and their infants. She also examines the effects of parenting behavior on the socioemotional and cognitive development of infants.

Michelle L. Batchelder is a doctoral candidate in child development and family relationships in the Department of Human Ecology at the University of Texas at Austin. She received her master's degree in developmental psychology from the Sorbonne in Paris. In her work she has examined the transformation of individuals' subjective perspectives in the context of changing close relationships, for example, adolescents and parental divorce, and children in self-care. With Dr. Catherine Surra, she has developed a coding scheme to analyze the degree of overlap between coupled partners' accounts of changes in commitment. Her dissertation is a study of dating partners' shared knowledge about their own relationships and its association with changing commitment and interpersonal processes.

Gary L. Bowen (Ph.D., University of North Carolina at Greensboro, 1981) is William R. Kenan, Jr., Distinguished Professor of Social Work at the University of North Carolina at Chapel Hill. He also holds a joint appointment in the Department of Communication Studies. His current research is examining how structural and dynamic aspects of the work environment influence the adaptation of employees and families. He is also serving as co-principal investigator, with Jack Richman, on a grant from BellSouth Foundation to establish an evaluation system for informing the intervention plans and monitoring the progress of students who participate in the Cities/Communities-in-School Program, the largest U.S.

public-private partnership for school dropout prevention. He is author of *Navigating the Marital Journey* (1991); coeditor, with Joe F. Pittman, of *The Work and Family Interface: Toward a Contextual Effects Perspective* (in press); and coeditor, with Dennis K. Orthner, of *The Organization Family* (1989).

Brant R. Burleson (Ph.D., University of Illinois at Urbana-Champaign, 1982) is Professor in the Department of Communication at Purdue University, where he teaches courses in communication theory, interpersonal communication, and the philosophy of the social sciences. His research interests include communication skills acquisition and development, social-cognitive foundations of strategic communication, effects of communication skills on relationship formation and development, and prosocial forms of communication. His research has appeared in several edited volumes and journals, and he has served on the editorial boards of more than a dozen major journals. Recently, he coedited *Communication of Social Support: Messages, Interactions, Relationships, and Community.* He is currently serving as editor for *Communication Yearbook.*

Nancy A. Burrell (Ph.D., Michigan State University, 1987) is Associate Professor in the Communication Department at the University of Wisconsin—Milwaukee. Her research interests include interpersonal and organizational conflict and its resolution. She has been working with the Milwaukee Public Schools to evaluate peer mediation training in a program designed to address violence in the schools and with the Family Court Counseling Services of Milwaukee County to assess the divorce mediation program. Her research interests extend to stepfamilies and the reorganizing processes that stepfamily members experience. She has published in *Human Communication Research, Communication Monographs, Mediation Quarterly, Conciliation Court Review, Management Communication Quarterly,* and various edited volumes.

William R. Cupach (Ph.D., University of Southern California, 1981) is Professor in the Department of Communication at Illinois

State University. The central theme of his research is relational competence. Currently, he is exploring how individuals manage awkward, difficult, and challenging interactions in interpersonal relationships. He serves as associate editor for the communication section of the *Journal of Social and Personal Relationships,* and his scholarly work has appeared in various journals, including *Human Communication Research, Communication Monographs, Journal of Social and Personal Relationships,* and *Journal of Language and Social Psychology.* He is coauthor, with Brian Spitzberg, of *Interpersonal Communication Competence* (in the Sage Series on Interpersonal Communication) and the *Handbook of Interpersonal Competence Research.* Recently, he and Spitzberg published an edited volume of essays titled *The Dark Side of Interpersonal Communication.*

Jesse G. Delia (Ph.D., University of Kansas, 1970) is Dean of the College of Liberal Arts and Sciences at the University of Illinois at Urbana-Champaign, where he is also Professor in the Department of Speech Communication and Research Professor in the Institute of Communication Research. His research interests include the development of cognitive and communicative abilities in varied cultural milieus, communication in interpersonal relationships, and the history of communication as an academic area of study. He has published widely in both communication and psychology journals. He received the Speech Communication Association's Distinguished Scholar Award in 1993 for career contributions to the study of human communication.

Frank D. Fincham (Ph.D., University of Oxford, 1980) is Professor at the University of Wales College of Cardiff. He is the author of numerous articles on marriage, coeditor of *The Psychology of Marriage and Cognition in Close Relationships,* and coauthor of *Communicating in Relationships: A Guide for Couples and Professionals.* He also serves on the editorial boards of several journals in social, clinical, and family psychology. A Fellow of the American Psychological Association, British Psychological Society, and American Psychological Society, he has been the recipient of numerous professional awards, including a Rhodes Scholarship, an early career award from the British Psychological Society, and, most recently, the Berscheid-Hatfield Award from the International Network on Personal Relationships for "sustained, substantial, and distinguished contributions to the field of personal relationships."

Susan Gano-Phillips (Ph.D., University of Illinois at Urbana-Champaign, 1995) is Lecturer cum Assistant Professor in the Department of Psychology at the University of Michigan, Flint. She has published articles in the *Journal of Marriage and the Family* and *Journal of Family Psychology*. She completed her doctoral studies in clinical psychology at the University of Illinois at Urbana-Champaign and a pediatric psychology internship at the University of Oklahoma Health Sciences Center. Her research and clinical interests include children's divorce adjustment, sex roles in marriage, and normative sexual development in children. She has worked in school, community, and clinical settings with children from divorcing families, and has conducted workshops for both laypersons and professionals on the impact of divorce on child adjustment.

Debra K. Hughes is a doctoral candidate in the Department of Human Ecology, Division of Child Development and Family Relationships, at the University of Texas at Austin. She has presented her research on the causal structure of commitment at national and international conferences. These presentations concerned types of commitment processes and their association with relationship satisfaction and stability, and the effects of research participation on couples' relationships. Results from this work have led to the topic of her dissertation research, which is the interface between commitment in close relationships and commitment to work. Her future research will include the development of a subjective, multidimensional measure of work commitment.

Ted L. Huston (Ph.D., State University of New York at Albany, 1972) is Amy Johnson McLaughlin Centennial Professor of Psychology and Human Ecology at the University of Texas at Austin and former President of the International Society for the Study of Personal Relationships. After receiving his doctorate in psychology, he was on the faculty at the Pennsylvania State University until moving to Texas in 1984. His work has appeared in various journals, including the *Journal of Personality and Social Psychology, Journal of Marriage and the Family, Personality and Social Psychology Bulletin,* and *Personal Relationships.* A coauthor of the seminal *Close Relationships* volume, he has made contributions to the conceptualization of relationships and the development of procedures for gathering data about them.

Marie-Louise Mares (Ph.D., University of Wisconsin—Madison, 1994) is Assistant Professor at the Annenberg School for Communication, University of Pennsylvania. Her research interests include media use and effects among elderly viewers, as well as interpersonal relationships in old age. Her work has been published in *Communication Research* and is to be published in the *Handbook of Communication and Aging Research.*

Sandra Metts (Ph.D., University of Iowa, 1983) is Professor in the Department of Communication at Illinois State University. Her research interests focus on the management of problematic social and relational episodes, including embarrassment, relationship disengagement, deception, relational transgressions, and sexual communication. Two of her recently completed books, *Self-Disclosure* (coauthored with Val Derlega, Sandra Petronio, and Stephen Margulis) and *Facework* (coauthored with William Cupach) appear in the Sage Series on Close Relationships. Her work has also appeared in a variety of journals, including *Communication Monographs, Human Communication Research,* and *Journal of Social and Personal Relationships,* as well as in several edited volumes. Her professional responsibilities include serving as associate editor of *Personal Relationships,* and editor of *Communication Reports.*

Patricia Noller (Ph.D, University of Queensland, 1981) is Reader in Psychology at the University of Queensland. She is author of *Nonverbal Communication and Marital Interaction;* coauthor, with Victor Callan, of *Marriage and the Family* and *The Adolescent in the Family;* and coauthor, with Victor Callan, Cynthia Gallois, and

Yoshi Kashima, of *Social Psychology*. She is coeditor, with Mary Anne Fitzpatrick, of *Perspectives on Marital Interaction* and coauthor with Fitzpatrick of *Communication in Family Relationships*. Her research has been published in the *Journal of Personality and Social Psychology, Developmental Psychology, Journal of Marriage and the Family, Journal of Social and Personal Relationships, Multivariate Behavioral Research, Journal of Adolescence,* and as chapters in a number of books. She has served on the editorial boards of several major journals and is the founding editor of *Personal Relationships: Journal of the International Society for the Study of Personal Relationships*. She is a Fellow of the Academy of the Social Sciences in Australia.

Jack M. Richman (Ph.D., Florida State University, 1977) is Associate Professor of Social Work, University of North Carolina at Chapel Hill. He teaches graduate courses in the area of family social work practice and consults with several social agencies regarding family practice issues. His research in the area of family communication has appeared in *Pediatric Clinics of North America, Research on Social Work Practice,* and *Journal of Social Work Education*. He is co-principal investigator and codirector of the North Carolina Family and Children's Resource Program, a program to strengthen families that provides curricular development, training, and technical assistance to departments of social services and other public agencies. Also, he is co-principal investigator with Gary Bowen on a grant from BellSouth Foundation to establish an evaluation and monitoring system for students in the Cities/Communities-in-School Program, a public-private partnership for school dropout prevention.

Lawrence B. Rosenfeld (Ph.D., Pennsylvania State University, 1971) is Professor of Communication Studies, University of North Carolina at Chapel Hill. His current research in the area of family communication focuses primarily on intimacy and social support. His recent publications in these areas have appeared in the *Journal of Couples Therapy, Western Journal of Speech Communication,* and *Research on Social Work Practice*. Also, he is the author or coauthor of 14 books, the most recent of which are *Connecting: A Culture-Sensitive Approach to Interpersonal Communication Competency* (with Roy M. Berko and Larry A. Samovar) and the sixth edition of *Interplay: The Process of Interpersonal Communication* (with Ronald B. Adler and Neil Towne). He was editor of *Communication Education* and the *Western Journal of Speech Communication*. He received the Robert J. Kibler Memorial Award from the Speech Communication Association in 1987.

Pepper Schwartz (Ph.D., Yale University, 1974) is Professor of Sociology at the University of Washngton in Seattle. She is a past president of the Society for the Scientific Study of Sexuality and coauthor with Philip Blumstein, of *American Couples, Money, Work and Sex* (1983) as well as author of *Peer Marriage: How Love Between Equals Really Works* (1994). She has served on the boards of Planned Parenthood and the AIDS Foundation in Seattle and writes monthly or bimonthly for several magazines and newspapers including *Glamour, American Baby,* and *The New York Times' Parent and Child* column.

Alan L. Sillars (Ph.D., University of Wisconsin, 1980) is Professor of Communication Studies at the University of Montana. His past publications in the area of marital and family communication have dealt mainly with conflict, interpersonal perception, relationship types, and life-span issues.

Sara Steen is a graduate student at the University of Washington. She has done work on such diverse topics as condom use in romantic relationships, racial disproportionality in juvenile justice, and juvenile sex offenders.

Catherine A. Surra (Ph.D., Pensylvania State University, 1980) is Associate Professor in the Department of Human Ecology, Division of Child Development and Family Relationships, at the University of Texas at Austin. Her research interests concern the development of close relationships, with a focus on the development of marital commitment and the premarital predictors of marital outcomes. She has published in the *Journal of Marriage and the Family, Journal of Personality and Social Psychology,* and *Journal of Social and Personal Relationships.*

Samuel Vuchinich (Ph.D., University of Michigan, 1975) is Director of the Graduate Program in Human Development and Family Studies at Oregon State University. He has published in the areas of psycholinguistics, semiotics, social psychology, developmental psychology, family studies, family therapy, and conflict resolution. His most influential work has been in the areas of family conflict, coalitions within the family, and family problem solving, where his research has effectively merged videotaping of naturalistic family interaction in the home (especially family dinners) with rigorous statistical analysis, including sequential models. He is currently applying his research to the development of parent education programs for the prevention of antisocial behavior in preadolescents. He is a member of the Society for Research in Child Development, the National Council on Family Relations, and the Society for Research in Adolescence, and is on the editorial board of the journal *Developmental Psychology.*